Advances in Spatial Science

Titles in the Series

Aura Reggiani · Laurie A. Schintler

Editors

Methods and Models in Transport and Telecommunications

Cross Atlantic Perspectives

With 46 Figures
and 33 Tables

 Springer

Professor Dr. Aura Reggiani
Department of Economics
Faculty of Statistics
Piazza Scaravilli 2
40126 Bologna
Italy
E-mail: aura.reggiani@unibo.it

Professor Dr. Laurie A. Schintler
George Mason University
4400 University Drive
Fairfax, VA 22030
USA
E-mail: lschintl@gmu.edu

ISBN-13 978-3-642-06522-4   e-ISBN-13 978-3-540-28550-2

Springer is a part of Springer Science+Business Media
springeronline.com

© Springer-Verlag Berlin Heidelberg 2010
Printed in Germany

Cover design: Erich Kirchner

Printed on acid-free paper – 88/3153 – 5 4 3 2 1 0

To Our Evolving Small World Network

Preface

One aspect of the new economy is a transition to a networked society, and the emergence of a highly interconnected, interdependent and complex system of networks to move people, goods and information. An example of this is the increasing reliance of networked systems (e.g., air transportation networks, electric power grid, maritime transport, etc.) on telecommunications and information infrastructure. Many of the networks that evolved today have an added complexity in that they have both a spatial structure – i.e., they are located in physical space but also an a-spatial dimension brought on largely by their dependence on information technology. They are also often just one component of a larger system of geographically integrated and overlapping networks operating at different spatial levels.

An understanding of these complexities is imperative for the design of plans and policies that can be used to optimize the efficiency, performance and safety of transportation, telecommunications and other networked systems. In one sense, technological advances along with economic forces that encourage the clustering of activities in space to reduce transaction costs have led to more efficient network structures. At the same time the very properties that make these networks more efficient have also put them at a greater risk for becoming disconnected or significantly disrupted when super connected nodes are removed either intentionally or through a targeted attack. There is also often a "congested hub" phenomenon, as is seen in aviation networks, which raises questions regarding congestion pricing.

Our ability to visualize and analyze spatial systems has been greatly enhanced with the development of methods and models emerging from spatial economics, geographic information systems, mathematical modelling and simulation. More traditional techniques, such as multicriteria analysis and adaptive conjoint analysis, hold some promise in aiding with decision-making when there are a large number and complex set of alternatives to consider. The ability to do this has become even more important as spatial economic networks have become increasingly interconnected and interdependent and the task of planning for these systems more complex.

Knowledge of complex networks is enriched through international scholarly exchange and comparative analyses of networked systems that span different geographic boundaries and diverse cultural, political and economic cultures. This is the premise for this book. The volume intends to provide new insights into the modelling and analysis of transportation and telecommunications networks, utilizing perspectives from North America, Europe and other areas of the world. The papers in this volume begin to probe a number of interesting questions that can help us to understand the dynamics of our modern networked society. Do properties found in one network fail to exist in other networks and are there geographic factors that can explain this? Further, are there social, economic or cultural factors that contribute to differences in network properties and dynamics across regions? Can planning models such as those used for traffic forecasting or freight demand modelling be universally applied to networks situated in different regions, and how should this problem be dealt with when a system spans multiple spatial locations? What are the implications for policy analysis and decision-making?

The concept of the book originates from STELLA (Sustainable Transport in Europe and Links and Liaisons with America) an organization of the European Commission dedicated to fostering transatlantic transportation research. North American partners come from the STAR network (Sustainable Transportation Analysis and Research) supported by the National Science Foundation. The authors would like to give special thanks to the individuals who gave birth to STELLA and STAR and who continue to help move things forward (Peter Nijkamp, Bill Black and their colleagues) as well as all of the other international scholars who have participated in the organizations' activities and have offered knowledge on a variety of subjects along the way. Many of the papers contained in this volume were presented at a special STELLA session at the Conference of the European Regional Association held in Jyväskylä (Finland), in August of 2003. Additional papers were added later to provide a more comprehensive coverage of the topic and to offer a balance of insight from both North America and abroad. We are grateful to all the authors and referees for their efforts and careful collaboration, by providing new input and suggestions in the field.

The editors would also like to thank the Editorial Board of the series of *Advances in Spatial Science* for their support of the idea, Roberto Patuelli who helped out immensely in editing the volume and in soliciting referee reports and revised papers from the authors, and also Katharina Wetzel-Vandai from Springer for her support and assistance in making the book happen.

Aura Reggiani and Laurie Schintler
Bologna (Italy) and Fairfax (US)   Spring 2005

Contents

Part D: Sustainable Transport and Policy Perspectives

1 Introduction: Cross Atlantic Perspectives in Methods and Models Analysing Transport and Telecommunications

Aura Reggiani[1] and Laurie A. Schintler[2]

[1] University of Bologna, Bologna, Italy
[2] George Mason University, Fairfax, Virginia, USA

1.1 Prologue

Our modern world is in a continuous state of flux. Modern transport systems and the emerging new style of behaviour have created an unprecedented rise in mobility, at all spatial levels. The ever rising mobility patterns apply to all types of movement work, business, shopping and leisure, as well as to freight transport. Globalisation certainly plays a key role in this dynamic framework.

Globalisation refers to the broad area of increasing internationalisation of markets, changing consumption patterns and the shifting of industrial activities all over the world, with clear consequences for (international) transport and the environment.

The increasing awareness of globalisation phenomena has, in fact, not only demonstrated the complexity of the transport phenomenon, but also the fragility of the system and its links (e.g., the events in the recent years, like terrorist attacks, SARS and the war in Iraq). Globalisation appears then to be the underlying framework in the consumer/user (economic) activities with an immediate impact on the related transport activities (see, among others, Beuthe et al. 2004; van Geenhuizen et al. 2005; Hensher et al. 2004).

The above mentioned trends call for a thorough exploration of contrasts and similarities in both Europe and United States/Canada. For example, concerning the event of deregulation, this started in the US in the years 1977 and 1978 (for freight and passenger transport, respectively), while in Europe there was a gradual 'deregulation' movement starting in the eighties to the end of the nineties. Concerning the evolution of transport modes, Europe showed – after the year 1990 – a strong increase in air transport, which reached, in the year 2000, the amount of the EU rail traffic volume, while in US there has been a steady growth in air transport in contrast to a very stable low traffic volume in the rail sector. These two simple examples show undoubtedly the need of exploring the effects – on EU and US transport, at all spatial and transport mode levels – of our economic globalised era. In this context, particular attention has to be given to the multiplicity of goals involved in sustainable mobility policy, and consequently, to the related multiplicity of policy strategies.

These main concerns are also related to the need for a 'methodological' Trans-atlantic synthesis of the various approaches adopted so far in transport analysis and applications. The book attempts to offer a prospectus in this respect, together with the emerging reflections on the desirable future evolution of research.

The scientific platform underlying these fascinating challenges is constituted by the findings developed during the STELLA-STAR project. In particular, the STELLA (Sustainable Transport in Europe and Links and Liaisons with America) thematic network – together with the STAR (Sustainable Transportation Analysis and Research) network – aims at stimulating a thorough debate in both Europe and North America/Canada on the future perspectives of transport research and the foundations of policy analysis in this field, including the issue of the formulation of policy lessons (Button and Nijkamp 2004) An introduction to the main objectives and themes of STELLA-STAR is briefly designed in the next section.

1.2 Towards Sustainable Transport: The STELLA-STAR Network

STELLA is a thematic network funded by the European Commission. It started on January, 1st 2002. The aim of STELLA is to generate a clear added value from knowledge exchange and a common research perspective that is applicable at both sides of the Atlantic (see the EU-STELLA Deliverables 2002–2004).

The following three objectives are the basis of the STELLA project:

- the creation of an institutionalised *platform for exchange* of scientific information;
- a *better understanding* of the (common and different) causes and backgrounds of mobility behaviour in both Europe and North America;
- to foster and create conditions for applied *comparative research* in both Europe and North America regarding behavioural motives, innovative strategies and policy assessment in the transportation sector with a view to sustainable transport.

In this perspective, the STELLA network, in conjunction with the STAR network, has identified the complex force field of spatial mobility, according to five major building blocks, which are the following:

1. Globalisation, E-economy and Trade
2. ICT, Innovation and the Transport System
3. Society, Behaviour and Private/Public Transport
4. Environment, Safety, Health, Land Use and Congestion
5. Institutions, Regulations and Markets in Transportation

These research areas and their interrelationships with their transferability/implementation in applied and policy frameworks have constituted the main activity challenges of the STELLA-STAR Network. In particular, much emphasis has been given on the complexity of the spatial dynamic interrelationships – and related feedback effects – among transport, land use, and socio economic systems, inter alia with a view to their impact on sustainability.

In the light of globalisation effects, the same five forces might be rephrased as depicted in Fig. 1.1, by synthesising the research framework from which to depart. From the discussion that has emerged in the various STELLA-STAR meetings we can extrapolate the following main research issues:

• Relevance and necessity of clarification on transport sustainability scope, concept and measurements
• Impact and feedback (space-time) effects among transport, growth of e-commerce, ICT, travel behaviour, policy decisions and implementation.

In addition, the emerging common policy issues appear to be as follows:

• Space-time scale of transport policy implementation.
• Equity, efficiency and environmental issues in the implementation of transport policies.
• Barriers to implementation of transport policy.

The fundamental research directions for the STELLA-STAR activities mainly concern the exploration of agenda for future research in the field of sustainable mobility, linked to institutions and regulatory policy.

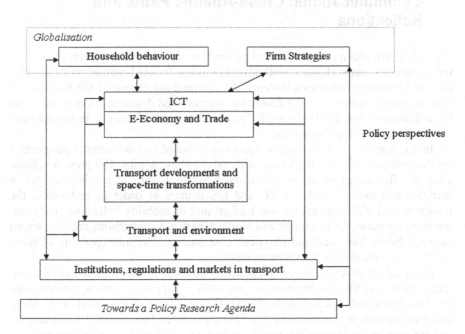

Fig. 1.1. The complex force field of transport and spatial mobility in a globalisation context. Source: EU-STELLA (2003)

In this context, the following methodological steps can be identified:

- Transatlantic comparative transport research: theories, empirical analyses and prospects
- Operational frameworks for advanced transport research:
  - Data assessments
  - Common research designs in different regional settings
  - Future (critical) trends and scenarios
- Road map from theory and research to policy implementation at different space-time scales.

Consequently, transferability of models in different networks and markets are a challenging research issue, towards a meta-analysis oriented to different policy users and institutions.

Having said this, it seems worth to respond to the above research agenda, by proposing, as a starting point, the insights emerging from the following chapters, devoted to the analysis and modelling of transportation and telecommunications networks, utilizing perspectives from North America, Europe and other areas of the world.

1.3 Method and Models in Transport and Communications: Cross-Atlantic Paths and Reflections

This book provides a compendium of papers that highlight recent advances in spatial economics, network they, methods and models focused mainly on transportation and telecommunications systems. An overarching theme of the book is the role of space in influencing the economic structure and dynamics of networks, and the adjustments that need to be made to our existing set of analytic techniques and models to capture any disparities.

In this framework it is certainly necessary to adopt an international perspective for the exchange of scientific information on the above topics. The present volume aims to offer contributions in this respect by discussing recent innovations in methods and models made by EU and US authors in order to understand the (common and different) causes and background of mobility behaviour and communications networks in Europe and North America. Comparisons are also drawn between North American and European case studies. The transferability of these models is a critical issue for future research.

The need for cross-Atlantic comparative studies of transportation and telecommunications and the development of new tools in support of this is formally outlined by Black and Nijkamp in the chapter (Chap. 2) that follows next. They argue that recent trends in the strengthening interdependency between ICT and transport and the growing interest in "sustainability" as a goal of policy actions are creating the demand for models that can capture these elements and trends. The chapter concludes with a road map for further research in this area.

The body of the manuscript contains four major sections. The chapters in Part A offer some new perspectives on traffic forecasting, the visualization of transportation networks and the emerging interdependencies between transportation networks, the electric power grid and regional economies. Part B focuses on commercial transport, addresses the issue of transferability of freight models across the Atlantic and offers some innovative approaches for analyzing freight alternatives. The chapters in Part C focus on aviation and telecommunications networks. The issue of congestion pricing at airports the effects of September 11 on the economic behaviour of European airlines, and the structure and dynamics of telecommunications networks are considered. The book concludes in Part D with some policy perspectives and directions for future research to encourage more comparative research across Europe and North America aimed at transport sustainability issues.

In Chap. 3, Boyce and Williams describe the status of urban travel forecasting modelling and how developments in this area have compared across the Atlantic (United States and the United Kingdom). The two regions have different demands in the type of evaluation measures desired as output from these models resulting in variations in the modelling frameworks themselves and software available. They examine how model requirements and applications vary in different policy, program and even geographic contexts. You and Kim in Chap. 4 focus on travel time forecasting models which have become necessary features of many types of Intelligent Transportation Systems (ITS). The authors provide a survey of existing methodologies that range from mathematical optimization, computer simulation, statistics and artificial intelligence. An emerging trend they identify is the use of Geographic Information Systems (GIS) to store and manage real-time and historical traffic data as well as statistics that are generated from travel-time forecasting models and this is discussed as well. Chapter 5 by Li and Waters also looks at the use of GIS in transportation analysis although their focus is on traffic safety.

Donaghy et al. (Chap. 6) develop a methodological approach for modelling interdependencies between different types of critical infrastructure and their ties to regional economies. The model captures elements of a multi-modal transportation system and the network of power generation and distribution. The model is designed to explore spatial hierarchies of the networked infrastructure, cross-sectoral and inter-regional demands on infrastructure and the location of potential bottlenecks in the system and how the trustworthiness of interdependent systems can be increased.

The issue of freight transport modelling is addressed in Part B. All of the authors recognize that this is an area of growing concern and also one that is grossly underdeveloped. Button introduces the topic in Chap. 7 and explores whether or not freight transport models can be universally applied across different geographic regions, or transferred from applications involving passenger movements to those focussed on commodity flow. Geographic transferability issues are discussed mainly in the context of the United States and the EU. According to Button, these two regions are good candidates given that they are similar in size and economic structures, and they are beginning to develop new linkages, e.g., in the air traffic market. The chapter stresses that the development of a completely new analytical framework for freight transport may neither be necessary or pragmatic. Rather it may be more useful to explore what already exists and assess the applicability of these models in different geographic and functional contexts. The paper concludes that the transferability of models from the US to the EU and vice versa may be difficult due to differences in policy processes and approaches, network characteristics, the market for freight transportation, institutional frameworks and modelling frameworks. While somewhat pessimistic, there are some compelling reasons to move forward with further research in this area.

Friesz and Veras discuss the difficulties associated with modelling freight transport and just how complex the problem in Chap. 8. They present a modelling framework based on dynamic game theory and differential variational inequalities that can be used to effectively capture many of the key elements and dynamics of the freight transport problem, and offer some suggestions for further research. The next two chapters focus on modelling the choices of freight operators. Beuthe et al. in Chap. 9 use stated preference data combined with multicriteria analysis to understand the preference ranking of Belgian freight operators for different alternatives. They specify an additive utility comprised of a non-linear partial utility function that are piecewise linear and use linear programming to estimate the functions and weights and also to derive information on willingness-to-pay and willingness-to-compensate. In Chap. 10, Bergantino and Bolis demonstrate how the method of adaptive conjoint analysis can be used to apply a different technique, adaptive conjoint analysis, to model maritime freight service alternatives. The method identifies the value that a user assigns to each alternative, the tradeoffs associated with these choices and the willingness-to-pay for various service upgrades. It is applied to the northwest region of Italy to assess maritime ro-ro service from the ports of Genoa or La Spezia.

Telecommunications and aviation networks are the focus of Part C. Chapter 11 by Schintler et al. uses frequency distributions to examine and compare the topological structure of three different communications networks: the IP backbone network of the United States, the landline phone traffic model in Italy and a peer-to-peer musical data exchange network. This analysis finds some differences in the structures of each of these networks as represented by different types of frequency distributions, e.g., exponential versus power law. The findings provoke the need for further research particularly to understand how comparable types of telecommunications networks differ between the United States and Europe, and what social, political, technological and economic factors contribute to these distinctions or to any noted similarities in network structure. Campisi et al. in Chap. 12 also examine the telecommunications sector and attempt to understand the diffusion of wireline and wireless technologies and market potential of these systems in Italian regions, with a comparison to the United States. This process is modelled for the time period of 1996 to 2000 using a framework base on Pearl-Verhulst equations or logistic S-Shaped curves.

The next two chapters deal specifically with aviation networks. Chapter 13 develops a method for modelling to analyze congestion pricing at capacity-constrained and congested airports with free access. The analytical framework consists of three components, a queuing model, a model of the delay externalities imposed by different flights and a model to assess what impact congestion pricing has on the profitability of airlines. The model is also used to conduct a sensitivity analysis under varying assumptions regarding traffic levels, aircraft mix and airport capacities. New York (NY) La Guardia airport is used as a case study to demonstrate the practicality of the approach and to draw specific inferences about the impact of congestion pricing in a stylized setting. Alderighi and Cento in Chap. 14 focus their analysis on European aviation markets and present a theoretical framework based on continuous-time dynamics for examining the short-term and long-term reaction of airlines to shocks in demand. The analysis reveals information on how carriers reaction to such events varies given their own internal strategies and expectations, financial situation, market structure, adjustment costs, etc. This is demonstrated for two recent events; the September 11 terrorist attacks in the United States and the SARS epidemic in the Fair East.

The remaining section focuses more on transportation policy with some specific implications for the environment. In Chap. 15, Hirota and Poot examine the effect of taxing on auto ownership and demand using an econometric model. Potter in Chap. 16 reviews taxation schemes for vehicle and fuel use in the countries of the EU. He argues for a new taxation scheme targeted at improving the environment. The last chapter (Chap. 17) by Banister in a way summarizes the manuscript and emphasizes the importance of "time" as a variable in enhancing models aimed at understanding transportation and telecommunications networks, and the interdependencies between these systems. He also makes an interesting point that time should not be viewed solely as a constraint but also as a mechanism for creating new opportunities for travel, and that different "time" dimensions (long-term versus short-term) as well as the social elements of the attribute should be explored. The importance and value of fostering cross-Atlantic research to explore these issues and to enhance the accuracy our models for transportation and telecommunications models and the relevance of these methods for decision-makers is stressed.

In conclusion, the present volume, by attempting to provide a Cross-Atlantic prospective view of recent theories, methods and models in transport and communication, offers a platform from which the different spatial economic dimensions of networks start to be better understood. In this context, further research agenda can be traced also in the light of the STELLA-STAR network. For example, one question is whether the properties found in one network exist in other networks, and whether economic geography plays in role in creating any differences. Consequently, it might be interesting to explore: a) whether one uncover disparities when comparing similar infrastructure networks between the United States and Europe; further, b) whether social, economic or cultural factors contribute to differences in network properties and dynamics across regions. Clearly a 'global' assessment of data infrastructures is essential in this respect. It may also be important – in future research – to examine whether or not planning models such as those used for traffic forecasting or freight demand modelling can be universally applied to networks situated in different regions, and should this problem be dealt with when a system spans multiple geographic locations.

Research could then take place along the following main lines:

– Inventory research: trying to identify the different network typologies and different ways of measuring and analyzing such typologies *(typological approach)*
– Research strategies: trying to identify appropriate research strategies for different network typologies *(policy research approach)*.

References

Beuthe M, Himanen V, Reggiani A, Zamparini L (eds) (2004) Transport developments and innovations in an evolving world. Springer, Berlin Heidelberg New York

Button K, Nijkamp P (eds) (2004) Special Issue: Challenges in conducting Transatlantic work on sustainable transport and the STELLA/STAR initiative. Transport Reviews 24

EU-STELLA (2003) Deliverable 6. European Commission, DG TREN E4, Brussels. Available at www.stellaproject.org

van Geenhuizen M, Reggiani A, Rietveld P (eds) (2005) Policy analysis of transport networks. Ashgate, Aldershot (forthcoming)

Hensher DA, Button KJ, Haynes KE, Stopher PR (eds) (2004) Handbook of transport geography and spatial systems. Elsevier, Amsterdam

2 Transportation, Communication and Sustainability: In Search of a Pathway to Comparative Research

William R. Black[1] and Peter Nijkamp[2]

[1] Indiana University, Bloomington, Indiana, USA
[2] Free University, Amsterdam, The Netherlands

2.1 Transportation, Mobility and Communication

The past decades have witnessed an enormous and unprecedented increase in the volume of intercontinental transport (e.g., between Europe and North-America, and between Asia and North-America). Wide-body airplanes and mega container ships have shaped the conditions under which our world is becoming smaller all the time. Interestingly enough, a similar development is taking place at a local level, where the action radius is not only increasing, but also the frequency of trips. Geographically, our world is becoming less global and distant, but on the contrary more local and close-by.

Since the early history of mankind, people have tried to expand their geographical action radius. Spatial mobility, either on a daily basis (e.g. commuting) or on a structural basis (e.g. migration), has become a prominent feature of human behaviour. With the advent of the Industrial Revolution, new and unprecedented opportunities emerged for extending the spatial range of human activity, thanks to the train, the steamship, the telegraph, the car and the airplane. The 'homo economicus' has also become a 'homo mobilis'.

Nowadays, human behaviour is largely synonymous with movement. The old dream of the flying carpet has not yet fully materialized, as the distance friction costs have not vanished, but we are gradually moving toward a space-economy where the death of distance tends to become – to some degree at least – reality. Admittedly, bridging physical distance still incorporates costs (i.e. financial, psychological, time), but over the years these costs tend to decline gradually. Clearly, distance friction continues to play a role in agglomeration phenomena, as geographic proximity (i.e. physical, socio-psychological) generates a great variety of economies of density that compensate for geographic interaction costs. Economies of density seem to run parallel to economies of motion.

More interaction and communication between different parts of our world (at all geographic scales) prompt also an interconnectivity between previously distinct markets. Markets for goods tend to get not only a global uniformity, but they are also becoming spatially more competitive. With the advent of trade liberalisation (thanks to the WTO, the enlargement of the EU, the NAFTA etc.) more physical movement of people and goods is unavoidable.

In our modern network, one cannot imagine an advanced economy without spatial mobility and interaction. And, with an increasing number of people on our earth, more people are becoming more mobile. Since the 1970s, the world population has risen from 4 billion to 6.5 billion, and the US population from approx. 200 million to 300 million. In the same period, the number of vehicles in the US almost doubled, while the total mileage by all cars in the US has almost tripled since the 1970s. These figures illustrate the mobility explosion in our world, but also highlight some of the negative externalities (pollution, fatalities, congestion, etc.) of a mobile world. Though there is a phase difference with respect to other countries (e.g., in Europe or in Asia), the pattern of rapid increase in car ownership and use is largely similar all over the world.

Mobility as a key feature of a modern society takes place at all geographic scales. In the past decades, we have not only seen a drastic increase of transport at metropolitan or local levels, but also witnessed a globalization of trade and transport of goods, a phenomenon induced by the fact that mass and scale have more impact on the transport prices of goods than distance. Consequently, the smart organization of goods flows, ranging from local to global scales by means of sophisticated logistics, has become an enormous challenge for transport operators. In this context, the rise of information and communication technology (ICT) has been a breakthrough.

The emergence of the ICT era has indeed prompted a new phenomenon, viz. the transport of information and data on a world-wide scale at almost zero costs. The emerging e-society has had – and will continue to have – far-reaching impacts on our modes of production, consumption, knowledge acquisition, and leisure. In recent years, we have witnessed the emergence of interesting scenarios where virtual transportation takes over physical movement. So far, however, we have not observed a substitution between physical movement and virtual transport (i.e., telecommunication). In fact, both phenomena are still on a rising edge and seem to exhibit – at least at a macro scale-complementarity.

Transportation and communication have developed over the centuries in a dependent manner, in which the former was very much a precursor of the latter. The transmission of information was, for all practical purposes, a transportation process as well as a communication process. Letters and packets sent during the centuries prior to 1844 moved at the same speed as the mode of transport, which therefore dictated the speed of communication, whether the carriers were post riders, stage coaches, or sailing ships. Although pigeons had been used since the time of the Roman Empire for short messages, Samuel Morse's invention of the telegraph in 1844 was probably the first significant break in this communication-transport dependence. Of course, the spread of the telegraph was also intimately involved with the spread of the railroad, the transport mode for which schedules and time were far more important than other early modes. The Atlantic cable of the 1860s and Bell's telephone invention of the 1880s further widened the developing chasm between transport and communication.

This dependence continues to the present day, when the rapid development of ICT has not only meant an enormous rise in productivity caused by our information and communication economy but has also facilitated the better logistic handling of both passenger and goods transportation. Nevertheless, even though the technological drivers of our mobile world share common features in many countries, there may be different patterns of mobility among various countries as a result of varying adoption mechanisms of new technologies, different lifestyles and residential living patterns, different land use patterns and different transportation policies (see Stead 2003). Therefore, it is important to investigate the commonalities and contrasts in the transport field in different countries more thoroughly. In particular, at the transatlantic edge we witness rather drastic differences in both behaviour and policy, which warrants an ambitious effort to draw lessons from comparative study. Comparative transportation analysis would need systematically collected databases, not only on actual transport movements but also on transport policies and the negative impacts of transportation (such as congestion).

The above mentioned trends prompt a scientific investigation along two complementary lines. First, the rapid increase in transatlantic transport calls for applied, modelling and policy research on actual flows, impediments to mobility, risks of large-scale transport volumes (e.g., security), modern logistics and ICT, as well as policy arrangements on international transport (e.g., open skies or open seas agreements). In the second place, almost all countries face similar problems associated with the mobility revolution (such as congestion, environmental decay, traffic fatalities, just-in-time logistics). Such issues demand a thorough analysis and an exchange of experiences from different regions in our world could be extremely useful in finding solutions and remedies for mobility impediments, not only in the field of technological progress but also in the area of behavioural adjustments. From a policy perspective, attempts to establish new forms of policy coordination, to ensure a liberalisation of the transport markets, to develop new forms of effective traffic management, or to design an environmentally-benign lay-out of new urban areas would lead to intriguing questions on comparability and transferability of policy lessons between e.g. Europe and the United States.

It is no surprise that the dynamics in transportation and communication have prompted a search for new research tools in the form of operational methods and models. The present volume offers an interesting collection of innovative approaches. Our introductory chapter aims to provide a contextual exploration of new analytical perspectives for understanding the drivers of the above mentioned dynamics. We will address in particular the opportunities for the comparative analysis of mobility flows and interests in Europe and North America, while taking into account differences in technological development paths, in regulatory trajectories and in behavioural responses at both the supply and demand side.

The remainder of this contribution is therefore organized as follows. In Sect. 2.2, we will address the strong relationship between transport and communication, as well as the negative externalities of transport in a mobile society; and the analytical potential of scenarios in an uncertain environment will also be highlighted. Next, Sect. 2.3 will address the complex interdependency between ICT and sustainable transport, while Sect. 2.4 will focus on the sustainability of ICT. Then Sect. 2.5 will pay attention to similarities and differences in transportation, as seen from a transatlantic perspective. That section also discusses the associated possibilities for comparative research on the transatlantic edge. Finally, Sect. 2.6 will make some suggestions regarding a future research agenda.

2.2 Transport and Communication

The railroads of the early 20th century were the primary mode of transport for moving mail between major cities. In the United States this led to the creation of railway post offices (RPOs): rail cars where mail was processed and bagged for distribution at various points along the railroad's route. These RPOs actually had their own cancellation equipment that carried the name of the railroad on the cancelled postage. Although these mobile post offices continued for several decades, they ceased to be of real importance probably by the middle of the century.

The use of wireless radio communication became common in the early years of the century. It was useful for ensuring travel safety and the scheduling of arrivals for different transport modes, but not for much else.

During this same period, various inventors and entrepreneurs were experimenting with the development of automobiles. Innovations in this area were evident on both sides of the Atlantic, and it was ultimately Ford's assembly line that enabled the internal combustion engine to win out over the electric and steam automobiles of the day. Although the automobile brought about many changes, its development is notable here as a transport mode that was initially completely independent of communication.

World War I saw the further development of motorized vehicles. Airplanes also developed during this era and, in the beginning, these too functioned without any communication. In the immediate post-war period we saw the development of airmail, a faster way of moving communication than the railroad at that time, but the latter was still used for the movement of express mail at night.

Communication technology was used as early as 1929 in aviation. In this case radio beams were used to assist pilots with navigation. During the 1930s, radio communication began to appear in aircraft and this was significant in the general field of aviation safety and as a device to assist with navigation. It was in the 1940s, after World War II, that radar became common in the commercial aviation sector for air traffic control and as a way of monitoring aircraft location, landings, take-offs, and so forth — once again, a significant safety improvement.

Major changes in communication capabilities of the other transport modes were slow. The motor carriers began using citizen band radios, but these were not major developments. By mid-century, a new set of problems was emerging. These were problems brought on by the rapid growth of the automobile and the rise of commercial aviation. From this time until the end of the 20th century, these problems for the most part simply increased.

Such problems were, however, the proverbial tip of the iceberg in terms of what we refer to today as problems of sustainable transport. At that time, these new problems began to manifest themselves as problems with local air quality due to automotive exhaust emissions, general problems attributable to, and defined by, congestion, and, in its wake, problems of equity. Although the first of these needs no explanation, it was in attempts to solve the congestion problems that the equity problem arose. These equity problems had to do primarily with the household relocation effects created by attempts in the U.S. and elsewhere to build more highways as a solution to the congestion problem.

The availability of petroleum also emerged as a problem of transportation sustainability. Petroleum is the major fuel source for all motorized transport. The distribution of this resource is not uniform, and it is anticipated that reserves of this fuel may be depleted by the mid-21st century. In addition, the developed world is very much dependent on the developing world for this resource but, in many cases, the former lacks the control of the resource that it would like and this also has an impact on its transport sustainability.

Fatalities and injuries had been increasing since the beginning of the 20th century, though very few viewed this as something that could be resolved. During that century, in the U.S. motor vehicle accidents resulted in more than three million fatalities. By the 1960s, concern was being expressed about the safety of motor vehicles and this concern led first to the use of seat belts and much later air bags (see also WHO 2004).

In the U.S., the equity problem was resolved partially by the Relocation Assistance Act which remedied many of the early equity problems. But local air quality problems have still not been resolved and congestion continues to be a major transport problem globally. In addition, there has been greater recognition of the association between global warming and carbon dioxide emissions.

A mobile society undoubtedly offers a wide variety of positive outcomes, such as better access to facilities, more opportunities for social interaction, and many trade gains. Some of these outcomes may be regarded as positive externalities in an economic sense. Recently, however, there has been an overwhelming interest in the shadow side or disadvantages of large-scale transport, in particular in the negative externalities (Gudmundsson 2003; Nijkamp and Vleugel 1995; Steg 2003).

These negative externalities have prompted extensive research, e.g. on the assessment of the social costs of transport (incurred by congestion, fatalities, pollution, landscape destruction etc.). The ongoing debate on the feasibility of road pricing exemplifies the complexity of the issues involved. In recent years, many studies have also addressed the technological uncertainty in future transportation systems (such as those using electric cars, zero-emission cars, hydrogen vehicles, etc.). To map out the future (or at least the intrinsic uncertainties of the future), many researchers and policymakers have resorted to scenario experiments (see van Geenhuizen and Nijkamp 2003).

Scenarios could play an interesting role in complex decision issues, as scenario analysis is in agreement with the desire to unfold a panorama of possible futures, which are probably generated in the light of past causalities, and offer an integrated future picture of part of a complex reality. They can be seen as coherent mappings of likely, feasible or desirable future states of (a part of) society, including the trajectory between the present and the future. Scenarios are different from policy strategies, in that they cannot be chosen by policymakers, in contrast to policy strategies. Strategies are the responses to exogenously given developments. There are two types of scenarios, viz. those which look forward and those which are of a backcasting nature. The use of scenarios has several advantages for decision making under uncertainty and risky decisions, because scenarios:

- are a rational way to judge future uncertainty in a cohesive way;
- depict uncertainty from the viewpoint of driving forces;
- offer an intellectual framework for a sensitivity analysis in terms of robustness of strategies;
- are strategic learning tools for decision makers;
- may act as communication tools in an uncertain multi-actor situation;
- stimulate creative thinking on an open future.

Scenario analysis – including in the transportation policy sector – has gained much popularity. In Nijkamp et al. (1998) several approaches to scenario building in the transportation sector are presented. In their study they used a distinction of future images of transportation into expected and preferred developments, using survey techniques among a wide range of transportation experts. The estimated transport implications of these images (in terms of person kms or tonne kms) were next translated into emissions of air pollution, through which tests on sustainability consequences could be carried out.

Various classes of scenario building experiments may be distinguished. From the perspective of the involvement and views of the designer, one may distinguish inter alia: intuitive scenarios, idealistic scenarios, qualitative scenarios, quantitative scenarios and participatory scenarios. From the perspective of application fields of scenarios, one may distinguish, inter alia, projective and prospective scenarios, autonomous (background) scenarios, reference (trend) scenarios, surprise-free and challenge scenarios, contrast (borderline) scenarios, and conflict scenarios. In all cases, scenarios are analytical and visionary mental constructs. They are not necessarily valid, but provide a frame for thinking in a rational way about the future. They are meant to prompt proper action in terms of policy strategies, but are not intended to play a role as valid predictions.

In recent years, various extensive scenario studies on the feasibility of future sustainable transport systems have been undertaken. Examples can be found in, amongst others, Banister et al. (2000), Nijkamp et al. (1998), and Rodenburg et al. (2001). These studies not only presented a systematic constellation of transport scenarios at different geographic scale levels, but also an exploration of policy strategies aimed at achieving more sustainable development. Policy instruments and measures to be used are, for instance, regulation, subsidies, and fair and efficient pricing.

2.3 ICT and Sustainable Transport

ICT entered the transport sustainability battle in the mid-20th century. Traffic signals on expressway ramps that controlled the entrance of vehicles onto major highways and freeways were controlled by television signals that informed central traffic control operators of the density of vehicles on these roads. In this way, the signals were controlled and this prevented vehicle density from increasing to congestion levels, at least some of the time.

Since then, the involvement of ICT in the area of transport sustainability has continued. The entire area of air traffic control is essentially an ICT field. It controls the flights of all commercial aircraft and most general aviation traffic as well. Its fundamental importance is well-illustrated by the complete paralysis of this network when the system goes down for one reason or another. This is one example of the manner in which transport has become virtually dependent on communication technology. This is a complete reverse of the situation of 150 years ago when virtually all communication relied on transportation.

Congestion control in motor vehicle transport has also continued to develop over the years. The television cameras of mid-20th century are now suspended above thousands of intersections. Instead of an individual monitoring all this, the system is set to change signals when it perceives a traffic jam building up. Humans are not involved after the equipment is installed, unless things go wrong. Communication with the drivers takes place through the use of the traffic signal. There are also demand-activated signals where the presence of one or more vehicles at a signalized intersection is "perceived" by sensors in the highway surface. The signal responds depending on where the volume is the greatest and this facilitates traffic flow and reduces congestion.

Within urban areas, it has been common to use cameras to record vehicles proceeding against a stop traffic signal for some time. This technology is also being used to keep track of vehicles moving within certain areas where congestion fees apply. This is the case in London where a fee was initiated in February 2003 for motor vehicles moving within a defined central area of that city during certain times of the day. Currently, there are discussions about ultimately increasing this zone to include all areas within the M25 orbital highway that surrounds London, but this will most likely require the use of a different technology: the use of transponders and cell-tower based technology.

Satellite and cell-tower technology are also being considered as a way of identifying the road use taxes due from highway, road and street users in the United States. Hitherto, these taxes were based on gallons of gasoline sold, but the improvement in the fuel efficiency of current vehicles and the increasing use of alternate fuels and hybrid fuel vehicles will decrease the revenues received. A global positioning system (GPS) and a geographic information system (GIS) along with transponders would enable users to be taxed on the basis of miles over which their vehicle used different types of roadways. Prototypes of this system are currently being tested in the U.S..

A similar GPS/GIS system is used in the more expensive motor vehicles being sold today. This system has the capability of communicating directly with the driver of these vehicles in the event that an air bag deploys. It also has the capability of dispatching local emergency vehicles to the location of the vehicle. In addition, the system can be used to assist with navigation and in this way decrease fuel use and emissions attributable to way-finding.

Nowadays, in several European cities, sensors record the entry and exit of vehicles into multi-level garages, and information about the availability of parking spaces is sent to electronic displays along highways. This prevents drivers from wandering through the street system in search of a parking space, adding to congestion, fuel use and pollution.

Still further examples of ICT involvement with transportation are on the horizon with the use of front, rear, and side radar on vehicles. These innovations would virtually prevent vehicles from running off the road or into other vehicles. The sensors would inform the driver of the approaching difficulties and, in the process, decrease the risk of accidents, injuries, and fatalities, and this would make transport more sustainable.

ICT has thus various implications for the transport sector. It may help to encourage greater efficiency in transport, but in the long run it may also stimulate more mobility, as intensified interaction and communication tends to create more physical transport. But is may do so at lower environmental costs.

As the above examples demonstrate, ICT is making transport far more sustainable than it would otherwise be. It also is making the current and future transport system far more dependent on ICT. A word of caution is in order here. The above sketch of the potential of ICT was mainly supply-oriented and offered an optimistic picture. But institutional, political, behavioural and logistic bottlenecks may preclude a full achievement of all the potential benefits of ICT. The limited success of these potentials in countries like Germany, France or Italy is illustrative. This raises the question: Just how sustainable is ICT? In the realm of transport we recognize resource depletion, congestion, injuries and fatalities, and emissions as problems arising from transport not being sustainable. Are there similar or analogous situations in the realm of ICT?

2.4 The Sustainability of ICT and Transport

Certain nations of the world today do not have sufficient petroleum to power the fleets of vehicles that operate on their transport systems. They find that they are essentially at the mercy of other nations who may control the availability and price of this fuel. The imposition of oil embargoes of the 1970s was one of the primary reasons why the U.S. government began to look at alternate fuels at that time. Today, certain nations find that if they base control of their public systems (possibly transport systems) on ICT software available only from major vendors, then they are virtually controlled by the vendor concerned. The lack of standardization and the unavailability of computer source code in much software makes it impossible for most users to modify it and, as a result, whenever the vendor upgrades or alters its software, or switches technologies, the user is obliged to make the same changes. This is hardly a sustainable situation and it is very significant in the developing nations of the world.

The major attempt to counter this problem has been the development of free and open-source software (FOSS). FOSS is software for which the source code has been made public and may be altered by the user. Aside from enabling countries to be independent of vendors, it also allows these same countries to develop expertise in the area as programmers to see the manner in which certain systems are put together. Programs may be modified for specialized uses and then shared with other users. Most of this software has been developed in such a way that it will run on virtually any machine.

We usually do not think of the world of ICT as having accidents resulting in fatalities and injuries to humans using such a system. In the case of motor vehicles, these accidents are generally attributable to three fundamental causes: human error, environmental factors and design defects. The question is whether these causal factors could also have an impact on ICT and consequently on its sustainability. If experience to date is representative, then these factors could also play a role in the realm of ICT. Programming errors (i.e. human errors) will most likely be found in the software of any system and situations arise that are never anticipated. Some of these (for example, digitizing errors) have already occurred and been corrected, but others will undoubtedly occur in the future as new data input is added to information systems.

Environmental errors may be particularly daunting since reliance on GPS satellite systems is subject to blackouts caused by solar activity. This is quite disturbing today when one watches television relayed by satellites, but it could actually be hazardous if that GPS is monitoring or controlling the movement of vehicles.

Design defects are less obvious, but just as much of a potential problem. We can not, at this point, anticipate what exactly these might be, for if we had such prescience they would not occur.

ICT will definitely influence spatial behaviour and hence impact on the transport of people and goods. The latter aspect deserves indeed due attention, as the emerging e-society and sophisticated logistics will most likely shape new patterns of spatial interaction.

Congestion in the transport sector must also have a counterpart in the communication sector, but this is rarely discussed. Concern here is not with the additional geosynchronous satellites that may have to be placed in orbit, but rather with the potential confusion of the multitude of signals to and from these satellites. What are the potential problems that could occur? How secure would such systems be? These are just a couple of the questions that one might pose if we begin to rely too heavily on ICT as a way of moving toward transport sustainability.

One final area in which ICT is playing a role in improving the sustainability of transport and travel is the substitution of communication for travel or movement. There are several areas in which this is viewed as having some potential. The first of these is in the straight substitution of a communications link-up for workers travel to their place of work. This is referred to as telecommuting in the U.S. and teleworking in Europe. 'Teleworking' is actually the better term since such employees are actually working at a distance.

There is no doubt that teleworking actually is possible, and that numerous employees in the U.S. and Europe do practice this type of substitution. However, it is very unlikely that they are teleworking five days a week. Because of this, it is reasonable to ask: is this limited use of teleworking actually enough to decrease accidents, congestion, emissions, and fuel use? Probably not, but this does not mean teleworking is insignificant. The major problem is that there are still too few jobs to which it can be applied.

Another form of substitution is the replacement of a certain amount of travel by e-commerce. Recent data suggests that e-commerce in the U.S. and EU is approximately 1.5% of total retail sales in each area. Under the premise that every little bit helps, we do not want to cast this completely aside, but we also should not expect this to be a source of significant reduction in motor vehicle traffic. How much of the e-commerce taking place is merely a substitution of the Internet for sales that were previously done by telephone or mail-order or catalogue sales? If this is the case, is this type of substitution having any impact at all on the transport sector?

Certainly e-commerce in the business-to-business transactions is much more significant; it represents about 15% of such transactions. But, once again, how much of this business was previously done over telephone lines and, therefore, does it really represent a reduction in transportation? Probably not. There is already a significant increase in small-scale deliveries of parcels etc. as a result of internet use for shopping.

To summarize, this section has looked at the historical linkages between transportation and communication and noted the manner in which the virtual dependence of the latter on the former for most of recorded history has changed in the last 150 years in such a way that communication has become independent of transport. This independence continued through the first half of the 20th century, but transport then began to depend more and more on communication and information technology (ICT) in response to problems in the area of transportation sustainability.

At present, the role of ICT in moving toward a more sustainable transport system is becoming of growing importance and one must query whether ICT is sustainable, or, as in the case of transport, if we increase our dependence on this sector, will it also become non-sustainable. ICT may have significant impacts on spatial behaviour and hence on urban interaction patterns and in the long run on urban structure, by allowing more dispersion. Preliminary analysis would suggest that is the potential outcome.

Also important from many perspectives is the substitution of communication in areas of the journey to work and in the purchasing of retail goods; these are teleworking, in the former case, and e-commerce in the latter. In the area of teleworking, we find the number of individuals involved is often too small in most cases to have a major impact on any of the factors that make transport non-sustainable: congestion, accidents, fuel use, and emissions. In the area of e-commerce we conclude that the substitution is merely of one form of communication for another, and the transport portion of the commerce is little affected by this change.

A final remark concerns aviation. The airline sector is strongly driven by the ICT sector, and will continue to be structurally influenced by new developments in ICT. This will generate more long-distance mobility, while ensuring higher levels of sustainability. Lessons from the airline sector (e.g., safety requirements) will increasingly be adopted by other transport sectors.

2.5 Similarities and Differences in Transportation and Communication: Toward a Transatlantic Comparative Perspective

All countries in our world seem to be moving toward higher mobility levels. Less developed countries may have lower mileage figures, but sooner or later they tend to catch up, as is witnessed in European mobility data. Seen from this perspective, both North America and Europe might be expected to exhibit similar mobility phenomena. At first glance, this may seem to be true, but a closer investigation also reveals some interesting differences in terms of the structure of mobility patterns and related policy.

In the first place, it ought to be recognized that North America has a clear private car orientation that is instigated by individual market beliefs, whereas Europe has more a mixed (private car and public transport) orientation which makes the operation of the transport market different from that in North America. Second, a prominent feature is also that — as part of the North American life style - public transport does not play an essential role, and is mainly oriented towards specific target groups, whereas in Europe public transport has a great deal of public support and forms an indispensable part of the total transport system. And, finally, the transport market in Europe tends to be seen to a considerable extent as a public sector responsibility, while in North America liberal market perspectives tend to prevail.

In recent years, comparative study has become an enormous methodological challenge in many disciplines, as it may reveal important lessons from available information. The presence of extensive databases has undoubtedly contributed to the current popularity of comparative analysis in a quantitative sense, in particular, meta-analysis.

Comparative analysis may address relevant features of a complex phenomenon under consideration. For example, it may refer to the inputs of a process (e.g., expenditures for infrastructure) in order to assess their efficiency. But it may also address the performance of a system by investigating output indicators (e.g. the occurrence of congestion). And finally, comparative research may address the impacts of policies (e.g. the effect of road pricing schemes on congestion). In all such studies, the main aim is to identify causal or explanatory patterns in the functioning of a common set of complex features which exhibit considerable variation in space and time. Comparative studies may originate from various sources of interest, such as testing a causal relationship; identifying whether a proposition in a given study is also applicable in other studies; exploring whether a critical condition in a given case result also holds somewhere else; or observing whether there are commonalities in causal structures and in empirical results in different case studies. It goes without saying that the structure and the development of transportation on both sides of the Atlantic is particularly suitable for quantitative comparative research.

The main traditional method for a synthesis of research findings in economic research has been the literature review. As a method of research it is well developed. According to Van den Bergh et al. (1997), surveys have often tended to report findings in a tabular or narrative fashion with verbal comments and a discussion of the strengths and weaknesses of each study. Although useful, such studies are qualitative in character and neglect a full account of many quantitative aspects of the individual studies. Neither can they fully account for the difficulties underlying the application of synthesis, such as the incompatibility of pieces of knowledge.

Glass (1976) introduced the, then, new study of meta-analysis. Originally, this study approach, which finds its origin in experimental psychology, aimed at examining a well-defined collection of experiments in an integral way by using statistical methods. This study process has evolved towards a broader field of application. Meta-analysis has also found its way into economics, where an increasing number of quantitative studies are available.

In the literature many definitions of meta-analysis have been presented thus far. However, none of these is entirely satisfactory, and, in view of the necessity for a solid methodological underpinning, we offer a more precise definition. We consider meta-analysis as *a scientific investigation of a well-defined collection of previously presented individual (case)studies concerning a certain phenomenon, in which (mainly) quantitative research methods are applied which are able to test and assess qualitative as well as quantitative knowledge based on a well-defined collection of available study material with the aim to (i) gain new insight into the chosen phenomenon under study, and (ii) achieve a quantitative research experiment.*

The use of meta-analysis in economics has resulted in a rising tide of scientific contributions. But, clearly, it has also increasingly been recognized that economics is at best a quasi-experimental science, so that external study circumstances are hard to control. For example, the year of data collection, the geographical location, the sample size, or the functional forms of models in various empirical studies are usually not equal or uniform, and may have significant impacts on the study outcomes. In many cases, empirical studies were not intended for comparative analysis, so that statistical inference from a sample of previous studies is highly problematic. It is thus of critical importance to design an operational methodology that accounts to the maximum extent possible for differences in study design and execution. In general, meta-analysis is a proper methodological vehicle for those research questions that are investigated in comparable study designs and formats. Only then, can meta-analytical procedures generate additional information from an existing body of knowledge, by deploying proper methods for the quantitative research synthesis of findings from a range of prior studies.

In recent years, we have seen an avalanche of comparative studies and meta-analyses in the field of transportation. These contributions have highlighted the analytical vigour and have applied lessons from research syntheses in this field.

2.6 Prospect for a Research Agenda

There is certainly a need for thorough comparative analysis in the transportation sector. Despite different research traditions, different policy constellations, different lifestyles and mobility patterns and different socioeconomic conditions, it is of the utmost relevance to identify commonalities and contrasts in research findings and policy impacts. The following issues may serve as illustrations of a possible research agenda for comparative study:

• general transportation issues

Examples are access conditions to (public and private) transport, differences in environmental stress, contrasting views on mobility and social rights, or different shares of passenger and freight transport.

• problem identification in regard to the human dimension

In this setting, one may want to analyze and design megatrends of mobility (e.g. individualization, ageing, economic growth), the organization of our space-economy (urbanization, land use, etc.), or people's innate drive to benefit from the 'flying carpet' idea (see Sect. 2.1).

• strategic policy issues

Here one may think of policy scenario design for sustainable transport; the identification of constraints, goals and opportunities for sustainable mobility; or the exploration of different pathways and transitional roads to sustainable transport systems (e.g. hardware, information provision, attitude changes, or shifts in policy practices).

• social well-being and human behaviour

The following issues may illustrate this approach: the assessment of values and perceptions of the 'homo mobilis'; the social dilemma emerging from efficiency, equity, and quality in transport access; or the modelling of the social epidemiology of noise, stress or safety.

• policy handles and policy research

Important concerns in this context are: the transparent modelling of individual and collective interests in mobility behaviour, the assessment of sustainable transport impacts and perception by different socioeconomic target groups, or the systemic innovation of our land use-transportation systems (including industrial site development, satellite cities, etc.).

It goes without saying that a proper analysis and sophisticated modelling exercise of this complex force field means an enormous challenge for the transportation research community. There is clearly a need for a transition from speculative arguments to solid theory, from subjective reflections to testable models, from aggregate macro-oriented analysis to behavioural, micro-based experimental models, and from a mono-disciplinary approach to a creative exploration of the opportunities for sustainable mobility at the edges of different disciplines. And, most of all, there is a clear need for systematic fact-finding, leading to consistent and harmonized empirical databases so as to pave the road for international comparative research. This would be a sine qua non for a mature comparative study program on European and North-American mobility and transportation patterns, and elsewhere in the world.

References

Banister D, Stead D, Akerman P, Dreborg A, Steen P, Nijkamp P, Schleicher-Tappeser R (2000) European transport and sustainable development. SPON, London

van den Bergh, JCJM, Button KJ, Nijkamp P, Pepping G (1997) Meta-analysis in environmental economics. Kluwer Academic, Dordrecht

van Geenhuizen M, Nijkamp P (2003) Coping with uncertainty: an expedition into the field of new transport technology. Transportation Planning and Technology 26: 449–467

Glass GV (1976) Primary, secondary and meta-analysis of research. Educational Research 5: 3–8

Gudmundsson H (2003) Making concepts matter: sustainable mobility and indicator systems in transport policy. International Social Science Journal 176: 199–218

Nijkamp P, Vleugel J (1995) In search of sustainable transport systems. In: Banister D, Capello R, Nijkamp P (eds) European transport and communications networks. John Wiley, Chichester, pp 287–299

Nijkamp P, Rienstra S, Vleugel J (1998) Transportation planning and the future. John Wiley, New York

Rodenburg CA, Ubbels B, Nijkamp P (2001) Open windows of Europe. In: Columbus F (ed) European economic and political issues III. Nova Science Publishers, New York, pp 117–136

Stead D (2003) Transport and land-use planning: really joined up? International Social Science Journal 176: 333–348

Steg L (2003) Can public transport compete with the private car? IIATS Research 27: 27–36

WHO (2004) Report on traffic accidents. Available at http://www.who.int/world-health-day/2004/infomaterials/world_report/en/chapter1.pdf

Part A: Traffic Forecasting and Transport Network Analysis

3   Urban Travel Forecasting in the USA and UK

David E. Boyce[1] and Huw C. W. L. Williams[2]

[1] Northwestern University, Evanston, Illinois, USA
[2] Cardiff University, Cardiff, UK

3.1 Introduction[1]

Nearly five decades ago in the United States, urban transport was first subjected to a systematic analysis that became the forerunner of modern transport planning. The reasons for the emergence of this new kind of planning activity are well known and will not concern us here. Within ten years both the approach and the embedded travel forecasting models had been implemented at many major urban centres of the world including several in Europe. Although subject to refinements and reinterpretation, the models in widespread contemporary use in urban, regional, national and international transport studies are recognisably the descendants of those four-stage procedures defined in the late 1950s.

There have always been criticisms of travel forecasting models. In the early 1960s criticism was muted, but by the late 1970s voices in opposition had turned into a clamour. Following the celebrated San Francisco Bay Area lawsuit and the subsequent Clean Air Act Amendments of 1990 (Garrett and Wachs 1996) the critique of "conventional" models took on new urgency. And yet, nearly 50 years after its inception, the four-stage travel forecasting procedure is still in widespread use in large metropolitan areas.

The purpose of this chapter is to examine some of the tensions and conflicts between the multiple states of the art and the states of practice. We interpret the former as comprising the theory of models, conceptions of model systems, model prototypes, and possibly advanced model systems being applied in practical studies which may be on the point of wider acceptance. The latter are characterised by widely available practical applications.

We shall structure our discussion of state of the art developments around two related themes: firstly, those evolutionary approaches in which the multi-stage procedure has been significantly refined; and secondly, those attempts beginning in the early 1970s to model travel behaviour "from the ground up." In Sect. 3.2 we offer a view of the historical development focusing on model specification and equilibration, noting the consequences of some lost opportunities at the very outset

---

[1] Presented at the 43rd Congress of the European Regional Science Association, Jyväskylä, Finland, August 27–30, 2003.

of the discipline. This discussion forms an important point of contact with the various states of practice. In Sect. 3.3 we survey those attempts to rethink the field by constructive aggregation over microbehavioural relations, extending early microeconometric approaches based on the theory of discrete choice.

Models are not, of course, constructed in a vacuum but are strongly conditioned by their context, the planning and policy framework, the evaluation system and precision of information required. The selection of the United States (US) and the United Kingdom (UK) to exemplify our discussion in Sects. 3.4–5 is rather more than for the authors' convenience, as it illustrates the influence on model design of differences in historical development, institutional contexts, evaluation and information requirements, and the resources available to maintain and upgrade models. An assessment of progress, current problems and challenges is presented in Sect. 3.6, particularly in relation to what are key requirements for model validity and design. A brief conclusion follows.

3.2 Specification, Estimation and Solution Methods for Integrated Equilibrium Models

Throughout history, traffic congestion has been a phenomenon that mankind finds wasteful and offensive. So it was in the early 1950s when mathematical economics, a new and rapidly developing field, sought to tackle practical problems. A team of young economists (Beckmann et al. 1956) took up the problem of congestion in a transport network, and succeeded in devising a mathematical model of travel and route choices that contributed in a fundamental way to this new field. Assuming that travel between each pair of origins and destinations decreases with increasing cost, that used routes connecting each pair have minimal and equal travel costs, and that the travel costs on the links of the network are increasing functions of the total link flow, Beckmann devised an optimization problem whose solution simultaneously satisfies these three conditions. Although the solution properties of the problem were thoroughly analyzed, no solution method was devised. Concurrently, Wardrop (1952) succinctly described the properties of such equilibria.

This work, completed in 1954, and published in book form only in 1956, did not appear in academic journals. It was summarized in only one professional journal as late as 1967. It did not impact the urban transportation studies that began in those same years in the United States, perhaps because the mathematical treatment was not accessible to the engineers and planners who staffed those agencies. As a result, one of the most important innovations of this field was effectively lost for over ten years.

In place of this integrated model of travel and route choices proposed by Beckmann, a four-stage travel forecasting procedure evolved from 1956 onwards, as described by Martin et al. (1961), in which the authors depicted the procedure in a complex, multi-page diagram. At its heart lay four stages or steps: trip generation (G); trip distribution (D); modal split (MS) and traffic assignment (A). Each was depicted as a separate stage that received inputs from the former and provided outputs to its successor.

Following the acceptance of the four-stage paradigm, most researchers and professionals became engaged in the improvement of the models and methods described in the individual stages. Of particular relevance here, household-based category analysis replaced zone-based regression models for trip productions (Wooton and Pick 1967), and utilities or generalised costs derived in early studies of modal choice with models specified and estimated at the individual level (Quarmby 1967; Warner 1962) were embedded in assignment, modal split and distribution models (Wilson et al. 1969). The incorporated generalised costs, specified as linear functions of objectively measured attributes with travel time suitably scaled to money units, served as an interface between policies, behavioural response and benefit evaluation. The numerical estimate of the "value of time" has, arguably, proved to be one of the most important parameters in the whole of planning.

From an analytic viewpoint, the earliest distribution and modal split models, which involved apportioning trips between different locations and modes, adopted empirically derived functions – sometimes referred to as deterrence functions (for spatial interaction), and diversion curves (for modal shares) – and these were determined through "goodness-of-fit" criteria. By the late 1960s these started to be replaced by analytic functions, and share models of the multinomial logit form were widely adopted (Manheim 1979; Wilson 1970; Wilson et al. 1969). These were conceptually appealing, analytically tractable and consistent with several theoretical constructs that were starting to be used for interpreting dispersion associated with travel (Erlander and Stewart 1990; McFadden 1973; Wilson 1970).

A problem that exercised the earliest modellers was the ordering of the G, D, MS and A segments and how they should be "linked" together. There were, from the start, informal behavioural assumptions underpinning the four-stage approach in terms of a sequence of decisions that mapped onto the individual submodels. However, the correspondence between the Generation (G), Distribution (D), Modal Split (MS) and Assignment (A), with frequency (f), location (l), mode (m) and route (r) choice of the trip, respectively, remained tenuous.

Various alternative structures for the demand model were proposed reflecting, it was assumed, the conditionality of a sequence of decisions, the most popular being whether the distribution submodel preceded (G/D/MS/A), followed (G/MS/D/A) or was combined (G/D-MS/A) with the modal split submodel. The first two constructions involved the formation of "composite costs" that represented "average costs" at what were referred to as "later stages of the models." As late as the mid 1970s no detailed theoretical basis for the entire model existed; for a given ordering, which was suggested *a priori* from behavioural assumptions, the form of the composite cost was regarded as an extra degree of freedom for achieving improved "goodness-of-fit;" see Senior and Williams (1977) for a review of model structures adopted in practice.

The derivation of the nested logit model within discrete choice theory provided one resolution to these ambiguities (Daly and Zachary 1978; McFadden 1978; Williams 1977). This development endowed the whole model with a behavioural rationale in which the analytical structure of the demand function reflected under-lying utility functions, imposing two important restrictions on the overall model. Firstly, the composite costs that interfaced the different submodels needed to be formulated in a particular way; for logit-type models these were in the form of a "log sum" function, a form that had already been implemented with microdata by Ben-Akiva (1974). Secondly, the parameters that determined the sensitivity of trip choices to changes in times or costs, had to decrease as one progressed from route choice, through mode to locational and frequency selection in the G/D/MS/A structure. Only then would it be ensured that the *estimated* direct- and cross-elasticity parameters had the appropriate sign, requiring the demand for an alterna-tive to fall when its cost rose or the cost of a substitute fell. The nested logit model thus provided a consistent way of combining the various constituent choices with differential cross substitution between alternatives, and made the ordering of asso-ciated logit share functions subject to empirical test. It is important to note that the specification of the demand model with empirically derived functions for loca-tional and/or modal shares is not immune from this strict requirement for appro-priate response properties derived from the calibrated model.

Williams and Senior (1977) reconfigured the four-stage procedure as a nested logit structure, experimented with different orderings of the distribution and modal split models, and showed that many models in UK practice did not satisfy the nec-essary parameter inequalities implied by the chosen structure. The specific impli-cation of this finding was that such models could have produced counter-intuitive results. The more general implication was that calibration and the traditional no-tion of validation based on goodness-of-fit and held-back samples was not a suffi-cient test for the validity of such cross-sectional models for policy appraisal.

A fundamental problem that confronted theoreticians and practitioners since the earliest days was the design of solution procedures to generate equilibrium states of required precision, in which the costs (or times) of travel through the networks are consistent with the demands that created them. The practical difficulties of this problem almost certainly have resulted from the mathematical statement of the problem that Beckmann had produced years earlier being unknown to the profes-sionals who initially proposed the *ad hoc* four-stage procedure.

Until 1975 the problem of equilibrium was almost entirely seen to be confined to the assignment of fixed trip matrices. Several *ad hoc* approximate procedures were devised before rigorous solution algorithms based on the Beckmann formula-tion emerged. In the morass of numerical detail involved in handling several trip matrices and large urban networks, the additional complexity of seeking self-consistency throughout the entire procedure tended to be seen as an unnecessary luxury or was simply unrecognised or ignored.

Where it was considered, the notion of "feedback" of costs from the assignment to other segments of the model began to be discussed. The congested costs were simply recycled back to the modal split and possibly to the distribution model, and amended modal matrices returned to the assignment process. A few scholars, however, had already begun to investigate ways to combine the trip distribution, mode split and traffic assignment stages, and eventually rediscovered Beckmann's formulation. The first to embark on this line of thinking was Murchland (1970), but his efforts were largely unsuccessful. Subsequently, Evans (1976) and Florian and Nguyen (1975, 1978) proposed formulations, which were special cases or elaborations of Beckmann's original formulation, and solution algorithms. Upon evaluation, only the algorithm of Evans proved to be practical for solving problems of realistic size (Boyce et al. 1988).

Even with this advance in understanding, these combined models were largely a research curiosity and effectively unknown to practitioners. Initial efforts to implement such models occurred in the early 1980s and continued through the 1990s. These early combined, or integrated, models had serious limitations as compared with professional practice, representing only a single class of travel or trip purpose, and being much smaller in scale than the models used in practice.

During the past ten years, several multiclass, integrated models have been implemented and applied. The first multiclass integrated model was implemented by Lam and Huang (1992); however, since classes in their model correspond to modes, it is not comparable to other multiclass models. The second model represents the work of de Cea et al. (2003), and is arguably the most advanced model available today. The third example is by Boyce and Bar-Gera (2003), a two-class research model for the Chicago Region implemented at the same scale and detail used in professional practice. Each of these models was estimated from available travel surveys and validated against census data. In the case of Santiago, Chile, the model has evolved to the status of commercially available software, called *ESTRAUS*. Each model is solved with algorithms that may be traced to Evans (1976). Subsequent to these developments, Bar-Gera and Boyce (2003) integrated the origin-based assignment algorithm of Bar-Gera (2002) into a single class integrated model. For a review of operational multiclass models, see Boyce and Bar-Gera (2004).

There is a close correspondence between the Evans algorithm for solving an integrated model and the four-stage procedure; in effect the four-stage procedure is actually a primitive algorithm, or solution procedure, for solving an unstated, integrated model. Current understanding of integrated models is providing guidance for solving the four-stage procedure with feedback, as is now required in the US. The gist of this insight is to recognize that the trip tables and road link flows are the solution variables of the problem, which need to be adjusted from iteration to iteration to drive the solution towards equilibrium. One difficulty from the four-stage perspective is the lack of a well-defined objective on which to base this adjustment procedure.

3.3 Specification, Estimation and Solution Methods for Microanalytic Models

In a rallying call to accompany the early stages of the Travel Model Improvement Program, Wachs expressed a view that resonated with many: "the state of practice in transportation planning consists of an obsolete approach to modelling which has been marginally updated and adapted by clever technicians but which has not been fundamentally rethought from the ground up" (Wachs 1996, p 213). The four-stage procedure was deemed to belong to another age, essentially one of large infrastructure development, quite inappropriate for a new generation of travel demand management policies. There was a widely held view that what was needed was a finer representation and understanding of both the demand for and supply of transport services more closely attuned to the contexts of application.

In fact, attempts to model travel and transport systems "from the ground up" started to appear in the early 1970s in the work of, among others, Ben-Akiva (1974) and Domencich and McFadden (1975). Systems of disaggregate demand models were specified and estimated at the individual level and were then subjected to aggregation to generate the desired forecasts. This approach contrasted with the traditional one of specifying models for broad groups and then subjecting them to parameter estimation.

The basic motivation for this style of work was to consider the full variability in individual behaviour and avoid or ameliorate aggregation bias, to provide efficient sampling procedures for model estimation, and above all to furnish the model system with a behavioural theory based on individual choice that would, it was hoped, yield a more suitable and stable basis for forecasting. We shall discuss this "ground up" approach and its emergence as an operational competitor to models of the traditional form. Further developments based on activity-travel frameworks are then considered briefly.

By the late 1970s the microeconomic theory of discrete choice had taken root and provided a behavioural basis for travel forecasting. For the last 25 years this theory has been the dominant paradigm within which predictions of travel behaviour have been made; see Ben-Akiva and Lerman (1985), Oppenheim (1995), Ortúzar and Willumsen (2001), as well as McFadden (2001) for a 30-year retrospective review of the approach. The discrete choice framework, based on random utility theory, proved to be a particularly powerful one capable of wide application, and many of the locational and travel-related models were reinterpreted from this viewpoint. Spatial interaction models were explicitly treated as models of locational choice within housing markets (Anas 1981; McFadden 1978; Williams and Senior 1978). Modal choice models were studied in great detail and the traditional two or three way choices were extended to a variety of private, public transport and slow (walk and cycle) modes. For these purposes, the multinomial and nested logit models were widely used, the latter incorporating "similarity" and differential substitution between alternative choices, and being preferred to the more general but computationally less tractable multinomial probit function. More general specifications, such as General Extreme Value (McFadden 1978) and mixed logit (McFadden and Train 2000) models are now increasingly applied in academic studies, but it may be some time before the multinomial and nested logit are replaced in practice.

While the revealed preference (RP) approach dominated the early studies of discrete choice, stated preference (SP) methods emerged in the 1980s as a powerful and widely used technique; see, for example, Bates (1988) and Hensher (1994). The use of micro-computers to implement stated preference experiments to study and forecast travel behaviour dates from the mid-1980s. *MINT* is a prominent example of software developed at that time for the generation of different SP designs. The version *WinMINT* resulted from a collaboration between Hague Consulting Group and Accent Marketing and Research (Hague Consulting Group 2001). The relative strengths of the revealed and stated preference approaches are now widely recognised and mixed data designs are increasingly used to exploit the strengths and avoid the weaknesses of each.

Much theoretical and applied developmental work on specification, estimation and aggregation was undertaken in the 1970s and 1980s by Ben-Akiva and by McFadden, and their colleagues. In Europe the contribution of Andrew Daly was particularly significant, not least in the development of the software *ALOGIT* for nested logit estimation (Daly 1987).

In its selective review of world practice in the late 1990s, Hague Consulting Group (1997) critically discussed, among others, applications of the microeconometric approach in the San Francisco Bay Area, The Netherlands, Stockholm and Sydney. The authors advanced the claim that "the evidence from the Review indicates that disaggregate models now provide a practical alternative to aggregate models in terms of providing trip tables to load onto networks. In terms of ability to capture aspects of behaviour that may affect forecasts of demand, they consistently outperform their aggregate counterparts." They also note: "Representations of travel patterns as trips or tours have both been able to form the basis for operational systems; they are to be deemed 'available technology.'"

Research over the last twenty years aimed at relaxing some restrictions involved in the formation of simple utility models, by incorporating imperfect information, limited choice sets and satisficing behaviour – which are clearly present to differing degrees in all choice contexts (see, for example, Bhat 2002; McFadden 2001; Williams and Ortúzar 1982). These developments led to the question of how to refine existing models to improve the representation of behaviour, and the more philosophical problem of how much "understanding" is required for satisfactory prediction, questions that continue to divide social scientists.

For the last 25 years the major question confronted by travel behaviour theorists has been how to embed spatial and temporal choices and preferences within a rich constraint-based environment formed by household interdependencies, activity scheduling and the transport supply. Although the activity-travel framework has flourished as a *descriptive* basis for travel demand analysis since the late 1970s (see, for example, Jones 1979; Jones et al. 1983), synthesis of the activity-travel framework based on constraints and the discrete choice paradigm for *forecasting* travel had to await the late 1980s and 1990s before significant development was achieved. The broad distinction between activity-travel models under development, and in particular between econometric and hybrid simulation approaches, has been provided by, among others, Wachs (1996), Rossi and Shiftan (1997) and Bowman and Ben-Akiva (2001).

3.4 States of Practice in the USA

Urban travel forecasting may be regarded as beginning in 1955 with the Chicago Area Transportation Study, the first to implement a procedure that resembles the four stages described above. Significantly, it was the first study to assign a trip table (origin-destination flows) to a road network taking into account the effects of congestion. Concurrently, engineers at the Bureau of Public Roads were devising other procedures and computer programs for assigning trips to congested road networks.

Model and computer code development in the US prior to 1970 may be summarized as follows: use of household surveys to estimate daily trip frequencies (trip generation); development and application of two trip distribution models, the doubly-constrained gravity model and the intervening opportunities model; use of simple diversion curves to allocate trips to modes, either before or after trip distribution; implementation of heuristic procedures for assigning trips to congested road networks with travel times increasing with flow, but without solving a well-specified equilibrium problem; development and application of main-frame computer programs to solve this sequence of models, but without taking account of inconsistencies among the models.

This fragmented activity led in the early 1970s to a more coordinated effort within the US Department of Transportation. Some of the achievements of the Urban Transportation Planning System (*UTPS*) may be summarized as follows: introduction of the multinomial logit function for forecasting mode choice; introduction of a user-equilibrium algorithm (effectively, the Frank-Wolfe method) for assigning auto trips to congested road networks; improvements in the coding of transit networks and the assignment of transit trips; recognition of the need to achieve consistency among the four stages, with some concern about solving the procedure with feedback. The creation and distribution of *UTPS* also led to the preparation of manuals and training courses (US DOT 1977).

Changes in federal policy in 1981 led to a decision to terminate the development of *UTPS*. Comsis, a private organization that had been involved in its development, then launched their product, *MinUTP*. A somewhat similar product called *TranPlan* had been under development for some years, initially by Control Data Corporation. These two software systems, either directly or indirectly encompassing the model and code development efforts of US DOT, were the initial versions of PC-based travel forecasting models and software. Other software systems from the same period have effectively not survived.

In parallel with these developments, researchers at the University of Montreal, Canada, had implemented an equilibrium-based two-mode urban travel forecasting model called *EMME*, drawing on research findings cited above (Florian et al. 1979). Subsequently, this method became the basis for *EMME/2*, a commercial software system first released in the late 1980s for linking and solving the models of the four-stage procedure (INRO 2004). In addition to a rigorous implementation of a user-equilibrium road assignment algorithm and a probabilistic transit route choice algorithm, *EMME/2* includes tools for solving the doubly-constrained trip distribution model, stochastic mode choice models, network coding procedures and related utilities.

Building on the capabilities of the emerging field of Geographical Information Systems, a group of travel modellers assembled a system known as *TransCAD* based on PC technology (Caliper Corporation 2004). This system sought to embrace and incorporate various research advances throughout the US and beyond, including an early version of the combined model described above. Another US-developed research-based software system, which has been found to be useful for smaller regions, is *Quick Response System II* (*QRS II*), developed by AJH Associates (2004). *EMME/2* and *TransCAD* have enjoyed considerable success throughout the US during the 1990s; *EMME/2* also succeeded in developing an international following in the UK, Sweden, Canada, Australia and New Zealand, and South Africa, to name several.

The late 1980s was a period of change in the US, as environmental-based interest groups successfully sought to challenge the status quo of transportation planning in the courts (Garrett and Wachs 1996). The Bay Area lawsuit led to the Clean Air Act Amendments of 1990, and the requirement of conformity analysis for MPOs. To qualify a transportation plan for federal aid, each MPO had to demonstrate that building the proposed system would not result in the deterioration in air quality. One implication of this requirement is the need to determine road link flows and speeds by time periods of the typical weekday, in order to forecast atmospheric emissions. Since available travel forecasting methods were based on a 24-hour period, an ad hoc factoring method, based only on surveys, was devised to allocate flows by time periods of the day (Deakin et al.1993).

Attempts to reform transportation planning practice also led to new provisions in the Intermodal Surface Transportation Efficiency Act of 1991 (ISTEA). Many new requirements were placed on planners and MPOs by this legislation, but the one most pertinent to this discussion is the requirement to solve the four-stage procedure with "feedback." During the early 1990s many MPOs updated their travel forecasting models for the first time in many years, which often resulted in adoption of a different software system.

In response to these legislative mandates, model updates and related technical requirements, US DOT and US Environmental Protection Agency (US EPA) created the Travel Model Improvement Program, as mentioned earlier. The agencies had begun to devise a series of short and longer run model improvement tasks, when they were directed by the US Congress to fund a large-scale systems simulation project at the Los Alamos National Laboratory dubbed TRANSIMS. This ambitious effort set out to apply microsimulation techniques to represent interrelated travel and location-based decisions of each inhabitant of a metropolitan area throughout the 24-hour weekday. The result was not a new, integrated model so much as a system of computer programs related to choice of when, where, and how to travel, and the associated computation of atmospheric emissions. An attempt to implement the system was initially made for the Portland, Oregon, metropolitan area, but was not completed by 2001, as intended. At that time a transportation modelling consultant was retained to make a final attempt to implement and validate the system. This effort remains a work in progress.

3.5 States of Practice in the UK

By the middle of the 1970s the era of the large urban transport studies was coming to an end and few city authorities had the resources or inclination to maintain large transport models. With few exceptions, most notably in London, model systems constructed a decade or more earlier, and the databases that supported them, were allowed to atrophy. Much local expertise dispersed, and the under-resourced and lonely task of local authority modellers fell on fewer and fewer shoulders. Where necessary, international consultants, some with the founders of the discipline at their helm, were called upon to address strategic and tactical issues, often in the form of urban development projects and traffic studies. Large urban transport projects were relatively few in number. Partly in an attempt to wrest control in a deregulated public transport environment, however, renewed interest was shown in Light Rapid Transit schemes for which the estimation of decongestion benefits was a significant component of the external benefit of such schemes and central to mounting the case for Central Government funding support. Throughout the 1990s there was also an increasing interest in demand restraint; several metropolitan areas conducted modelling exercises involving public transport, traffic restraint and, in some cases, limited highway investment.

For such purposes many software packages were available in the private sector. Indeed, a key feature of the 1980s and early 1990s was one of fragmentation of the transport planning software suite, and its organisation within management information systems as a collection of submodels that were refined and integrated on a "pick-and-mix" basis (see Williams 2004 for an overview of developments). In turn, large consultancies found it in their interest to join forces with smaller specialist companies, particularly in the context of implementation of land use models, microeconometric studies of discrete choice (typically multimodal studies), and stated preference exercises.

A prominent example, and one of the most widely used and innovative, was the *TRIPS* suite (now *CUBE*) of Martin, Voorhees and Associates (MVA 2004). The various submodels of the four-stage approach had been enhanced and available in both synthetic and incremental (pivot point) forms (Bates et al. 1987). In the former travel behaviour is modelled at the cross section and elasticity parameters estimated prior to forecasting, while in the latter, changes from a given state (e.g. the base state) are estimated utilising given elasticity parameters. Both are available for application at the micro (individual data) or aggregate (grouped data) level.

Since the mid-1980s *SATURN* (Van Vliet 1982) was extensively applied in and beyond the UK. Matrix updating was a standard part of the package and was widely applied to breathe new life into dated trip matrices. Initially promoted as a "modern" assignment program, it was the first to incorporate a rigorous approach to equilibrium assignment in UK transport planning applications. *SATURN* not only had the capability of working at different levels of network resolutions, requiring different and compatible specifications, but in the 1990s became a framework within which research was conducted on consistently integrating demand and assignment models. A further important development in the 1990s was the extension of microsimulation models from their traditional junction applications to treat wider urban networks. In the UK the *PARAMICS* model system developed by SIAS Limited is an example of a microsimulation approach which has been applied to a wide range of towns and cities (Druit 2000).

In the late 1980s and early 1990s there was considerable interest in both the US and UK in the effect of congestion on travel, and of additional traffic (and vehicle miles) that might be induced by capacity expansion and new roads. In the US the effect of induced traffic on atmospheric emissions and energy consumption was a matter of particular concern (TRB 1995), while in the UK it was the effect on congestion, traffic growth and economic benefits (SACTRA 1994). The report of the Standing Advisory Committee for Trunk Road Assessment had a substantial impact on the methods by which travel forecasting and the appraisal of schemes were conducted in the UK (Williams 2004).

Congestion problems on interurban networks were traditionally addressed within a single mode planning framework. Within an essentially "predict and provide" approach, construction of more highway capacity almost inevitably resulted. By the mid-1990s this approach was officially questioned and, in an attempt to establish sound environmental credentials, the 'New Labour' Government elected in 1997 sought to re-examine the problems of development and transport in the major corridors, drawing in the large urban areas or conurbations of which they were part. The policy terms of reference of the 22 Multimodal Studies set up in 1998 embraced all modes, and demand restraint in addition to road and public transport investment. The studies were accompanied by an enhanced evaluation framework that sought to establish a "level playing field" between the modes and is based on environment, safety, economy, accessibility and integration criteria.

The Department for Transport issued modelling and evaluation advice to accompany the Multimodal Studies and for Local Transport Planning (DETR 2000; DfT 2002). The methodological framework is not narrowly prescriptive and allows considerable discretion on the part of consulting teams according to the nature of the local areas and their problems. The wide range of approaches applied so far for the Multimodal Studies has included: both integrated land use-transport models and independent estimates of trip ends; four- and five-stage structures down to two-stage models with a simple bridge between modal networks; and synthetic and incremental (pivot point) approaches.

Both the Multimodal Studies and Local Transport Planning are being conducted within the overall framework of the Government's Ten Year Plan (which includes national targets for congestion, accidents and pollution), and each has the requirement to examine a whole range of initiatives which will encourage more sustainable transport arrangements and particularly improve integration, both between modes and between land use and transport. Land use, infrastructure investment, fiscal and regulatory policies, as well as a range of "soft" measures, such as workplace travel plans, school travel plans, teleworking, cycling and walking strategies, are to be considered. The evidence base for travel forecasting for some of these policies is not strong and transferability of experience will likely be considered of more value than model-based prediction as a guide to implementation.

As part of the guidance issued by the Department for Transport in relation to infrastructure investment appraisal, the advice on variable demand analysis, to be released in 2005 (Department for Transport, personal communication) is likely to have significant implications for both strategic and tactical model development in the UK. Following earlier advice (Highways Agency 1997), the emphasis will be on model design, and will be much enhanced in terms of the discussion of: model complexity, proposed structures, model parameters, design and convergence of equilibrium-seeking algorithms, model validation and sensitivity analysis. Of particular interest in the present context is the research conducted on the model system DIADEM (Development of Integrated Assignment and Demand Modelling) and the development of improved equilibrium models and solution algorithms. Further information about this research on variable demand modelling in general, and DIADEM in particular, can be found in Department for Transport (2003).

As part of the research underpinning the on-going scrutiny of impact models and appraisal methods by the Department for Transport, Bly et al. (2001) have reviewed the structure, parameters and validation of 24 of those models that have been implemented in the last ten years or so, drawing largely but not exclusively from UK applications. Some have been applied in Multimodal Studies, others in strategic assessments in major cities. The models exhibit wide variation in their explicit representation of responses and range from five-level nested structures in the form G/D/MS/T/A (with T representing the journey timing choice) to 2-stage models. Many models are in the form of nested (logit) functions, some in incremental form (Bates et al. 1987). Following our discussion in Sect. 3.2, it is interesting and sobering to note the finding by Bly et al. (2001) that several of the synthetic models, with nested structures, are endowed with estimated parameter values that are *inconsistent* with the structures selected. We would suggest that model validation is here deficient and some of the predictions may have been unreliable. Where incremental nested logit forms have been adopted, parameter values have been inserted that are consistent with the selected specifications. This UK experience suggests that current US practice, in which distribution models often include empirically derived deterrence functions, be scrutinised to confirm that the demand functions are endowed with acceptable elasticity properties.

3.6 Assessment of Progress, Problems and Prospects

The experience of the past 50 years, both in practice and research, offers many insights and lessons for the future development of our field of urban travel forecasting. In this section, we offer a very brief assessment of progress, problems and future prospects and some directions. To give some structure to the discussion we present our points under a number of key themes as shown below.

3.6.1 Contexts of Model Development

Although many of the core issues of our field, particularly congestion mitigation, accessibility provision and urban growth management have long been key concerns, the sustainability agenda, including air quality and environmental justice, have imposed new information and appraisal considerations. Future developments will be driven in part by these changes and information requirements. While we have cited much progress in the development of theory, method and technique over the last fifty years, the lead time of new ideas is uncomfortably long and we are even now questioning issues such as the impact of that most common of policies, highway development, that were once taken for granted. While infrastructure investment and pricing remain prominent policy instruments, new initiatives are now widely advocated. The field is still not well placed to deal with the full range of demand management policies. Although the generalised cost function is very flexible, and much ingenuity is shown in representing the "policy-model interface," the knowledge base in many areas is currently weak. Indeed, some estimates for the implication of lifestyle changes, technological initiatives (such as e-commerce and telecommuting), and even some price-based demand management policies, are often little better than guesses and rely on minimal empirical evidence. Transferability of experience will be particularly important in this context.

3.6.2 Distinct Alternatives for Practice

We agree with the view expressed by the Hague Consulting Group (1997) that there is no generally accepted state of the art or state of practice in travel forecasting, but rather large classes of models and model systems, some at distinct stages of development and in a process of continual refinement. These classes of models may achieve particular significance in different periods of the development of the field. Thirty years ago "aggregate" and "disaggregate" models and "simultaneous" and "sequential" structures were distinctions that stimulated considerable debate. Nowadays, the former remains - whether aggregation precedes or follows estimation - but the unit of demand, be it trip-based, tour-based and activity-travel based, has become a prominent distinction. In the future, microanalysis specifications and estimates with cross sectional or longitudinal (panel) data may well become a further key distinction. Although the four-stage procedure has dominated applications over this period, they have long since absorbed different "disaggregate" concepts, becoming hybrid forms, and have been applied in anything from two- to five-stages or levels. Such is the variation in this approach, both in detail and quality of specification, that care is needed in applying a single collective description to the genus.

3.6.3 Theoretical Developments

Although still a technical and rather esoteric specialisation, travel forecasting has long since emerged from its exclusive traffic engineering, operational research and regional science roots, and now widely embraces economic, statistical, geographical and psychological theories and constructs. The award of a Nobel Prize to Daniel McFadden in 2000 affirmed both the contribution of transport applications to consumer econometrics, and the ascendancy of the discrete choice paradigm as a basis for describing, understanding and predicting travel behaviour. That said, from a behavioural standpoint, the field of practice is still theoretically immature. Although activity-based travel demand models are now developing rapidly, hitherto they have had little impact on forecasting in practice.

One of the original motivations for the development of the field, to gain an improved understanding of the interrelationship between land use and transport has been achieved and several operational, if cumbersome, integrated land use-transport models based on inter-related markets have emerged. Within the activity-travel framework, uncovering the detailed relationship between the travel behaviour of individuals and households and the structure of neighbourhoods and cities, which is showing considerable advances, (see, for example, Kitamura et al. 1997) will have important implications for our understanding of the sustainability of cities and regions.

The equilibrium paradigm remains dominant in our field and this is likely to continue. The analytical framework set out by Beckmann was rediscovered and is now being exploited more fully for the specification and solution of models. The representation of travel behaviour as a system of constraints, both equalities and inequalities with embedded choice functions, allows for the derivation and solution of families of models that may be widely adapted to different contexts. By focusing attention on the identification of this system and its relationships to benefits of engaging in activities, as well as travel costs, broadly defined, we can extract the essence of accumulated knowledge from multi-stage procedures.

3.6.4 Specification of Models and Model Design

Travel forecasting models are now characterised by greater precision in their representation of behaviour. We point to the increased stratification of traditional models by passenger groups, trip purposes, and time periods, and the greater refinement of the supply side. Time-of-day modelling and time-switching are now key aspects of our understanding of behavioural responses to congestion and transport policies. Experience with temporally stratified models, and current policy concerns, strongly suggest that 24-hour forecasts with factoring to time-of-day periods should no longer be used.

Highway network coding procedures have much improved the representation of supply, and may relate to demand in the form of individual vehicles, vehicle packets and flow groups. In particular they provide much greater appreciation of the significance of interacting flows at junctions. Public transport networks also now offer crowding effects. Transport networks should be represented in terms of road and transit link functions that depend upon the conflicting flows encountered on that link. Simpler functions that depend only on the links own flow may suffice for more aggregated representations suitable for long range, general models, but more detailed functions are needed for depicting the interactions of person and vehicle flows. The implications of network specification for solution algorithms and solution properties are important, and should be clarified for practitioners.

More information is needed about the costs and benefits of implementing models at different levels of resolution and the balance between over-elaboration and misspecification, given current knowledge and the information requirements. In many areas of our field, and in particular, the treatment of the inter-relationships between land use and transport, and the detailed specification of network models, the value added by greater resolution must be subject to detailed design criteria.

3.6.5 Estimation of Response Parameters

Stated preference methods have emerged as a powerful technique to augment revealed preference studies of individual choice behaviour. A current issue of major importance is the extent to which such methods yield useful results when the time or cost changes representing policies are small (less than 5 minutes). See the discussions in Mackie et al. (2003) and Hague Consultant Group (1996). This is a significant and unresolved problem, given the value of typical travel time changes accompanying many transport policies. A considerable amount of effort is now being directed towards reconciling demand responses from different types of data, specifically longitudinal and cross-sectional data sets. Contributions to impacts from different short and long run response mechanisms require clarification, given their importance to the economics of projects.

3.6.6 Solution of Models

The need to measure small differences between equilibrium states, particularly associated with economic benefits and emissions, imposes strict requirements for the precise solution of models. Considerable progress has been achieved in the design of algorithms to solve models in an internally consistent manner. The concept of solving for travel choices in stages should be de-emphasized, and replaced with convergent solution methods now becoming available. These solution procedures should be imbedded in future software systems in ways that can be readily applied by practitioners. Software vendors need to incorporate these new approaches, allowing users to specify a system of functions and constraints to be solved by specific or general purpose solution procedures.

3.6.7 Validation of Models

Validation is often and, in our view, incorrectly viewed simply as constructing models that satisfactorily replicate aspects of travel behaviour in a base year. This approach is necessary but far from being sufficient for forecasting the *response* to policies that requires adequate elasticity measures. Many models have been applied that do not attain the necessary standards for the purposes specified. As long as this notion continues to dominate the field, inappropriately specified models will slip through the validation net and little progress will be made in the comparison of model systems.

3.7 Conclusions

In 50 years travel forecasting has evolved from a fledgling field in North America to a worldwide activity in the support of public and increasingly private policy decision making. It is also a greatly expanded academic discipline in which understanding of travel behaviour is an end in itself, which requires different assessment criteria than for travel forecasting.

Perhaps travel forecasting models have failed to deliver their initial promise; we have pointed to lost opportunities in the early years and to inappropriate notions of validity. Theoretical deficiencies, predictive inaccuracies, and a general battering by those with a different approach to promote are evident. Travel forecasting activity has itself been undermined by a discredited "predict and provide" approach to planning within which it was housed. The remarkable longevity of those models of the "traditional form," however, is due to their capacity to absorb innovations; it has been suggested many times that in spite of known deficiencies, professionals trained in the use of these methods are, on the whole, comfortable with their results. There is also perceived to be a lack of a clear alternative for generating the required information. Assessment of the models is rightly seen as a relative not absolute activity, in relation to the next best alternative.

In conclusion we offer the following recommendations.

1. All models should be subjected to a detailed audit, particularly in relation to their descriptive, forecasting and policy testing characteristics. In particular, equilibration methods and qualitative and quantitative response properties should be assessed in order to screen for perverse behaviour.
2. Urban travel model development should be viewed as an ongoing process, requiring continual funding. It may well be context specific, and that one size will not necessarily fit all MPOs. It should also be seen as a technical matter. Legislative and administrative mandates are unlikely to be productive.
3. We, like many others, regard enrichment of the knowledge base in the form of case studies and before-and-after studies to be a priority for the development of the field. Case studies combining experience of transport system design and management with modelling of travel choices on these systems will be most useful in understanding both policies and how to model them.

We believe that the field is best served by taking a more eclectic view than is fashionable, avoidance of exaggerated claims and resisting model comparisons at different stages of their development. In this comparative exercise, nothing is obsolete until it is replaced by a model system fully tested in the arena of practice. The lack of standardisation of the models, and the protracted stages of development (from concepts, through prototypes to applications in the field) all suggest careful scrutiny of available alternatives for undertaking a specific task and caution against hasty and possibly ill-directed comparisons between models.

Acknowledgements

The contributions of the first author to this paper were initiated while he was an Erskine Fellow at the University of Canterbury, Christchurch, New Zealand, April–June 2003; revisions were made while he was a Visiting Professor at the University of Pennsylvania during the Fall Term 2003. The authors wish to acknowledge the helpful comments of two anonymous referees.

References

AJH Associates (2004) Quick response system II. Available at http://my.execpc.com/~ajh/ (accessed 19 September 2004)

Anas A (1981) Residential location markets and urban transportation: economic theory, econometrics and policy analysis with discrete choice models. Academic, New York

Bar-Gera H (2002) Origin-based algorithm for the traffic assignment problem. Transportation Science 36: 398–417

Bar-Gera H, Boyce D (2003) Origin-based algorithms for combined travel forecasting models. Transportation Research 37B: 405–422

Bates JJ, Ashley DJ, Hyman G (1987) The nested incremental logit model: theory and application to modal choice. Proceedings 15th PTRC Summer Annual Meeting, Seminar C, University of Bath

Bates JJ (ed) (1988) Stated preference methods in transport research. Journal of Transport Economics and Policy 22: 1–137

Beckmann M, McGuire CB, Winsten CB (1956) Studies in the economics of transportation. Yale University Press, New Haven

Ben-Akiva ME (1974) Structure of passenger travel demand models. Transportation Research Record 526: 26–42

Ben-Akiva ME, Lerman S (1985) Discrete choice analysis: theory and applications to travel demand. MIT Press, Cambridge

Bhat CR (2002) Recent methodological advances relevant to activity and travel behaviour analysis. In: Mahmassani HS (ed) In perpetual motion: travel behavior research opportunities and application challenges. Pergamon, Oxford, pp 381–414

Bly P, Emmerson P, van Vuren T, Ash A, Paulley N (2001) User-friendly multistage modelling advice. Phase 2: Modelling parameters, calibration and validation. Project report for ITEA Division, DTLR

Bowman JL, Ben-Akiva ME (2001) Activity-based disaggregate travel demand model system with activity schedules. Transportation Research 35A: 1–28

Boyce DE, LeBlanc LJ, Chon KS (1988) Network equilibrium models of urban location and travel choices: a retrospective survey. Journal of Regional Science 28: 159–183

Boyce D, Bar-Gera H (2003) Validation of multiclass urban travel forecasting models combining origin-destination, mode, and route choices. Journal of Regional Science 43: 517–540

Boyce D, Bar-Gera H (2004) Multiclass combined models for urban travel forecasting. Network and Spatial Economics 4: 115–124

Caliper Corporation (2004) TransCAD. Available at http://www.caliper.com (accessed 19 September 2004)

Daly AJ, Zachary S (1978) Improved multiple choice models. In: Hensher DA, Dalvi MQ (eds) Determinants of travel choice. Saxon House, Westmead

Daly AJ (1987) ALOGIT 3.2 user's guide. Hague Consulting Group, The Hague. The latest version ALOGIT4 is described at www.hpgholding.nl/software/welcsoft.htm (accessed 19 September 2004)

Deakin, Harvey, Skabardonis, Inc. (1993) Manual of regional transportation modeling practice for air quality. National Association of Regional Councils, Washington, DC.

De Cea J, Fernandez JL, Dekock V, Soto A (2003) ESTRAUS: a computer package for solving supply-demand equilibrium problems on multimodal urban transportation networks with multiple user classes. Presented at the Annual Meeting of the Transportation Research Board, Washington, DC.

Department of the Environment, Transport and the Regions (DETR) (2000) Guidance on the methodology for multi-modal studies (GOMMMS). Available at http://www.dft.gov.uk (accessed 19 September 2004)

Department for Transport (2002) Major scheme appraisal in local transport plans, parts 1, 2, 3 detailed guidance on public transport and highway schemes. Available at http://www.local-transport.dft.gov.uk (accessed 19 September 2004)

Department for Transport (2003) Variable demand modelling consultation advice background papers. Available at http://www.dft.gov.uk/stellent/groups/dft_econappr/ /documents/divisionhomepage/032181.hcsp (accessed 4 February 2005)

Domencich TA, McFadden D (1975) Urban travel demand: A behavioral analysis. North-Holland, Amsterdam

Druit S (2000) An introduction to PARAMICS. Available at http://www.sias.com/sias/ /paramics/articles/article1.html (accessed 19 September 2004)

Erlander S, Stewart NF (1990) The gravity model in transportation analysis. VSP, Utrecht

Evans SP (1976) Derivation and analysis of some models for combining trip distribution and assignment. Transportation Research 10: 37–57

Florian M, Nguyen S, Ferland J (1975) On the combined distribution-assignment of traffic. Transportation Science 9: 43–53

Florian M, Chapleau R, Nguyen S, Achim S, James-Lefebvre L, Galarneau S, Lefebvre J, Fisk C (1979) Validation and application of an equilibrium-based two-mode urban transportation planning method (EMME). Transportation Research Record 728: 14–23

Florian M, Nguyen S (1978) A combined trip distribution, modal split and trip assignment model. Transportation Research 12: 241–246

Garrett M, Wachs M (1996) Transportation planning on trial. Sage, Thousand Oaks

Hague Consulting Group (1997) A review of current world practice: a report for New South Wales Department of Transport. The Hague

Hague Consulting Group (2001) WinMINT 2.1. Available at http://www.hpgholding.nl/ /software/mint.htm (accessed 19 September 2004)

Hague Consulting Group, Accent Marketing and Research (1996) The value of travel time on UK roads. Prepared for the Department of Transport. Available at www.hpgholding.nl/publica/vot-uk.htm (accessed 19 September 2004)

Hensher DA (ed) (1994) Stated preference methods: Special issue. Transportation 21: 135–288

Highways Agency (1997) Design manual for roads and bridges, Volume 12, Traffic appraisal of road schemes. Section 2, Part 2: Induced traffic appraisal. The Stationery Office, London

INRO Consultants, Inc. (2004) EMME/2. Available at http://www.inro.ca/ (accessed 19 September 2004)

Jones PM (1979) New approaches to understanding travel behaviour: the human activity approach. In: Hensher DA, Stopher PR (eds) Behavioral travel modelling. Croom Helm, London

Jones PM, Dix MC, Clarke MI, Heggie IG (1983) Understanding travel behaviour. Gower, Aldershot

Kitamura R, Mokhtarian PL, Laidet L (1997) A microanalysis of land use and travel in five neighborhoods in the San Francisco Bay Area. Transportation 24: 125–158

Lam WHK, Huang H-J (1992) A combined trip distribution and assignment model for multiple user classes. Transportation Research 26B: 275–287

Mackie PJ, Wardman M, Fowkes AS, Whelan G, Nellthorp J, Bates J (2003) Values of travel time savings in the UK. Report to the Department for Transport. Institute for Transport Studies, University of Leeds, Leeds

Manheim ML (1979) Fundamentals of transportation systems analysis. MIT Press, Cambridge

Martin BV, Memmott 3rd FW, Bone AJ (1961) Principles and techniques of predicting future demand for urban area transportation. Research Report No. 38, M.I.T., Cambridge

Martin, Voorhees and Associates (MVA) (2004) CUBE. Available at http://www.mva-group.com (accessed 19 September 2004)

McFadden D (1973) Conditional logit analysis of qualitative choice behavior. In: Zarembka P (ed) Frontiers in econometrics. Academic, New York.

McFadden D (1978) Modeling the choice of residential location. In: Karlqvist A, Lundqvist L, Snickars F, Weibull J (eds) Spatial interaction theory and planning models. North-Holland, Amsterdam, pp 75–96

McFadden D (2001) Disaggregate behavioral travel demand's RUM side: a 30-year retrospective. In: Hensher D (ed) Travel behaviour research: The leading edge. Pergamon, Amsterdam, pp 17–64

McFadden D, Train K (2000) Mixed MNL models for discrete response. Journal of Applied Econometrics 15: 447–470

Murchland JD (1970) Road network traffic distribution in equilibrium. In: Henn R, Kunzi HP, Schubert H (eds) Mathematical models in the social sciences 8. Anton Hain Verlag, Meisenheim am Glan, Germany, pp 145–183 (in German translation)

Oppenheim N (1995) Urban travel demand modeling, Wiley, New York

Ortúzar JD, Willumsen L (2001) Modelling transport, 3rd edn. Wiley, Chichester

Quarmby DA (1967) Choice of travel mode for the journey to work: some findings. Journal of Transport Economics and Policy 1: 273–413

Rossi TF, Shiftan Y (1997) Tour based travel demand modelling in the US. Transportation systems 1997. In: Papageorgiou M, Pouliezos A (eds) Proceedings of the 8th IFAC/IFIP/IFORS symposium, Chania, Greece, Vol. 1. Pergamon, Oxford, pp 381–386

Standing Advisory Committee for Trunk Road Assessment (SACTRA) (1994) Trunk roads and the generation of traffic. The Stationery Office, London

Senior ML, Williams HCWL (1977) Model-based transport policy assessment; Part I: The use of alternative forecasting models, Traffic Engineering and Control 18: 402–406

Transportation Research Board (1995) Expanding metropolitan highways: implications for air quality and energy use. Special Report 245, Washington, DC.

US DOT (1977) An introduction to travel demand forecasting: A self-instructional text. Federal Highway Administration and Urban Mass Transportation Administration, Washington, D.C.

van Vliet D (1982) SATURN: A modern assignment model. Traffic Engineering and Control 23: 575–581

Wachs M (ed) (1996) A new generation of travel demand models: special issue. Transportation 2: 213–352

Wardrop JG (1952) Some theoretical aspects of road traffic research. Proceedings of the Institution of Civil Engineers, Part II 1: 325–378

Warner SL (1962) Stochastic choice of mode in urban travel: a study in binary choice. Northwestern University Press, Evanston

Williams HCWL (1977) On the formation of travel demand models and economic evaluation measures of user benefit. Environment and Planning A 9: 285–344

Williams HCWL (2004) Themes in the development and application of transport planning models. In Lee D-H (ed) Urban and regional transportation modeling. Edward Elgar, Cheltenham Northampton, pp 1–24

Williams HCWL, Ortúzar JD (1982) Behavioural theories of dispersion and the mis-specification of travel demand models. Transportation Research 16B: 167–219

Williams HCWL, Senior ML (1977) Model-based transport policy assessment; part II: removing fundamental inconsistencies from the models. Traffic Engineering and Control 18: 464–469

Williams HCWL, Senior ML (1978) Accessibility, spatial interaction and the spatial benefit analysis of land-use transportation plans. In: Karlqvist A, Lundqvist L, Snickars F, Weibull JW (eds) Spatial interaction theory and planning models. North-Holland, Amsterdam, pp 253–287

Wilson AG, Hawkins AF, Hill GJ, Wagon DJ (1969) Calibrating and testing the SELNEC transport model. Regional Studies 3: 337–350

Wilson AG (1970) Entropy in urban and regional modelling. Pion, London

Wooton HJ, Pick GW (1967) A model for trips generated by households. Journal of Transport Economics and Policy 1: 137–153

4 Towards Developing a Travel Time Forecasting Model for Location-Based Services: A Review

Jinsoo You[1] and Tschangho John Kim[2]

[1] InComKorea Co., Ltd., Seoul, South Korea
[2] University of Illinois at Urbana-Champaign, Champaign, Illinois, USA

4.1 Introduction

Public and private sectors often deal with decision making issues that are related to spatial and locational consideration. The rapid development of information technologies made various and adequate locational information available for decision makers.

The location-based services (LBS) are the new face of the wireless Internet. Advertising and e-commerce consulting firms predicts that by 2005 LBS market will reach $11–$15 billion in revenue and as many as one billion Internet-enabled handsets will be in use.1 With this growth potential, LBS present a substantial emerging market opportunity for wireless providers.[2]

Travel time forecasting models primarily have two functional areas in ITS and LBS applications: traffic management and traveller information. While travel time forecasting systems assist in avoiding delayed controls of traffic flow in traffic management, predicted travel time information can support commercial vehicle operators and individual travellers who seek appropriate travel routes.

In general, travel time forecasting tasks are initiated by forecasting future traffic conditions such as traffic volumes, speeds, and occupancies, and thus research that deal with traffic forecasting is directly related to travel time forecasting. Future travel times can be directly predicted or indirectly estimated after forecasting traffic data, depending on the types of real-time data that comes from various traffic surveillance systems such as closed-circuit video cameras, loop detectors, and probe vehicles. For instance, loop detectors installed on highways can transmit traffic volumes and speeds to traffic management information centres (TMICs) or LBS service providers. Thus, future travel time information can be estimated after future traffic conditions are predicted, or future travel time can be predicted using estimated travel time information that is based on collected raw traffic data. Probe

---

[1] See Jim VanderMeer (2001), "Location Content Drives Wireless Telecommunications" (http://www.geoplace.com/bg/2001/0201/0201pay.asp).
[2] http://www.isotc211.org.

vehicles on arterial roads, on the other hand, can transmit link travel times as raw data to TMICs. Thus, future travel times can be predicted directly using the transmitted travel time data.

4.2 What Is LBS?

In order to implement location based services, there are a number of technologies that need to be integrated, including information technology, GIS, positioning technology, ITS technology and Internet. LBS applications combine hardware devices, wireless communication networks, geographic information and software components that provide location-related guidance for customers (see Fig. 4.1). It differs from mobile position determination systems, such as global positioning systems (GPS), in that LBS provide much broader application-oriented location services, such as the following:

"You are about to join a ten-kilometre traffic queue. Turn right on Washington Street, 1 km ahead."

"Help, I'm having a heart attack!" or "Help, my car has broken down!"

"I need to buy a dozen roses and a birthday cake. Where can I buy the least expensive ones while spending the minimum amount of time on my way home from the office?"

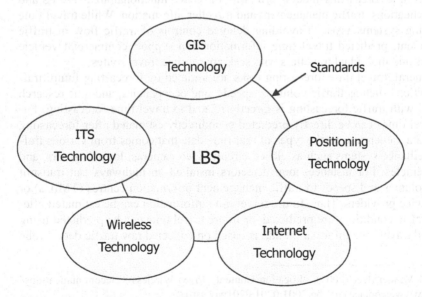

Fig. 4.1. Technology context of LBS

A typical example of LBS for personal navigation would include the followings:

- Entering address to desired destination (Geocoding and Reverse geocoding).
- Subscriber wishes to start from their current position and add one stop along the way (Gateway).
- Determining the route (Route Determination).
- Presenting route summary to subscriber (Route Summary).
- Presenting turn-by-turn directions to subscriber (Route Instruction).
- Subscriber wants to see a map overview with the route shown (Presentation).
- Subscriber is now in transit and wants to see manoeuvres (Gateway and Presentation).

A typical example of LBS for finding Point of Interest (POI) would include the followings:

- Subscriber wants to go to a nearby pizza restaurant. The address may be known (Gateway)
1. Subscriber wishes no more than 10 selections and no more than 2 miles from their current location.
2. Now search an online directory containing local restaurants (Directory)
3. The 10 restaurant choices are displayed. The subscriber's position is also shown using such as a star (Presentation)
4. The subscriber selects a nearby location (Presentation).
5. Subscriber also selects starting address and obtains its location (Reverse Geocoding)
6. Determine the fastest route from starting location to the restaurant (Route Determination)
7. Subscriber displays the route and begins the trip to the restaurant (Presentation).

While most of these services are either available or will soon become available by commercial providers of LBS, the followings issues need to be researched for providing efficient and accurate location-based services for personal productivity:

1. Utilization of Real Time Data in Spatio-Temporal Context in GIS
2. Development of Spatio-Temporal Topology in GIS.
3. Development of Efficient Means to handle Large Data Set for LBS
4. Interoperability among Contents Providers and Interface Standardization for Efficient Request-Response Services.
5. Efficient and Cost-effective Means to collect Real-Time traffic data.
6. Development of Alternative Theories for utilizing Population Data vs. Sample Data in GIS
7. Development of routing and navigation models for LBS
8. Development of Heuristic Solution Algorithms for routing and navigation models for LBS.

Among those, the following sections describe issues related to providing services for routing and navigation in LBS and issues related to solving such complex functions in few seconds to be able to respond to users' requests.

4.3 Travel Time Forecasting in ITS

While many researchers have studied travel time forecasting issues (Palacharla and Nelson 1995; Sen et al. 1997; Shbaklo et al. 1992; Sisiopiku et al. 1994; Yasui et al. 1994), a number of researchers (Ben-Akiva et al. 1993, 1994, 1995; Camus et al. 1995; Davis and Nihan 1991; Kaysi et al. 1993; Moorthy and Ratcliffe 1988; Smith and Demetsky 1997; Uchida and Yamasita 1997; Vythoulkas 1992; You and Kim 1999, 2000) have also studied traffic forecasting issues due to various types of real-time traffic data. This research focuses on both traffic and travel time forecasting efforts, so that a travel time forecasting model can be applied for a broad range of real-time traffic data types.

Among various ITS applications, there are two important applications that can primarily and immediately utilize travel time forecasting models for LBS: advanced traffic management systems (ATMS) and advanced traveller information systems (ATIS). In conventional ATMS and ATIS applications, which do not consider travel time forecasting, both applications estimate current travel time. Real-time traffic data are transmitted from traffic surveillance systems to TMICs. Transmitted real-time traffic data are processed and current link travel times are estimated. Estimated link travel times are disseminated within TMICs and sent to external users via communication networks, including local area network (LAN), the Internet, and wireless communications.

Nonetheless, these estimated current travel times from conventional ATMS and ATIS are not exactly current when users utilize them on road networks. In fact, these estimated travel times are delayed information in a strict sense due to the dynamic nature of network traffic. Without exception, traffic conditions change rapidly and dynamically as time goes by, and thus traffic conditions cannot be the same as the conditions when travel times are initially estimated in TMICs. With this concept in mind, it is understood that predicted travel times might reduce the gaps between current travel time estimation and actual travel times. Therefore, it is recognized that travel time forecasting models be utilized as an important module in ATMS and ATIS applications.

In general, travel time forecasting models could reduce the difference between estimated and actual link travel times. For example, real-time traffic data are initially transmitted to traffic management and information centres, and stored in historical databases. Transmitted raw traffic data and historical data are then screened, filtered, and fused in data pre-processing modules, after which a travel time forecasting module performs short-term link travel time predictions. Predicted link travel times are finally disseminated within a TMIC and sent to external users.

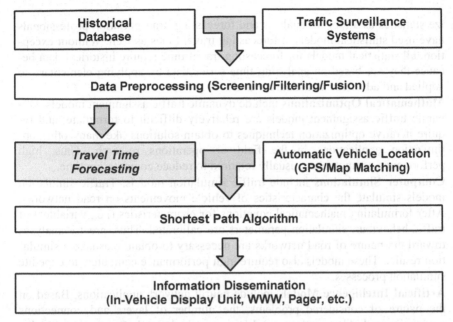

Fig. 4.2. A possible application of travel time forecasting with shortest paths algorithms

Travel time forecasting models could play more important roles when LBS applications intend to provide shortest path information to travellers. Predicted travel times can be used to calculate shortest paths as shown in Fig. 4.2. TMICs search shortest paths between user-defined origins and destinations using predicted link travel times. Travel time forecasting models require tremendous amounts of calculations, and thus high performance computers are necessary to reduce computation time. Thus, conceptual applications discussed in this section assume that travel time forecasting tasks are performed in TMICs or LBS service providers.

4.4 Existing Travel Time Forecasting Models

For many years, various types of travel time forecasting models have been developed, including historical profile approaches, time series models, neural network applications, nonparametric regression models, traffic simulation models, and dynamic traffic assignment (DTA) models. By analyzing the original formulations of these existing models, they can be categorized as statistical models, mathematical optimizations, computer simulations, and artificial intelligence models.

- **Statistical Models** include historical profile approaches, time series models and nonparametric regression models. Like many other scientific areas that utilize statistics as a tool for analysis and forecasting, transportation professionals have used statistical models in forecasting travel times as well. Without exception, all statistical models for forecasting travel time require historical data because they are based on analyzing time series data by applying elementary to applied and advanced statistical methods.

- **Mathematical Optimizations** include dynamic traffic assignment models. Dynamic traffic assignment models are relatively difficult to formulate, and require iterative optimization techniques to obtain solutions like many other optimization applications in the field of operations research. Thus, high performance computers are usually required to reduce computation time.
- **Computer Simulations** include traffic simulation models. Traffic simulation models simulate the characteristics of vehicle movements on road networks. After formulating mathematical equations for characteristics (i.e., variables) of traffic behaviour, simulation parameters are calibrated. Thus, precise analyses toward the nature of road networks are necessary to obtain reasonable simulation results. These models also require high performance computers to expedite simulation processes.
- **Artificial Intelligence Models** include neural network applications. Based on the nature of considered problems, the number of layers and connections among input, hidden, and output layers are predefined. Connection weights among layers are estimated based on network learning procedures (for example, supervised and unsupervised learning). Most of neural network forecasting models perform predictions based on learned information from historical data patterns. Thus, these models generally produce better results when the pattern learning is performed more frequently.

Table 4.1 shows researches related to travel time forecasting in the four categories from a variety of international researchers, including those in the US and Europe. The most widely applied methods are the statistical models. They have been applied in the field of traffic forecasting since the early 1970s. Early applications utilized simple historical profile approaches, but they have adopted other advanced approaches such as time series and nonparametric regression models later on. Traffic simulation models have been developed much earlier than their applications in travel time forecasting, but the massive computation in simulating traffic behaviours has hindered their applications in travel time forecasting for many years.

As a result, some formulations in simulating traffic behaviours have adopted parallel computing technologies (Berkbigler et al. 1997; Bush 1999; Nagel et al. 1998). Neural network applications became popular in travel time forecasting during the 1990s, and the recent development of neural network applications have a strong influence in forecasting travel time. Nevertheless, their current formulations are still difficult to deal with real-time applications due to complex learning processes.

Table 4.1. Types of traffic forecasting models

Types	Models	Applications
	Historical Profile Approaches	– Jeffrey et al. 1987 – Kaysi et al. 1993 – Kreer 1975 – Stephanedes et al. 1981
Statistical Models	Time Series Models	– Ben-Akiva et al. 1993, 1995 – Davis et al. 1990 – Moorthy and Ratcliffe 1988 – Shimizu et al. 1995 – Smith and Demetsky 1997 – Uchida and Yamasita 1997 – Vythoulkas 1992 – Yasui et al. 1995
	Nonparametric Regression Models	– Davis and Nihan 1991 – Smith and Demetsky 1997
	Hybrid Model	– You and Kim 2000
Computer Simulations	Traffic Simulations	– Berkbigler et al. 1997 – Bush 1999 – Junchaya et al. 1992 – McShane et al. 1998 – Nagel et al. 1998 – Yang, Q. 1997
Mathematical Optimizations	Dynamic Traffic Assignment Models	– Ben-Akiva et al. 1993, 1994, 1995 – Gilmore and Abe 1995 – Mahmassani et al. 1991 – Ran and Boyce 1996 – Sadek et al. 1997
Artificial Intelligence Models	Neural Network Applications	– Dochy et al. 1995 – Dougherty et al. 1993 – Gilmore and Abe 1995 – Palacharla and Nelson 1995 – Smith and Demetsky 1997

The next subsections will briefly illustrate the different approaches introduced above.

4.4.1 Historical Profile Approaches

The historical profile approach is based on the assumption that a historical profile can be obtained for traffic volume or travel time (Shbaklo et al. 1992). It solely relies upon the cyclical nature of traffic flow. For instance, this approach simply uses an average of past traffic volume to forecast future traffic volume. The advantage of this approach is its relatively easy implementation and its fast computation speed. However, this approach has a serious disadvantage due to its static nature; i.e., if traffic incidents occur, it has no way to react to the changes (Smith and Demetsky 1997). This approach has been tested in many traffic management and information systems such as the Urban Traffic Control System (UTCS) (Kreer 1975; Stephanedes et al. 1981), as well as in several traveller information systems in Europe including AUTOGUIDE (Jeffrey et al. 1987) and LISB (Kaysi et al. 1993).

4.4.2 Time Series Models

Time series models have been used particularly for short term travel time forecasting. These methods include various time-series analysis such as autoregressive moving average (ARMA) and autoregressive integrated moving average (ARIMA). In order to enhance forecasting accuracy, many research projects have also adopted data filtering methods such as Kalman filtering, fixed interval smoother, and m-interval polynomial approximation Kalman filtering that is defined as an optimal recursive data processing algorithm for estimation of system state.

A time series is defined as a set of statistical observations, arranged in chronological order. For instance, an observed traffic volume series consists of two parts: the series generated by the real process and the noise that is not directly related to the real process. Therefore, elimination of the noise, which is the result of outside disturbances, is the main target of time series models (Moorthy and Ratcliffe 1988). In order to eliminate the noise, autoregressive (AR) and moving average (MA) models have been mainly utilized. Based on these basic models, it has been shown that any discrete stationary time series can be analyzed using an autoregressive moving average (ARMA) model. Later the Box-Jenkins model was introduced based on ARMA (Box and Jenkins 1977). An improved version of ARMA, Box-Jenkins model, is called an autoregressive integrated moving average model (ARIMA). ARIMA models have been applied to the UTCS and freeway volume forecasting (Davis et al. 1990; Smith and Demetsky 1997).

One of the most advanced time series methods, Kalman filtering, has also been utilized to minimize estimation errors in time series analyses (Ben-Akiva et al. 1995, 1993; Shimizu et al. 1995; Vythoulkas 1992). In addition, a vector autoregressive moving average (VARMA) model has been applied to a multivariate time series analysis by segmenting road network and considering correlation between road segments (Uchida and Yamasita 1997).

4.4.3 Neural Network Applications

A neural network application is an information processing system that is non-algorithmic, non-digital, and intensely parallel. Because neural network applications are capable of learning how to classify and associate input and output patterns, they are distinguished from other traditional computing systems. Their learning capabilities make themselves a suitable approach for solving complicated problems like estimating current travel times from traffic flow patterns (Palacharla and Nelson 1995). Recently, neural network applications have gained a significant attention for transportation applications such as traffic flow modelling, traffic signal control, and transportation planning (Dochy et al. 1995; Gilmore and Abe 1995; Smith and Demetsky 1997). Among a number of neural network paradigms, back-propagation, a multi-layer learning regime, has been often applied to forecast traffic flow and congestion because of its ability to model relationships among continuously valued variables (Dougherty et al. 1993; Smith and Demetsky 1997).

4.4.4 Nonparametric Regression Analysis

Nonparametric regression can be thought of as a dynamic clustering model, which attempts to identify groups of past cases whose input values or states are similar to the state of the system at prediction time. It is considered dynamic because it defines a group of similar past cases (or the neighbourhood) around the current input state, instead of defining a number of groupings prior to the time of prediction. Nonparametric regression is applicable to analyzing multiple links, which is an extension of single link analysis where traffic flow prediction on a link is based on previous flow information from that link and from other neighbouring links (Shbaklo et al. 1992). Nonetheless, few nonparametric regression models have been used in travel time forecasting due to the complexity of search tasks for "neighbours" (Davis and Nihan 1991; Smith and Demetsky 1997). Thus, nonparametric regression models generally require an effective and efficient search algorithm with a well-structured data model.

4.4.5 Traffic Simulation Models

Simulation models are designed to mimic the behaviour of real-world systems. Transportation researchers have developed various types of traffic simulation models such as discrete time/discrete event models, micro/mesoscopic/macro models, and deterministic/stochastic models. In fact, most traffic simulation models are discrete time models, which segment time into a succession of known time interval (Lieberman and Rathi 1997; McShane et al. 1998). Most of traffic simulation models are micro models as well as stochastic models. Though simulation-based models are capable of analyzing various types of situations, they require estimating the entering and exiting traffic flows when they are used in travel time forecasting (Smith and Demetsky 1997).

4.4.6 Dynamic Traffic Assignment Models

Dynamic traffic assignment (DTA) models have evolved from traditional static equilibrium assignment models. In general, traffic assignment models can be categorized as two distinctive types: descriptive and normative models. The descriptive models attempt to capture how the users behave given a set of traffic conditions (i.e., user optimal). Whereas, normative models seek to determine how the system should behave in order to optimize some system-wide criteria (i.e., system optimal) (Mahmassani et al. 1991; Ran and Boyce 1996).

Unlike static assignment models, dynamic models assume link flows and link trip times change over the duration of the peak period, so that they are appropriate for real-time traffic control during peak periods on congested networks, where constant steady-state conditions hardly occur. Thus, DTA models have been used for relatively long term travel time forecasting. To apply DTA models in forecasting travel time, it is necessary to estimate dynamic travel demand, and hence obtaining dynamic origin-destination (OD) tables is a major issue for a successful DTA model. In addition to traditional DTA models, which are mostly based on static user equilibrium and system optimal traffic assignment models, there are several variations that have adopted genetic algorithms and neural networks (Gilmore and Abe 1995; Sadek et al. 1997).

4.5 A Comparison of Existing Travel Time Forecasting Models

It is difficult to decide a suitable method in travel time forecasting because existing models have both advantages and disadvantages as shown in Table 4.2. For instance, time series and simulation models are relatively accurate for very short-term (i.e., less than 15 minutes) predictions, but they become unreliable when prediction time periods get longer and longer (i.e., more than 15 minutes). In a study, DTA models have been considered in travel time forecasting for 15 to 60 minutes time interval (Ben-Akiva et al. 1995). However, dynamic assignment formulations have often encountered problems with regard to their tractability and solvability in realistic network settings (Mahmassani et al. 1991; Sen et al. 1997).

Toward developing a more reliable travel time forecasting model, a generalized comparison has been conducted, based on six evaluation categories: (1) Utilization of Historical Database, (2) Capability of Online Data Use, (3) Transferability of Forecasting Procedure, (4) Effectiveness of Forecasting Procedure, (5) Accuracy of Forecasting Procedure, and (6) Capability of Forecasting with Traffic Incidents.

Table 4.2. Advantages and Disadvantages of Travel Time Forecasting Models (Adapted from Sen et al. 1997; Smith and Demetsky 1997)

Model	Advantages	Disadvantages
Historical Profile Approach	– Relatively easy to implement – Fast execution speed	– Difficult to respond to traffic incidents
Time Series Analysis	– Well-defined model formulation	– Difficult to handle missing data
Neural Network	– Suitable for complex, non-linear relationships	– Forecasting in black box – Complex training procedure
Nonparametric Regression Analysis	– Requires no assumption of underlying relationship	– Complexity of search in identifying "neighbours"
Traffic Simulation	– Possible to simulate various situations	– Requires traffic flow prediction in priori
Dynamic Traffic Assignment	– Various types of models available – Models are relatively well known	– Not suitable to Microsimulation

- **Utilization of Historical Database**: Historical profile approaches, nonparametric regression models, and time series models utilize historical databases relatively well. For instance, historical profile approaches compute historical averages of traffic data using historical databases. Within historical databases, nonparametric regression models search similar conditions that occurred in the past. Time series models can perform autoregressive (AR) and moving average (MA) analyses using time series data stored in historical databases.
- **Capability of Online Data Use**: A travel time forecasting model should be able to promptly produce outputs using real-time data. In general, historical profile approaches involve static models that do not consider real-time data. Time series models should persistently accomplish complicated parameter estimations, and neural network applications have to learn input patterns continuously. Moreover, DTA models require complex dynamic O-D estimations whenever input data are changed. Therefore, with time series models, neural network applications, and DTA models it is difficult to utilize real time data with currently available computing technologies. On the other hand, nonparametric regression models, which are based on pattern recognition techniques that search similar conditions that have occurred in the past, do not require any assumptions, and thus they can effectively utilize real-time data. However, nonparametric regression models need a well-designed search algorithm for large size historical databases to reduce search time.
- **Transferability of Forecasting Procedure**: A forecasting model needs to be adopted easily among TMICs that are usually equipped with various types of computer systems. It is economical that a forecasting model is readily custom-

ized among these centres. DTA models, time series models, traffic simulation models, and neural network applications usually require intensive calibration processes for different road networks. On the other hand, historical profile approaches and nonparametric regression models do not require any assumption, and thus they can be applied in travel time forecasting with relatively simple calibration processes.

- **Effectiveness of Forecasting Procedure**: Computation time strongly affects the success of a forecasting model development. For instance, forecasting results should be calculated at least within a specified forecasting range. Thus total computation time should be no longer than 15 minutes to perform a "15-minute ahead" forecasting. It is always necessary to minimize computation time, so that the forecasted results can be disseminated within TMICs and to public. In real-time applications, high performance and parallel processing capable computer systems are often considered for DTA models that repeatedly calculate dynamic O-D tables. In traffic simulation models, the computing time grows quickly when input road networks become larger. Nonparametric regression models require relatively simple calculations, but they have to optimize search processes to minimize computation time (Smith and Demetsky 1997).

- **Accuracy of Forecasting Procedure**: A forecasting algorithm should be able to produce accurate forecasting results. In general, neural network applications are relatively accurate when they learn input networks sufficiently (Weigend and Gershenfeld 1994). Nonetheless, computation time in neural network applications grows rapidly when more accurate results are required; i.e., more network learning processes are required. Like neural network applications, nonparametric regression models have shown relatively accurate forecasting results while their computation times are much shorter than neural network applications.

- **Capability of Forecasting with Traffic Incidents**: A forecasting model should be able to deal with traffic incidents. In this category, none of the existing models is satisfactory. Historical profile approaches and time series models have difficulty in dealing with online traffic data with incidents. Nonparametric regression models, neural network applications, traffic simulation models, and DTA models need to be modified and enhanced to deal with traffic incidents.

In order to shed light on the issue of adopting a core-forecasting algorithm for the development of a travel time forecasting model, which requires the use of historical database and real-time data concurrently, Table 4.3 shows a generalized comparison. Basically, historical profile approaches do not consider real-time data. Therefore, they could not be the core algorithms in developing a travel time forecasting model that utilizes real-time data. DTA models, time series models and traffic simulation models require intensive computations and complex parameter estimations. Thus, they are extremely cumbersome to implement among TMICs, particularly in dealing with real-time data. Neural network applications show relatively accurate output, but they require complex network learning algorithms and additional computations for real-time data input.

Table 4.3. Generalized comparison of existing forecasting models

Model \ Evaluation Category	Utilization of Historical Database	Capability of Online Data Use	Transferability of Forecasting Procedure	Effectiveness of Forecasting Procedure	Accuracy of Forecasting Procedure	Capability of Forecasting with Traffic Incidents
Historical Profile Approaches	O	×	O	O	×	×
Time Series Models	O	Δ	×	Δ	Δ	×
Neural Network Applications	O	Δ	×	×	O	Δ
Nonparametric Regression	O	O	O	Δ	O	Δ
Traffic Simulation	Δ	O	Δ	Δ	Δ	Δ
Dynamic Traffic Assignment Models	Δ	O	×	×	Δ	Δ

O excellent, Δ good, × poor.

On the other hand, nonparametric regression models provide relatively simple forecasting mechanisms with reasonably high forecasting accuracy. However, in order to implement an effective nonparametric regression model with limited computer resources, it is necessary to optimize its complex search processes. In addition, a supplementary algorithm should be developed to make nonparametric regression models capable of dealing with traffic incidents, which could cause conventional nonparametric regression models to generate inaccurate forecasting results.

4.6 Potential Roles of GIS in Travel Time Forecasting for LBS

Upon reviewing various functions of GIS-based applications (Abkowitz et al. 1990; Azad and Cook 1993; Choi and Kim 1994; Gillespie 1993; Loukes 1992; Nygard et al. 1995; Ries 1993), data management, technology management, and information management – the three important roles of GIS could be employed to support the operation of a travel time forecasting model.

- *Data Management*: Travel time forecasting requires various types of traffic data including traffic speed, traffic volume, occupancy rate, number of lanes, and so forth. Therefore, GIS should be able to provide mechanisms for data aggregation and manipulation.
- *Technology Management*: Travel time forecasting requires various functions including display, computation, and analysis. Therefore, GIS should provide

flexible tools to integrate and customize the required functions. Moreover, GIS should support a travel time forecasting model to deal with various types of raw traffic data from loop detector, mobile communication, and Global Positioning Systems (GPS).

- *Information Management*: After forecasting future travel times, the results are validated and classified, so that traffic management and information centres can utilize them to manage network traffic. It is expected that GIS will eventually become an information gateway to the public, through various types of communication tools such as the Internet, telecommunications, broadcasting, etc.

In addition, it is also expected that GIS provide important functions to expedite the development of a travel time forecasting model as follows:

- Creating and maintaining traffic networks,
- Assisting in both managing and visualizing historical and real-time traffic data,
- Providing various tools for graphic user interfaces,
- Supporting application development environments for the integration of forecasting algorithms, and
- Providing flexible spatial data analysis tools using search and query tools when a forecasting model is implemented.

4.7 Summary

In this paper, preliminary discussions regarding both existing travel time forecasting models and GIS technologies have been made for the development of a reliable travel time forecasting model. The characteristics of travel time forecasting models have been presented and existing travel time forecasting models have been reviewed. In addition, the theoretical aspects of GIS implementation have been discussed to identify the potential roles of GIS in travel time forecasting. In the future research, it is recommended that findings in this research be further analyzed and compared for a more reliable travel time forecasting model, which could effectively utilize the existing forecasting models with GIS technologies in an integrated system framework (Kim, 2004).

Acknowledgement

Research fund from the Korean Agency for Technology and Standards (KATS), the Ministry of Commerce, Industry, and Energy (MOCIE), Republic of Korea through Korea Standard Association (KSA) is gratefully acknowledged.

References

Abkowitz M, Walsh S, Hauser E (1990) Adaptation of geographic information systems to highway management. Journal of Transportation Engineering 116: 310–327

Azad B, Cook P (1993) The management/organizational challenges of the "Server-Net" model of GIS-T as recommended by the NCHRP 20–27. In: Proceedings of GIS-T '93: Geographical Information Systems for Transportation Symposium, pp 327–342

Ben-Akiva M, Cascetta E, Gunn H (1995) An on-line dynamic traffic prediction model for an inter-urban motorway network. In: Gartner NH, Improta G (eds) Urban traffic betworks: dynamic flow modeling and control. Springer, Berlin Heidelberg New York, pp 83–122

Ben-Akiva M, Koutsopoulos HN, Mukundan A (1994) A dynamic traffic model system for ATMS/ATIS operations. IVHS Journal 2: 1–19

Ben-Akiva M, Cascetta E, Whittaker J (1993) Recent progress in short-range traffic prediction. Compendium of Technical Papers, Institute of Transportation Engineers (ITE), pp 262–265

Berkbigler KP, Bush BW, Davis JF (1997) TRANSIMS software architecture for IOC-1. Report Number: LA-UR-97-1242, Los Alamos National Laboratory

Box GEP, Jenkins GM (1977) Time series analysis: forecasting and control, revised edn. Holden-Day, San Francisco

Bush BW (1999) The TRANSIMS framework. TRANSIMS Opportunity Forum, Santa Fe, 28 June 1999

Camus R, Longo G, Santorini F (1995) A short term forecasting model for freeway traffic monitoring and control. In: Applications of advanced technologies in transportation engineering: proceedings of the 4th International Conference, pp 418–422

Choi K, Kim TJ (1994) Integrating transportation planning models with GIS: issues and prospects. Journal of Planning Education and Research 13: 199–207

Davis GA, Nihan NL (1991) Nonparametric regression and short-term freeway traffic forecasting. Journal of Transportation Engineering 117: 178–188

Davis GA, Nihan NL, Hamed MM, Jacobson LN (1990) Adaptive forecasting of traffic congestion. Transportation Research Record 1287: 29–33

Dochy T, Danech-Pajouh M, Lechevallier Y (1995) Short-term road forecasting using neural network. Recherche-Transports-Securite (English issue) 11: 73–82

Dougherty MS, Kirby HR, Boyle RD (1993) The use of neural networks to recognise and predict traffic congestion. Traffic Engineering and Control 34: 311–314

Elmasri R, Navathe SB (1994) Fundamentals of database systems, 2nd edn. The Benjamin/Cummings Publishing Company, Inc.

Emery JC (1969) Organizational planning and control systems: theory and technology. The Macmillan Company, Collier-Macmillan Limited, Houndmills

ESRI (1992a) Dynamic segmentation, ARC/INFO user's guide. Environmental Systems Research Institute, Inc., Redlands

ESRI (1992b) Network analysis, ARC/INFO user's guide. Environmental Systems Research Institute, Inc., Redlands

Gillespie S (1993) The benefits of GIS use for transportation. In: Proceedings of GIS-T '93: Geographical Information Systems for Transportation Symposium, pp 34–41

Gilmore JF, Abe N (1995) Neural network models for traffic control and congestion prediction. IVHS Journal 2: 231–252

Goodchild MF (1987) Towards an enumeration and classification of GIS functions. In: Proceedings of the International Geographic Information Systems (IGIS) Symposium: The Research Agenda, Arlington, pp 67–77

Guo B, Poling AD (1995) Geographic information systems/global positioning systems design for network travel time study. Transportation Research Record 1497: 135–139

Jeffrey DJ, Russam K, Robertson DI (1987) Electronic route guidance by AUTOGUIDE: the research background. Traffic Engineering and Control 28: 525–529

Junchaya T, Chang G, Santiago A (1992) Advanced traffic management system: real-time network traffic simulation methodology with a massively parallel computing architecture. Transportation Research Record 1358: 13–21

Kaysi I, Ben-Akiva M, Koutsopoulos H (1993) An integrated approach to vehicle routing and congestion prediction for real-time driver guidance. Transportation Research Record 1408: 66–74

Kim TJ (2004) Multi-modal routing and navigation cost functions for location-based services (LBS). In: Der-Horng L (ed) Urban and regional transportation modeling: essays in honor of David Boyce. Edward Elgar, Cheltenham Northampton, pp 278–288

Kreer JB (1975) A comparison of predictor algorithms for computerized control. Traffic Engineering 45: 51–56

Lieberman E, Rathi AK (1997) Traffic simulation. In: Traffic flow theory: a state-of-the-art report. Oak Ridge National Laboratory.

Loukes D (1992) Geographic Information Systems in Transportation (GIS-T): an infrastructure management information systems tool. In: Proceedings of 1992 TAC Annual Conference, vol. 3, pp B27–B42

Mahmassani HS, Peeta S, Chang GL, Junchaya T (1991) A review of dynamic assignment and traffic simulation models for ADIS/ATMS applications. Technical Report DTFH61-90-R-00074, Center for Transportation Research, The University of Texas at Austin

McShane WR, Roess RP, Prassas ES (1998) Traffic engineering, 2nd edn. Prentice-Hall, Inc., Upper Saddle River, New Jersey

Moorthy CK, Ratcliffe BG (1988) Short term traffic forecasting using time series methods. Transportation Planning Technology 12: 45–56

Nagel K, Rickert M, Simon PM (1998) The dynamics of iterated transportation simulations. Paper presented at TRISTAN-III, Report Number: LA-UR 98-2168. Los Alamos National Laboratory

Nygard K, Vellanki R, Xie T (1995) Issues in GIS for transportation. MPC Report No. 95-43, Mountain-Plains Consortium, Fargo

Palacharla PV, Nelson PC (1995) On-line travel time estimation using fuzzy neural network. In: Proceedings of 1995 ITS World Congress, Yokohama, Japan, pp 112–116

Ran B, Boyce D (1996) Modeling dynamic transportation networks: an intelligent transportation system oriented approach, 2nd edn. Springer, Berlin Heidelberg New York

Ries T (1993) Design requirements for location as a foundation for transportation information systems. In: Proceedings of GIS-T '93: Geographical Information Systems for Transportation Symposium, pp 48–66

Sadek AW, Smith BL, Demetsky MJ (1997) Dynamic traffic assignment: a genetic algorithm approach. Preprint at the Transportation Research Board 76th Annual meeting, Washington, D.C.

Scholten HJ, Stillwell JCH (1990) Geographical information systems: the emerging requirements. In: Scholten HJ, Stillwell JCH (eds) Geographical information systems for
urban and regional planning. Kluwer Academic Publishers, Dordrecht Boston, pp 3–14

Sen A, Sööt S, Ligas J, Tian X (1997) Arterial link travel time estimation: probes, detectors
and assignment-type models. Preprint at the Transportation Research Board 76th Annual meeting, Washington, D.C.

Shbaklo S, Bhat C, Koppelman F, Li J, Thakuriah P, Sen A, Rouphail N (1992) Short-term
travel time prediction. ADVANCE Project Report, TRF-TT-01, Illinois University
Transportation Research Consortium

Shimizu H, Yamagami K, Watanabe E (1995) Applications of state estimation algorithms
to hourly traffic volume system. In: Proceedings of 1995 ITS World Congress, Yokohama, Japan, pp 72–77

Sisiopiku VP, Rouphail NM, Tarko A (1994) Estimating travel times on freeway segments.
Advance Working Paper Series, no. 32

Smith BL, Demetsky MJ (1997) Traffic flow forecasting: comparison of modeling approaches. Journal of Transportation Engineering 123: 261–266

Stephanedes YJ, Michalopoulos PG, Plum RA (1981) Improved estimation of traffic flow
for real-time control. Transportation Research Record 795: 28–39

UchidaT, Yamasita S (1997) Vector ARMA time series models for short-term prediction of
traffic demand. Journal of the Eastern Asia Society for Transportation Studies 2:
1247–1261

Vythoulkas PC (1992) Short term traffic forecasting for dynamic driver information systems. In: Traffic management and road safety: proceedings of Seminar G, pp 225–238

Weigend AS, Gershenfeld NA (1994) The future of time series: learning and understanding. In: Weigend AS, Gershenfeld (eds) Time series prediction: forecasting the future
and understanding the past, a proceeding volume in the Santa Fe Institute Studies in
the Sciences of Complexity. Addison Wesley, Reading

Yang Q (1997) A simulation laboratory for evaluation of dynamic traffic management systems. Ph.D. Thesis, Massachusetts Institute of Technology

Yasui K, Ikenoue K, Takeuchi H (1994) Use of AVI information linked up with detector
output in travel time prediction and O-D flow estimation. In: Proceedings of 1995 ITS
World Congress, Yokohama, pp 94–99

You J, Kim TJ (1999) Implementation of a hybrid travel time forecasting model with GIS-
T. In: Proceedings of the 3rd Bi-Annual Conference of the Eastern Asia Society for
Transportation Studies, September 14–17, 1999, Taipei

You J, Kim TJ (2000) Development and evaluation of a hybrid travel time forecasting
model. Transportation Research Part C 8: 231–256

5 Transportation Networks, Case-Based Reasoning and Traffic Collision Analysis: A Methodology for the 21st Century

Kaidong Li and Nigel M. Waters

University of Calgary, Calgary, Canada

5.1 Introduction

An average of 400 people are killed and 23,000 injured each year as a result of motor vehicle collisions in the western Canadian province of Alberta (population of 3,146,066; Statistics Canada estimate for 2003). Motor vehicle collisions are the leading cause of death for Albertans under the age of 30 (AMA 2003). These statistics, on a *per capita* basis, are similar to those that might be obtained for many developed states, provinces and nations and their reduction through the application of computer technology is the goal of much recent research in traffic safety analysis (Arthur 2002).

Traffic safety is of paramount concern to not only police and traffic safety engineers, but also to the insurance industry, health care organizations, social workers and the public at large. There is a need for efficient and *intelligent* facilities to study, and eventually enhance, safety on road and other transportation networks. The provision of such a facility is an integral component of work currently being conducted in Calgary's intelligent transportation systems (ITS) community (City of Calgary ITS Workshop No.3, 2003).

Geographic information systems (GIS) have recently received substantial attention in the ITS and traffic safety literature (Arthur 2002; Panchanathan and Faghri 1995; Smith 2000; Spring and Hummer 1995; Waters 2002). The benefits of using a GIS include spatial query, multi-source data overlay and network analysis, among others.

Rule-based expert systems, that embody specialist knowledge in a computer based decision support system (Chris Naylor Research Limited 2003, p. 1), have been used as decision support systems in transportation and road safety research in the past decade (Herland et al. 2000; Panchanathan and Faghri 1995; Paniati and Hughes 2000; Suttayamully et al. 1995). Case-based reasoning (CBR), a parallel methodology to rule-based reasoning, is of increasing interest to the ITS community (Boury-Brisset and Tourigny 2000; Capus and Tourigny 1998; Waters 2002). In CBR, prior experiences are reused and adapted for solving new problems (Leake et al. 1996; Richter et al. 1998). Prior experiences, whether successful or failed, carry valuable information. Similar to human learning and reasoning activities, the system can become more efficient over time as a result of collecting and indexing additional experiences (Leake 1996). CBR approaches are more appealing than the rule-based ones in areas where situations are complex or rules are difficult to generalize (Capus and Tourigny 1998; Khattak and Renski 1999). Traffic safety is a complex function of a wide range of factors, such as road network and environmental conditions, driver behaviour and vehicle condition. Prior experiences rather than general rules might provide more site-specific or case-specific solutions to a given safety problem.

5.2 Applications of GIS in Traffic Safety Analysis

GIS have been widely used in transportation research and management since the late 1980s (ESRI 2003; Thill 2000). Over the past two decades, GIS for Transportation (GIS-T) has evolved and matured to a sophisticated technology that is now applied to a wide range of transportation research (Miller and Shaw 2001; Nyerges 2005; Waters 1999). Traffic safety, an important aspect of transportation research, also shares the benefits of this technology. Early efforts to provide workstation capacities for GIS-based safety analysis were developed in the 1990s for the Federal Highway Administration (FHWA) in the United States. These GIS-based software packages were capable of performing functions that ranged from identifying hazardous intersections to analyzing corridors.

One of the main advantages of a GIS is its ability to access promptly and analyze accurately data distributed across a transportation network. This benefit of GIS enables the analysis of traffic safety at specific sites, along the whole network as well as on the area-wide transportation system. Another advantage of a GIS is its ability to retrieve rapidly relevant information from various sources, such as traffic flow, land use, environmental and socioeconomic databases. Other capabilities of a GIS include: spatial analysis, user-friendly visual representation, thematic mapping and charting. Furthermore, most GIS software provides the capability of interfacing external programs for decision support and database management. For example, a Visual Basic for Application (VBA) development kit packaged with the ArcGIS software produced by the Environmental Systems Research Institute (ESRI) allows users to call external stand-alone software within a GIS environment (Lang 1999).

A review of recent traffic safety studies and projects shows that safety engineers primarily apply GIS technology in investigations that fall into three, overlapping categories: 1: Data collection and access; 2: Data processing and analysis; and 3: Decision support.

5.2.1 Data Collection and Analysis

Locating traffic collisions. In many jurisdictions, including Alberta, collision data is manually transcribed from paper collision report forms and then georeferenced as a separate operation. In this process the quality and quantity of the original data may affect accuracy in the developed GIS database. The employment of GIS techniques, such as batch processing, intersection matching and conflation, as well as the incorporation of road attributes from multiple sources, increases the percentage of identified and located collisions (Carreker and Bachman. 2000; Thompson 2001).

Transportation network data. Safety engineers must have accurate data on the physical characteristics of a transportation network and its traffic characteristics. For a road network this would include: roadway geometry, roadway condition, traffic control devices, roadside features and traffic volumes. Conventionally, this information is stored in spreadsheets, or database tables. In these spreadsheets and tables, locational information can only be described by text. GIS enable the acquisition and display of roadway characteristic data *visually*, and hence, *efficiently*. GIS also allow simultaneous access to multiple data layers, as well as the ability to interface with external information such as census tracts and municipal land use zoning areas. (Panchanathan and Faghri 1995). An example of a GIS that performs such a role is the on-going development of a road network inventory in the City of Calgary (Nelson 2002).

5.2.2 Data Processing and Analysis

Traffic safety studies, in this category, emphasize the analytical capabilities of GIS. These capabilities range from simple buffer and overlay operations to spatial query (Spring and Hummer 1995), time series analysis (Arthur 2002), network analysis (HSIS Summary Report 1999) and dynamic segmentation (Bayapureddy 1996). A review of the literature and recent projects shows five trends in the use of GIS to analyze accident data: (1) identifying the high-accident locations, (2) identifying the accident characteristics, (3) determining the causes, (4) determining the countermeasures, and (5) evaluating the countermeasures (Bayapureddy 1996).

Identification of hazardous roadway locations. The identification of hazardous or high-accident locations is one of the most commonly used GIS approaches in traffic safety studies. Spring and Hummer (1995) state that the *sole* use of traditional statistical methods for the determination of high-accident locations presents several limitations. One of which is that the determination is based on experiential data. Thus problem locations are not revealed until a significant number of accidents has occurred. Another limitation is the "regression to the mean" phenomenon and high accident levels may be due to this statistical anomaly, and not to a road network problem (Spring and Hummer 1995). The third limitation is the "accident-matching" problem whereby differently formatted data can cause distortion and misunderstanding when displaying high-accident locations on the network (Bayapureddy 1996). Within the GIS software, different types of data are easily related, either graphically or in report forms, thus making the data more easily accessible and providing a more intuitive and flexible user interface (Arthur 2002; Bayapureddy 1996). By providing consistent access to a common pool of accident and roadway data, GIS can "identify and predict hazardous highway locations before accidents occur" (Spring and Hummer 1995, p. 83).

Accident pattern analysis and remediation. GIS has the potential to improve traffic accident analysis in several significant ways. First, GIS provides visual acquisition and display of accident locations. This equates to a minimum one-year advance in knowledge of accident information, since in the past it would have taken up to one year to enter and geocode these data (Hall et al. 2000). Additionally, the individual accident characteristics become immediately available for site analysis. Rapid access to individual accident information enhances the appropriate application of countermeasures for accident remediation. GIS facilitate analysis of accident locations by integrating previously disparate data elements. For example, incorporation of accident types and conditions in conjunction with road network characteristics, such as lane width, surface type and friction index number, allow substantially more multivariate analyses (Hall et al. 2000).

Network analysis. The Linear Referencing System (LRS) provides GIS with network analysis capability, allowing multiple routes to be linked together in a manner that enables the analyst to assess the overall safety performance within a transportation network. A common use of network analysis is to examine truck crashes along designated truck routes. On a network-wide basis, a particular element may have a high accident rate and thus it may be more cost-effective to make a network-wide correction of a common element than to correct only a high-accident location (HSIS Summary Report 1999).

5.2.3 Decision Support

Another potential application of GIS in traffic safety is to support decisions for policy makers, transportation planners and safety engineers. Such decision support systems (DSS) are useful to traffic safety management organizations. Efforts have been made to integrate GIS and other DSS to manage traffic safety in the Federal Department of Transportation (DOT) in the United States. For example, Ozbay and Mukherjee (2000) developed a web-based expert GIS, called WIMSI, to provide operators with high-level analyses and recommendations concerning incident response. This system integrated a rule-based reasoner, the incident and network database in MS Access and the web-enabled GIS developed in ArcView IMS to provide a real-time, incident management DSS. Panchanathan and Faghri (1995) developed a knowledge-based GIS system to manage safety at rail-highway at-grade crossings in Delaware. The advanced functionality of a GIS, including spatial query, multi-source data overlay and network analysis, make it a powerful platform and database to support an intelligent system for decision makers.

5.2.4 A Synopsis of the Impact of GIS in Traffic Safety Studies

Although GIS have been successfully employed in recent traffic safety studies, Smith (2000) noted that, except for reporting a picture of crash locations, the majority of safety engineers were not using the full range of GIS capabilities. According to Smith the reasons why GIS is not popular for safety analyses with many safety engineers include: the need for a GIS champion; the need for progressive communications between the GIS leader and safety engineers; a lack of GIS knowledge; a lack of resources for GIS development; and not using GIS to manage the linear referencing system for the transportation network (Smith 2000, p. 12).

Smith (2000) also addressed some obvious barriers in implementing GIS-based safety applications within the traffic safety authorizations in the United Sates. These barriers included: not seeing the benefits that GIS has to offer in safety analyses; not using a common technical language, for the needs, and requirements, of both the highway safety engineers and the GIS systems engineers; not having, or supporting, standards for data consistency; an absence of appropriate data, such as transportation network inventory, accident data and work zone, necessary to perform safety analyses; and problems understanding the various linear referencing systems (Smith 2000, p. 3).

GIS has proven to be a promising technology in traffic safety studies. It provides functionality to display visually and analyze spatially distributed safety data by their actual locations. Applications of GIS in traffic safety research are still at an initial stage. The slow diffusion of GIS in traffic safety research might possibly be explained by the complexity of these systems and the misconstrued perception that they are not qualitatively different from the older computer aided design and drafting (CADD) packages. Increased productivity and well-trained personnel are the two most important variables in applying GIS in traffic safety research.

5.3 Applications of Case-Based Reasoning in Traffic Safety Analysis

The term "case-based reasoning" (CBR) is used in both cognitive science, which studies the human behaviours of reasoning and learning and in artificial intelligence (AI), in which CBR is implemented to make AI systems more efficient. In the context of artificial intelligence, CBR is normally applied in the development of expert systems (ES) (Waters 1988). However, CBR tools reason differently from rule-based expert systems that draw conclusions by chaining together generalized rules, starting from scratch. In CBR new solutions are generated by retrieving the most relevant cases from memory and adapting them to fit the new situations (Leake 1996). CBR systems retrieve previous cases that are similar to the current problem and attempt to reuse, or adapt, relevant solutions in the new situation (Kolodner and Leake 1996).

This approach is based on two tenets about the real world: first, the world is regular, similar problems have similar solutions; second, the types of problems an agent encounters tend to recur (Leake 1996). The diffusion of ES was not as broad and as rapid as predicted. One crucial reason is the so-called "knowledge elicitation bottleneck" (Waters 1989). In a rule-based ES, much time and effort are required in order to elicit and generalize a series of rules, thus creating a "bottleneck."

Roger Schank first proposed CBR, in 1982, as a model for human reasoning processes (Joh 1997). Since the early 1980s, CBR research has matured and the methodology has been widely used in various research programs and practical applications (Capus and Tourigny 2000; Kolodner 1996). Compared to a rule-based system, a case-based system has advantages in the following five aspects:

Knowledge acquisition. The first step in building a rule-based system is to provide rules for the inference engine. In some domains, however, rules are difficult to formalize or become unmanageably large (Capus and Tourigny 1998; Leake 1996). CBR systems utilize previous cases to infer a new solution, thus making it unnecessary to decompose experiences and to elicit rules to support the reasoning processes. CBR avoids the "knowledge elicitation bottleneck" problem in rule-based systems and is especially useful when conceptual knowledge is limited (Khattak and Renski 1999).

Knowledge base maintenance. A conventional rule-based system requires the definition of a complete and "perfect" knowledge base. However, initial understanding of the problem is usually imperfect and circumstances and requirements may change over time. In CBR, the knowledge base is scalable and adaptable on an ongoing basis (Wisdo 1997). CBR systems "can be operated with only a partial case base, and are always expected to add new cases" (Clayton and Waters 1999, p. 279) or update existing cases. The knowledge base in a CBR system can evolve and grow simply by adding new experiences.

Problem-solving efficiency. Reuse of prior solutions in CBR systems greatly reduces the need to repeat prior effort, thus increasing problem-solving efficiency. In addition, reuse can avoid potentially problematic solutions by saving failed cases.

Solution quality and consistency. Rules can be imperfect and unreliable when the principles of a domain are not well understood. In this situation, solutions suggested by actual cases might be more accurate and reliable since they reflect real world circumstances. Consistent solutions are guaranteed for problems under similar situations (Leake 1996; Richter 1998).

User acceptance. Most rule-based systems produce unsatisfactory results because of their limited explanatory capabilities. End users of the system often find it difficult to understand, and accept, the solutions suggested by chains of rules. In CBR, solutions and explanations are given based on actual prior cases rather than on the basis of generalized rules (as in rule-based systems) or by "black boxes" (as in a neural network). These solutions and explanations are more acceptable and interpretable to the users of the system (Boury-Brisset and Tourigny 2000; Burkhard 1998; Leake 1996).

5.3.1 Applications of CBR

Since the early 1980s, CBR methodology has been used by many prominent corporations such as Lockheed, GTE, DEC, Boeing and Martin Marietta (Clayton et al. 1998). As the technology becomes more mature, CBR has been successfully applied in various fields such as medical diagnosis, software development, planning and decision support. Recently, CBR has proven to be quite a useful and efficient tool for electronic commerce (E-commerce), such as customer support, hotlines and helpdesks. Software companies that provide CBR tools and consulting services include eGain Communication Corporation, US (Knowledge product family) and, in Europe, empolis Knowledge Management GmbH (CBR-Works) (see University of Kaiserslautern 2003 for a detailed list). CBR applications can be sorted by different task types (Richter 1998; University of Kaiserslautern 2003):

Diagnosis, Classification, and Decision Support. This category contains the most common applications of CBR, such as medical diagnosis, information classification (Richter 1998), legal reasoning (University of Kaiserslautern 2003), troubleshooting (Lenz et al. 1998), tutoring (Weber and Schult 1998) and helpdesk (Haley Enterprise Inc. 2003). Algorithms to calculate the nearest neighbour in the knowledge base appear crucial for applications in this category.

CBR Supported Planning and Design. Experience plays an important role in planning and design activities. However, planning and design activities introduce variable degrees of creativity. Solutions taken from a case base almost always need modification before reuse in an actual planning or design problems (Richter 1998). Hence, the adaptation capability of a CBR is an important issue in this group of applications. Example projects include *Aircraft Conflict Resolution – CBR support for Air-Traffic Control* by Artificial Intelligence Group at Trinity College Dublin and *Bioplan – Planning of Bioprocess Recipes* by Bioprocesses Group at VTT Biotechnology and Food Research (University of Kaiserslautern 2003). Reuse of parts, software and knowledge also falls into this category.

Information Retrieval. Applications in this group include E-commerce on line catalogue sales (Vollrath et al. 1998), intelligent Internet search (Vollrath et al. 1998) and hotline support (Lenz et al. 1998). The most essential issue for this type of task is the inexact matches of textual information. CBR is a natural problem solving technique that makes reference to the specific context of a particular problem. For example, when one searches the Internet for a certain product only the intended use of the project and not its various features are known (Richter 1998).

5.3.2 Challenges and Limitations of CBR

The major limitation of CBR is that an optimal solution cannot be guaranteed. Solutions provided by a CBR system are restricted to its case library and thus have only a certain degree of flexibility. The efficiency of the solution provided by a CBR system relies on the coverage of the case base, thus making it very difficult to be evaluated *quantitatively* (Leake 1996). Another challenge is associated with designing the adaptation rules. The definition of adaptation rules can be a complicated task that depends on the knowledge domain. Although several techniques have been applied in CBR for adaptation, most commercial CBR tools remain only case retrieval systems with adaptation being left to human intervention (Watson & Marir 1994).

The third challenge involves finding an appropriate indexing scheme (Haddad 2003). Relevant cases in human memory can be retrieved quickly when needed due to the efficient methods of indexing in a human brain. Although many algorithms have been developed for automated indexing methods in a case-based reasoner, Kolodner (1993) believed that people tend to be better at choosing indices than algorithms, and therefore, for practical applications, indices should be chosen by hand.

5.3.3 CBR Applications in Traffic Safety Analysis

Waters (2002) noted that traffic accidents and traffic safety studies are complex phenomena in a technical sense. Accordingly, existing regulations and safety measures tend not to reflect reality nor do they necessarily protect the driver. One of the first uses of CBR in road safety analysis (ROSAC – Road Safety Analysis with Cases) was proposed and developed by Capus and Tourigny (1998). ROSAC is a knowledge-based system that provides safety improvement solutions at road intersections based on previous, similar cases. Domain knowledge and expertise is represented by individual cases instead of rules. The system has two main functions: the first function is to manage a case base of road intersections as a conventional database while the second function allows the system to search for cases most similar to the situation encountered and, as needed, to reuse, adapt and save them as new cases. The developers of ROSAC found that the results of tests on hypothetical cases and a small sample of real cases were "satisfactory" (Capus and Tourigny 1998, p. 7).

Further to the development of this prototype, researchers at Laval University have designed an organizational memory (OM) using a hybrid approach that combines rule-based reasoning and case-based reasoning for road safety analysis (Boury-Brisset and Tourigny 2000). An OM consists of the integration of different knowledge assets in an organization, including both theoretical knowledge and practical know-how. This system is called SICAS (System with Intelligent and Cooperative functions to help in the Analysis of Sites). It shares domain expertise of road safety analysis among experts and analysts within the organization. It assists the analysts by identifying safety problems on a given site, determining possible causes and identifying proper correcting actions. Within SICAS, domain expertise is stored in a knowledge base while individual cases are stored in a case base. The developers realized that the domain expertise was efficient for solving "easy cases." However, as it grew, users could more effectively exploit the case base as a DSS for handling more complex cases. The developers also realized that the CBR approach enabled communication between experts and end users. Solutions to a complex case were proposed by the experts according to the features of the case reported by the end users. Moreover, detailed follow-up studies were facilitated and made possible since both the features *and* solutions of the case were saved in the case base (Boury-Brisset and Tourigny 2000). Lin et al. (2003) state that the CBR approach is useful in estimating safety benefits of road improvements. In order to evaluate the effectiveness of countermeasures that have been applied to a problematic road site, collision reduction factors (CRF) were calculated. Lin et al. argued that the estimation of CRF should also account for specific circumstances (e.g. location characteristics and surrounding environment, etc.) and the random nature of collisions. They reviewed 450 previous safety studies that described the effectiveness of various safety improvements. The reported CRF of these cases together with their physical and traffic attributes, and countermeasure types were documented in a CBR system, named ISECR. The effectiveness of safety countermeasures on a new study project can then be estimated based on similar previous cases in the case base. The developers tested the system and found that it "does provide valid results" (Lin et al. 2003, p. 389). CBR applications in traffic safety analysis are still limited to the research stage. Potential challenges of applying CBR to traffic safety analyses in the real world are: first, problems associated with scaling up the case base from test bed systems (Leake 1996) and, second, gaining user acceptance (Boury-Brisset and Tourigny 2000).

5.3.4 Summary of the Importance of CBR in Traffic Safety Studies

CBR is an information-retrieval methodology that uses the most similar prior cases as references for suggesting solutions to solve new problems (Leake 1996). The information-retrieval method, adaptation capability, and learning process are the major advantages of CBR compared to other database and information retrieval systems (Waters 2002). In addition, CBR systems are more interactive and allow communication between the experts and the end users (Boury-Brisset and Tourigny 2000).

5.4 Integrating Case-Based Reasoning and Geographic Information Systems

Making decisions is a complex activity that often involves the interaction of many disciplines. It is agreed that the key to useful computer-based DSS is integration (Abel et al. 1996; Cortes 2000). Tools obtained from different sources should be interoperable and, at best, combined in a common framework. GIS provides a rich solution for simultaneously integrating, analyzing and distributing data. Data manipulation operations (e.g. overlay) in most GIS applications overcome the heterogeneity of data coming from different sources with different levels of precision (Cortes 2000; ESRI 2003; Cusack 2003). Further, the mapping capability in GIS is optimal for visualizing data distributed across a network.

New research has sought to incorporate knowledge-based systems with GIS in order to create intelligent information systems. A knowledge-based GIS for safety analysis at rail-highway crossings in Delaware was developed on the TransCAD platform (Caliper Corporation 2003) to store and retrieve safety-related information at state-wide crossings (Panchanathan and Faghri 1995). Abel et al. (1996) used a KBS as a programming tool to perform queries while GIS worked as a "toolbox" and a database to enable spatial analysis. They also discussed the "re-use" of prior experiences as an intelligent component in the next generation of DSS. According to Cortes's (2000) review, the integration of GIS and ES can benefit an environmental decision support system (EDSS) with respect to data integration, data mining, problem diagnosis and decision support. The integration of CBR and GIS also shows promising results in some recent research. Examples include Clayton et al.'s (1998) work of integrating Traditional Environment Knowledge (TEK) in Gwich'in, Northern Territories within a GIS and Khattak and Renski's (1999) project of reusing and adapting prior cases for High-Occupancy-Vehicle (HOV) lane planning.

5.4.1 Options for Integrating CBR Tools with a GIS

There are several options when integrating CBR tools with GIS (Clayton and Waters 1999): 1. attach GIS layers at the end of CBR actions or answers; 2. operate both the CBR and the GIS through a common interface on a network; 3. have the GIS operate as a client program for CBR, sending requests and initiating the CBR when required; 4. run CBR as a client program in the GIS context using VBA; or 5. implement the CBR methodology and algorithms directly within a GIS environment. Clayton and Waters (1999) explored the first two options in their study of integrating traditional environment knowledge within a GIS. They found that the best option was to attach the GIS layers as "browsable" files over a common network because it "does not require the user to be an expert in GIS" (Clayton and Waters 1999, p. 299). A web-based expert GIS was also found to be highly useful and quite user-friendly for applications that involve multiple users (Ozbay and Mukherjee 2000). However, there are a number of drawbacks to this approach. First, the user's access to the GIS files is limited since the GIS files are always the end result of the search. Second, it takes significant efforts to link the database and case base without a powerful relational database server. The feasibility of having the GIS operate as a client program greatly depends on the interoperability of the CBR software. Most readily usable CBR programs are commercial applications; they are usually specific and offer very limited capability of accommodating other software. On the other hand, most GIS software has the capability of interfacing external software such as CBR tools. Khattak and Renski (1999) developed a CBR tool for HOV lane analysis in the ESRI's ArcView 3.0 environment (www.esri.com). They applied CBR methodology and algorithms using the Avenue programming language to query historical HOV cases. The direct application of CBR algorithms in GIS is a truly intelligent system that enables the immediate query and analysis of historical cases, adaptation of previous solutions and the display of final results all in one database and on one software platform.

5.4.2 The Potential for Integrating CBR and GIS in Traffic Safety Research

The above discussion outlined how GIS and expert systems have been applied to solve traffic safety problems, and how the integration of case-based reasoning and GIS can provide new opportunities for the design and application of intelligent systems for traffic safety analysis. Recent efforts have contributed to applying new AI technologies such as case-based reasoning (Boury-Brisset and Tourigny 2000; Capus and Tourigny 1998) and integrating AI with other technologies such as GIS (Ozbay and Mukherjee 2000) to build more efficient intelligent systems for traffic safety analysis. As Guariso and Werthner (1994) pointed out, all these intelligent systems cannot, and will not, do the work that remains to be done by humans. *Better computer support does not necessarily imply a better decision*; it is still the safety professional's responsibility to validate decisions provided by these systems.

5.5 A Case Study: Integrating GIS Network and CBR Approaches for Traffic Safety

The Calgary Light Rail Transit (LRT) system has been serving Calgarians for more than two decades and will continue to serve as a major public transit system in the City. The Calgary LRT system is a relatively safe system and in recent years has produced few collisions. Light-rail vehicle (LRV) related collisions from 1996 to 2000 averaged only 2.4 per annum. However, collisions involving an LRV are generally more severe, affect more people and take more time to clear up. Safety engineers, transit planners and transit organizations seek to reduce potential traffic collisions and conflicts among LRV, motor vehicles and pedestrians along LRT corridors and to provide a safer and more reliable service.

Based on the potential conflicts between LRV and motor vehicles, bicycles and pedestrians, light rail alignments can be classified into three categories (TCRP Report 69 2001):

Exclusive: light rail and roadways are fully grade separated or at-grade without crossings; examples in Calgary include short sections along the northwest line, where both below-grade and elevated structures are used;
Semi-excusive: light rail and roadways use separate rights-of-way, or shared rights-of-way protected by barriers, this occurs in various parts of the Calgary network including just east of the downtown area;
Non-exclusive: mixed traffic operations or LRT/pedestrian malls, such as in the central downtown portion of the network.

Semi-exclusive and non-exclusive systems experience variable degrees of mixed operation with other traffic and with pedestrians. Seventy percent of the total track length of the Calgary LRT is classified as semi-exclusive or non-exclusive alignment (TCRP Report 69 2001). The main advantage of semi-exclusive or non-exclusive LRT systems is their cost efficiency. However, the at-grade design of light rail can result in traffic collisions or conflicts among trains, motor vehicles, bicycles and pedestrians.

For example, all 12 LRV-related collisions 1996 to 2000 occurred at rail-roadway grade crossings, including one fatality and four injuries (Fig. 5.1). Questions occur when implementing safety strategies along existing LRT, and planning future LRT systems: how safe are the existing light rail/roadway at-grade crossings in Calgary? Did they experience higher collision rates and/or more severe consequences due to the presence of LRT? Are there ways to improve the safety at these crossings? Or is it essential to grade-separate light rail and roadways in the City? This case study aims at implementing a methodology to help traffic safety professionals to answer these, and related, questions.

5.5.1 Methodology

Traffic safety studies typically involve analyzing collision history, addressing existing safety problems and providing countermeasures. This methodology requires a robust sample size of collision data in order to minimize variations due to external effects (Hamilton-Finn 2000) and is thus questionable for analyzing LRT safety since LRV-related collisions are relatively rare. When LRV-related collision data are insufficient, analyzing the patterns of non LRV-related collisions at rail/roadway grade crossings might provide useful information to predict potential LRV-related collisions, and to examine safety issues at these crossings. However, the occurrence of a traffic collision is a complex function of three major factors: human, vehicle and environment, each considered before, during and after the collision (Haddon et al. 1964). The variations in collision patterns are the results of the differences of these three major factors among sites and time. Thus the relationship between non LRV-related collisions and LRV-related safety issues at a given site cannot be modelled using a simple equation. Rather, another, more holistic reasoning approach that takes into account site-specific characteristics should be considered. As noted above, the CBR approach that values the details of each individual case may be used to explore the relationships among such complex events.

The purpose of this case study was to review traffic safety at Calgary's light rail/roadway grade crossings, by employing GIS technology and CBR tools, to analyze the collision history and site-specific characteristics at these crossings. In this study, GIS played an important role as a framework enabling the manipulation and analysis of collision data, as well as the retrieval of other relevant information. CBR tools were employed to assist in the identification of potential safety problems at rail/roadway at grade crossings based on the analysis of collision histories and the site-specific network characteristics.

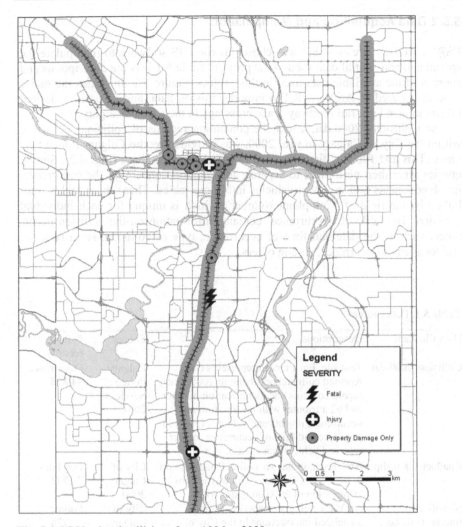

Fig. 5.1. LRV-related collisions from 1996 to 2000

The CBR system was then used to recommend possible solutions.

The case-study objectives were: 1. to import, manipulate and analyze the collision data in a GIS environment; 2. to retrieve relevant site-specific information from multiple sources using GIS analysis; 3. to determine potential safety problems at these light rail/roadway grade crossings and to recommend solutions using CBR tools.

5.5.2 Data Acquisition and Manipulation

ESRI's ArcGIS ArcView 8.2 was chosen as the GIS software to manipulate the spatial and non-spatial data used in the project. Table 5.1 lists the descriptions and sources of the available data used in this project. Figure 5.2 illustrates the major procedures used in ArcView 8.2 to import collision data, and to retrieve desired information at light rail/roadway grade crossings in the City of Calgary.

The Collisions_2000.dat, a text file containing records of collisions occurring within the City of Calgary in year 2000, was provided by the Calgary Police Services. This text file was first imported to MS Access database (Fig. 5.2). Simple queries were then performed to separate information concerning the occurrence, involved objects and involved vehicles into three tables. These three tables were linked by the field of 'Complaint Number', which is unique for each individual collision. The table of 'Occurrence' contains information on the collision occurrence, such as the date and time of occurrence, type of collision, severity level, and location of occurrence, among others.

Table 5.1. Data sources

Data file name	Descriptions	Source	# of records
Collision_2000.dat	Text file. Each record represents one reported collision occurring in 2000. Each record contains one identification number and 62 attributes with information on occurrence, objects and vehicles involved (e.g. date and time of occurrence, object type and vehicle make, etc.).	Calgary Police Services. 2001	Occurrence: 34,825
Roadnet_2000.shp	ArcView polyline shapefile. Road network in the City of Calgary, with traffic flow information of 2000 on major roads.	City of Calgary, 2000	Polylines: 76,774
Signalized_ Intersection.shp	ArcView polygon shapefile. Major signalized intersections in the City of Calgary	City of Calgary, 2003	Points: 778
Lightrail.shp	ArcView polyline shapefile. Existing LRT tracks in the City of Calgary (by May, 2003)	City of Calgary, 2003	Polylines: 13,598
Landuse.shp	ArcView polygon shapefile. Land use type information within the City limit	City of Calgary, 2000	Polygons: 5,549
LRT_crossings.shp	ArcView point shapefile. 47 light rail/roadway crossings along the City's existing LRT tracks.	Digitized by Li, K., 2002	Points: 47
LRT_stations.shp	ArcView point shapefile. 31 existing LRT stations by December, 2001.	Digitized by Raza, W., 2001	Points: 31

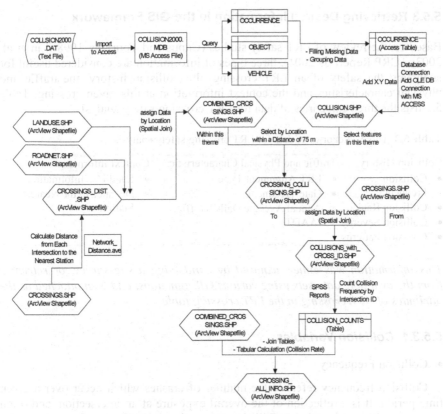

Fig. 5.2. Procedures for importing and retrieving information in GIS

Collision locations are represented by X,Y coordinates, and thus can be displayed geographically in a GIS. 30,717 collisions with valid X,Y coordinates were converted to the ArcView shapefile format. LRT crossings were digitized based on the Calgary Transit Map 2002. Attributes, such as type of light rail alignment and gate treatment, were added to each LRT crossing. Eight of the 47 LRT crossings in Calgary were classified as exclusive alignments with underpass structures, while the other 39 are at-grade crossings. Since the goal of this project was to examine the safety of those at-grade crossings, only the 39 at-grade crossings were extracted and analyzed. Thirty one LRT stations were digitized based on the same transit map. Most of the data used in this project were provided by the City of Calgary. Therefore, the City's standard coordinate system was used in this project. The City of Calgary currently uses datum NAD83, projection 3TM (a modified UTM system) to represent transportation data.

5.5.3 Retrieving Desired Information in the GIS Framework

Based on the review of LRT safety studies (Capus and Tourigny 1998; Lin et al. 2003; TCRP Report 69 2001), three types of information are considered useful for analyzing the safety of an LRT crossing: the collision history, the traffic and physical characteristics and the context information at this given crossing. Table 5.2 lists the three categories of data for LRT crossing safety analysis.

Table 5.2. Three categories of data for LRT crossing safety analysis

Collision History	Traffic and Physical Characteristics	Context Information
• Collision Frequency • Collision Rate • Collision Severity • Collision Patterns	• LRT Alignment Type • Gate Treatment • Annual Average Daily Traffic (AADT)	• Land Use Information • Distance to the Nearest Station

This information was either acquired by conducting a site survey, or retrieved from the available data sets using various GIS functions, and then attached as the attributes of each crossing in the LRT crossing table.

5.5.3.1 Collision Variables

• Collision Frequency

Collision frequency refers to the number of crashes which occur over a given time period. It is a reflection of the overall exposure at an intersection, and often increases with traffic volume. Collisions occurring in 2000 were first selected by locations within a radius of 75 meters of each LRT at-grade crossings.

• Collision Rate

Collision rate indicates the collision risk relative to the traffic volumes at a given location. It is an estimate of the chance that a vehicle at any point in time will be involved in a crash. It is usually expressed in terms of the number of collisions per million entering vehicles. The collision rate for each LRT at-grade crossing was calculated using the following equation:

$$CollisionRate = \frac{CollisionFrequency}{(AADT*365)/1,000,000} \qquad (5.1)$$

where AADT is the average annual daily traffic volume in 2000.

- Collision Severity

Collision severity is classified into three categories: fatal, injury and property damage only (PDO). Safety professionals are typically interested in the fatal and injury rate at a study site.

- Collision Patterns

Collision patterns represent general trends and common characteristics of collisions occurring at a given site. These trends and characteristics can be useful in identifying collision causes and can reveal safety problems at the collision site. The determination of variable(s) in the collision dataset for pattern analysis is discussed below.

5.5.3.2 Traffic Data

The only available traffic data are the AADT volumes from the ROADNET_2000 shapefiles. AADT ranges from 1,000 to 10,600 at the LRT at grade crossings. The information concerning the LRT alignment type and gate treatment type was digitized based on field surveys.

5.5.3.3 Context Information

Land use information was retrieved by locations, and attached as attributes of the LRT at-grade crossings. Land use types at these crossings, together with the number of occurrences in parentheses, are: agricultural (1), commercial (7), direct control (13), industrial (9), public education and recreation (4), public services (1) and urban reserve (4).

An Avenue script was used to calculate the distance from each at-grade crossing to the nearest LRT station (Wang 2000). This script allows the user to calculate the nearest network distance from one point data set (crossings) to another point data set (stations). The shortest distance between an at-grade and an LRT station is 25 meters, occurring in downtown.

5.5.3.4 Comparing Samples

To allow a comparison between signalized intersections and the at-grade LRT crossings, the same types of attributes were retrieved for each signalized intersection, and attached in the intersection table using similar procedures. Signalized intersections with the same land use type and falling into the same AADT range as that of the at-grade crossings were extracted for comparison.

5.5.4 Multiple Correspondence Analysis: Exploring the Collision Data Structure

There are 24 variables describing each collision occurrence in the data set. These variables include date of occurrence, time of occurrence, location of occurrence, collision type, collision consequence and environmental condition, among others. Some variables contain redundant information; it would be inefficient to include all these variables in the analysis. Hence, it is necessary to explore the data structure and reduce the data dimensions before further analyzing the collision data. Correspondence analysis (CA) is an exploratory technique for categorical and higher level data. The results of a CA provide statistics that are similar to those produced by factor analysis techniques. CA allows the exploration of the structure of categorical variables, and is a useful way to reduce redundant information in the data set, producing fewer data dimensions. Multiple correspondence analysis (MCA) or optimal scaling (SPSS 2000) may be considered an extension of simple correspondence analysis to more than two variables (StatSoft Inc. 2003, Fellenberg et al. 2001). A multiple correspondence analysis was carried out using SPSS v.11.5 to explore the data set of collisions occurring at LRT grade crossings. Figure 5.3 shows the 'Eigenvalues' of each dimension. The eigenvalues measure "how much of the categorical information is accounted for by each dimension" (SPSS 2000, p. 181). They are a measure of the total variance accounted for by the model. The higher the eigenvalue, the larger the amount of the total variance among the variables that loads on to that dimension. The largest possible eigenvalue for each dimension is 1.0. Ideally, the first two or three dimensions contain high eigenvalues (e.g. higher than 0.5) while the others express much lower values. Data dimensions are therefore reduced to the first two or three according to the eigenvalues. In our case the maximum eigenvalue in the first dimension was only 0.222, and there was not a significant "cut-off point" to determine which dimensions could be removed.

Dimension	Eigenvalue
1	0.222
2	0.165
3	0.150
4	0.121
5	0.111
6	0.106
7	0.100
8	0.094
9	0.089
10	0.087

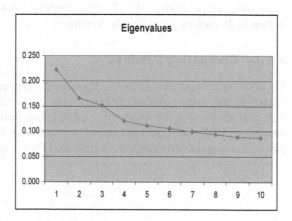

Fig. 5.3. Eigenvalues for the Intersection-collision data

The similarly low eigenvalues in each dimension indicated that the variables in the collision data are heterogeneous and all carry, to some extent, unique information. Reducing any of the variables might result in losing useful information concerning the observations. The heterogeneity of the collision variables reflects the random nature of collision occurrence. Traffic collisions can occur anywhere, anytime.

Table 5.3 shows the 'Discrimination Measures' of each variable in each dimension.[1] A discrimination measure, which can be regarded as a "squared component loading", is the variance of the quantified variable in that dimension (SPSS 2000, p. 184).

Large discrimination measures indicate that the categories of a variable are better separated along that dimension. Similar discrimination measures for different variables in the same dimensions indicate that these variables are related to each other. Related variables provide redundant information and therefore, some of them can be removed.

Since the eigenvalues are not very large in this analysis, discrimination measures in all ten dimensions were examined. The main findings were:

First, the variables 'Surface Condition', 'Environment Condition' and 'Month of the Year' were highly related as they all have high discrimination measures in dimension 3 and 4, but relatively low discrimination measures in other dimensions. These related variables described the winter road conditions in Calgary, when it is snowing (Environment Condition) and the roads are wet, slushy, snowy or icy (Surface Condition).

Second, the variables of 'Special Facility', 'Road Class' and 'Collision Location,' were related since they had similar discrimination measures in dimensions 1, 2 and 5. These variables described the locational information of collision occurrence.

Table 5.3. Discrimination measures for the Intersection_collision data

	Dimension									
	1	2	3	4	5	6	7	8	9	10
PRI_EVEN	0.460	0.229	0.125	0.008	0.112	0.370	0.438	0.552	0.335	0.331
SEVERITY	0.139	0.044	0.004	0.009	0.009	0.009	0.033	0.019	0.026	0.004
HIT_RUN	0.192	0.086	0.005	0.004	0.025	0.053	0.167	0.060	0.016	0.001
SCENE	0.408	0.239	0.013	0.001	0.001	0.005	0.025	0.006	0.004	0.000
DIAGRAM	0.118	0.107	0.006	0.003	0.003	0.011	0.028	0.013	0.004	0.000
SUR_CON	0.044	0.138	0.693	0.698	0.009	0.008	0.005	0.002	0.006	0.002
ENV_CON	0.024	0.086	0.442	0.743	0.013	0.024	0.015	0.024	0.036	0.025
SPE_FAC	0.521	0.189	0.040	0.006	0.203	0.114	0.030	0.069	0.151	0.422
RD_AL_A	0.070	0.072	0.035	0.003	0.291	0.073	0.012	0.036	0.015	0.044
RD_AL_B	0.064	0.072	0.015	0.004	0.320	0.126	0.023	0.020	0.001	0.004
RD_CLAS	0.375	0.278	0.053	0.004	0.347	0.102	0.157	0.327	0.049	0.023
LOCAT	0.673	0.623	0.116	0.019	0.183	0.534	0.147	0.020	0.034	0.022
MONTH	0.014	0.123	0.505	0.170	0.026	0.049	0.061	0.137	0.417	0.226
GRP_HOUR	0.011	0.030	0.049	0.017	0.019	0.008	0.256	0.028	0.152	0.113

[1] Further details on this analysis are available upon request from the authors.

The relatively homogeneous nature of these variables indicated that collisions tend to occur at certain types of location, such as, on undivided two-way roads (Road Class), at intersections (Collision Location), on divided roads (Road Class) and on highway interchange ramps (Special Facility). Third, the discrimination measures for the variable of 'Primary Event' (type of collision) were high in dimension 1, 6, 7, 8, 9 and 10. Conclusions can be drawn that this variable accounted for significant variance in the data set. The type of collision was related to the location of collision occurrence (dimensions 1, 6, 8 and 10) and time of occurrence (dimensions 7 and 9).

Fourth, discrimination measures appeared low in almost all dimensions for the binary variables of 'Hit and Run', 'Scene Visit' and 'Diagram Available' (the only exception was the relatively high value for the variable of 'Scene Visit' on the first dimension). These variables might be considered as noise in the dataset, and were ignored.

5.5.5 Crosstabulation, Confirming the Significant Variable

According to the results of a multiple correspondence analysis, the "Primary Event" variable appeared to be the most important variable in the collision dataset. A crosstabulation table was used to examine if the pattern of values for the "Primary Event" variable was associated with the two types of intersection (i.e. LRT or non-LRT crossing). Crosstabulation can be used to examine frequencies of observations that belong to specific categories on more than one variable (StatSoft Inc. 2003). By examining these frequencies, we can identify relations between crosstabulated variables. In this analysis, 13 categories of "Primary Event" (column variable) were crosstabulated with the two types of intersection (row variable). The Pearson Chi-square was 98.152. The significance value (0.00) indicated that there was a highly significant relationship between the variables of "Primary Event" and "Type of Intersection."

Although the Pearson Chi-Square showed a significant relationship between the tested variables, the phi value of 0.094 in this test indicated that the relationship was quite weak and this was probably due to the large number of accidents.

5.5.6 Interpretations

Multiple correspondence analysis is a useful statistical technique to explore the structure of categorical data and reduce the data dimensions. The MCA results showed that some of the variables, such as the variables of 'Surface Condition', 'Environment Condition' and 'Month of the Year', in the data set provide exactly the same information, and could therefore be removed from the analysis. These results can also be used to structure a more efficient case base.

The crosstabulation analysis further confirmed that the variable "Primary Event" was associated with the variable "Type of Intersection". LRT crossings experienced a different pattern of collision types. The pattern of the "Primary Event" variable at each crossing will be reviewed therefore, to determine the safety attributes of the various crossings.

5.5.7 Case Base Construction

The construction of a case base is crucial, since prior cases are the fundamental elements of a CBR system. New solutions are generated by retrieving the most relevant cases from memory and adapting them to fit the new situations. In CBR, knowledge is organized by cases. The CBR tool used in this study is the Knowledge software family from eGain Communication Corporation (eGain 2003). Knowledge Central functions as the administrator that manages the case bases and their users. Knowledge Author is the key tool for case input, modification and adaptation. Search results of the most relevant cases are presented in Knowledge Agent. In eGain Knowledge, the knowledge, or the descriptions of a case, are represented by "questions" and then grouped by "clusters." Answers to these questions are used to refine the search results, or to lead to another question or cluster by actions. Answers in eGain Knowledge can be formatted as text (e.g. "LRT at-grade crossings"), HTML links, lists (e.g. a list of safety issues at a given LRT at-grade crossing), tables (e.g. numeric tables), and controls (to enable actions within the eGain Knowledge Software).

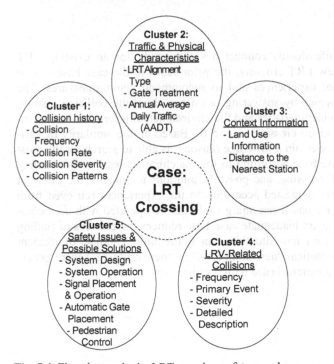

Fig. 5.4. Five clusters in the LRT crossing safety case base

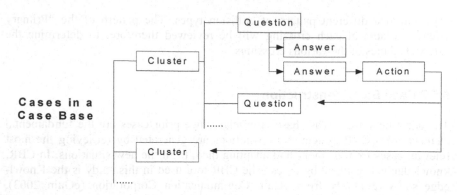

Fig. 5.5. Case base structure in eGain knowledge

The structure of a case base in eGain Knowledge is shown in Fig. 5.4.

In this project, traffic safety studies at the LRT at-grade crossings were considered cases. Five clusters were defined in the case base (Fig. 5.4). Cluster 1–3 contain criteria for searching matched cases, while Cluster 4 and 5 provide LRV-related collision prediction and possible solutions to enhance traffic safety at the study crossing. Figure 5.5 shows the case tree structure of these clusters in eGain Knowledge.

5.5.8 Case Retrieval

When traffic safety professionals conduct a safety study for an existing LRT crossing, or design a new LRT crossing, the prior cases in the case base can be used to provide relevant experiences and to recommend countermeasures. The case retrieval process begins by answering questions about the collision history, the traffic and physical characteristics and the environmental information concerning past collisions of a given crossing (Fig. 5.6). Based on the similarity of variables in these clusters, the eGain knowledge reasoner is able to search for the most relevant cases in the case base according to the matching scores. Potential safety issues at the given LRT crossing, and possible solutions to enhance the safety at this crossing can then be suggested according to the experiences retrieved from prior cases. Although case based reasoning tools can be operated with an incomplete and small case base, an inadequate case base reduces the chances of finding perfectly matched cases for a new situation. Due to the limited number of accident cases in this study, hypothetical "new situations" or "new crossings" were generated in order to retrieve a matched case with a satisfactory score.

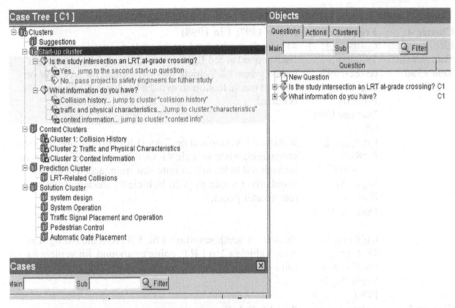

Fig. 5.6. A portion of the case tree in eGain author

Table 5.4 shows the case of 7th Avenue and 4th Street S.W. intersection. Detailed descriptions of the traffic collision history, traffic and physical characteristics and context information of the crossing were stored in the criterion clusters (Clusters 1, 2 and 3).

Table 5.4. One case example for 7th Avenue and 4th Street

Cluster 1:	Collision	
Collision	Frequency	8
History (2000)	Collision Rate	1.37
	Severity	Injury: 1 (12.5%); PDO: 7
	Primary Event Pattern	

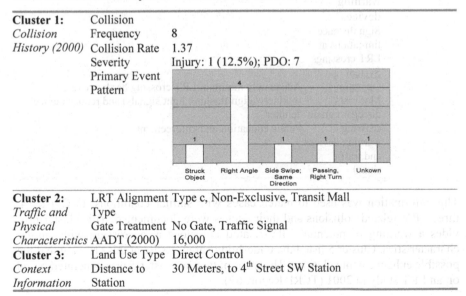

Cluster 2:	LRT Alignment Type	Type c, Non-Exclusive, Transit Mall
Traffic and		
Physical	Gate Treatment	No Gate, Traffic Signal
Characteristics	AADT (2000)	16,000
Cluster 3:	Land Use Type	Direct Control
Context	Distance to	30 Meters, to 4th Street SW Station
Information	Station	

Table 5.4. (cont.)

Cluster 4:	Frequency	3 (2 in 1997; 1 in 1998)
LRV-Related	Collision 1:	#1 vehicle northbound on 4 St. SW in east Centre lane.
Collisions	19:00pm,	Had stopped at red light. Proceed through light before it
from 1996	03-22-1997	turned green. #2 Vehicle was westbound on 7Av. SW on
to 2000	Right Angle	tracks. Unable to stop to avoid #1 vehicle. Collision
	Property	occurred.
	Damage Only	
	(PDO)	
	Collision 2:	Vehicle #2 westbound on 7 Av (LRT) proceeding through
	6:58am,	green light, when vehicle #1 southbound on 4 St. SW went
	04-8-1997	through red light, last minute saw train, accelerated to
	Right Angle	avoid driver's side impact. Vehicle #1 stuck by train right
	Property	rear quarter panel.
	Damage Only	
	Collision 3:	Vehicle #1 southbound on 4 St. SW. Ran the red light at 7
	18:42pm,	Ave. Vehicle #2, a LRT, going eastbound, hit vehicle #1.
	06-27-1998	Little damage
	Right Angle	
	PDO	
Cluster 5:	**Safety Issues**	**Possible Solutions**
	System Design	
	Motorist	Avoid excessive use of signs
	disregard for	Photo-enforcement
	regulatory	Maximize sight distance by limiting potential obstructions
	signs at LRT	to 1.1 m (3.5 ft.) in height within about 30 to 60 m (100 to
	crossings and	200 ft.) of the LRT crossings (measured parallel to the
	grade crossing	tracks back from the crossing)
	warning	
	devices	
	Sign distance	
	limitations at	
	LRT crossings	
	System	
	Operations	Adequately maintain LRT crossing hardware (e.g.,
	Motorists	routinely align flashing light signals) and reduce device
	disregard grade	"clutter"
	crossing	Public education and enforcement
	warning devices	
	and traffic	
	signal	

This information was used to match cases with similar conditions. In Cluster 4, three LRV-related collisions and their causes were documented. This cluster provides a warning of potential LRV-related collisions at a crossing with similar characteristics. Cluster 5 listed the underlying safety issues at this crossing and the possible enhancement solutions. The information in Cluster 5 was generated based on an LRT study in 2001 (TCRP Report 69).

5.5.9 Conclusions

In this project, traffic collision records within the City of Calgary were imported to ESRI's ArcView 8.2 GIS software, where collisions were analyzed by their locations. Collision history and site-specific roadway characteristics of the LRT at-grade crossings were retrieved using various GIS functions. Traffic safety at these crossings was reviewed. The results of the studies were documented in eGain Knowledge, a case-based reasoning system, to enable more efficient and intelligent referencing for future safety studies of LRT crossings of the road network. GIS is an effective framework for integrating data from various sources, and for manipulating this multi-source data geographically. The acquisition of collision history and other site-specific characteristics of the study crossings would have been extremely difficult and time-consuming without a GIS solution. Moreover, the fully relational database architecture within ArcView GIS makes it possible to integrate with other database applications, such as most case based reasoning tools.

Case based reasoning methodology takes advantage of prior experiences when solving new situations. This reasoning approach is similar to the problem solving activities of a human brain. It also appears as a common research method in traffic safety, in which experience plays an important role. Another advantage within a case based system is that previous safety studies or projects can be documented and stored in a more interactive fashion. In such an interactive system, expertise and solutions to the previous problems are more reviewable and reusable. Thus professional knowledge can be circulated more efficiently within the traffic safety community.

Future efforts should be devoted to developing a more advanced system that implements CBR tools directly in a GIS environment, in order to monitor traffic safety at LRT crossings. Such a system would have several advantages. First, information retrieved from GIS layers could remain within the GIS database. CBR tools would provide a new indexing system to this information for performing queries to obtain matching cases. This would save the time and effort of converting database tables between the GIS and CBR systems. Second, the existing CBR tools are mostly focused on dealing with text information. Searches are triggered by entering key words, or answering questions. The integrated system would enable graphical representation of knowledge in the case base. For example, by pointing to a potential LRT crossing on a GIS map, relevant information concerning this crossing would be retrieved and the most similar existing crossings would be highlighted. Third, the fully integrated system would avoid requiring the user to switch between two applications, and thus would be more user-friendly.

Acknowledgements

The authors would like to thank Drs. Laurence Capus and Nicole Tourigny at Laval University who kindly provided a copy of their unpublished paper from the

1998 TRB conference and Mr. Cam Nelson for the use of the City of Calgary Accident database. Special thanks go to Mr. David Baines and eGain Corporation for providing the Knowledge package without which this research would not have been possible.

References

Abel D. et al. (1996) Decision support systems for sustainable development experience and potential: a position paper. Macau Workshop. Available at http://www.fes.uwaterloo.ca/Tools/docs/dssfsd_pp.pdf (Accessed on 08/19/2003)

Aha DW (2003) Case-based reasoning sources. Available at http://www.aic.nrl.navy.mil/~aha/research/case-based-reasoning.html (Accessed on 11/18/2003)

Alberta Motor Association (2003) Available at http://www.ama.ab.ca/mission_possible/mission.html (Accessed on 06/19/2003)

Arthur R (2002) Modeling hazardous locations with geographic information system. In: Rothe P (ed) Driving lessons, exploring systems that makes traffic safer. Edmonton AB: University of Alberta Press, pp 257–270

Arthur R, Waters N (1997) Formal scientific research of traffic collision data utilizing GIS. Transportation Planning and Technology 21: 121–37

Bayapureddy D (1996) Geographic information system for identification of high accident locations. Available at http://www.esri.com/library/userconf/proc96/PAP105/P105.htm (Accessed on 12/03/2001)

Boury-Brisset A, Tourigny N (2000) Knowledge capitalisation through case bases and knowledge engineering for road safety analysis. Knowledge-Based Systems 13: 297–305

Burkhard H (1998) Extending some concepts of CBR – Foundations of case retrieval nets. In: Lenz M, Bartsch-Spörl B, Burkhard H-D, Wess S (eds) Case-based reasoning technology: from foundations to applications. Lecture Notes in Artificial Intelligence 1400, Springer, Berlin Heidelberg New York, pp 17–50

Capus L, Tourigny N (1998) Road safety analysis: a case-based reasoning approach. Paper presented at Transpiration Research Board 77th Annual Meeting. Washington, D.C.

Carreker L, Bachman W (2000) Geographic information system procedures to improve speed and accuracy in locating cashes. Transportation Research Record 1719, National Academy Press, Washington, D.C.

Chris Naylor Research Limited (2003) Expert systems: a definition. Available at http://www.chrisnaylor.co.uk/Definition.html (Accessed on 09/04/2003)

Cirillo J, Council F, Griffith M, Hauer E, Paniati J (2000) Making safety management knowledge based. Transportation in the new millennium. Transportation Research Board, Washington, D.C.

City of Calgary (2003) ITS strategic plan, stakeholder consultation workbook. Workshop No.3, City of Calgary

Clayton D, Waters N (1999) Distributed knowledge, distributed processing, distributed users: integrating case-based reasoning and GIS for multicriteria decision making. In: Thill JC (ed) Spatial multicriteria decision making and analysis, a geographic information science approach. Ashgate, Aldershot, pp 275–304

Clayton D, Charlie R, Waters N (1998) Developing a knowledge base to incorporate traditional knowledge with GIS. Paper presented at Twelfth Annual Symposium on Geographic Information Systems. Toronto

Cortes U, Sanchez-Marre M, Ceccaroni I (2000) Artificial intelligence and environmental decision support systems. Applied Intelligence 13: 77–91

Cusack M (2003) Knowledge presentation in GIS-T for ITS decision support systems. Available at http://www.albany.edu/rcinf/students/KnowledgeRepresentationinGIS-TforITS.pdf (Accessed on 08/19/2003)

Dieng R, Giboin A, Amerge C, Corby O (1996) Building of a corporate memory for traffic accident analysis. Available at http://www-sop.inria.fr/acacia/Publications/1996/dieng-kaw96.html (Accessed on 03/25/2003)

eGain Communication Corporation (2003) Knowledge user's manual. Available at www.egain.com

ESRI Website (2003) Available at http://www.esri.com

Fellenberg K, Hauser NC, Brors B, Neutzner A, Hoheisel JD, Vingron M (2001) Correspondence analysis applied to microarray data. In: Proceeding of the National Academic of Sciences of the United States of America, Vol.98, no.19

Glauz W, Bauer K, Migletz D (1985) Expected traffic conflict rates and their use in predicting accidents. Transportation Research Record 1026. National Academy Press, Washington, D.C.

Guariso G, Werthner H (eds) (1994) Environmental Decision Support Systems. Ellis Horwood-Wiley, Chichester New York

Haddad M (2003) Case-based reasoning case study: a case-based reasoning system for automated image interpretation of myocardial perfusion scintigraphy. Available at http://escher.cs.ucdavis.edu/mdi207/CBR.pdf (Accessed on 08/07/2003)

Haddon W, Jr., Suchman EA, Klein D (1964) Accident research – Methods and approaches. Harper and Row, New York

Haley Enterprise Inc. (2003) Available at http://www.haley.com/2045129008650259//THE.html (Accessed on 09/16/2003)

Hall J, Kim T, Darter M (2000) Cost-benefit analysis of geographic information system implementation. Transportation Research Record 1719. National Academy Press, Washington, D.C.

Hamilton-Finn Road Safety Consultants Ltd. (2000) Calgary blackspot pilot study. Available at http://www.hamiltonfinn.ca/

Herland L, Moller B, Schandersson R (2000) Knowledge acquisition, verification, and validation in an expert system for improved traffic safety. Transportation Research Record 1739. National Academy Press, Washington, D.C.

HSIS Summary Report (1999) GIS-based crash referencing and analysis system. (http://www.tfhrc.gov/safety/hsis/99-081.pdf (Accessed on 12/04/2001)

Joh D (1997) CBR in a changing environment. In: Leake DB, Plaza (eds) Case-based reasoning research and development. Lecture Notes in Artificial Intelligence. No. 1266. Springer, Berlin Heidelberg New York

Khattak AJ, Renski H (1999) PLAN◇HOV: case-based reasoning planning tool for high-occupancy vehicle lane analysis in a geographic information system environment. Transportation Research Record 1682. National Academy Press, Washington, D.C.

Kolodner J (1993) Case-based reasoning. Morgan Kaufmann, San Francisco

Kolodner J (1996) Making the implicit explicit: clarifying the principles of case-based reasoning. In: Leake DB (ed) Case-based reasoning, experiences, lessons, & future directions. AAAI Press, Menlo Park, pp 349–370

Lang L (1999) Transportation GIS. ESRI Press, Redlands

Leake DB (1996) CBR in context: the present and future. In: Leake DB (ed) Case-based reasoning, experiences, lessons, & future directions. AAAI Press, Menlo Park, pp 3–30

Leake DB, Kolodner J (1996) A tutorial introduction to case-based reasoning. In: Leake DB (ed) Case-based reasoning, experiences, lessons, & future directions. AAAI Press, Menlo Park, pp 31–66

Lenz M, Auriol E, Manago M (1998) Diagnosis and decision support. In: Lenz M, Bartsch-Spörl B, Burkhard H-D, Wess S (eds) Case-based reasoning technology: from foundations to applications. Lecture Notes in Artificial Intelligence 1400. Springer, Berlin Heidelberg New York, pp 51–90

Lin F, Sayed T, Deleur P (2003) Estimating safety benefits of road improvements: case based approach. Journal of Transportation Engineering 129: 385–391

Miller J (2000) The unique analytical capabilities geographic information systems can offer the traffic safety community. Transportation Research Board 79th Annual Meeting. Washington, D.C.

Nelson C (2003) Personal communication. (Traffic Safety Coordinator, City of Calgary)

Nyerges TL (2004) GIS in urban and regional transportation planning. In: Hanson S, Giuliano G (eds) The geography of urban transportation. The Guilford Press, New York, pp 163–95

Ozbay K, Mukherjee S (2000) Web-based expert geographical information system for advanced transportation management systems. Transportation Research Record 1719, National Academy Press, Washington, D.C.

Panchanathan S, Faghri A (1995) Knowledge-based geographic information system for safety analysis at rail-highway grade crossings. Transportation Research Record 1497. National Academy Press, Washington, D.C.

Paniati JF, Hughes W (2000) Making safety management knowledge based. Transportation in the New Millennium, Washington, D.C.

Parker MR, Jr., Zegeer CV (1988) Traffic conflict techniques for safety and operations: engineers guide. Report FHWA-IP-88-026, FHWA, U.S. Department of Transportation, Washington, D.C.

Peled A, Haj-Yehia B, Hakkert A (1996) Arc/Info-based geographic information system for road safety analysis & improvement. Available at http://www.esri.com/library//userconf/proc96/TO50/PAP005/P5.htm (Accessed on 02/09/2002)

Richter M (1998) Introduction. In: Lenz M, Bartsch-Spörl B, Burkhard H-D, Wess S (ed) Case-based reasoning technology: from foundations to applications. Lecture Notes in Artificial Intelligence 1400. Springer, Berlin Heidelberg New York, pp 1–16

Riesbeck C (1996) What next? The future of case-based reasoning in postmodern AI. In: Leake DB (ed) Case-based reasoning, experiences, lessons, & future directions. AAAI Press, Menlo Park, pp 371–388

Saccomanno F, Fu L, Roy R (2003) GIS-based integrated model for road accident analysis and prediction. Available at http://www.civil.uwaterloo.ca/saccomanno/Publications//GIS_PapTRB.doc (Accessed on 04/28/2003)

Smith R (2000) Implementing GIS-based highway safety analyses: bridge the gap. Available at http://www.esri.com/library/userconf/proc00/professionalpapers/PAP888//p888.htm (Accessed on 11/28/2001)

Souleyrette R, Strauss T, Estochen B, Pawlovich M (1998) GIS-based accident location and analysis system (GIS-ALAS). Project Report: Phase 1. Available at http://www.ctre.iastate.edu/Research/gis-alas/papers/gisalasph1.pdf (Accessed on 03/26/2002)

Spring G, Hummer J (1995) Identification of hazardous highway locations using knowledge-based GIS: a case study. Transportation Research Record 1497. National Academy Press, Washington, D.C.

SPSS Inc. (2000) SPSS user's manual

StatSoft, Inc. (2003) The statistics homepage. Correspondence analysis. Available at http://www.statsoftinc.com/textbook/stcoran.html (Accessed on 06/19/2003)

Suttayamully S, Hardpriono F, Hemeth Z (1995) Knowledge acquisition, representation, and knowledge base development of intelligent traffic evaluation for prompt incident diagnosis. Transportation Research Record 1497. National Academy Press, Washington, D.C.

TCRP Report 17 (1996) Integration of light rail transit into city streets. Transportation Research Board. National Academy Press, Washington, D.C.

TCRP Report 69 (2001) Light rail service: pedestrian and vehicular safety. Transportation Research Board. National Academy Press, Washington, D.C.

Thill J (2000) (ed) Geographic information systems for transportation in perspective. Transportation Research C 8: 1–144

Thompson R (2001) Targeting traffic problems through an automated collision database. Project presented at 27th International Forum on Traffic Records & Highway Information Systems. Available at http://www.traffic-records.org/forum2001/ /Best%20Practices/Thompson.htm (Accessed on 11/10/2002)

University of Kaiserslautern (2003) Case-based reasoning on the web. Available at http://www.cbr-web.org/CBR-Web (Accessed on 06/19/2003)

Vollrath I, Wilke W, Bergmann R (1998) Case-based reasoning support for online catalog sales. IEEE Internet Computing 2: 47–54

Wang L (2000) Network distance.ave. (Downloaded from ESRI website at www.esri.com)

Waters N (1988) Expert systems and systems of experts. In: Coffey W (ed) Geographical systems and systems of geography, essays in honour of William Warntz. Dept. of Geography, University of Western Ontario, London, pp 173–187

Waters N (1989) Expert systems within a GIS: knowledge acquisition for spatial decision support systems. In: Proceedings of the National Conference for Geographic Information Systems. The Canadian Institute for Surveying and Mapping, Ottawa, pp 740–759

Waters N (1999) Transportation GIS: GIS-T. In: Geographic information systems, vol 2, Management Issues and Applications, Second Edition

Waters N (2002) Geographic information systems, case-based reasoning and system design. In: Rothe P (ed) Driving lessons, exploring systems that makes traffic safer. University of Alberta Press, Edmonton, pp 247–256

Watson I, Marir F (1994) Case-based reasoning: a review. Available at http://www.ai-cbr.org/classroom/cbr-review.html (Accessed on 08/07/2003)

Weber G, Schult T (1998) CBR for tutoring and help systems. In: Lenz M, Bartsch-Spörl B, Burkhard H-D, Wess S (ed) Case-based reasoning technology: from foundations to applications. Lecture Notes in Artificial Intelligence 1400. Springer, Berlin Heidelberg New York, pp 255–272

Webnox Corp. (2003) Hyper dictionary. Available at http://www.hyperdictionary.com/ /computing (Accessed on 09/06/2003)

Wisdo C (1997) A scalable approach for question based indexing of encyclopedic texts. In: Leake, Plaza (ed) Case-based reasoning research and development. Lecture Notes in Artificial Intelligence. No. 1266. Springer, Berlin Heidelberg New York

6 A Sketch and Simulation of an Integrated Modelling Framework for the Study of Interdependent Infrastructure-Based Networked Systems

Kieran P. Donaghy, Jose F. Vial, Geoffrey J.D. Hewings and Nazmiye Balta

University of Illinois at Urbana-Champaign, Champaign, Illinois, USA

6.1 Introduction[1]

Before revelations about how Enron and other energy trading firms contributed to the plight of utilities in California, the rolling brownouts experienced by the state in the 1990s were in large part written off as an isolated lesson in how not to deregulate a utility industry (Krugman 2003). Then, on August 14, 2003, the northeastern United States and parts of Canada experienced the largest power outage in North American history, affecting more than 50 million people. The cascading blackouts associated with the outage were triggered when transmission lines owned by an Ohio electric utility came into contact with trees. In the same month hundreds of thousands of Londoners lost power in an outage that shut down the public transport system. Late in the following month the lights went out on five million Danes and Swedes after a faulty transmission line closed a nuclear power plant. And on the early morning of September 28, 2003 a massive blackout left nearly all of Italy powerless for much of the day. Each of these power failures caused massive disruptions in transportation and communication systems as well as considerable losses in economic production. Power failures are not the only source of widespread systemic disruptions. Technical problems with a communications satellite in the late 1990s also disrupted important flows of business information leading to sizeable losses of income (Rinaldi et al. 2001). Each of these events signifies an increasingly prevalent phenomenon – the interdependence of infrastructure-based networked systems, all of which can be brought down by a disruption to a component system.

Through the development of information and communications technologies (ICT), the logistics revolution to which it has given rise, business mergers, and the deregulation of utility industries, an environment has evolved in which infrastructure-based networked systems are much more interdependent than before, have little or no cush-

[1] The research reported in this chapter was supported with a grant from the Center for Trustworthy Networked Systems at the University of Illinois at Urbana Champaign.

ion for failure, and have few if any alternative sources of services (Rinaldi et al. 2001). Many of such systems are interregional, if not international, in scope and can have higher-order interdependencies and complex interactions. The criticality of this state of affairs has not been lost on the United States government, which, in the report of the President's Commission on Critical Infrastructure Protection (1997), has warned of the dangers of increasing and uncontrolled interdependencies (see also Branscomb 2004; National Academies 2002).

Interdependent infrastructure-based networked systems (henceforth, interdependent networks) are becoming an important subject of study. Such systems are complex, adaptive, and capable of emergent behaviour. The nature of system interdependence can be physical, cyber or informational, spatial, and logical. Interdependent networks can fail in a number of ways: through rolling or cascading disruptions, disruptions that escalate in magnitude, or from common causes which take out several systems simultaneously. Characteristics to which attention must be paid include spatial scales and temporal ranges of interdependencies, operational factors that affect reactions of systems when stressed, and organizational considerations, such as the regulatory environment of a system. For each system, it needs to be determined which other systems it depends on continuously, during times of high stress, and when service is restored after failure (see Rinaldi et al. 2001 on these points). To make such a determination, and to learn more about the implications of systems interdependence, research with integrated models is needed.

Frameworks that allow the coupling of models of multiple interdependent systems to address issues of infrastructure protection, problem mitigation, and response and recovery are only just beginning to be developed. Difficulties faced by modellers include coping with the variety of models in use for the study of different systems, software incompatibilities, limited access to distributed data, capturing dynamic interplay of systems, and accommodating a range of scenarios. In the literature of regional science there are, nonetheless, suggestions of how to proceed under such conditions. (See, *inter alia*, Boyce 2000; Nagurney and Dong 2002; Nijkamp and Reggiani 1998; Rose et al. 1997)

Because of the critical roles that transportation, power, and natural gas networks play in the regional economies of the United States and the Midwest in particular, and because of the existence of studies that have investigated potential impacts on the Midwest economy of natural disasters (Kim et al. 2002; Sohn et al. 2003) we explore in this chapter how the behaviour of these three interdependent networks can be modelled to begin to research some of the questions raised above. We suggest how freestanding static-equilibrium network models can be integrated and demonstrate the use of an integrated framework in numerical simulations. We also indicate how the framework might be given a dynamic cast and applied in several different analyses. In the second section we set up the problematic that motivates the modelling exercise and in the third we set out the network models. We present the results of the numerical simulations with the model in the chapter's fourth section, discuss the transition from statics to dynamics in the fifth, and offer concluding observations in the sixth.

6.2 Interdependent Networks in the Regional Economy of the Midwest United States

The regional economy of the Midwest United States has a number of salient features. Trade between the five states that make up this economy is of a very high volume as is trade that passes through these states. On average, 40% of the interstate exports from one state moves to the other four states and 39% of the imports of any one state originate in the Midwest. Furthermore, approximately 22% of the nation's interstate commodity trade originates in, is destined for or travels across the Midwest. While increasing volumes of trade in the new e-economy are in services, shipments of physical commodities along highways, rails, and rivers of the Midwest continue to grow.

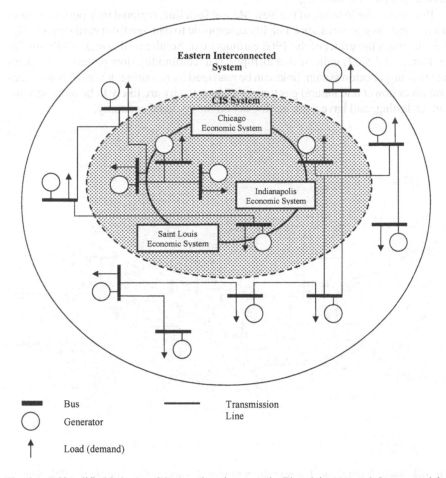

Bus   Transmission
Generator   Line

Load (demand)

Fig. 6.1. A Simplified Scheme of Connections between the Electricity Network System and the Economic Systems in the Chicago-Indianapolis-St. Louis (CIS) Area

For the country as a whole, over the period 1993–2002, Gross Domestic Product increased by 34% while the volume of commodity trade increased by 45%, paralleling similar processes observed at the international level (see Munroe and Hewings 1999). Worldwide, transportation systems through which goods are shipped have become increasingly important as the character of production itself has become progressively fragmented both horizontally and vertically and more transportation intensive (Jones and Kierzkowski 2001). This fragmentation process is evident in the Midwest regional economy as indices of trade overlap indicate that trade between Wisconsin, Illinois, Indiana, Michigan and Ohio is dominated by intra-industry trade (Munroe and Hewings 1999).

While the economy of the Midwest is highly dependent upon the smooth functioning of the regional power grid, or network for the generation and distribution of electricity, regional electrical power generation is itself highly dependent on the supply of natural gas (see Figs.6.1–2).

Because of the location of the New Madrid fault line, regional transportation, electricity, and gas networks are all highly susceptible to damage from earthquakes (Fig. 6.3 illustrates the effect of the 1968 earthquake in Southern Illinois.). While studies by Kim et al. (2002) indicate that disruptions to commodity flow patterns from damage to transportation system links can be managed by rerouting, losses of power generation or power and natural gas transmission capacity are likely to be more serious, longer-lasting, and have a greater impact on the regional economy.

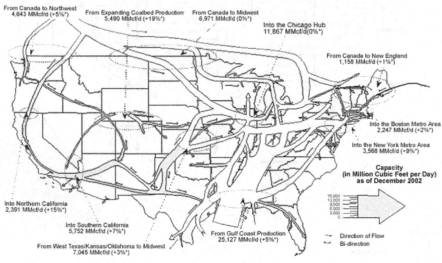

*Percent change since 2000.
Source: Energy Information Administration, GasTran Gas Transportation Information System, Natural Gas Pipeline State Border Capacity Database.

Fig. 6.2. Major Natural Gas Transportation Routes at Selected Key Locations, 2002. Source: EIA

Fig. 6.3. Isoseismal map: Southern Illinois earthquake of November, 1968. Notes: Southern Illinois, 1968 11 09 17:01:40.5 UTC. Magnitude 5.3. Intensity VII. Contour lines indicate isoseismals and Roman numbers indicate Modified Mercalli I intensity. Source: Stover and Coffman (1993)

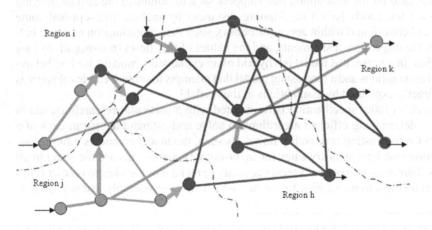

Fig. 6.4. Interdependent networks involving different sets of nodes

Even as the transportation network over which commodities flow and the power and natural gas networks are interdependent, the physical nodes and links of these networks seldom coincide. This state of affairs, which is depicted in Fig. 6.4, poses some challenges for characterizing the workings of the models in a common framework, discussed below. In addition to differences in spatial scales there are also differences in natural units of time for characterizing network flows. And while physical commodities and gas may be stored or inventoried at nodes, electricity cannot.

6.3 Static Equilibrium Interdependent Network Models

Our aim is to begin to elaborate a characterization of three interdependent networks: a transportation network through which commodities flow (henceforth, transportation network), an electricity network (or power grid), and a natural gas network. Our point of departure is a set of free-standing static equilibrium models, taken from the literature, which we modify and integrate into a common framework. We demonstrate the use of the integrated modelling framework in several *proof-of-concept* exercises and then suggest ways in which this framework might be given a dynamic cast. The models we employ are spare in detail as our primary intent is to provide a heuristic sketch of how network interdependence can be captured and studied in models.

6.3.1 Combined Model of Interregional Commodity Flows on a Transportation Network

The transportation network model which informs this analysis is the combined model of interregional commodity flows on a transportation network set out by Boyce (2000). This model has antecedents in Leontief and Strout (1963) and Wilson (1970) and a version of it is employed in Kim et al. (2002) and Sohn et al. (2003). The model is predicated on the assumption that shippers seek to minimize the cost of meeting demands for goods (effective shipping distance) by making user-optimal route choices between and within zones (or nodes), such that conditions on material balances, the dispersion of shipments, and the values of link flows (non-negativity) are satisfied. In a sense, this model is a hybrid of an explanatory model based on behavioural assumptions and a forecasting model that attempts to capture empirical patterns not directly explained by assumptions in the model.[2]

Boyce's (2000) specification is formulated with a particular research agenda in mind – determining efficient algorithms to solve and estimate the parameters of a model for forecasting commodity flows. As such, the model embodies a further assumption that inter-industry sales (or input-output) coefficients are the same in all zones. This assumption would seem necessary to make if one wishes to predict flows of commodities from one zone to another, which vary considerably, but not solve si-

---

[2] It is arguable, however, that the conditions on dispersion can be motivated from a behavioral model of spatial interaction. See Wilson (1971) and Boyce (2000).

multaneously for the sales coefficients. Our interest here is different in that we wish to specify a model that (in a dynamic orientation) can capture a stylized fact of economies undergoing structural changes associated with globalization: that interregional inter-industry sales coefficients vary considerably and are continuing to evolve as industries undergo vertical and horizontal fragmentation. And because we are interested in capturing dependencies of local industries upon what is happening both locally and remotely in electricity and natural gas networks, we also wish to take into account inter-industry sales of services that are not in the form of shipped physical commodities. Consequently the specification of the material balance condition of our model will differ from that of Boyce's (2000).

We adopt the following notation to characterize network flows over a fixed period of time, which is in keeping with the interregional input-output modelling conventions of Miller and Blair (1985). Nodes of the network through which goods are shipped are indexed by l and m. The set of nodes at which production occurs is $A_x | l, m \in A_x$. Links joining such nodes are indexed by a and routes comprising contiguous links are indexed by r. $R_x | r \in R_x$ is the set of routes through the network. The length of some link a connecting two nodes is denoted by d_a. If link a is part of a route r connecting nodes l and m, an indicator variable δ_{lmr}^a assumes the value 1. It is 0 otherwise. The length of a given route from some node l to another node m, D_{lmr}, is given by the sum of link distances along the route:

$$D_{lmr} \equiv \sum_a d_a \delta_{lmr}^a . \tag{6.1}$$

Turning now to quantities shipped through the network, let x_l^i be the total sales (in dollars) of sector i produced at node (or in region or zone) l and a_{lm}^{ij} be the amount of sector i's output at l needed to produce a dollar of sector j's output at m. FD_m^k denotes final demand of type k in region m and b_{lm}^{ik} is the dollar amount of sector i's output at l required to meet a dollar of final demand of type k at m. The physical flow of sector i's product from l to m along route r is h_{lmr}^i. This quantity is obtained by converting the value flow, $a_{lm}^{ij} x_l^i$, from dollars to tons by means of the ratio of total interregional economic flow to annual physical flow, q_x^i. The total physical flow of all commodities shipped on a link a via all routes using the link is defined by

$$f_a^x \equiv \sum_i \sum_{lmr} h_{lmr}^i \delta_{lmr}^x . \tag{6.2}$$

Conditions that the network must satisfy in any period are as follows.

Material balance constraint:

$$x_l^i = \sum_m \sum_j a_{lm}^{ij} x_m^j + \sum_m \sum_k b_{lm}^{ik} FD_m^k, \forall i, \forall l \; ;^3 \tag{6.3}$$

Conservation of flow of goods constraint:

$$\sum_r h_{lmr}^i = \sum_j a_{lm}^{ij} x_m^j / q_x^i, \forall i, \forall l, \forall m \; ; \tag{6.4}$$

Dispersion of the flow of goods constraint:

$$-\sum_{lm} \sum_j a_{lm}^{ij} x_m^j \ln(a_{lm}^{ij} x_m^j) = S_i^x, \forall i \; ; \tag{6.5}$$

Capacity constraint on flow of goods:

$$\sum_i \sum_{lmr} h_{lmr}^i \delta_{lmr}^x \equiv f_{lm}^x \le k_{lm}^k, \forall l, m \in A_x \; ; \tag{6.6}$$

Non-negativity and feasibility constraints:

$$h_{lmr}^i \ge 0, \forall i, \forall l, \forall m, \forall r \; . \tag{6.7}$$

In Eq. (6.5), S_i^x is the entropy of shipments of good i in the system. Typically, one seeks to minimize the cost of shipping commodities through the network (or total shipping distance) such that conditions (6.1–7) are satisfied. There are two components to costs: those incurred from interregional and intraregional shipments. The interregional part of transportation costs is expressed in two ways. In the first, use is made of Eq. (6.1) above:

$$\sum_i \sum_a d_a f_a^x \equiv \sum_i \sum_{lm} D_{lmr} h_{lmr}^i \tag{6.8}$$

This formulation fails to account for congestion, however. A second formulation, which does account for congestion, is:

---

[3] In Boyce's (2000) model the material balance constraint for sector i at location l is of the form $\sum x_{lm}^i = \sum a_{ij} (\sum x_{lm}^j) + y_l^i$ in which x_{lm}^i is the amount of commodity j shipped from location l to location m and y_i^l is the final demand for sector i's output at location l. We employ this specification as a simplification in simulations with an integrated modeling framework discussed in Sect. 6.4 below.

$$\sum_a \int_0^{f_a} d_a(w)dw \tag{6.9}$$

in which d_a is now the effective distance at flow f_a. The functional form adopted for d_a in Kim et al. (2002) and Sohn et al. (2003) is the Bureau of Public Roads (1964) congestion function. Intraregional transportation costs can be represented by:

$$\sum_l \sum_{ij} p_l^z a_{ll}^{ij} x_l^j / q_x^i \tag{6.10}$$

in which p_l^z is the price of shipping a ton of a commodity the mean intrazonal distance and q_x^i is the conversion factor defined above.

Boyce (2000) and Kim et al. (2002) have shown that first-order necessary conditions for a solution to the implied minimization problem can be solved efficiently by the Evans/DSD algorithm and the model's parameters can be estimated by making use of an experimental method developed by Sacks et al. (1989).

6.3.2 Electricity Network Model

The electricity model we consider next is of a generic formulation characterizing the so-called economic dispatch problem. (see, e.g., Del Toro 1992 and, more generally, Wagner 1975.) The underlying assumption of the model is that a network manager seeks to minimize the cost of generating electricity such that demands for the electricity at all nodes of the network are satisfied and certain technical limitations are respected. The form of the objective function is usually derived from heat rate functions, which relate heat energy (in British thermal units, or BTUs) required per megawatt-hour of generated electrical output and which are approximated by second- or third-order polynomials. Let A_e denote the set of nodes l and m which are connected by the power grid, $A_e | l, m \in A_e$. The cost of power generation in the network, $\sum_l C_l^e(e_l)$, is minimized subject to several constraints. The first constraint ensures that a technical relationship between electricity flows and net power injections (differences between power generated and power demanded) is satisfied. In this case, the sum of flows of electricity from and to all neighbouring nodes m of some node l is related to net power injections at all nodes by:

Relationship between energy flows and power injections

$$\sum_{m \in N(l)} f_{ml}^e = \sum_m w_{lm}(e_m - e_m^d), \forall l ; \tag{6.11}$$

where $e_l^d = \sum_m \sum_j a_{lm}^{ej} x_i^j / q_e + \sum_m \sum_k b_{lm}^{ek} FD_m^k / q_e$ is the power demanded at l. In Eq. (6.11), e_l denotes electricity (in megawatt-hours) produced at node l, f_{lm}^e is the flow of electricity from l to m and w_{lm} is a technical coefficient accounting for the resistance, reactance, and phase angle of the transmission line between l and m.[4] On the right-hand side of the expression defining the demand for power are the sum of sales by the utility industry, indexed by e, to all other economic sectors j converted by coefficient q_e, which gives the value in dollars of a megawatt-hour.

A second constraint characterizes the conservation of electricity generated and flowing through the network.

Conservation of flow of electricity constraint

$$\sum_l e_l + e_{ref} = \sum_l e_l^d + \sum_{l,m \in A_e} (f_{lm}^e)^2 R_{lm} \tag{6.12}$$

The second term on the left-hand side of Eq. (6.12) denotes the power generated by a reference power bus. The second term on the right-hand side of Eq. (6.12) accounts for power lost in transmission. In this term, R_{lm} denotes the resistance of the transmission line connecting nodes l and m. The solution to the economic dispatch problem must also satisfy capacity constraints on power transmission and generation.

Capacity constraints on power transmission and generation

$$|f_{lm}^e| \le k_{lm}^e, \forall l, m \in A_e; \tag{6.13}$$

$$e_l \le e_l^{max};$$

in which k_{lm}^e denotes the transmission line capacity of the line connecting l and m and e_l^{max} denotes the maximum amount of power that can be generated at node l. The economic dispatch problem for electricity networks is typically solved by one of several computationally efficient non-linear programming algorithms.

---

[4] The coefficient w_{lm} is the element in the lth row and m^{th} column of the matrix W, which is defined by $W \equiv \Omega C (C^T \Omega C)^{-1}$, where C is a submatrix of the incidence matrix, $\tilde{C}$, indicating positive and negative directions of flows of electricity, and $\Omega = \alpha R^{-1}$ is a diagonal matrix. The elements on the diagonal matrix, αR_{lm} are the resistances of network transmission lines scaled by a constant fixed proportion of assumed to relate resistances to reactance's. C is $N+1$ x N in size, where N is the number of transmission lines linking nodes in the network.

6.3.3 Natural Gas Network Model

The natural gas network model we consider is also of common provenance (see, e.g., Munoz et al. 2003). The optimization problem that this model characterizes is one of minimizing the cost of natural gas purchases needed by the network manager to supply consumers and the electrical utility. In this case we shall assume that costs of purchases, $C_l^g(g_l^s)$, may be represented by a polynomial function. Let A_g denote the set of nodes l and m which are connected by the gas network, $A_g \mid l, m \in A_g$. Conditions that the solution to this problem must satisfy include constraints that are similar to those placed on the other network models' solutions and some that are not. First, and as before, there is a conservation of flow constraint,

Conservation of flow of natural gas constraint

$$\sum_m f_{lm}^g + g_l^d + g_l^e = \sum_m f_{ml}^g + g_l^s, \forall l ; \tag{6.14}$$

where f_{lm}^g denotes the flow of gas in cubic feet from l to m and g_l^e, g_l^d, g_l^s are volumes of natural gas purchased at node l by, respectively, a combined cycle electricity producing utility, households and local industry, and the natural gas network manager.

Unlike in the previous two cases there is also a constraint on the differential between gas pressure measured at the end nodes of a link.

Natural gas pressure differential condition at link nodes

$$(f_{lm}^g)^2 \geq -c_{lm}^2 (P_l^2 - P_m^2), \forall l, m \in A_g ; \tag{6.15}$$

where P_l^2 denotes pipeline pressure at node l and c_{lm} is a constant depending on length, diameter, and rugosity of the pipeline.[5]

The solution must satisfy local demands for natural gas,

Satisfaction of local demands for natural gas

---

[5] In Eq. 6.15, the value of the constant c_{lm}^2 is given by the relationship $c_{lm}^2 = K \dfrac{D_{lm}^5}{\lambda_{lm} z T L_{lm} d}$, in which K is a constant, D_{lm} is the interior diameter of the pipeline, T is the gas temperature, z is the gas compressibility factor, d is the density of the gas relative to the air, and L_{lm} is the length of the pipe section. The variable λ_{lm} is defined by the following relationship between the diameter of the pipeline and its absolute rugosity, ε, $\lambda_{lm} = \left[2 \log(\dfrac{K D_{lm}}{\varepsilon}) \right]^2$ (De Wolf and Smeers 2000).

$$g_l^e = y_l e_l, \forall l \in A_e \cap A_g ;$$ (6.16)

$$g_l^d = \sum_m \sum_{j \neq g} a_{lm}^{gj} x_m^j / q_g + \sum_m \sum_k b_{lm}^{gk} FD_m^k / q_g, \forall l \in A_g \cap A_x ;$$ (6.17)

where γ_l is a technical coefficient, q_g is a factor that converts natural gas sales in value terms to volume terms, and g indexes the natural gas sector, and requirement that the sum of gas purchases by the network manager are absorbed by the demands in the system:

$$\sum_l g_l^s = \sum_l g_l^d + \sum_l g_l^e ;$$ (6.18)

a capacity constraint on link flows,

Capacity constraint on the flow of gas

$$f_{lm}^g \leq k_{lm}^g, \forall l, m \in A_g$$ (6.19)

and constraints on the flow, provision and pressure of natural gas,

Constraints on flow, provision, and pressure of Natural Gas

$$f_{lm}^g \geq 0, \forall l, m \in A_g ;$$ (6.20)

$$g_l^{d\,min} \leq g_l^d \leq g_l^{d\,max}, \forall l \in A_g ;$$ (6.21)

$$g_l^{e\,min} \leq g_l^e \leq g_l^{e\,max}, \forall l \in A_g ;$$ (6.22)

$$g_l^{s\,min} \leq g_l^s \leq g_l^{s\,max}, \forall l \in A_g ;$$ (6.23)

$$P_l^{min} \leq P_l \leq P_l^{max}, \forall l \in A_g .$$ (6.24)

Solutions to natural gas network problems as posed above can be solved by an extension of the simplex algorithm (DeWolf and Smears 2000).

In the last two decades, most research effort has been directed to the enhancement of existing models – for example, improving their reliability, increasing the degree of endogeneity, and providing greater spatial and sectoral disaggregation. Relatively modest attention has been directed to ways in which networks interface and yet it is here that some of the major challenges arise. Consider the problem of linking commodity flow and electricity networks, covered in this section. Disruption in electricity supply (as a result of a catastrophic event like an earthquake or a hurricane) may occur for intervals as brief as several hours or as extensive as several days or cur for intervals as brief as several hours or as extensive as several days or months. However, commodity flow models are most often calibrated with annual data. Linking systems models of electricity supply and commodity shipment will thus require new thinking about the resolution of temporal scales and the sharing of data.

6.4 Numerical Simulations with a Stylized Integrated Model of Interdependent Networks

As a proof-of-concept exercise, we implement a simple 3-region version of an interdependent networks model. Economic activity is described by three sectors, which produce a generic commodity, electricity, and natural gas. Physical flows of those three commodities are supported by three networks: a transportation network, an electric power transmission network, and a natural gas pipeline network. The objective function of the model comprises the costs of operating the three networks, which are to be minimized. The model is not intended as a characterization of any particular set of regional economies. The point of the exercise is to demonstrate how in principle implementations of interdependent network models may be carried out and some of the systems behavioural characteristics that emerge even in cases of this level of simplification.

Each regional economy is characterised by an input-output matrix and a set of final demands. Infrastructure networks have been modelled in very simple way both in terms of their topology and in terms of their technical details. Nodes and links are laid out so that regions are connected directly by routes, transmission lines, and pipelines. Other simplifications have been made to bring the model's specification into conformance with a nonlinear programming problem, which can be solved with GAMS or some other available nonlinear equation solver. Figure 6.5 depicts the set of networks.

The main characteristics of the simplifications considered in each network are as follows.

Transportation Network. Routes connect regions directly without intermediate nodes or link sharing. Flow directions are predetermined over routes and a pair of routes (in opposite directions) connect each pair of regions. An average unit cost is considered to mobilise the physical counterpart of economic flows in each route. Physical flows are limited by link capacity constraints.

Electric Power Distribution Network. There is a bus per each region that has associated with it one load and one generator. Region 1 also has a reference bus which is needed to solve the power flow equations. Power generation is limited by the maximum generating capacities at the 3 nodes. Generating costs are assumed to be quadratic. A direct-current (or DC) approximation is used to model the alternating-current (or AC) system and only real power flows are considered, i.e. we have abstracted from considering reactive power flows and other ancillary services. Transmission lines are characterized in terms of resistances and exhibit transmission limits.

Natural Gas Pipeline Network. Gas production is limited at each node and quadratic functions describe the production cost. Only active pipelines are considered, i.e. they have predetermined flow directions, but a pair of pipelines, between each pair of nodes, allows for flows in both directions. Gas flows are dependent on a technical co-efficient that is related to the rugosity, length and diameter of the pipe, and to the difference between pressures at each end of the pipe. Those pressures are bounded in the model.

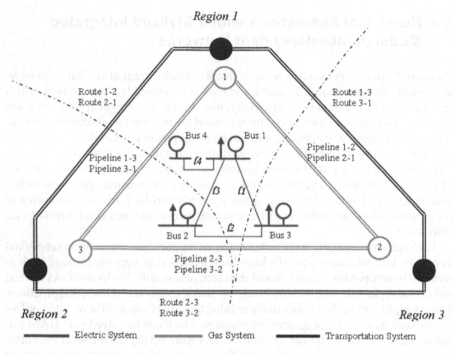

Fig. 6.5. Interdependent networks of stylized integrated model

Details of the model are presented in Appendix 6.A. Here we present the main results of some numerical simulations carried out with the model. We concentrate on major features of these results as their specificity is highly related to the specific figures chosen in this example.

6.4.1 Solution of the Model in the Base Case

The base case can be described as follows. Electric generation and gas production are characterised by high costs in Region 3, medium costs in Region 2, and low costs in Region 1. Coupled with a larger final demand for the generic commodity of Region 1, this region exhibits the largest gross product of the generic commodity. As expected the energy generation tends to concentrate in Region 1 (see Table 6.1 below).

Table 6.1. Base case

	Region 1	Region 2	Region 3
Final demand for generic commodity	1400	500	600
Final demand for electricity	500	600	400
Final demand for natural gas	600	550	500
Generic commodity production ($)	4,739	2643	0
Electric generation (MW)	690	185	64
Gas production (m3)	2,880	482	361

Units are given as a reference, but magnitudes do not keep any dimension with real situations.

Transmission line 1, which connects Region 1 to Region 3, is fully utilised. Transmission line 2, which connects Region 3 to Region 2, is used at 59% of capacity and transmission line 3, which connects Region 1 to Region 2, is used at 81% of its capacity. Transportation routes from Region 2 to Region 1 and from Region 2 to Region 3 are also fully utilised. None of the generic commodity is produced in Region 3 because of the high cost of energy that would be required to produce it. Nonetheless, technical and capacity constraints imply positive production of electricity and gas. The gas pipeline connecting Region 1 with 3 is fully utilised as is the electricity transmission line connecting those regions.[6]

6.4.2 Alternative Scenarios: Increased Final Demand

In the first set of alternative scenarios considered, the final demand for the generic commodity is increased separately by region by the same amount. If final demand for the generic commodity in Region 1 is increased by $392, the production of that commodity increases in 15% in Region 1, while in the other regions the effect is negligible. Electric power generation and gas production increase in all regions but by less than 1%. The flow patterns of electricity and gas do change significantly, however, as usage of line 1 drops by 8%, the direction of the flow is reversed in line 2, and in lines 3 and 4 there are significant reductions in the use of transmission capacity. Gas flows from Region 1 to Region 2 and from Region 2 to Region 3 decrease, but flows from Region 3 to Region 1 increase.

When final demand in Region 2 is increased by $392, increased production of the generic commodity is concentrated in the region, while the effect on the other regions is negligible. There is also a slight increase in the regional production of gas and electricity in every region, though the magnitude is smaller than in the previous case. The effects on electricity and gas flows, with respect to the base case, are similar to the ones described above. Attempting to increase final demand for the generic community by $392 in Region 3 results in an unfeasible solution.

---

[6] The choice of a quadratic cost function precludes that some source to be less expensive than the others at any production level.

This first set of simulation exercises illustrates several important features of inter-dependent network models, which distinguish them from models without explicit consideration of network and production constraints. First, though, production of the commodity intended for final consumption is increased by a common amount in each region and the absolute output effects are rather small, flows of electric and natural gas change markedly. These changes occur not only because of the multiple feed-backs in the system but also because of the nonlinearity of flow equations. Since electric power flows must observe Kirchoff's laws, the contract path of electricity does not necessarily coincide with the actual path of electric power. In other words, if we intend to send some amount of electric power through a line that connects a generator with a load, even without considering transmission capacity constraints we would observe power flows moving across parallel lines (see Chao and Peck 1996; Hogan 1992). Moreover, as noted by Chao and Peck (1996) the effective transmission capacity constraints depend upon the specific set of generations and loads in the system.

Secondly, as can be expected, some sets of final demands are incompatible with the transmission and production capacity constraints of the model depending on their dimension, sector, and location. In the model solutions under the scenarios considered above one can see that the same increment in final demand for the generic commodity that is feasible when applied in Region 1 and Region 2, is unfeasible when applied in Region 3.

6.4.3 Alternative Scenarios: Changes in Network Capacity

We now consider a second type of scenario in which the capacities of electric trans-mission lines connecting Region 1 to the system are reduced from 150 to 100 (*line 1*) and from 400 to 300 (*line 3*). In this case, production of the generic commodity de-creases in Region 1 by 3%, while it increases in Region 2 by 2.7%, and becomes posi-tive in Region 3. Electricity generation decreases by 13% in Region 1, while it in-creases by 29% and 49% in Regions 2 and 3. Purchases of gas supplies are increased slightly in Region 1 and reduced slightly in Regions 2 and 3. Transmission line 1 is now fully utilised, while the flows in line 2 change direction. Noticeable changes also occur in the gas flows.

In the solution under this second scenario one can see that a reduction in transmis-sion line capacity brings about a reduction in output of the region that tends to be a net exporter of the generic commodity and electricity, while stimulating production in the less competitive regions with excess capacity.[7]

---

[7] These results depend on the fact that final demands are fixed, and the system accommodates to satisfy those demands without price changes. An increase in the total cost of production and generation results from reducing transmission capacity in this case.

6.5 From Statics to Dynamics

Static-equilibrium models of interdependent networks can be used to examine a number of critical issues, including where infrastructure maintenance priorities should lie, via 'what if' scenario analyses. They are less helpful in addressing questions of how impacts will be staged over space and time or how systems should be restored to operation once they fail. Moreover, questions about emergent behaviour that arises in interactions between systems cannot be addressed in a static framework. Hence we turn from statics to dynamics. While acknowledging that the modelling of individual dynamic networks is a mature subject (see, e.g., Aronson 1989), our focus will be on motivation of the dynamics in interdependent networks.

The first question we need to ask is from whence dynamics in the set of interdependent networks we are considering might emanate. Logical suggestions would include changes in the composition of final demands for goods and services and changes in interregional inter-industrial sales patterns to which producers and network managers must respond. In view of the lack of time series data on interregional inter-industry sales (especially commodity flow data), it will be necessary to derive updated estimates of coefficients for such sales. A demonstration of how such estimates may be derived from the solution of a regional econometric input-output model is provided in the appendix. A second question concerns the nature of the optimization problem the model's solution is intended to address and from whose perspective.

If our primary purpose for developing a dynamic model of interdependent networks is to test hypothetical explanations of the evolution of network structures, forecast future flows, and identify potential bottlenecks or links whose performance is critical for functionality across networks, we may turn to characterizations of cost-minimizing behaviour, which we believe has contributed to fragmentation of production, elimination of redundant capacity, and increased reliance upon logistics. This might be done initially in one of two ways. We might adopt the perspective of an intertemporally optimizing representative agent who seeks to minimize the costs of maintaining flows of goods, electricity, and natural gas through the interdependent networks, subject to the technical constraints encompassed by the static models we have considered and additional constraints upon changes in link capacity conditions brought about by physical depreciation or additions to capacity. An objective functional capturing costs of inter- and intra-zonal shipment of goods, the cost of natural gas that must be purchased by the gas network manager, the cost of electricity that must be generated in solving the economic dispatch problem of the electricity network manager, costs of purchasing and bringing online new capacity and costs of maintaining the networks might be written as follows:

$$
\int_0^1 \left\{
\begin{aligned}
& \sum_{a \in A_a} p^c \int_0^{f_a} d_{a(w)dw} + \sum_{l \in A_x} \sum_{ij} p^z a_{ll}^{ij} x_l^j / q_x^i + \sum_{l \in A_g} C_l^g (g_l^s) + \sum_{l \in A_e} C_l^e (e_l) \\
& + \sum_{a \in A_a} ucc_a^x (k_a^x) I_a^x + \sum_{l,m \in A_e} ucc_{lm}^e (k_{lm}^e) I_{lm}^e + \sum_{l,m \in A_g} ucc_{lm}^g (k_{lm}^g) I_{lm}^g \\
& + \sum_{a \in A_a} mc^x (k_a^x, f_a^x) + \sum_{l,m \in A_e} mc^e (k_{lm}^e, f_{lm}^e) + \sum_{l,m \in A_g} mc^g (k_{lm}^g, f_{lm}^g)
\end{aligned}
\right\} dt \qquad (6.25)
$$

In this expression all notation is as previously defined, with the exception of several new terms. The ton-mile cost of shipping goods interzonally is denoted by p^c. User costs of capital, including adjustment costs, for unit additions to flow capacity of links in transportation, electricity, and gas networks are denoted by ucc_a^x, ucc_{lm}^e, and ucc_{lm}^g, and are assumed to be variable functions of existing link capacities. Costs of operating and maintaining a link in a transportation, electricity, or natural gas network are denoted by mc_a^x, mc_{lm}^e, and mc_{lm}^g, and are assumed to be variable functions of both link capacities and flows.

The representative agent would seek to minimize the above expression by choosing the time paths of $x_j^l, I_{lm}^x, I_{lm}^e, I_{lm}^g, e_l, f_{lm}^e, g_l^s, g_l^d, g_l^s, f_{lm}^g$, and P_l subject to constraints on network capital formation,

$$
\dot{k}_a^x = [1 - d_x (f_a)] k_a + I_a, \forall a \in A_a ; \qquad (6.26)
$$

$$
\dot{k}_{lm}^e = [1 - d_e (f_{lm}^e)] k_{lm}^e + I_{lm}^e, \forall l, m \in A_e ; \qquad (6.27)
$$

$$
\dot{k}_{lm}^g = [1 - d_g (f_{lm}^g)] k_{lm}^g + I_{lm}^g, \forall l, m \in A_g ; \qquad (6.28)
$$

and constraints (6.1–7) and (6.11–24) given above.

The first-order-necessary conditions for the solution to this problem can be generated from the appropriate augmented Hamiltonian (intertemporal Lagrangian) (see Syerstaad and Seidseiter 1978) and solved subject to boundary-point conditions via a numerical nonlinear differential-equation solution algorithm, such as the variable-step, variable-order Adams method employed in the software developed by Wymer (various dates) (see Donaghy and Schintler 1998 for a demonstration of the approach.) A variational-inequality approach involving discretisation of the model might also be taken (see Friesz et al. 1996; Nagurney and Dong 2002). Given time series of sufficient length, Donaghy et al. (2001) demonstrate how the parameters of a non-linear continuous-time model can be estimated using a quasi-full-information-maximum-likelihood estimator. Existence, uniqueness, and stability of the solution can be promoted through judicious selection of functional forms (Diewert and Wales 1987). But we may wish to allow for the possibility that alternative solutions may have been possible and that the current 'solution' that has been arrived at may not be stable.

The case considered above is consistent with the formulation of a cooperative differential game in which three agents, or network managers, seek to minimize the collective costs of operating their networks, where all contributions to total cost are weighted equally. Another way to set up the problem would be as a non-cooperative differential game, of either the open- or closed-loop type, in which each network manager takes the choices of the other two as given and proceeds to minimize costs. Whereas in the above formulation prices are given, they might well be endogenised and determined via an excess demand formulation (for an alternative set up of a non-cooperative differential game in which networked systems are involved, see Chap.8).

If our intent is promote a resilient set of interdependent networks we might follow a suggestion of Nijkamp and Reggiani (1998) and pose the optimization problem as that of determining what spatial and temporal combination of goods production, network infrastructure investments, electricity generation, natural gas purchases, and electricity and gas flows would maximize the combination of all links' performances in terms of diversity.[8] In this case the expression to be maximized would be:

$$\int_0^{t_1} e^{-pt} \left\{ \sum_i S_i^x \ln(S_i^x) + S^e \ln(S^e) + S^g \ln(S^g) \right\} dt \tag{6.29}$$

where

$$S_i^x = - \sum_{l,m \in A_x} \sum_j a_{ij}^{lm} x_j^m \ln(a_{ij}^{lm} x_j^m), \forall i ; \tag{6.30}$$

$$S^e = - \sum_{l,m \in A_e} f_{lm}^e \ln(f_{lm}^e) ; \tag{6.31}$$

$$S^g = - \sum_{l,m \in A_g} f_{lm}^g \ln(f_{lm}^g) ; \tag{6.32}$$

The alternative framings of dynamic optimization problems suggested above represent only a first cut. While the mechanics of moving between discrete and continuous-time specifications are well known, important issues regarding the characterization of adjustment dynamics (other than of capacity or prices) in the different networks remain to be resolved. Gross temporal differences in lag structures, alluded to above, owe to technological and institutional factors that need to be explicitly accounted for. To characterize these properly (and adequately) adjustment mechanisms with theoretical foundations or of a more ad hoc nature will need to be developed.

---

[8] Diversity of network performance is defined by Nijkamp and Reggiani (1998) for some network of type n (in terms of the notation we have employed) as $S_i^n = -\sum f_{lm}^n \ln(f_{lm}^n)$, where $l,m = 1,...,n$ represent the nodes connected by network links.

6.6 Conclusions

In the foregoing our concern has been to provide a sketch of how behaviour in transportation, power, and natural gas networks can be modelled in a common framework to permit consideration of issues raised by their interdependence. We have suggested how static-equilibrium network models might be integrated and employed in numerical simulations. We have also suggested how the static framework might be given a dynamic cast and applied in a number of different types of analysis which involve dynamics in a meaningful way.

References

Aronson JA (1989) A survey of dynamic network flows. Annals of Operations Research 20: 1–66

Bennett RJ, Haining RP, Wilson AG (1985) Spatial structure, spatial interaction, and their integration: a review of alternative models. Environment and Planning A 17: 625–645

Boyce DE (2002) Combined model of interregional commodity flows on a transportation network. In: Hewings GJD, Sonis M, Boyce D (eds) Trade, networks and hierarchies. Springer, Berlin Heidelberg New York, pp 29–40

Branscomb LM (2004) Protecting civil society from terrorism: the search for a sustainable strategy. Technology in Society 26: 271–285

Bureau of Public Roads (1964) Traffic assignment manual. U.S. Department of Commerce, Washington, D.C.

Chao HP, Peck S (1996) A market mechanism for electric power transmission. Journal of Regulatory Economics 10: 25–59

Del Toro V (1992) Electric power systems. Prentice-Hall, Englewood Cliffs

De Wolf D, Smears Y (2000) The gas transmission problem solved by an extension of the simplex algorithm. Management Science 46: 1454–1465

Diewert EW, Wales TJ (1987) Flexible functional forms and global curvature conditions. Econometrica 55: 43–68

Donaghy KP, Federici, D, Gandolfo G (2001) Continuous-time estimation of an endogenous-growth model of an open economy. Annals of Regional Science 35: 449–461

Donaghy KP, Schintler LA (1998) Managing congestion, pollution, and infrastructure in a dynamic transportation network model. Transportation Research D 3: 59–80

Elgerd. OI (1982) Electric energy systems theory: an introduction. McGraw-Hill, New York.

Friesz TL, Bernstein D, Stough R (1996) Dynamic systems, variational inequalities and control theoretic models for predicting time-varying urban network flows. Transportation Science 30: 14–31

Hogan WW (1992) Contract networks for electric power transmission. Journal of Regulatory Economics 4: 211–242

Israilevich PR, Hewings GJD, Sonis M, Schindler GR (1997) Forecasting structural change with a regional econometric input-output model. Journal of Regional Science 37: 565–590

Jones RW, Kierzkowski H (2001) A framework for fragmentation. In: Arndt SW, Kierzkowski H (eds) Fragmentation: new production patterns in the world economy. Oxford University Press, New York

Kim TJ, Ham H, Boyce DE (2002) Economic impacts of transportation network changes: implementation of a combined transportation network and input-output model. Papers in Regional Science 81: 223–246

Krugman P (2003) The great unraveling. Norton, New York

Leontief WW, Strout A (1963) Multiregional input-output analysis. In: Barna T (ed) Structural interdependence and economic development. Macmillan, London

Miller RE, Blair PD (1985) Input-output analysis: foundations and extensions. Prentice-Hall, Englewood Cliffs

Munoz J, Jimenez-Redondo N, Barquain J (2003) Natural gas network modeling for power system reliability studies. Working Paper, Academic Workshop and Discussion 6/7 May, Amsterdam, Insuring Against Disruptions of Energy Supply (INDES) Project. Energy Research Centre of the Netherlands

Munroe DK, Hewings GJD (1999) The role of intraindustry trade in interregional trade in the Midwest of the US. Discussion Paper 99-T-7, Regional Economics Applications Laboratory, University of Illinois, Urbana. Available at www.uiuc.edu/unit/real

Nagurney A, Dong J (2002) Supernetworks. Edward Elgar, Cheltenham Northampton

National Academies (Committee on Science and Technology for Countering Terrorism, L.M. Branscomb and R. Klausner, co-chairs) (2002) Making the nation safer: the role of science and technology in countering terrorism. National Academies Press, Washington, D.C.

Nijkamp P, Reggiani A (1998) The economics of complex spatial systems. Elsevier, Amsterdam

President's Commission on Critical Infrastructure Protection (1997) Critical foundations: protecting America's infrastructure. Available at http://www.ciao.gov

Rinaldi SM, Peerenboom JP, Kelly TK (2001) Critical infrastructure interdependencies. IEEE Control System Magazine, December: 11–25

Rose A, Benvenides J, Chang SE, Szczesniak P, Lim D (1997) The regional economic impact of an earthquake: direct and indirect effects of electricity lifeline disruption. Journal of Regional Science 37: 437–458

Sacks J, Welch W, Mitchell T, Wynn H (1989) Design and analysis of computer experiments. Statistical Science 4: 409–435

Schweppe FC, Caraminis MV, Tabors RD, Bohn RE (1988) Spot pricing of electricity. Kluwer, Boston

Seierstad A, Sydsaeter K (1977) Sufficient conditions in optimal control theory. International Economic Review 18: 367–391

Sohn J, Kim TJ, Hewings GJD, Lee JS, Jang S-G (2003) Retrofit priority of transport network links under an earthquake. Journal of Urban Planning & Development 129: 195–210

Stover CW, JL Coffman (1993) Seismicity of the United States, 1568-1989 (U.S. Geological Survey Professional Paper, 1527), revised edn. United States Geological, Reston

Wagner HM (1975) Principles of operations research, 2nd edn. Prentice-Hall, Englewood Cliffs

Wilson AG (1970) Interregional commodity flows: entropy maximizing procedures. Geographical Analysis 2: 255–282

Wilson AG (1971) Entropy in urban and regional modeling. Pion, London

Wood AJ, Wollenberg, BF (1984) Power generation, operation, and control. John Wiley & Sons, New York

Wymer CR [various dates] WYSEA software package for systems estimation and analysis. Takapuna, New Zealand

Zeeman EC (1977) Catastrophe theory. Addison-Wesley, Reading

Appendix 6.A: A Stylized Integrated Model of Interdependent Networks

In the integrated network model we employ in simulations discussed above, we incorporate the specification of the direct-current model of electricity transmission developed by Schweppe et al. (1988). We characterize the general optimization problem as follows. A manager of 3 integrated networks must choose $x_c^{lm}, e_l, e_{ref}, g_l, f_{lm}^e, f_{lm}^g$ to minimize:

$$\sum_{lm} p_x d_{lm} x_{lm}^c / q_x + \sum_l C_l^e (e_l + \phi_l e_{ref}) + \sum_l C_l^g (g_l) \tag{6.A1}$$

where

$$C_l^e = c_{0e} + c_{1e}(e_l + \phi_l e_{ref}) + c_{2e}(e_l + \phi_l e_{ref})^2, \text{ and}$$

$$C_l^g = c_{0g} + c_{1g} g_l + c_{2g} g_l^2;$$

subject to

$$\sum_m x_{ml}^c = a_l^{cc} \sum_l x_{lm}^c + a_l^{ce} e_l / q_e + a_{lm}^{cg} g_l^s / q_g + y_l^c, \forall l ; \tag{6.A2}$$

$$\sum_m f_{lm}^e = \sum_m w_{lm} (e_m - e_m^d), \forall l ; \tag{6.A3}$$

$$\sum_l e_l + e_{ref} = \sum_l e_l^d + \sum_{l,m \in A_e} (f_{lm}^e)^2 R_l ; \tag{6.A4}$$

$$e_l^d = (a_l^{ec} \sum_m x_{lm}^c + y_l^e + a_l^{eg} q_g g_l^s) / q_e, \forall l ; \tag{6. A5}$$

$$\sum_m f_{lm}^g + g_l^d = \sum_m f_{ml}^g + g_l^s, \forall l ; \tag{6.A6}$$

$$g_l^d = (a_l^{gc} \sum_m x_{lm}^c + y_l^g + a_l^{ge} q_e e_l) / q_g, \forall l ; \tag{6.A7}$$

$$\sum_i g_i^s = \sum_i g_i^d, \forall l ; \tag{6.A8}$$

$$(f_{lm}^g)^2 \ge -c_{lm}^2 (P_l^2 - P_m^2), \forall l, m ; \tag{6.A9}$$

$$P_l^{\min} \leq P_l \leq P_l^{\max}, \forall l, m ; \qquad (6.A10)$$

$$x_{lm}^c / q_x \leq h_{lm}^{\max}, \forall l, m ; \qquad (6.A11)$$

$$x_c^{lm} \geq 0; e_l \geq 0; g_l^s \geq 0, \left| f_{lm}^e \right| \geq 0; f_{lm}^g \geq 0, \forall l, m ; \qquad (6.A12)$$

$$\left| f_{lm}^e \right| \leq k_{lm}^e, \forall l, m ; \qquad (6.A13)$$

$$e_l \leq e_l^{\max}, \forall l, m \qquad (6.A14)$$

$$\phi_l = 1 \text{ if } i = 1; 0 \text{ otherwise.}$$

Parameters for the model used in simulations are as follows.

Table 6.A1. Cost function coefficients

	Electric Generation			Gas production		
	Region 1	Region 2	Region 3	Region 1	Region 2	Region 3
C0	50	100	130	40	100	130
C1	4	10	14	6	10	12
C2	100	200	500	50	200	400

Table 6.A2. Interregional inter-industry sales coefficients

	0.4555	0.3452	0.3216		0.5626	0.2973	0.2386		0.6116	0.5027	0.5306
$A_l =$	0.0127	0.0000	0.0462	$A_l =$	0.0218	0.0000	0.0343	$A_l =$	0.0115	0.0000	0.0536
	0.0059	0.0037	0.0000		0.0091	0.0077	0.0000		0.0129	0.0126	0.0000

Table 6.A3. Quantity to value conversion factors

$$q_x = 0.7 \quad q_e = 0.04 \quad q_g = 2.5$$

Table 6.A4. Link capacities for commodity flows ($h_{lm}^{\max}$)

	1	2	3
1	∞	250	400
2	250	∞	100
3	350	140	∞

Table 6.A5. Effective costs of shipping via links ($p_x d_{lm}$)

	1	2	3
1	500	971	785
2	971	500	1000
3	1142	1000	500

Table 6.A6. Coefficients relating power injections to power flows at buses (w_{lm})

	1	2	3
1	0.0	0.3	0.6
2	0.0	0.3	−0.3
3	0.0	−0.6	−0.3
4	−1.0	−1.0	−1.0

Table 6.A7. Incidence matrix (Ω)

	1	2	3	ref
1	1	−1	0	0
2	0	1	−1	0
3	−1	0	1	0
4	0	0	−1	1

Table 6.A8. Maximum flows of electricity along transmission lines (absolute values)

$$k^e_{12} = 150; k^e_{23} = 300; k^e_{31} = 400; k^e_{ref,1} = 350$$

Table 6.A9. Limits on power generation

$$e^{max}_1 = 450; e^{max}_2 = 500; e^{max}_3 = 300$$

The gas pressure coefficient, c^2_{lm}, is set to 9.0 for all lines.

Appendix 6.B: Deriving Updated Estimates of Interregional Inter-Industry Sales Coefficients in a Regional Econometric Input-Output Model

In view of the lack of time series data on interregional inter-industry sales, noted above, it will be necessary to derive updated estimates of coefficients for such sales. We employ the following notation in demonstrating how such estimates can be derived from the solution of a regional econometric input-output (I-O) model (REIM). (See Israilevich et al. 1997)

Let Z denote an $n \times 1$ column vector of regional industrial outputs (sales) forecasted by the fundamental accounting identities in the REIM – i.e., $Z = A*X + B*FD$, where X is an $n \times 1$ column vector of observed regional industrial outputs (sales) - i.e., historical time series - or solution values of the disequilibrium adjustment equations of the REIM, FD is an $m \times 1$ matrix of final-demand levels, A is the original $n \times n$ matrix of I-O coefficients for the benchmark year, and B is an $n \times m$ matrix of final demand coefficients for the benchmark year.

Now define A_t to be an $n \times n$ matrix of I-O coefficients corresponding to year t (or time t if intervals other than years are used in a continuous-time framework) and B_t to be an *n* x *m* matrix of final demand coefficients for year *t*. (It may be the case that $B_t = B$ by assumption, or the elements of B_t can be inferred from trends.)

The following relationships hold by definition:

$$X = A_t \cdot X + B_t \cdot FD \tag{6.B1}$$

$$Z = A^* X + B^* FD \tag{6.B2}$$

Subtracting Eq. (6.B2) from Eq. (6.B1) yields:

$$X - Z = A_t \cdot X - A^* X + B_t \cdot FD - B^* FD \tag{6.B3}$$

which upon rearranging gives the updated values of the I-O coefficients in terms of the benchmarked values, the changes in the final demand coefficients, the observed levels of final demand and the observed and forecasted levels of industrial outputs:

$$A_t = A + I - Z^* X' \left(X^* X' \right)^{-1} - \left(B_t - B \right) FD^* X' \left(X^* X' \right)^{-1} \tag{6.B4}$$

The last three terms together provide the updating of *A*. Collecting terms in the ordinary-least-squares type of expression, $X' \left(X^* X' \right)^{-1}$, we can also write the updating equation as:

$$A_t = \left\{ A^* X + X - Z - \left(B_t - B \right) FD \right\} X' \left(X^* X' \right)^{-1} \tag{6.B5}$$

Following Zeeman (1977), Bennett, Haining, and Wilson (1985) argued that spatial interaction modelling, which informs the commodity flow modelling discussed above, will mature as a science when we can account for the behaviour of both fast and slow changing variables (e.g., 'variables' and 'parameters'). The formulation given above indicates how the values of the slow changing variables (reflecting changes in shipment patterns) can be derived. The real challenge to modellers of evolving networks is to explain the changes in the regional industrial outputs in X in terms of factors that are teasing out fragmentation and other manifestations of globalization.

Part B: Freight Transport

7 Can Freight Transport Models Be Transferred Across the Atlantic?

Kenneth Button

George Mason University, Fairfax, Virginia, USA

7.1 Introduction[1]

There is an increasing focus on economizing with data and with the speeding up of the analysis in such areas as transport forecasting and assessment. Most of this work has concerned passenger movements (e.g., in terms of travel-time savings values) or the external effects of transport (e.g., noise valuations). The work done in the freight sector is limited. Recent years have, however, seen a considerable increase in the number and sophistication of studies that have sought to explore changing structures in freight movement. Some of these changes have been in the way that freight activities themselves are viewed (e.g., because of the focus on just-in-time production) but in other cases they have embodied wider structural and institutional changes in economies (e.g., in communications, production technologies and in economic regulation).

The issue addressed here is initially whether these sorts of techniques can readily be applied to freight transportation and then on whether, in light of the various changes that are taking place, there is scope for deploying models developed for

[1] The author would like to thank three referees of this paper and those that offered useful comments when an earlier draft was presented at the 2003 European Regional Science Association annual meeting held in Jyväskyla. This paper ties in with the on-going work of the STELLA/STAR initiative looking at common themes in transatlantic transportation and in transportation research. The genesis of this paper comes from both an interest in the use of meta analysis and similar techniques in applied transportation work, but also a more fundamental interest in the question of the extent that transportation behavior is really 'understood'. There are arguments as to what exactly constitutes 'understanding', but if any analysis does genuinely explain a phenomenon then it should be able to give fairly good guidance as to what will happen in the future. It should be able to forecast. Without that, there would seem to be no reason to suppose that anything is really being understood. Equally, if the analysis of transportation behavior is genuinely scientific then it should be governed by rules that are transferable across situations.

more advanced systems to be transferred elsewhere.[2] The potential for transference across the Atlantic forms the basis for much of this assessment. The examination is less concerned about the usefulness of value transfers than with the usefulness of model transfers. This has implications not only for analysis, but from a larger policy point of view, if models are similar this would indicate greater ease in developing global supply chains.

This paper is thus about models rather than about any particular model. Its focus is on the potential for transferring models developed in one context for use in another context. The particular interest is that of freight transportation models, and the transfer is from the US to Europe, but similar issues would seem relevant to many other forms of forecasting models used in applied regional science work. From a purely theoretical level whether a model is transferable says a lot about its generality, and from a pragmatic perspective transferability is usually correlated with economy in application.

Given the increased interest in using a wider range of policy tools to enhance the efficiency of transportation, and thus reduce the impediments to spatial interaction, there has been a strong interest in improving transportation models. At the very least they must now be more flexible in their ability to help decision-makers assess portfolios of actions comprising a more diverse set of policy instruments. There is thus a pragmatic case for being able to deploy models across a range of spatial applications. But there are also intellectual arguments that if there is a genuine 'social science' that underlay these models then there should be consistency in the types of model that can be applied, and that these models should be broadly transferable across cases. If this were not so, then there is nothing but a set of *ad hoc* observations.

The aim of this paper is therefore not to develop any new model of freight transportation but rather to look at what is available, and to see if there is transferability of models. The focus is almost entirely on freight demand modelling. This is because these types of model play a larger part in policy analysis than do supply models that are more closely entwined with operational considerations.[3] There are also impact models (e.g., dealing with the impact of freight transportation on the environment), but these fall more directly in the field of benefit transfers that is covered in another literature.

Freight transportation modelling has been selected for study because there has been relatively less work done in this field than with regard to passenger transportation, but freight traffic is growing, is important in inter-regional trade and can inflict heavy societal costs. The US/EU spatial dimension is chosen because the economic structure and size of the two areas are similar. There are also close links between the US and Europe with a gradual opening of freer trade taking place –

---

[2] The transferability is largely treated in terms of moving from the US to Europe. This is done to keep the paper within manageable bounds. Useful accounts of some recent thinking in Europe are to be found in Tavasszy et al. (2003) and Bolis and Maggi (2003).

[3] Shippers and consignors use various forms of forecasting models and these are discussed in contributions to Brewer et al. (2001).

the on-going efforts to develop and open the transatlantic air market being the most recent manifestation.[4]

Initially the paper provides a general discussion of meta-analysis and of value transfers.[5] The former offers a means of extracting general models from a much larger set of specific case studies. While there may be a case for transferring a particular model, its robustness and its potential local specificity are often in need of wider support. In particular there is a focus on the criteria that seem important if one is seeking to deploy a model developed in one region to a different region – its transfer. It then considers the development of freight transportation models in recent years and focuses on some of their aspects that may be important for allowing transfers between locations. This is supplemented by a very brief look at the differences between the modelling requirements in Europe and those of the US.

7.2 The Background to Modern Freight Models

The initial focus of regional science in the 19th and early 20th centuries took a rather simplistic view of the role of transportation in determining location and regional trade patterns. Distance was a standard proxy for transportation costs if they were considered at all. The focus, probably understandable given the quantitative techniques and data available at the time, was on gaining a basic understanding of relationships. Estimations of parameters[6] and forecasting were not priorities, and in practical terms not really possibilities. The emergence of land-use planning and a greater interest in encouraging regional development through Keynesian stimuli changed this. Better data, more sophisticated estimation procedures and the advent of computers allowed the application of theory to particular cases.

Much of the focus from the 1960s was, however, on the forecasting of passenger transportation demand. Engineering models that treated humans as fluids flowing through systems, or apples falling from trees were used in the absence of economic, behaviour based models to meet the needs of the infrastructure driven urban policies of the time. It should be said if fairness, however, some of this problem must lay at the door of economics and other social sciences that gave relatively little attention to transportation modelling. The later appreciation that human beings have evolved, not because they are mobile drops of fluid or falling

---

[4] From a trade perspective, negotiations and the subsequent monitoring of compliance with agreements normally require understanding and forecasts of what other economies are doing. This applies at the sector level as much as the national level. The ability to transfer local models to other situations can help in this.

[5] An initial aim of the paper was to conduct some meta analysis of US work to see how useful the parameters would be for modeling purposes in Europe. This proved impractical at this time.

[6] The term parameter is used in a very general sense in the paper. Models take a wide variety of forms and the term parameter should not be seen as being limited to econometric and related frameworks as is often the case.

fruit, but because they are concerned with more complex objective sets led to a basis of analysis more firmly founded in the social sciences, and in particular, economics (McFadden 2001; Quandt and Baumol 1966).[7]

The number of models that are now used to examine and forecast passenger transportation demand are numerous. Although few retrospective studies have been done,[8] there is also some confidence that Milton Friedman's criterion for a good model, namely its ability to predict, is being met. Or at least models are improving in that their predictions are not missing the mark by several orders of magnitude. A lot of effort has gone into trying to enhance our understanding of personal travel behaviour and into related areas such as the valuation of travel time savings. The initial work focused on commuter travel, quite understandably in the 1960s when 25% of trips in the US were for this purpose. The emphasis has gradually, although probably more slowly than it should, moved to complex matters of trip-chaining and non-commuter trips as journeys to work have fallen to about 15% of all urban trips.

In all of this, the amount of effort devoted to understanding and forecasting freight transportation has been comparatively limited. One reason for this is that the number of freight vehicles on roads is usually a relatively small proportion of the total. Another is that in some countries such as the US, a large amount of the ton-miles are done on dedicated private rail track and by commercial carriers that do their own business forecasts. The details of their models are not always publicly available, but at least there is a high degree of internal accountability. Certainly less is needed for parallel official forecasts to be produced.

For the most part, the bulk of early freight transportation modelling applications were nothing more than adaptations of established transportation modelling methodologies originally designed for passenger transportation, especially in the urban context (Meyburg and Stopher 1974).[9] They were usually little more than simple derivatives of passenger demand models, often of the four-stage model (Button and Pearman 1981; Federal Highways Administration 1988).[10] They tended to overlook fundamental differences between freight movement and passenger transportation. However, on the other hand some new advances in passen-

---

[7] Added to this explicit development of freight transport models should be the work of regional scientists such as Walter Isard, and those more interested in aggregate trade flows, for example as they affected input output flows.

[8] A cursory glance through the advertising publicity of a dozen major transportation modeling and forecasting consultancy companies setting out their experiences and skills found not a single reference to completed forecasts that had been retrospectively verified. I must assume, as a tax payer, that local and other authorities that hire consultants at least have this type of information prior to awarding contracts.

[9] More explicit analysis of the freight transport market began to emerge from the management literature in the 1970s but did not penetrate the engineering side of transportation modeling (Baumol and Vinod, 1970). And an occasional economics paper was published (e.g., Allen, 1977).

[10] An outline of this approach, albeit set in the context of passenger transportation is contained in McNally (2000).

ger demand modelling – e.g., activity based models – have not yet made it to freight modelling. It is sometimes not a simple matter of applying an approach developed for one area (passenger) to another area (freight).

This situation has changed somewhat in recent years. In part this is because there is more freight transportation and, although still a relatively small part of aggregate traffic, it does cause a disproportionate amount of congestion. There are additionally inter-urban and urban road corridors that do have very significant amounts of truck traffic.[11] The numbers here are rising. It has also become appreciated that simply tweaking models designed for passenger transportation forecasting is inadequate. The unique features of freight transportation include additional dimensions that have to be accounted for such as vehicle configuration, weight, freight volume, type and value of commodity, chain-of-custody and locus of decision-making issues, freight ownership issues, and the multiple stakeholders common to freight shipments.

In addition, perceptions of the economic importance of freight transportation have changed. Transportation costs were traditionally seen as a relatively small part of overall production costs, and then usually only viewed in financial terms. In cases such as those involving the extractive industries, transportation's share of total costs were higher but felt to be unalterable. This picture has changed as the structure of western economies has shifted aware from raw material production. It has also changed with refinements to supply-chain management and the adoption of just-in-time logistics and related techniques. It is now accepted that the economic concept of margins is important and that average costs play a more limited role. The financial costs of a movement are now seen as only part of a more complex generalized cost function that embraces time costs and reliability considerations amongst others.

There are concerns that the current transportation infrastructure and the way that it is used is inadequate to meet current demands let alone growth. For example a recent Transportation Research Board (2003) publication begins with the words, 'In every sector of the US freight transportation industry during the past decade, alarms were sounded, by service providers and their customers, that facilities were becoming inadequate to deal with the demands of traffic growth.' This issue is certainly not exclusively one felt in the US, and the European Union's (EU) white paper outlining the Union's transportation policy ambitions spends considerable time outlining the congestion being experienced on the various European networks (Commission of the European Union 2001).

Freight transportation can also be responsible for significant environmental external costs. Trucks generate a variety of atmospheric pollutants, railways are noisy and their infrastructure leads to serious implications for drainage, and maritime transportation can result in spillage and coastal damage around ports. Finally the most rapidly growing, and possibly by value of the goods carried (which is usually a fairly good guide to how individuals and companies assess the importance of something, if not planners) the most important freight mode, air transpor-

---

[11] For example on the I-81 corridor in Virginia, truck-trailer combinations accounted for about 25% of the vehicles in 1997 – some 40% of the road's capacity.

tation, is noisy and produces a variety of air pollutants. The environmental costs of moving freight are, therefore, high and growing in societies with rising incomes and greater environmental sensitivities. Environmental predictions require reliable freight transportation models (Björner 1999).

These changes in perspective have led to the development of many new models of freight transportation demand. The complexity of freight demand modelling has increased and the models used are more diverse (Cambridge Systematics, Inc. 1997; D'Este 2001; Friesz 2000; Ogden 1992). Freight demand modelling is also now often substantially different from passenger demand modelling – having a different focus. Data availability has also played a part in the ways in which freight models have been developed.

These new models also come at a time when the perception of the wider role of transportation in influencing land-use and in sustaining regional growth is going through something of a revision. There is an appreciation that new forms of urban structure are emerging, for example edge cities (Garreau 1991), and our understanding of regional development processes have been enhanced by the New Economic Geography (Fujita et al. 1999). These developments are also a reflection of new ways of providing freight transportation services to meet both emerging spatial forms and new logistics pressures. Hub-and-spoke operations have grown that both enhance the efficiency of traditional freight transportation services and additionally serve the needs of the new world of e-commerce. New communications technologies and applications – e.g., electronic data interchange (EDI) – also influence the ways that freight can be handled and tracked.

7.3 Meta Analysis

Acceptance of a particular model based upon one case is a normal practice. But this has limitations if the objective is to take the model and employ it in a different spatial context. The model may not have wider applicability in the immediate geographical area let alone a different continent. Strong arguments can be made for pooling information across a range of applications and cases before attempting any for spatial transfer.

Meta-analysis is a collection of quantitative techniques that aim to derive additional knowledge from analyzing a well-defined collection of independent, but similar studies undertaken over periods of time or at different places.[12] It has been increasingly used as the number of individual studies has grown with the advent of improved quantitative techniques and the ready accessibility of a wide range of computer software. Quite simply the raw material for synthesis has become larger. It has also become an attractive proposition as resources for primary research have become tighter.

Glass (1976) provides a widely accepted formal definition of meta-analysis,[13]

---

[12] There are a number of other techniques, and for a comparative review see Button (1998).
[13] See also Hunter and Schmidt (1990).

'Meta-analysis refers to the analysis of analysis...the statistical analysis of a large collection of analysis results from individual studies for the purpose of integrating the findings. In connotes a rigorous alternative to the casual, narrative discussions of research studies which typify our attempts to make sense of the rapidly expanding research literature.'

Meta-analysis provides for examining a number of results found in previous studies. It offers parameters that can be transferred to other studies (e.g., in constrained regression analysis), it offers insights into factors (moderators) that distinguish various cases (Bal et al. 2002),[14] and it offers the potential for the transfer of relationships, or models to new cases.

There are a variety of approaches to conducting this form of synthesis. Meta-regression analysis forms the basis of most work in the economic and transportation forecasting fields. The general form is:

$$b_j = \alpha + \sum b_k Z_{jk} + u_j \quad (j = 1,2,3...L)(k = 1,2,3...M), \qquad (7.1)$$

where b_j is the reported estimate of the relationship of interest in the j_{th} study from a total of L studies; Σ is the summary value of b_j; Z_{jk} are variables that reflect the relevant characteristics of an empirical study that could explain variations amongst studies (moderator variables); β_k are the coefficients of the M different study characteristics that are controlled for, and u_j is the error term.

While they differ according to the subject under consideration, the types of moderator variable that have been used in meta-regressions deployed in transportation work fit within the broad framework:

$$Y = f(P, X, R, T, S), \qquad (7.2)$$

where, taking analysis of a set of studies on the valuations of traffic noise amelioration, Y represents the values obtained (here the valuations of noise reduction), P is a specific cause of the noise (car, plane), X is the features of those affected (age, income), R is the research method to derive the values (stated preference, revealed preference), T is the date of the study, and S is the location of the study (urban, rural).[15]

---

[14] In regional science perhaps the most recent important focus on moderator type variables, albeit not explicitly in a meta-analytical context is the work by Barro and Sala-I-Martin (1992) on the conditional β convergence of regional economic growth.

[15] Below is a very simple example of a meta-regression analysis conducted by Schipper (1999). The study looks at reasons why there are variations in the implications of increased airport noise on house values. Changes in house prices are widely used to evaluate noise nuisance. The analysis looked at 29 different independent studies. It finds that the results of these studies can be influenced by such exogenous factors as 'when the

The approach differs from conventional literature reviews or epistemological analysis in that it seeks to test statistically for commonality in studies and for factors that explain diversity. A literature review have immense value when dealing with qualitative analysis where there are serious doubts about the quality of data used in various studies or the methods used. They permit comment on the less quantifiable difference between various analyses. Meta-analysis provides a more rigorous statistical approach.[16]

Studies using meta-techniques in areas such as management science, medicine and social psychology are quite widespread, with an increasing application in economics (Button et al. 1999). Perhaps the most successful application of the technique in transportation has been in the area of environmental impact evaluations where Kerry Smith (Smith and Kaoru 1990) has explored large numbers of studies and found, deploying only a limited number of moderators, robust valuations of recreational amenity. The outcomes of other efforts in the transportation field have produced a diversity of results, some indicating that there are underlying robust parameters and models that can vary because of explicit and quantifiable effects.

Meta-analysis has therefore several interesting features as a method of synthesis. First, it can deal with qualitative and, ever more completely using modern statistical techniques, quantitative, knowledge. Second, meta-analytical techniques can isolate relevant knowledge from a well-defined collection of previous studies. Compared to other such techniques, it makes more knowledge available for value transfers. Third, variables can be quantified and corrected for biases. Fourth, meta-analysis reduces the context-dependency of research findings and of models.

7.4 Transferability

For purposes of value transfer, meta-analysis is becoming of increasing importance (Loomis 1992; Parsons and Kealy 1994). The idea of value transfer is that

---

work was done', 'the nature of the model used', and 'the type of client the work was conducted for'. Other meta-studies have covered a range of topics and used a variety of estimation techniques. The one cited here is intended but as an example of what meta-analysis entails.

$$Y = 0.11 + 0.45X_1 - 0.04X_2 + 2.71X_3 + 1.30X_4 - 0.27X_5 + 0.88X_6 + 0.69X_7$$
$$\text{Adj } R^2 = 0.95$$

where: Y is the percentage change in house price, X_1 is the natural log of relative house price, X_2 is the year of data collection, X_3 is a dummy variable reflecting 1960, X_4 is a dummy variable reflecting whether the material was published in an academic source, X_5 is a dummy variable as to whether a log-linear model was used, X_5 is a measure of access, and X_7 is an indicator of the type of neighborhood.

[16] Meta- analysis is not without its limitations. In particular it relies upon the availability of suitable case studies where variables are expressed in a consistent manner. Without this the strength of the approach is diluted (van der Bergh et al. 1997).

knowledge cumulated over time may be transferred to a new, similar type of study. Value transfer further aims to use cumulated knowledge generated by previous research to draw inferences on hitherto unexplored cases. It has the practical merit of many mining techniques that it is relatively resource frugal.

The notion of value transfer is fairly well established in some fields of econometrics where various forms of pooling techniques have been long deployed. This may, for example, involve the use of restricted regression procedures where parameters in the primary model are restricted to values found in a secondary model or sets of models. In other cases it may just mean the adoption of values or parameters statistically extracted from other studies and used in such exercises as the cost-benefit analysis of transportation investments.

Institutionally, value transfer has been adopted in many contexts as a way of not only reducing the need for new bespoke quantification, and with this comes economies in resource utilization, but also as a means of improving consistency across decisions. While specific studies may allow for a more complete incorporation of local nuances, they do not allow for consistence across a series of decisions.[17] A long established transportation example is the use of standard values for travel time savings, vehicle operating costs and for changes in the value of the risk of having an accident that has been used across small and medium road investment computerized analysis in the UK – the COBA analytical framework. The use of common values across studies is less common in the US.

The number of studies that provide any genuine cross US/EU comparisons of parameters for freight transportation is, however, limited. Such comparisons are thought important prerequisites to see if there is a wider opportunity for transferability.

Beuthe et al. (2001), using their NODUS module, compare their European elasticity estimates with those obtained by Abdewahab (1998) for the US and conclude that '...our estimates are of about the same order of magnitude with the exception of some rail elasticities over short distances.' But 'about' seems to be used in a rather generous way in this particular instance. Additionally, the comparison, as the authors admit, is limited by differences in the techniques used. Abdewahab uses a simultaneous three stage econometric model based upon observed data to derive real price elasticities, whereas Beuthe and his colleagues look at cross and direct general cost elasticities using a simulation framework based upon synthetic networks for Belgium.

There has also been some effort to examine the international consistency of the valuation of freight travel time-savings – important if the cost-minimizing paradigm of many models is to be adopted across borders. Looking across a wide range of studies, De Jong (2000) finds that results tend to be highly contextual, especially when stated-preference methods are employed. Even very broad conclusions seem difficult to draw. Oum et al. (1992) provides summary of estimates of freight demand elasticities in their wider survey of demand parameters. Besides finding them much more variable than for passenger transportation, the study also

---

[17] This is a problem that at the extreme can lead to such things as the Skitovsky paradox in cost-benefit analysis.

found considerable variance across commodity classifications and within commodity classifications. The variability in the parameters was found to increase the more disaggregate the nature of the studies they examined.

Transferring values can thus experience severe problems if the underlying *ceteris paribus* assumptions of the original studies (essentially the importance of the moderator variables in meta-regression) are significantly different from those relevant at the transfer location. This has not only been found in the comparative analyses that have been undertaken but also in debates over the application of transfer values. In the UK context of using common values in investment appraisal cited above, for example, there have been long standing debates about whether a common value of travel time-savings is appropriate across a country with significant spatial variations in income.[18]

This has led to the argument that whilst value transfers (the term 'benefit transfer' is more common in the environmental literature) has limitations, there may be more utility in seeking to transfer functional forms – in effect, transferring models that are then re-calibrated or otherwise adjusted using local data. The degree and nature of any transfer may vary. In some cases it is the operational form of model that is transferred with the parameters (moderators) being part of the transfer. Local values of the independent variables in an econometric based model are then used for forecasting. In other cases the general form of the model may be transferred but local parameters are then calculated for the new situation. One major consideration is whether this is possible with freight transportation models at the international level, and if so what types of models are the most suitable.

7.5 Types of Model

There is a wide range of approaches emerging in the modelling of freight transportation, and of features of the larger field of freight logistics. Some are essentially theoretical constructs that have been developed from deductive methodologies, but there is also a trend towards more inductive modelling (Button et al. 2001).These can be divided up in a number of ways including by methods used and by the degree of spatial aggregation.

7.5.1 Modelling Techniques/Frameworks

An extensive variety of modelling frameworks has been used to try to capture the essentials of the freight transportation market. As suggested earlier, many are efforts at transference from passenger driven models. These include non-network econometric models (Oum 1979), mathematical models, (Vanek 2001), dis-

---

[18] There have in the past been heated debates about whether it is more rational to reduce all effects included in an appraisal exercise to 'generalized time units' rather than to monetary units since time allocations are equal across groups and individuals (Goodwin 1974).

crete/continuous choice models of mode and shipment size (Abdelwahab 1998), multinomial probit models (Garrido and Mahmassani 2000), and a variety of network based approaches (Beuthe et al. 2001; Friesz et al. 1998).[19]

One form of modelling gaining acceptance in the passenger arena but barely explored by freight transport modellers is activity analysis. The development of activity-based modelling is derived from the early work of Hagerstrand (1970) in time-space geography. The idea of activity-based modelling is that the demand for transportation is derived from the demand for activities (Horowitz 1985) and that people face temporal-spatial constraints in performing these activities. Such models of passenger behaviour have gained in importance as it has become appreciated that transportation decisions are part of a wider set of interactive choices.[20] There are, however, substantial methodological challenges and differences between passenger transportation and freight transportation. An activity-based approach that derives the demand for travel from the demand for activities may offer a completely different and new approach for freight, allowing modellers, logisticians, and policy-makers to better understand the complex dependencies and inter-relationships in freight logistics under conditions of uncertainty or external shocks.

Boerkamps et al. (2000) discuss the need for behavioural urban freight models that can predict goods flows and vehicle flows, and outlines a conceptual framework consisting of the markets, actors and supply chain elements of freight movements. This proposal suggests a new activity-based approach to freight demand and logistics, deriving demand conditions from the demand for freight activities

However, such approaches have not been developed, applied, or observed in the literature for freight. One step that can be considered in this direction is the work of Holguin-Veras and Thorson (2003) who have applied the idea of trip chaining to model the flow of empty commercial vehicles as a function of a given matrix of commodity flows. Trip chaining refers to the pattern where trips are chained together, and the chain becomes the basic element of activity-based models.

It is interesting, however, that some of the work in developing passenger activity-based models use notions and ideas from freight and logistics. Kitamura (1988) noted that the problem at its simplest is a discrete choice-continuous allocation problem with correlated multiple alternatives, combined with the travelling salesman problem, the problem of collective decision making, and household coupling constraints, all of which are, in part, a logistics problem. Recker (1995) posed the

---

[19] Pendyala et al. (2000) provides a synthesis of approaches and the body of knowledge of freight transportation factors, freight travel demand modeling methods, freight transportation planning issues and freight data needs, deficiencies and collection methods. McKinnon et al. (2002) offer a collection of papers dealing with logistics models. For a survey of the work specifically on urban freight models see, Taniguchi et al. (1999) and D'Este (2000).

[20] Kitamura (1988) provides an extensive evaluation of the field, covering approximately 120 studies.

household activity pattern problem as a variant of the pickup and delivery problem with time windows. In his most general case, the model addresses the optimization (relative to a household's utility function) of the interrelated paths through the time/space continuum of a series of household members with a prescribed activity agenda and a stable of vehicles and ride-sharing options available.

7.5.2 Macro-Models/Strategic Models

These models are mainly designed for strategic network analysis and are less focused on day-to-day freight flows and logistics operations than on the production of longer-term forecast over networks. They are fundamentally predictive models (Friesz 2000). They are usually couched in terms of a multi-modal, partial equilibrium transportation market to allow comparisons between various alternative policy scenarios that are under review. The nature of the problem and the constraints of the system generally make regression type approaches inoperable, and instead network models are examined in closed mathematical form as optimization or game thematic problems. The large size of the models normally means that estimation is through numerical methods.

Early attempts in the US at developing large-scale models along these lines stem from the work of Kresge and Roberts (1971), Bronzini (1980), and from consultancy companies such as ALK Associates – the Princeton Rial Network Model. More recently the freight network equilibrium model (FNEM) has emerged (Friesz and Viton 1985) and STAN (Crainic et al. 1990), a commercial venture, has been developed. Differences in these models lie in such things as the actors that are included (e.g., carriers and shippers) and the types of transportation features that are treated (e.g., backhaul). They are also sometimes especially tailored to serve specific purposes such as the demands of national security.

These types of model should in theory be readily transferable since they are based upon optimization principles. Provided it is possible to offer inputs on the various abstract features on any network then optimization is possible irrespective of the location. They are essentially abstractions very much along the lines, albeit rather more detailed, of an abstract mode model in transportation economics.

The various forms of these types of model are more easily delineated in terms of their features than their spatial specificity, It is a matter of which of the following types of features they include:

- Multiple modes
- Multiple commodities
- Sequential loading of commodities
- Simultaneous loading of commodities
- Explicit congestion
- Elastic transportation demand
- Explicit shippers
- Sequential shipper and carrier submodels
- Simultaneous shipper and carrier submodels

- Sequential computable equilibrium and network models
- Simultaneous computable equilibrium and network models

(In practice, as Friesz (2000) shows in a tabular comparison of three of the early models, none are comprehensive in their coverage.)

Thus, provided there is a US model that embodies the portfolio of features relevant for the European case under consideration, there should be little trouble in relating these types of model to different geographical situations. The chance of this being the case, however, seems unlikely, so inevitably transfer would seem to involve a degree of trade-off between what the US models embrace and what the European transfer situation seeks.

While of considerable academic interest there are very few actual cases where these US models have been validated – perhaps FNEM is the only case. But validation, knowledge of how well these models actually replicate actual freight flows, is important if they are to be used in policy analysis. In the case of FNEM, the results were mixed with good predictions for some commodity categories but not for others. This may be because of poor data, but equally it may reflect specification deficiencies. But whatever the cause, little confidence can be expressed in the idea that they could very easily be transferred to the European case.[21]

7.5.3 Micro-Models

Micro-models in this context can be viewed as more localized models that cover part of the geography of the network. Urban freight demand models can be seen as an example, as can those that relate to particular facilities such as a sea-port. They are much more data driven and often involve simplified networks. These types of model, because they are often designed to predict the impact of particular policy initiatives, tend to be location specific.[22]

As indicated above much of the analysis at this level still relies upon the four-stage model sequence, which for transfer purposes imposes the need to be able to transfer all stages in the sequence if there is to be any consistency in the exercise. Since much of the passenger traffic modelling in urban areas tends to still rely on this sequential framework there is an inevitable tendency for freight forecasts to be made on the same basis (D'Este 2000).

Where refinements have been made to the underlying passenger model, these have largely been in terms of simulation models. These have sometimes come as microscopic simulations (such as NETSIM, Mahmassani et al. 1990) that simulate the behaviour of individual vehicles and have been seen as improvements on the more macro frameworks that simulate traffic as groups of vehicles. Perhaps the

---

[21] There have been models that have captured part of elements of overall freight movements or types of commodity. For example, Harker and Friesz (1982) developed a shipper-carrier model that was applied to the US coal industry. There has been no attempt to see how this would perform in the European case.

[22] These types of model are more often used to provide parameters for value transfers than for model transfer in other contexts.

more impressive advances have, however, involved hybrids of these approaches (Fujii et al. 1994). While fine-tuning of individual stages in the four stage modelling sequence can help improve its performance, they do little to make it more easily transferable.

7.6 Differences Between the US and Europe

There are clear differences between the US and Europe, but the issue here is whether these make the transfer of the types of freight transportation models that have, say, been developed in the US useful or not for forecasting in the EU. If the differences are purely in terms of the parameters involved then this is simply a matter of local estimation and does not in itself prevent transferability.[23] The model parameters can be re-estimated. The issue is really a matter of degree in this case, and often involves data availability and compatibility of information. But there may be more fundamental differences that cannot at this time be easily overcome.

Many of the models used in freight transportation analysis have a neo-classical economic foundation – they assume cost-minimization at the very least and that actors are familiar with most of the opportunity costs of their actions. Economists are actually quite good at analyzing certain aspects of human behaviour, and econometricians at the quantification of key relationships. In particular the link between prices, both of the services being offered and of other competing/complementary services, and consumption is well explored, as is the link between income and consumption. What economists are not so adept at exploring is the black box called 'taste'. It is perhaps here, however, that the greatest issues of transferability emerge in the case of the US and Europe.

7.6.1 Different Policy Approaches

There are two broad approaches to transportation policy, and indeed policy in general. The Anglo-Saxon approach that is typified by the actions of the US and the UK is where the onus is on the market, and interventions and regulations have to be demonstrably superior. The Continental philosophy favoured by countries such as France takes the contrary position with the market only being seen as desirable when it is shown to be preferable to a command-and-control approach.

---

[23] This is true in theory but it may be much more difficult to put into practice. Models should be data neutral in the sense that one can 'plug-in' data from various locations, and while this affects parameters it should not affect the overall usefulness of the model. In practice, models are often developed with a particular data base in mind and these type of data may not be available or available in a comparable form at the new location. One example is that of air trucking. The US models of air freight demand actually assume that air freight or cargo as described on the air weight bills actually goes by air. In Europe a vast amount of this is actually trucked.

Underlying this is the objective of the Anglo-Saxon policy maker to make transportation efficient in itself whereas those pursuing a Continental approach treat transport as a policy tool to attain other objectives. US thinking is clearly dominated by the market efficiency argument, the situation in Europe is far less clear cut. In practice, the issue is not one of extremes but rather that of degree.

These varying approaches place differing demands on the types of output that policy-makers seek. The aggregate types of freight demand models that are being developed in the US seek to optimize network utilization. While this may be a technical objective of transportation planners in the EU they also embrace a much stronger concern for allocating traffic across modes. There is a policy objective in the EU to remove traffic, or at least contain the growth of traffic, that makes use of roads. The notion of optimization in a neo-classical sense is not part of this type of constrained framework. The type of model output being sought is more focused on numerical transfer of movements than on making economically efficient use of the network.

7.6.2 Different Networks

Models are seldom constructed so that all of their elements are equally refined. Pragmatism inevitably means that some elements are less well developed, and others are more complete. This may be because the user is more interested in certain parts of the of the freight transportation network – those concerned with 'last-mile problems' tend to have sophisticated urban networks but sparse inter-city, trunk networks. Data availability may also influence the way models are developed since it affects the ability to operationalise them in anything but a purely synthetic context.

The type of data available in Europe is significantly different to that in the US if for no other reason that it has not been systematically collected on an EU basis for the same length of time. This makes the use of many US models practically very difficult.

Conceptually more important is that the focus of many US models involves emphasizing elements of networks that are less important than in Europe. For example, air cargo network models in the states generally have extremely simplistic airport congestion sub-models. But airport congestion is a major concern in Europe. The main inter-city road network at the core of the EU is highly congested, and forecasting models thus require a fairly complex congestion component to cater for this. Some parts of the US also suffer from similar problems, but less sophisticated models are required as a whole and the four stage approach may often be a reasonable approximation (Transportation Research Board 2003).

A similar problem exists for trunk haul railways in that the primary function of the US rail network is for freight movement but that of Europe is largely a passenger network. Consequently, linked passenger rail models are largely absent in US freight railway modelling but are important for those making freight predictions for European railways. Intermodal transportation is significant in the US but limited in Europe despite concerted policy initiatives to support it. The types of model required to predict modal interchange in the two geographies would thus seem to require different specifications and emphasis.

7.6.3 Different Markets

The demand for freight transportation, as with most other transportation, is derived from the final demand for the goods that are carried. The goods carried in Europe differ significantly from those in the US as do such things as the length of haul. For example, the fact that only about 8% of the ton miles by the current 15 members of the EU are done by rail, compared to about 40% in the US is indicative of the differences in the markets on either side of the Atlantic.[24] The different types of commodity and the modes available not only make value transfers difficult but also suggest that there may major differences in the technical structure of the demand for freight services.

In particular, the geographical structure of markets is fundamentally different to that found in the US. There is a much greater concentration of population, production, and consumption at the spatial core of the EU – often called the 'Blue Banana' belt – than in the US, where economic activity is spread over a number of competing sub-national markets. The EU situation means there is limited need for hub-and-spoke operations in air cargo services (the vast majority of flights are of less than 90 minutes duration) and there is more opportunity to combine such carriage with passenger services. There is limited opportunity to exploit economies of distance for railroads, with US average hauls orders of magnitude greater than in the EU.

In theory these types of factors could be embraced in a US derived regression style model with inputs changed to reflect EU market conditions. But a difficulty is that the calculation of US parameters may in many cases be on ranges of observation outside of those found in Europe – estimates of rate elasticities based on a set of hauls of 1500 miles seem unlikely to be applicable to routes of 150 miles.[25] Further, the moderator variables used in meta-analysis in the US may not reflect variations across situations in Europe – transferability would, for example, imply similar degrees of multicollinearity between variables.

7.6.4 Different Institutions

Institutional structures are important. Institutional structures affect freight transportation in a number of distinct and potentially important ways. The Single European Market initiative of 1992 has essentially removed many of the obstacles to

---

[24] The figure for the accession countries joining the EU in 2004 is about 40% but is falling quite quickly.

[25] The accession of a number of former Soviet dominated countries to the EU in 2004 will significantly increase the potential for long-haul rail transportation. The problem is inevitably going to be one of management and efficiency.

the free movement of goods in Europe, and there are no restrictions of the right of establishment of transportation undertakings – a European company can locate and acquire anywhere in the Union. The documentation that is required to cross borders is minimal and more strictly related to the individuals involved in operating the transportation hardware than to the goods per se.

This does not, however, mean that there is a seamless service. Old practices die hard, and there are technical constraints on cross-border interoperability in some cases. The rail network in particular suffers from major problems in this respect (Commission of the European Union 2001). Labour is still largely organized on a national basis in the EU and there are inevitable differences in work practices on different national elements of the network. This is also true of short-sea shipping. This makes the development of cost functions more complex than in the US.

7.6.5 Different Modelling Requirements

The users of transportation forecasts in the EU often have somewhat different needs from their US counterparts. This is due mainly to the institutional structures in the two areas and the legal responsibilities of various levels of government. History is also a factor.

There is a current interest in Europe with macro and strategic modelling as the EU moves both to deepen its existing transportation networks – essentially the Trans-European Networks – and to widen the networks as membership of the Union is increased. The expansion to 25 members in 2004, involving countries often very distant from the core of the initial EU, poses challenges of access and economic integration. The EU has thus been engaged in a number of initiatives to develop appropriate models. The US, in contrast, confronted these challenges from the 1950s as the Interstate Highway system was planned and constructed. The need for large-scale strategic models is, therefore, largely absent in 21st USA. Where there have been some more extensive modelling at a near national level in the US has been when there has been legal actions concerning such things as railroad mergers. Here the interest has been on the degree of competition that exists over parts of networks. This has not, to date, been a major issue in Europe.[26]

They also have different interests in the implications of various types of policy interventions given their various powers. This need not be a problem if relevant policy instruments under review by the EU are a sub-set of those in effect in the US. For example, if the EU is interested in labour inputs such as truck driver's hours, on freight modal split, and this is a factor in parent US studies, then transferability may be possible. However, if the US rules pertain to numbers of hours worked in a week, but EU concerns are with the duration of shifts, the former offers little by way of insight.

The issue here is less whether a model may be transferred in terms of being able to replicate existing situations and do-nothing scenarios, but rather that of

---

[26] Where this type of issue has arisen in Europe it has been in the context of passenger airlines rather than freight.

whether transfer is possible if the EU users are interested in policy reactive predictions.

7.7 Conclusions

The objective here has not been to develop a new model or to suggest improved ways of estimating parameters in some existing freight transportation model. Rather the aim has been to see what scope there is for model transfer in transportation forecasting drawing upon freight models as a point of reference. It represents something of a musing about whether the freight transportation models that we now use have a genuine basis in social science or whether they are essentially ad hoc. To date, as far as I can find in the freight transportation field, there has been no attempt to take a model for one location, apply it to another and then to examine it subsequent predictive power. This makes it difficult to offer definitive conclusions, and the in this age of instant qualifications, the time it would take to do it makes it an unlikely topic for any PhD student to undertake.

What can be said is that transferring freight models is not easy. This may be an intrinsic problem with the exercise being attempted, but it may also be the result of models being deliberately location specific. This may also not be nation specific. For example, it may be more likely that a model developed for New York may predict well for Paris but not for Phoenix. The sad fact is that we simply do not know in most cases whether it actually predicts well for New York let alone other places.

As a result of this, the initial ambition of this exercise to produce a matrix that defined necessary and sufficient conditions for spatially transferring models has proved impossible. There are simply not enough data points to do this, and the topic may be too difficult anyway.

References

Abdelwahab WM (1998) Elasticities of mode choice probabilities and market elasticities of demand: evidence from a simultaneous mode choice/shipment-size freight transport model. Transportation Research E 34: 257–266

Allen WB (1977) The demand for freight transport: a micro approach. Transportation Research 11: 9–14

Bal F, Button KJ, Nijkamp P (2002) Ceteris paribus, meta-analysis and value transfer. Socio-economic Planning Science 36: 127–138

Barro RJ, Sala-I-Martin X (1992) Convergence. Journal of Political Economy 100: 223–251

Baumol WJ, Vinod HD (1970) An inventory theoretical model of freight transport demand. Management Science 16: 413–421

van den Bergh JCJM, Button KJ, Nijkamp P, Pepping GC (1997) Meta-analysis in environmental economics. Kluwer, Dordrecht

Beuthe M, Jourquin B, Geerts JF, Koul â Ndjang' Ha C (2001) Freight transportation demand elasticities: a geographic multimodal transportation network analysis. Transportation Research E 37: 253–266

Björner TB (1999) Environmental benefits from better freight transport management: freight traffic in a VAR model. Transportation Research D 4: 45–64

Boerkamps J, van Binsbergen AJ, Bovy PHL (2000) Modeling behavioral aspects of urban freight movement in supply chains. Transportation Research Record 1725: 17–25

Bolis S, Maggi R (2003) Logistics strategy and transport service choices: an adaptive stated preference experiment. Growth and Change 34: 490–504

Brewer AM, Button KJ, Hensher DA (eds) (2001) Handbook of logistics and supply-chain management. Pergamon, Oxford

Bronzini M (1980) Evolution of a multimodal freight transportation model. Proceeding of the Transportation Research Forum 21: 475–485

Button KJ (1998) The three faces of synthesis: bringing together quantitative findings in the field of transport and environmental policy. Environment and Planning C 16: 516–528

Button KJ, Kerr J (1996) Effectiveness of traffic restraint policies: a simple meta-regression analysis. International Journal of Transport Economics 23: 214–225

Button KJ, Pearman AD (1981) The economics of urban freight Transport. Macmillan, London

Button KJ, Jongma S, Kerr J (1999) Meta-analysis approaches and applied microeconomics. In: Dahiya SB (ed) The current state of economic science, volume 2: micro economics, macroeconomics, monetary economics. Spellbound Publications, Rohtak

Button KJ, Kulkarni R, Stough R (2001) Clustering of transport logistics centres in urban areas. In: Taniguchi E, Thompson RG (eds) City logistics II. Institute of Systems Science Research, Kyoto

Cambridge Systematics (1997) A guidebook for forecasting freight transportation demand NCHRP report #388, Transportation Research Board, Washington, D.C.

Commission of the European Union (2001) European transport policy for 2010: time to decide. European Commission, Brussels

Crainic TG, Florian M, Leal J-E (1990) A model for the strategic planning of national freight transportation by rail. Transportation Science 24: 1–24

De Jong G (2000) Value of freight travel-time savings. In: Hensher DA, Button KJ (eds), Handbook of transport modelling. Pergamon, Oxford

D'Este G (2000) Urban freight movement modeling. In: Hensher DA, Button KJ (eds), Handbook of transport modelling. Pergamon, Oxford

D'Este G (2001) Freight and logistics modelling. In: Brewer AM, Button KJ, Hensher DA (eds) Handbook of logistics and supply-chain management. Pergamon, Oxford

van Es J, Ruijgrok CJ (1969) Model choice in freight transport. In: Proceedings of the International Conference on Transportation Research, Bruges 1973. Cross, Oxford

Federal Highways Administration (1988) Quick response freight manual. Final report, Federal Highways Administration, Washington D.C.

Friesz TL (2000) Strategic freight network models. In: Hensher DA, Button KJ (eds), Handbook of transport modelling. Pergamon, Oxford

Friesz TL, Viton P (1985) Economic and computational aspects of freight network equilibrium: a synthesis. Journal of Regional Science 25: 29–49

Friesz TL, Gottfried J, Hacker PT (1983) The state of the art in predictive freight network models. Transportation Research A 17: 409–417

Friesz TL, Gottfried J, Morlok EK (1985) A sequential shipper-carrier network model for predicting freight flows. Transportation Science 20: 80–91

Fujii M, Iida Y, Uchida T (1994) Dynamic simulation to evaluate vehicle navigation In: Vehicle Navigation and Information Systems Conference Proceedings

Friesz TL, Soa ZG, Bernstein DH (1996) A dynamic disequilibrium interregional commodity flow model. Transportation Research B 32: 467–483

Fujita M, Krugman PR, Venables AJ (1999) The spatial economy: cities, regions and international trade. MIT Press, Cambridge

Garreau J (1991) Edge city: life at the new frontier. Doubleday, New York

Garrido RA, Mahmassani HS (2000) Forecasting freight transportation demand with the space-time multinomial probit model. Transportation Research B 34: 403–418

Glass GV (1976) Primary, secondary, and meta-analysis of research. Educational Research 5: 3–8

Goodwin PB (1974) Generalized time and the problem of equity in transport studies, Transportation 3: 1–24

Hagerstrand T (1970) What about people in regional science? Papers of the Regional Science Association 24: 7–21

Harker PT, Friesz TL (1986) A simultaneous freight network equilibrium model. Congressus Numerantium 20: 365–402

Holguín-Veras J, Thorson E (2003) Modeling commercial vehicle empty trips with a first order trip chain model. Transportation Research B 37: 129–148

Hunter JE, Schmidt FL (1990) Methods of meta-analysis. Sage Publications, London

Jones P, Koppelman F, Orfeuil JP (1990) Activity analysis: state-of-the-art and future directions. In: Jones P (ed) Developments in dynamic and activity-based approaches to travel analysis. Avebury, Aldershot

Kitamura R (1988) An evaluation of activity-based travel analysis. Transportation 15: 9–34

Kresge DT, Roberts PO (1971) Techniques of transportation planning: systems analysis and simulation models. Brookings Institution, Washington, D.C.

Loomis JB (1992) The evolution of a more rigorous approach to benefit transfer: benefit function transfer. Water Resources. Research 28: 701–705

Mahmassani HS, Jayakrishman R, Hermand R (1990) Network traffic flow theory: microscopic simulation experiments on a super computer. Transportation Research A 24: 149–162

McFadden D (2001) Economic choices. American Economic Review 91: 351–379

McKinnon A, Button KJ, Nijkamp P (eds) (2002) Transport logistics. Edward Elgar, Cheltenham Northampton

McNally MG (2000) The four step model. In: Hensher DA, Button KJ (eds) Handbook of transport modelling. Pergamon, Oxford

Meyburg A, Stopher PR (1974) A framework for the analysis of demand of urban goods movements. Transportation Research Record 496: 68–79

Ogden KW (1992) Urban goods movement – a guide to policy and planning. Ashgate, Aldershot

Oum TH (1979) A cross sectional study of freight demand and rail-truck competition in Canada. Bell Journal of Economics 10: 463–482

Oum TH, Waters WG, Young JS (1992) A survey of recent estimates of price elasticities of demand and recent empirical estimates: an interpretive essay. Journal of Transport Economics and Policy 26: 139–154

Parsons GR, Kealy MJ (1994) Benefits transfer in a random utility model of recreation. Water Resources Research 30: 2477–2484

Pendyala RM, Shankar VN, McCullough RG (2000) Freight travel demand modeling: synthesis of approaches and development of a framework. Transportation Research Record 1725: 9–16

Quandt RE, Baumol WJ (1966) The demand for abstract transport modes, theory and measurement. Journal of Regional Science 6: 13–26

Schipper Y (1999) Market structure and environmental costs in aviation: a welfare analysis of European air transport reform. Ph.D. thesis, Free University of Amsterdam

Smith VK, Kaoru Y (1990) Signals or noise – explaining variation in recreation benefit estimates. American Journal of Agricultural Economics 72: 419–433

Taniguchi E, Thompson RG, Yamada T (1999) Modelling city logistics. In: Taniguchi E, Thompson RG (eds) City logistics vol. 1. Institute for City Logistics, Kyoto

Tavasszy LA, Ruijgrok CJ, Thissen MKJPM (2003) Emerging logistics networks: implications for transport systems and policy, growth and change 34: 456–472

Transportation Research Board (2003) Freight capacity for the 21st century. TRB, Washington, D.C.

Vanek FM (2001) Analysis of the potential for spatial redistribution of freight using mathematical programming. European Journal of Operational Research 131: 62–77

8 Dynamic Game-Theoretic Models of Urban Freight: Formulation and Solution Approach

Terry L. Friesz[1] and Jose Holguín-Veras[2]

[1] The Pennsylvania State University, University Park, Pennsylvania, USA
[2] Rensselaer Polytechnic Institute, Troy, New York, USA

8.1 Introduction

Friesz et al. (1998) and Friesz (2001) have argued that, although during the past 20 years very significant progress has occurred in the understanding and modelling of inter-city freight networks, correspondingly significant advances in the understanding and modelling of urban freight movements have not yet occurred. This point of view is supported by Holguin-Veras (2000) and Holguin-Veras and Thorson (2003a) who show by empirical studies and simulation that there is much room to further improve the prediction and management of urban freight flows. These authors confirm that a deeper understanding of the fundamental processes driving urban freight supply and demand is required in order for urban freight transportation planning based on mathematical models and quantitative methods to become a widely accepted and widely practiced component of the urban transportation planning process.

Consideration of freight transportation in transportation planning and management is important for many reasons. On the positive side, an efficient freight transportation system is a *sine equa* non condition for economic competitiveness. On the negative side, there is increasing community pressure to ameliorate the negative externalities associated with freight transportation. As a result of the combined pressures of economic globalization, user expectations and community concerns, the freight transportation systems of the 21st Century will be expected to cover a larger geographic area, be more responsive to user needs and expectations, reduce the externalities of truck traffic, and do all of this in a context wherein the provision of additional freight infrastructure will be difficult and expensive. Simply put, the urban freight transportation system will have to do more with less. This immense challenge adds pressure to agencies that have to balance the conflicting objectives of multiple stakeholders. This is compounded by the complexity of freight movements and the lack of satisfactory urban freight modelling methodologies.

Concurrently, it is now widely recognized that electronic commerce (e-commerce), intelligent transportation systems and information technology provide a medium for the conveyance of information to enhance the efficiency of freight systems. There is anecdotal evidence suggesting that e-commerce and innovations in information technology have resulted in significant increases in the magnitude of urban freight flows as well as changes in the temporal fluctuations and spatial distribution of such flows. In particular, if telecommuting rates for passengers continue to rise in lock-step with e-commerce orders that generate more depot-to-home urban goods movements, the social costs of congestion generated by urban freight flows can only rise. As congestion costs rise, the potential deleterious impact on regional and national economic growth of each increment in urban goods flows must also rise. Adding to this the pervasive desire of traditional urban retailers to have narrow delivery windows for merchandise and of light manufacturers to have just-in-time delivery of factor inputs, so that both may control their inventory costs, one is led to the recognition that even very modest increases in the efficiency of urban goods movements will bring significant positive economic benefits to metropolitan areas with high levels of road network congestion.

Moreover, the Internet and electronic commerce associated with it can be both a blessing and a curse for urban freight efficiency. That is, the Internet and e-commerce generate more urban freight flows while holding the potential to reduce commuting and shopping trips. These considerations cannot be addressed within the framework of existing theories and models of freight systems, but instead require a new family of models that are explicitly dynamic and which directly treat the influence of the Internet and e-commerce.

In fact there are several factors that make urban goods movements extremely complex and the modelling of them very challenging; these include:

1. the undeniable dynamic nature of urban goods flows involving multiple time scales, since they vary by the season, week and day as well as the time of day;
2. the complex interactions among agents (e.g., shippers, receivers, carriers, freight forwarders) that take place in the context of commercially sensitive business transactions – not fully observable by planners and modellers – that determine urban goods flows;
3. the extremely diverse commodities (ranging from low value commodities such as waste to high value commodities like computer chips that are worth $1 million per ton) and the associated wide spectrum of opportunity costs which mandates diverse levels of service;
4. the wide array of metrics used to quantify urban freight traffic, most notably vehicle-trips, tonnage, volume and value;
5. the undeniable stochastic nature of urban goods movements arising out of the many unobservable and unknowable influences that impact goods traffic, including traffic incidents, weather, consumer utility, energy prices, and other fluctuations that may change supply, demand or the economic characteristics of the goods;
6. the lack of centralized control due to the presence of many decision agents and of economic competition taking the form of games in those markets that are generating demands for goods movements; and
7. the role that new technological innovations in transport and information technology may have on urban goods.

As game theory is concerned with the modelling of strategic interactions (that is, competition, coordination, collaboration and collusion) among agents, as well as broad classes of tactical decisions by individual agents active within the decision environment (market) of interest, it is a paradigm naturally suited to the study of urban freight network markets, which have the features cited immediately above. Consequently, we take the view in this paper that urban freight is best modelled using the perspective of game theory.

In fact most of the prior work on large scale predictive freight network models is based on static game theory (Friesz and Harker 1985). Because urban freight flows, as pointed out above, vary by season, week, day and time of day, they are intrinsically dynamic and models based on static game theory simply cannot be used. Moreover, because of the multiple time scales that characterize urban goods movements, recent work on dynamic network models of urban automobile traffic are of scant use since most of the latter involve only a single time scale (within-day) and none involve more than two time sales (within-day and day-to-day). As a consequence, the main systems modelling tool we advocate using the theory of differential games that directly treats the multiple time scales and stochasticity typical of urban freight flows. The models we describe may be divided into two main categories: (1) descriptive models that predict future flow patterns, freight prices and the like, and (2) prescriptive models that directly assist individual firms in constructing their transportation and physical distribution plans in light of the likely future states of the urban freight network in which they are immersed.

Urban freight models must also be computationally tractable. However, since our focus in this paper is primarily on strategy and general tactical rules there is no need for the models we present to be solved in real or near-real time. Instead we describe how well-known computational methods from applied mathematics may be used for computations.

8.2 Background

In order to provide a historical perspective for the models we present subsequently in this paper, it is useful to succinctly review the relevant portions of the five main bodies of antecedent literature: (1) lessons from intercity freight modelling, (2) complexity urban freight systems, (3) nature of urban demand for finished and semi-finished goods, (4) the interdependence of shippers and carriers, and (5) dynamic game theory and differential variational inequalities.

8.2.1 Lessons Learned from Intercity Freight Modelling

There has been considerable research to develop predictive inter-city freight models; see Friesz and Harker (1985), Crainic and Laporte (1997) and Friesz (2002) for comprehensive reviews of that literature. For our purposes in this proposal it is enough to highlight some of the lessons learned from inter-city freight modelling that are likely to be transferable to the study of urban freight movements. In particular, a list of lessons learned from inter-city modelling can be gleaned from three of the most representative static inter-city freight models: the Freight Network Equilibrium Model (FNEM), the model known as Freight Mathematical Program with Equilibrium Constraints (FMPEC), and the Generalized Spatial Price Equilibrium Model (GSPEM). Friesz et al. (1986) developed FNEM; the FMPEC was developed jointly by Friesz and Harker (1982), while GSPEM was developed by Harker and Friesz (1986a, 1986b). All three models are descriptive/predictive in nature and static. The list is:

1. Predictive freight network flow models must represent both shipper and carrier decision agents, in contrast to automobile flow network flow models that consider only a single category of agents (drivers).
2. The shippers' conceptual model of the freight network is substantially simpler than the actual network employed by carriers in meeting shippers' demands for freight services; specifically, shippers tend to only "see" origins (depots), end destinations and key transhipments nodes when choosing a carrier.
3. Consistency of assigned freight transportation network flows and shipment costs that generate the demand for freight transportation services make it necessary that shipper and carrier decisions be modelled simultaneously.
4. The demand for freight transportation services is a derived demand that devolves from spatially separated production and consumption activities served by a freight network.
5. In a steady state, spatially separated production and consumption activities served by a freight network may be modelled via either notions of generalized spatial price network equilibrium or spatial computable general equilibrium (where the latter includes multi-regional input-output models).
6. Fully general shipper-carrier freight network equilibrium models are intrinsically non-convex due to: (a) their potentially hierarchical structure leading to so-called mathematical programs with equilibrium constraints (Luo et al. 1996); and (b) the presence of so-called "U-shaped" generalized cost functions that reflect the transition from economies of scale and scope to diseconomies of scale and scope in distinct flow regimes.
7. Practical predictive equilibrium freight flow models require effective algorithms. This means that one must: (a) make modelling assumptions that avoid the aforementioned non-convexities, (b) be satisfied with non-unique equilibria, or (c) use computational intelligence to find those equilibria that provide the highest social welfare realizing that such solutions cannot be identified with probability one.

8.2.2 Complexity of Urban Freight Systems

The most significant methodological hurdle to the effective inclusion of freight transportation in the transportation modelling process is the lack of a fundamental understanding of the mechanisms of freight demand and supply. This situation is the result of the inherent complexity of freight processes, and of the fact that most modelling methodologies have been developed for passenger trips, not freight trips. In some cases, adaptation of passenger models has led to unreasonably simplistic urban freight models, such as estimating freight traffic as a function of the passenger car traffic. The use of such simplistic approaches may be an acceptable solution for small urban areas, where the amount of commercial vehicle traffic is of no major significance, but it is completely inadequate for major metropolitan areas, e.g., New York City, where the amount of truck traffic is of considerable importance. In such a situation, policy-sensitive freight demand models are required to examine the impact of freight specific policies upon commercial vehicle traffic. However, the development of policy-sensitive freight demand models faces significant hurdles which are a consequence of the inherent complexity of the mechanisms driving freight demand.

Although the complexity of freight demand has been discussed elsewhere (e.g., Holguín-Veras and Thorson 2000; Ogden 1992), we need to mention here the multi-dimensional character of freight movements. Contrary to passenger transportation, in which there is often only a single type of agent creating transportation demand, (the passenger/driver), freight transportation demand can be defined and measured according to multiple dimensions (e.g., value, volume, weight, and vehicle-trips). This multi-dimensionality of freight demand has given rise to two major modelling perspectives: commodity-based and trip-based modelling. However, these points of view are unable to provide a full depiction of freight movements. On the one hand, commodity-based models, which are able to capture the economic characteristics of cargoes, are unable to model empty trips – which require complementary models of empty trips (Holguín-Veras and Thorson 2003a). On the other hand, vehicle-trip models, which are able to consider both loaded and empty trips, are not able to take into account the cargoes' economic characteristics (Holguín-Veras and Thorson 2000). As shown in Holguín-Veras and Thorson (2000) these approaches produce significantly different estimates of truck traffic. Presently, due to strong empirical and theoretical evidence (Holguín-Veras 2002; Holguín-Veras and Jara-Díaz 1999) supporting the explicit consideration of the commodity types, it is presently widely believed that commodity-based formulations are the preferred modelling paradigm.

However, the use of commodity-based models are not naturally suited to the incorporation of empty trips – a fundamental characteristic of all freight systems. This limitation has been partially overcome by estimating empty trips from the commodity flows. Holguín-Veras and Thorson (2003b) developed formulations based on a simplified trip chaining model that estimates the number of commercial vehicle empty trips as a function of the commodity flow matrices which in essence act as a proxy for the routing decisions made by commercial vehicle operators. Such formulations have been successful in approximating empty trips made associated with both urban and intercity freight flows.

The paragraph above highlights a dilemma: if we use vehicle-trip models we cannot take into account the economic characteristics of the cargoes, and if we use commodity-based models we fail to model empty trips (unless we employ complementary empty trip models that, in turn, create statistical inefficiencies). This dilemma arises because, by focusing on either commodities or trips, the analysis takes into account only one dimension of freight movements: the user side, if commodity-based models are used; or the result of logistic decisions, if vehicle-trip based models are used. Attempting to overcome these limitations, provides the rationale for Thorson's Integrative Freight Market Simulation (IFMS). The IFMS provides an approximation of the freight related decision processes that take place in real life, involving producers, consumers, carriers and government agencies (as in Harker and Friesz 1986a). The IFMS relies on a set of simplifying assumptions: (a) among the potential set of players, the main focus is on producers, consumers, carriers, and a traffic management centre that provides real time traffic information and exercises traffic control; (b) the quantities of goods produced and consumed in the different transportation analysis zones are constant and estimated exogenously (that is, the relevant spatial price equilibrium is partial rather than general); and (c) the locations and the numbers of vehicles owned and operated by the different carriers are known. The IFMS estimates the trips made by freight transportation providers in the study area assuming that the problem could be decomposed into two sub-problems. The first sub-problem is the estimation of the amount of transportation service that maximize profits in a context of economic equilibrium. The second sub-problem is the estimation of routing patterns consistent with both the user equilibrium condition and the rest of the system constraints. The models proposed in this paper may be viewed as dynamic games that extend the IFMS framework to non-steady state settings using more rigorous mathematics.

8.2.3 Nature of Urban Demand for Finished and Semi-finished Goods

A key consideration in constructing an urban freight model is whether to endogenise determination of the spatial distribution of demand for finished and semi-finished goods (as in linked I-O and commodity-flow models). Doing so will give the desired urban freight model more of a general-equilibrium orientation. The real issue in this regard is whether to strive for a true general equilibrium or something that is more computationally tractable. This trade-off is forced on the urban freight model builder because of the network detail needed to accurately describe routing choices in an urban setting. We argue that the best trade-off possible with present computational tools is to determine the demand for finished and semi-finished goods with only crude information regarding freight rates and delivery time windows. This is then turned into detailed carrier plans by the carriers themselves, who are assumed to be efficient cost minimisers or profit maximisers. This perspective, while not a true general equilibrium, makes freight rates, service options and goods prices implicitly interdependent and allows all manner of sensitivity analyses.

8.2.4 The Interdependence of Shippers and Carriers

It is transparent that the shippers and carriers of urban freight are interdependent. This interdependence can arise for many reasons. For example, one may argue that there is a high percentage of freight in transit between cities made up of semi-finished goods that are being shuttled between firms' own far flung establishments, at which different processing operations are performed. Whatever its genesis, such interdependence has only one theoretical solution: the simultaneous determination of shipper and carrier actions. Yet that simultaneity has serious computational impacts. Until it is possible to assess the degree of inaccuracy that arises from treating shippers and carriers as sequential decision-makers, we argue that a sequential model of their interaction is dictated by computational considerations alone. There is also reason to argue that many shipper-carrier decisions are in fact sequential. Moreover, when the same firm or industry acts as both shipper and carrier at different spatio-temporal stages of its operations – as in the example cited above – it is quite plausible to invoke the notion of sub-game perfectness that is based on the view that the shippers and carriers will have evolved a relationship over time that assures sequential decomposition is identical to simultaneous play of a grand Cournot-Nash-Bertrand game.

8.2.5 Dynamic Game Theory and Differential Variational Inequalities

We are of the view that urban freight systems are seldom if ever in any kind of stationary equilibrium. We take this perspective because urban freight vehicles are sometimes demand responsive, have flexibility in routing and departure time choices, do not necessarily repeat delivery schedules with a predetermined periodicity, and are impacted by congestion-causing traffic incidents. As a consequence, a dynamic modelling framework that recognizes the equilibrium tending nature of freight flows which are interrupted by punctuated events that increase congestion is required. Moreover, this modelling framework must recognize that urban freight movements are frequently part of combined production-distribution policies by firms engaged in various forms of economic competition and that the urban freight vehicles also are engaged in non-cooperative competition with passenger traffic for available routes. These aspects of urban freight make it necessary to use non-equilibrium dynamic game-theoretic models to describe urban freight flows. Such a mathematical description of urban freight flows is – as commented on previously – a prerequisite to decision support calculations to develop transportation/distribution plans for individual firms.

The main body of technical literature relevant to game-theoretic disequilibria and moving equilibria is that pertaining to so-called differential games, a field of inquiry widely held to have been originated by Isaacs (1965). Although a rather substantial body of literature known as dynamic game theory has evolved from the work of Isaacs (1965), that literature continues to be strongly influenced by the emphasis of Isaacs on the relationship of such games to dynamic programming and to the Hamilton-Jacobi-Bellman partial differential equation. A consequence of this classical point of view is that full use of the mathematical apparatus of variational inequalities (VIs), discovered originally in the context of certain free boundary value problems in mathematical physics, has not occurred in the study of dynamic games. By contrast, in the last fifteen years, VIs have become the formalism of choice for applied game theorists and computational economists solving various static equilibrium models of competition. The "hole" in the dynamic game theory literature owing to this failure to fully exploit the VI perspective is significant, for VIs substantially simplify the study of existence and uniqueness. A VI perspective for infinite dimensional dynamic games also leads directly to function space equivalents of the standard finite dimensional algorithmic philosophies.

Non-cooperative dynamic competition among urban freight agents – especially shippers and carriers – modelling, may be placed in the form of a differential variational inequality wherein each individual agent (any firm or individual that generates or services an urban freight flow) develops for itself a distribution plan that is based on current and future knowledge of non-own flow patterns. Each such agent is, therefore, described by an optimal control problem for which the control variables are its distribution plan; this optimal control problem is constrained by dynamics that describe how the agent's distribution plan alters the flow on a network. The individual agent's optimal control problem may also have as control variables specific supply chain and production decisions that are within the purview of that agent, as discussed by Friesz (2002), Friesz et al. (2002), Kachani and Perakis (2002a) and Kachani and Perakis (2002b) who have studied flow models of distribution networks supply chains. Under the Cournot-Nash-Bertrand assumption that the agents are non-cooperative, the optimal control problems for individual agents may be combined to obtain a single differential variational inequality. This variational inequality may be made stochastic to describe the unobservable shipper and carrier behaviours. We do not explore such an extension in this paper.

Reduction of the problem of urban freight flow prediction to a variational inequality is more than a mathematical curiosity. Rather, by placing the dynamic gaming behaviour that underlies urban freight flows in the form of a variational inequality, we make available a substantial arsenal of mathematical and computational tools.

8.3 Obtaining a Dynamic Urban Freight Trip Table

We develop a dynamic urban freight model wherein demands for freight services are obtained by solving a model of oligopolistic network competition that describes the spatial competition of retailers in an urban setting. The oligopolistic firms of interest, embedded in a network economy, are in Cournot-Nash oligopolistic game theoretic competition according to dynamics that describe the trajectories of inventories/backorders and correspond to flow conservation for each firm at each node of the network of interest. The oligopolistic firms, acting as shippers, compete as price takers in the market for physical distribution services to distribute their merchandise to retail outlets within a dense urban environment character-ized by congestion. These firms view the market for physical distribution services as perfectly competitive. The time scale we consider is neither short nor long, but rather of sufficient length to allow output and shipping pattern adjustments but not long enough for firms to re-locate or enter or leave the network economy.

We employ the notation used in Miller, Friesz and Tobin (1996), augmented to handle temporal considerations. In particular, time is denoted by the scalar $t \in \mathfrak{R}_+^1$ and the analysis horizon is at $t_1 \in \mathfrak{R}_{++}^1$ so that $t \in [t_0, t_1] \subset \mathfrak{R}_+^1$. There are several sets important to articulating a model of oligopolistic competition on a network; these are as follow: F for firms, A for directed arcs, N for nodes and W for origin-destination (OD) pairs. Subsets of these sets are formed as is meaningful by using the subscript f for a specific firm, i for a specific node, and w for a specific OD pair.

Each firm controls production output rates q^f, allocation of output to meet demand c^f and shipping pattern s^f. Inventories I^f are state variables deter-mined by the controls. In particular, the c^f, q^f and s^f constitute concatenations of the following vectors:

$$c \in (L^2[t_0, t_1])^{|N| \times |F|}$$

$$q \in (L^2[t_0, t_1])^{|N| \times |F|}$$

$$s \in (L^2[t_0, t_1])^{|W| \times |F|}$$

$$I(c, q, s) : (L^2[t_0, t_1])^{|N| \times |F|} \times (L^2[t_0, t_1])^{|N| \times |F|} \times (L^2[t_0, t_1])^{|W| \times |F|}$$

$$\rightarrow (H^1[t_0, t_1])^{|N| \times |F|}$$

where $L^2[t_0, t_1]$ is the space of square-integrable functions and $H^1[t_0, t_1]$ is a Sobolev space for the real interval $[t_0, t_1] \in \mathfrak{R}_+^1$.

Each firm has an objective of maximizing net profit expressed as revenue less cost and taking the form of an operator acting on allocations of output to meet demands, production rates and shipment patterns. For each $f \in F$, net profit is

$$\vartheta_f(c^f, q^f, s^f; c^{-f}, q^{-f}) = \int_{t_0}^{t_1} e^{-\rho t} \left\{ \sum_{i \in N} \pi_i \left(\sum_{g \in F} c_i^g, t \right) c_i^f - \sum_{i \in N_f} V_i^f(q, t) \right.$$

$$\left. - \sum_{w \in W_f} r_w(t) s_w^f - \sum_{i \in N} \psi_i^f(I_i^f, t) \right\} dt$$

(8.1)

where $\rho \in \Re^1_{++}$ is a constant nominal rate of discount, $r_w \in \Re^1_{++}$ is the freight rate (tariff) charged per unit of flow s_w for OD pair $w \in W_f$, ψ^f_i is firm f's inventory cost at node i, and I^f_i is the inventory/backorder of firm f at node i. In Eq. (8.1), c^f_i is the allocation of the output of firm $f \in F$ at node $i \in N$ to consumption at that node. Our formulation is in terms of flows so we employ the inverse demand functions $\pi_i(c_i, t)$ where

$$c_i = \sum_{g \in F} c^g_i$$

is the total allocation of output to consumption for node i. Furthermore q^f_i is the output of firm $f \in F$ at node $i \in N$. Also $V^f_i(q, t)$ is the variable cost of production for firm $f \in F$ at node $i \in N$. Note that $\vartheta_f(c^f, q^f, s^f; c^{-f}, q^{-f})$ is a functional that is completely determined by the controls c^f, q^f and s^f when non-own allocations to demand

$$c^{-f} \equiv (c^{f'} : f' \neq f)$$

$$q^{-f} \equiv (q^{f'} : f' \neq f)$$

are taken as exogenous data by firm f. The first term of the functional $\vartheta_f(c^f, q^f, s^f; c^{-f}, q^{-f})$ in Eq. (8.1) is the firm's revenue; the second term is the firm's cost of production; the third term is the firm's shipping costs; and the last term is the firm's inventory or holding cost.

We also impose the terminal time constraints

$$I^f_i(t_1) = 0 \forall f \in F, i \in N_f \qquad (8.2)$$

All consumption, production and shipping variables are non-negative and bounded from above; that is

$$C^f \geq c^f \geq 0 \qquad (8.3)$$

$$Q^f \geq q^f \geq 0 \qquad (8.4)$$

$$S^f \geq s^f \geq 0 \qquad (8.5)$$

where

$$C^f \in \Re_{++}^{|F|}$$

$$Q^f \in \Re_{++}^{|F|}$$

$$S^f \in \Re_{++}^{|W_f|}$$

Constraints (8.3–5) are recognized as pure control constraints, while (8.2) are pure state space constraints. Naturally

$$\Omega_f = \left\{ (c^f, q^f s^f) : (8.3-5) \right\}$$

is the set of feasible controls.

Firm f solves an optimal control problem to determine its production q^f, allocation of production to meet demand c^f, and shipping pattern s^f – thereby also determining inventory I^f via dynamics we articulate momentarily – by maximizing its profit functional $\vartheta_f(c^f, q^f, s^f; c^{-f}, q^{-f})$ subject to inventory dynamics expressed as flow balance equations and pertinent production and inventory constraints. The inventory dynamics for firm $f \in F$, expressing simple flow conservation, obey

$$\frac{dI_i^f}{dt} = q_i^f + \sum_{w \in W_i^d} s_w^f - \sum_{w \in W_i^o} s_w^f - c_i^f \, \forall i \in N_f \tag{8.6}$$

$$I_i^f(t_0) = K_i^f \, \forall i \in N_f \tag{8.7}$$

where $K_i^f \in \Re_{++}^1$ is exogenous, while W_i^d is the set of OD pairs with destination node i and W_i^o is the set of OD pairs with origin node i. Consequently

$$I(c, q, s) = \arg \left\{ \frac{dI_i^f}{dt} = q_i^f + \sum_{w \in W_i^d} s_w^f - \sum_{w \in W_i^o} s_w^f - c_i^f, \right.$$
$$\left. I_i^f(t_0) = K_i^f, I_i^f(t_1) = 0, \forall f \in F, i \in N_f \right\}$$

where we implicitly assume that the dynamics have solutions for all feasible controls.

With the preceding development, we note that firm f's problem is: with the c^{-f} and q^{-f} as exogenous inputs, compute c^f, q^f and s^f (thereby finding I^f) in order to solve the following extremal problem:

$$
\left.
\begin{aligned}
& \max \vartheta_f(c^f, q^f, s^f; c^{-f}, q^{-f}) \\
& \text{subject to} \quad (c^f, q^f, s^f) \in \Omega_f
\end{aligned}
\right\} \forall f \in F
\tag{8.8}
$$

where

$$
\Omega_f = \left\{ (c^f, q^f s^f) : (8.2), (8.3), (8.4), (8.5) \text{hold} \right\}
$$

also for all $f \in F$. That is, each firm is a Cournot-Nash agent that knows and employs the current instantaneous values of the decision variables of other firms to make its own non-cooperative decisions. Note that Eq. (8.8) defines a Cournot-Nash game expressed as a set of coupled optimal control problems, one for each firm $f \in F$. As demonstrated formally by Friesz et al. (2003), the following differential variational inequality has solutions that are Cournot-Nash equilibria for the above game:

$$
\text{find } (c^{f*}, q^{f*}, s^{f*}) \in \Omega \text{ such that}
$$

$$
0 \geq \sum_{f \in F} \int_0^{t_1} \left[\sum_{i \in N_f} \frac{\partial \Phi_f^*}{\partial c_i^f} (c_i^f - c_i^{f*}) + \sum_{i \in N_f} \frac{\partial \Phi_f^*}{\partial q_i^f} (q_i^f - q_i^{f*}) \right.
$$

$$
\left. + \sum_{w \in W_f} \frac{\partial \Phi_f^*}{\partial s_w^f} (s_w^f - s_w^{f*}) \right] dt
\tag{8.9}
$$

$$
\text{for all } (c, q, s) \in \Omega
$$

where

$$
\Phi_f(c^f, q^f, s^f, I^f; c^{-f}, q^{-f}; t) = e^{-\rho t} \left\{ \sum_{i \in N} \pi_i \left(\sum_{g \in F} c_i^g, t \right) c_i^f \right.
$$

$$
- \sum_{i \in N_f} V_i^f(q, t) - \sum_{w \in W_f} r_w(t) s_w^f
\tag{8.10}
$$

$$
\left. - \sum_{i \in N} \psi_i^f (I_i^f(c, q, s), t) \right\}
$$

$$\Phi_f^* = \Phi_f(c^{f*}, q^{f*}, s^{f*}, I^{f*}; c^{-f*}, q^{-f*}; t) \tag{8.11}$$

$$\Omega = \prod_{f \in F} \Omega_f \tag{8.12}$$

The above variational inequality is a convenient way of expressing dynamic oligopolistic network competition. Solutions of this variational inequality provide a dynamic "trip table" for urban freight demand for the time interval $[t_0, t_1]$:

$$S^1(t) = \left[s_w^f(t)\right]_{w \in W_f}^{f \in F} \tag{8.13}$$

Clearly the model may be exercised for each of the time periods $[t_{l-1}, t_l]$ for $l = 1, 2, ..., n$ that comprise a larger time interval of interest $[0, t_n]$ and in so doing generate period-specific trip tables

$$S^l(t) = \left[s_w^{fl}(t)\right]_{w \in W_f}^{f \in F}$$

8.4 A Dynamic Carriers' Model for Urban Freight

The demand information obtained above may, as a first approximation, be used as input to a carriers' model to develop a more detailed model of freight flows within an urban setting, including coarse routing and distribution schedules. An essential question that must be answered before building the carriers' model is whether the carriers' flows will be voluminous enough to impact congestion or if carriers may be thought of as reacting to congestion created by passenger vehicles (automobiles) on urban streets. As our intent is to construct a preliminary model that suggests the general form a more advanced and theoretically rigorous model would take, we shall assume carriers are deterministically congestion-reactive. We will subsequently add a stochastic error to account for carriers' errors in assessing both own congestion and non-own congestion.

The set of freight carriers is K, and each freight carrier $k \in K$ controls its own efforts to secure a share of the shippers' demands for freight services y^{kl} which is a concatenation of the vectors

$$y^l \in (L^2[t_{l-1}, t])^{|W| \times |F| \times |K|}$$

We also have need to define the vector

$$y^{-kl} \equiv (y^{k'l} : k' \neq k)$$

which is recognized as non-own freight services relative to carrier k.

Following the approach developed in Friesz et al. (1986) for intercity freight flow predictions, we assume carriers use their extensive knowledge of the freight network (in this case the urban street network) in their decision making and competition with other carriers. In particular, we view the freight companies as Cournot-Nash oligopolistic competitors who develop strategies that non-cooperatively maximize their individual profits in meeting demand that is fixed for each individual time interval. In particular freight carrier k seeks to maximize its total cost on the time interval $[t_{l-1}, t_l]$ where $l = 1, 2, ..., n$, a circumstance we describe by

$$J^{kl}(y^{kl}; y^{-kl}) = \int_{t_{l-1}}^{t_l} e^{-\rho t} \left\{ \sum_{f \in F} \sum_{w \in W_f} \zeta_w^f \left(\sum_{g \in F} \sum_{i \in K} \sum_{v \in W_f} y_v^{gil}, t \right) y_w^{fkl} \right.$$

$$\left. - \sum_{k \in K} Z_c(y^{kl}, t) \right\} dt \qquad (8.14)$$

$$= \int_{t_{l-1}}^{t_l} e^{-\rho t} \Psi_{kl}(y^{kl}; y^{-kl}; t) dt$$

where

$$\Psi_{kl}(y^{kl}; y^{-kl}; t) = e^{-\rho t} \left\{ \sum_{f \in F} \sum_{w \in W_f} \zeta_w^f \left(\sum_{g \in F} \sum_{i \in K} \sum_{v \in W_f} y_v^{gil}, t \right) y_w^{fkl} - \sum_{k \in K} Z_c(y^{kl}, t) \right\}$$

Also $\zeta_w^f(.,.)$ is the inverse demand function of producer $f \in F$ for freight services between OD pair $w \in W_f$, while y_w^{fkl} is the kth carrier's share of the producer f demand for freight services between OD pair v during period $[t_{l-1}, t_l]$. Furthermore, $Z_c(.,.)$ is the total cost function for carrier $k \in K$.

The principal constraints are those which reconcile carrier OD flows with the freight OD trip tables obtained from the shippers' model; that is:

$$s_w^{fl} = \sum_{k \in K} y_w^{fkl} \tag{8.15}$$

for all $f \in F$, $w \in W_f$ and $l = 1,2,...,n$

There are, of course, also non-negativity constraints on the carrier OD flows:

$$y_w^{fkl} \geq 0 \text{ for all } k \in K, \ f \in F \ w \in W_f \text{ and } l = 1,2,...,n \tag{8.16}$$

In light of the above development, we note that carrier k's problem is: with the y^{-kl} as exogenous inputs, compute y^{kl} in order to solve the following extremal problem:

$$\left. \begin{array}{l} \max J^{kl} \left(y^{kl} ; y^{-kl} \right) \\ \text{subject to} \quad y^{kl} \in \Lambda_{kl} \end{array} \right\} \forall k \in K \text{ and } l = 1,2,...,n \tag{8.17}$$

where

$$\Lambda_{kl} = \left\{ y^{kl} : (8.15), (8.16) \text{hold} \right\}$$

also for all $f \in F$. Note that each problem of the type (8.17) is an infinite dimensional mathematical program rather than an optimal control problem.

As with the shippers' model, we may create a variational inequality for intercarrier non-cooperative competition. In fact the following differential variational inequality has solutions that are Cournot-Nash equilibria for the carriers' game described above:

find $y^{l*} \in \Lambda_l$ such that

$$\sum_{f \in F} \int_{l-1}^{l} \frac{\partial \Psi_{kl}^{*}}{\partial y_w^{fkl}} (y_w^{fkl} - y_w^{fkl*}) \geq 0 \tag{8.18}$$

for all $y^l \in \Lambda_l = \prod_{k \in K} \Lambda_{kl}$

where

$$\Psi_{kl}^* = \Psi_{kl}(y^{kl*}; y^{-kl*}; t)$$

8.5 Post-Processing to Identify Carrier Routes

Another issue – mentioned in our introductory remarks – is that of trip-chaining behaviour by carriers. We propose to address that consideration through post processing calculations based on traditional vehicle routing models that turn the flows, coarse routing and coarse distribution schedules calculated by the carriers' model into specific tactical delivery plans. Routing models reported in the literature as well as those tested in actual applications are numerous. Such models by their very design seek trip chains that offer efficiencies to carriers.

8.6 Algorithms for Dynamic Variational Inequalities

The shippers' and the carriers' models presented here are highly amenable to computation using discrete time and finite element methods in conjunction with efficient algorithms for complementarity problems. See Facchinei and Pang (2003) for a detailed exposition of those and related algorithms.

8.7 Future Research

The models presented above must be subject to qualitative mathematical analyses to ascertain regularity conditions that assure stability, existence and uniqueness and which allow an assessment of complexity. As part of such qualitative analyses, it would be useful to explore the inter-relationships of stability, speed of return to equilibrium, network architecture, self-healing, the Braess paradox, and the general vulnerability of urban freight systems. A key consideration in this regard is the development of a chain of necessity involving these notions, with the aim of developing regularity conditions that will tell us, for example, (1) when Lagrange stability leads to self-healing, (2) when exceeding a threshold speed of return to equilibrium ensures a bound on economic losses from security breaches, (3) whether dendritic (radial) or meshed network architectures are more or less conducive to self-healing, and (5) what architectures are least prone to exhibit the network paradoxes.

Much attention must also be devoted to algorithm refinement and testing, scenario development and policy analyses. In fact we believe the following set of tasks are fundamental to a comprehensive study of urban freight models;

Task 1. Qualitative Model Formulation. Define the players, strategic variables, exogenous variables, and market types to be used in our efforts to model urban freight flows. Representative example problems involving synthetic data should be created and used to define a set of scenarios for in-depth numerical analyses.

Task 2. Formulate Constrained Dynamics. Explore: (1) dynamics based on notions of "distance" from equilibrium, (2) dynamics based on extensions of classical tatonement models wherein price changes are proportional to excess demand, (3) projective dynamics that generalize the notion of tatonement and include embedded constraints, (4) differential inclusions wherein the rates of change obey point-to-set maps, and (5) stochastic dynamics describing Wiener processes.

Task 3. Building Dynamic Game-Theoretic Network Models. By varying assumptions about the type and nature of competition and dynamic adjustment processes, formulate a family of dynamic game-theoretic descriptive models of urban freight networks. These dynamic models should ultimately include noncooperative games and games with collusion and coalition formation based on the notion of the core of a game.

Task 4. Qualitative Analysis of Models. For the models constructed in Task 3, perform stability, existence, uniqueness and complexity analyses. Also give formal mathematical definitions of stability, speed of return to equilibrium, network architecture, self-healing, the Braess paradox, and vulnerability. Create new metrics for assessing vulnerability, using various notions of stability, including permanence and speed of return to equilibrium. Explore the inter-relationships of stability, speed of return to equilibrium, network architecture, self-healing, the Braess paradox, and general vulnerability. Based on the analyses of this task, further refine and shorten the list of most promising models created in Task 4.

Task 5. Qualitative Analyses and Preliminary Testing of Algorithms. For the refined list of most promising models created in Task 4, explore the qualitative properties (in particular, convergence) and numerical performance of the five algorithmic philosophies as outlined above. Note that, based on the computational demands posed by the scenarios identified in Task 2 as well as qualitative analyses of algorithms conducted as part of this task, only a subset of these solution perspectives will be translated into fully detailed algorithms and numerically tested. Preliminary testing of the remaining most promising algorithms will be conducted.

Task 6. Larger-Scale Testing of Computational Methods and Policy Analyses. For the game-theoretic models identified in Task 3 and using available data together with the most promising algorithms, calibrate an urban freight model. Use the calibrated model to analyze policy questions of interest, including the effects of market structure (e.g., number and location of generation firms, transmission network design, demand elasticity) and urban freight market design on economic efficiency.

References

Crainic T, Laporte G (1997) Planning models for freight transportation, design and operation of civil and environmental engineering systems. In: Revelle C, McGarity A (eds) Design and operation of civil and environmental engineering systems. Wiley, New York

Facchinei F, Pang J-S (2003) Finite dimensional variational inequalities: parts I and II, Springer, Berlin Heidelberg New York

Friesz TL (2001) Strategic freight network planning models. In: Hensher D, Button K (eds) Handbook of transport modelling. Pergamon, Oxford, pp 181–195

Friesz TL (2002) Strategic modeling of supply chains in dynamic oligopolistic network competition. Working Paper, Department of Systems Engineering & Operations Research, George Mason University, Fairfax

Friesz TL, Harker PT (1982) A simultaneous freight network equilibrium model. Congressus Numerantium 36: 365–402

Friesz TL, Harker PT (1985) Freight network equilibrium: a review of the state of the art. In: Daughety AF (ed) Analytical studies in transportation economics. Cambridge University Press, New York

Friesz TL, Gottfried JA, Morlok EK (1986) A sequential shipper-carrier network model for predicting freight flows. Transportation Science 20: 80–91

Friesz TL, Suo Z, Westin L (1998) Integration of freight network and computable general equilibrium models. In: Lundquist L, Mattsson L-G, Kim TJ (eds) Network infrastructure and the urban environment. Springer, Berlin Heidelberg New York, pp 212–223

Friesz TL, Lin CC, Kydes N (2002) A Brownian network model of the returns problem in supply chain management. Working Paper, Department of Systems Engineering & Operations Research, George Mason University, Fairfax

Friesz TL, Rigdon MA, Mookherjee R (2003) Self-regulating variational inequalities and dynamic oligopolistic network competition. Preprint, Department of Industrial and Manufacturing Engineering, The Pennsylvania State University, State College

Harker PT, Friesz TL (1986a) Prediction of intercity freight flows, I: theory. Transportation Research 20B: 139–153

Harker PT, Friesz TL (1986b) Prediction of intercity freight flows, II: mathematical formulations. Transportation Research 20B: 155–174

Holguín-Veras J (2000) A framework for an integrative freight market simulation. In: IEEE 3rd Annual Intelligent Transportation Systems Conference ITSC-2000, Dearborn Michigan October 2000, pp 476–481

Holguín-Veras J (2002) Revealed preference analysis of the commercial vehicle choice process. Journal of Transportation Engineering 128: 336–346

Holguín-Veras J, Jara-Díaz S (1999) Optimal space allocation and pricing for priority service at container ports. Transportation Research Part B 33: 81–106

Holguín-Veras J, Thorson E (2000) An investigation of the relationships between the trip length distributions in commodity-based and trip-based freight demand modelling. Transportation Research Record 1707, September, pp 37–48

Holguín-Veras J, Thorson E (2003a) Modeling commercial vehicle empty trips with a first order trip chain model. Transportation Research Part B 37: 129–148

Holguín-Veras J, Thorson E (2003b) Practical implications of modeling commercial vehicle empty trips. Transportation Research Record 1833: 87–94

Isaacs R (1965) Differential games, 1st edn. Wiley, New York

Kachani S, Perakis G (2002a) A fluid model of dynamic pricing and inventory management for make to stock manufacturing systems. Pre-print, Sloan School MIT, August

Kachani S, Perakis G (2002b) Fluid dynamics models and their application in transportation and pricing. Pre-print, Sloan School MIT, September

Luo ZQ, Pang J-S, Ralph D (1996) Mathematical programs with equilibrium constraints. Cambridge University Press, New York

Miller T, Friesz TL, Tobin RL (1996) Equilibrium facility location on networks. Springer, Berlin Heidelberg New York, pp 242

Ogden KW (1992) Urban goods movement. Ashgate, Aldershot

9 A Multi-Criteria Methodology for Stated Preferences Among Freight Transport Alternatives

Michel Beuthe[1], Christophe Bouffioux[1], Jan De Maeyer[2], Giovanna Santamaria[3], Marie Vandresse[3], Els Vandaele[4] and Frank Witlox[4]

[1] Catholic University of Mons, Mons, Belgium
[2] University of Antwerp, Antwerp, Belgium
[3] University of Louvain, Louvain, Belgium
[4] Ghent University, Ghent, Belgium

9.1 Introduction[1]

This paper presents a multi-criteria analysis of stated preference data, an approach we are experimenting to assess the relative importance of quality attributes in freight transportation, i.e. reliability, frequency, absence of losses, carrier's flexibility, and transport time. The overall objective is to better understand what determines the choice of a particular freight transport solution and/or mode. Given the continuous growth of freight transport, and the increasing congestion of roads and pollution, policy makers are attempting to promote a switch from trucking to other modes like inland waterways, short-sea shipping and rail, including combinations of these modes. Thus, it is particularly important to analyse how that can be organised and promoted given the determinants of transport mode choice.

Some useful information is available about freight transport price direct- and cross-elasticities, in Abdelwahab (1998), NEI (1999) and Beuthe et al. (2001) for instance. However, the problem of transportation choice cannot be reduced to the one of pricing alone but should also encompass the role of qualitative factors, which may bear upon the internal and external logistic organisation of the firms. These are not enough taken into account in previous studies. A stated preference approach can provide some additional information in that respect by assessing with transport managers the relative importance and value they give to service

[1] This paper is one preliminary output of a research led by a Belgian consortium directed by M. Beuthe (Catholic University of Mons), H. Meersman and E. Van de Voorde (University of Antwerp), M. Mouchart (Catholic University of Louvain), and F. Witlox (University of Ghent). We thank the Belgian Federal Office for Scientific, Technical and Cultural Affairs (OSTC) for the financial support it granted to this project. A first version of this paper was presented at the European Regional Science Association conference in Jyväskylä (Finland) in August 2003.

quality attributes. Hopefully, it should enable us to better value the real potential of a means/mode switching policy.

In Sect. 9.2, the paper gives a description of the questionnaire developed for this research and the experimental design that is used to elicit preferences from transport managers. Section 9.3 presents the multi-criteria methodology that we are experimenting with, the UTA multi-criteria method of preference des-aggregation of Jacquet-Lagrèze and Siskos (1978, 1982). It relies on a goal programming model to evaluate an additive non-linear utility function from an individual preference ranking of alternatives. It allows for the computation of the attributes' weights and equivalent money values for individual decision makers. Our survey is far from completed at this stage, so that Sect. 9.4 can only illustrate the methodology with some results obtained on a set of interviewed firms.

9.2 The Questionnaire and Stated Preference Experiment

Stated preference techniques are currently used in the field of transport economics for analysing transport choices, particularly choices made by travellers. Much information about this field of enquiry and techniques can be found, for instance, in the recent Manual published by the U.K. Department of transport (2002). Over the last few years, some researches using that methodology have also been published in the field of freight transportation, and some recent contributions certainly deserve to be mentioned here: Fowkes and Shingai, Bolis and Maggi, Fridstrom and Madslien, Maier and Bergman, all of them edited in the book by Danielis (2002), but also Bergkvist (1998), INRETS (2000), Jovicic (1998), Matear and Gray (1993), NERA (1997) and STRATEC (1999), to name just a few. However, most of them limit their research to very specific transport alternatives, like the choice between trucking and rail inter-modal transport along a corridor, the choice between an external carrier and own-transport, or simply the value of time, etc. Moreover, samples are sometimes rather small given the number of explanatory variables that could play a role. Altogether, more research in this field is needed, particularly in the transport context of Belgium where no wider scope study has ever been made. These are the reasons that determined our involvement.

The techniques of interviews, which are necessary to elicit the decision makers preferences are well developed, and are extensively used in many fields, particularly in marketing analyses. They still are somewhat delicate to use, because interviews must be adjusted to the problem at hand, the nature of the sample and the available budget. The associated questionnaire, including its experimental design, also raises many problems. Finally, the modelling of the decision problem and the techniques used to analyse the data constitute another area of research.

The stated preference data used in this paper are taken from a survey of Belgian freight transport managers, which is presently realised by a consortium of Belgian universities (Antwerp, Ghent, Louvain-la-Neuve, and Mons). The survey methodology and the questionnaire are based on an extensive survey of the transport, marketing and statistical literature in the field. Some contributors in the field are already mentioned in the introduction, but we should also cite Green and Srivini-san (1990), Huber and Zwerina (1996), Louvière et al. (2000), as well as Carmone and Schaffer (1995), Carroll and Green (1995), and Oppewal (1995a; 1995b) for reviews of techniques and available software. Additional references can be found in the survey paper by Louvière and Street (2000), as well as in the Manual of the U.K Department of Transport (2002).

Some preliminary in-depth interviews of transport managers were made in the course of preparing the questionnaire. Its feasibility was then pre-tested and adjusted accordingly. In the end, it is a compromise between a desire to gather as much useful information as possible and the practical consideration of a survey constraints. The choice of face-to-face interviews was made because it allowed the gathering of additional information in the course of the dialogue with the interviewee. The questionnaire and the stated preference experiment were administered on paper without any computer support. There are several reasons for this option that we discuss in the following paragraphs.

Previous studies on freight transport considered four to seven different attributes, among which our team was led to identify and define six relevant attributes. This is a number that the literature in the field considers as still feasible to handle in an interview. The purpose being to identify the attributes' relative importance in decision making, a full profile presentation of the six attributes characterizing each transport alternative was deemed more appropriate. To ease the task, we chose to present each alternative on a separate card; this conveniently permits to compare and rank all the alternatives, with the possibility of changing one's mind in the course of the interview. Also, we chose to demand only a full ranking of all alternatives, with no rating of preferences. Indeed, a ranking already provides a very rich information about the respondent's preference system. Additionally, we limited the number of alternatives by adopting a fixed orthogonal fractional factorial design of 25 alternatives, as proposed by Addelman (1962). Altogether, this task was deemed acceptable by a large majority of the people we have interviewed until now, i.e. about 100 people. Note that this experimental design implies that only the attributes' main effects on preferences can be analysed, whereas the effects of two attributes interaction are left aside.

The target population of the survey is the Belgian shippers of freight, which have at least 20 employees, in all industries and to any destination in Europe. Included among respondents are logistic operators and forwarders who manage shipments for industry. The modes of concern are: rail, road, waterway, short-sea-shipping, and their inter- and multi-modal combinations. Given the small size of the country, no location of origin is excluded, even though some modes may have a reduced accessibility like inland navigation in some provinces. Focusing on possible modal shifts, urban and distribution activities on short distances are excluded. Although there is a reduced opportunity over short distances for non-road transports, no minimum transport distance is set for the survey, since there are important cases of industrial goods that are transported over short distances by rail or inland navigation.

Unhappily, firms are often reluctant to be interviewed, so that a random sampling cannot be made, and the survey will be relatively small in size at around 125 firms. This led us to build a representative quota sample. Our target roughly is that each category of commodity in the sample should be in proportion to the shipments goods categories, that tonnages be in proportion to the shipments by each mode, and that shipments from different provinces be in proportion to their economic activities. Nevertheless, we should still be alert to the possibility that the assembled data could provide some biased information. A partial evaluation of that problem will be made by comparing the general characteristics of the firms that accepted the interview with those that refused the interview.

The face-to-face interviews are based on a questionnaire made of four parts: first, general questions about the characteristics of the firm and, more specifically, the characteristics and transport organisation of the plant from which shipping flows originate; second, the description of a typical transport flow that is used as a reference transport for the stated preference experiment; third, the stated preference experiment that aims at eliciting the relative importance of the quality attributes; fourth, a set of questions about the transport manager's readiness to accept a modal switch in order to obtain an alternative preferred to the reference situation.

The first set of questions concern the size of the firm, its type of operations, its accessibility to the transport network, how transport decisions are taken, etc. They provide information on the firms' transport situation and organisation that will be used as econometric explanatory variables in an ulterior phase of our research (when our survey will be completed). There is no point here to give more explanation about them.

The second part of the questionnaire is focused on a typical transport flow from the plant, which will be the reference shipment for the stated preference experiment. It leads the interviewee to choose and describe a typical specific flow: the specific good, its origin and destination, the distance, the annual tonnage, the shipments size and frequency, the type of consignee, the value and the characteristics of the transported good, etc. Then, the respondent must describe the typical flow in terms of the six transport attributes. Some of the criteria are defined in % of occurrences in order to encompass the idea of probability or risk affecting these criteria. They are defined in the following way:

- COST, i.e. out-of-pocket cost for transport, including loading and unloading;
- TIME, i.e. door-to-door transport time, including loading and unloading;
- LOSS as the % of commercial value lost from damages, stealing and accidents;
- FREQUENCY of service per week actually supplied by the carrier or the forwarder;
- RELIABILITY as the % of deliveries at the scheduled time;
- FLEXIBILITY as the % of times non-programmed shipments are executed without undue delay.

In the central part of the interview, the respondent is asked to rank various transport alternatives according to his/her preferences. The alternative solutions are defined in terms of all six attributes; it is a full profile representation, as explained above. The levels of attributes are given in percentages of variation from the status quo situation, the latter being the typical flow's current transport solution. The respondent is invited to keep in mind this typical flow and to interpret the percentage variations in terms of that reference situation. Some alternatives are shown in Table 9.1. Their definition conveniently allows the use of the same set of alternatives and cards for all respondents even though their reference typical flow is different. It also clearly defines the appropriate reference situation from which a potential switch should be envisaged (Department for Transport 2002, Chap.12).

As shown in Table 9.1, only five levels of variation are considered: plus or minus 10%, plus or minus 20%, and the status quo level of 0% variation. In this table, alternative 1, with zero percentage of variation for every attribute, obviously corresponds to the status quo solution. In contrast, alternative 2 compared to the status quo is characterized by a 10% increase of both transport time and reliability, a 20% increase of flexibility, a 10% decrease of loss and a 20% cost decrease. For example, this means that, if the cost of a reference typical flow is 100 EURO and its reliability is at the level of 70%, the cost of alternative 2 is only 80 EURO and its reliability improved at the level of 77%.[2]

Table 9.1. Some examples of full profile alternatives

	Frequency	Time	Reliability	Flexibility	Loss	Cost
1	0%	0%	0%	0%	0%	0%
2	0%	10%	10%	20%	−10%	−20%
3	0%	20%	20%	−20%	10%	−10%
4	0%	−10%	−10%	10%	−20%	20%
5	0%	−20%	−20%	−10%	20%	10%
6	10%	0%	10%	10%	10%	10%
-	-	-	-	-	-	-
15	20%	−20%	10%	0%	−20%	−10%
16	−10%	0%	−10%	−10%	−10%	−10%
17	−10%	10%	−20%	0%	10%	20%
-	-	-	-	-	-	-
23	−20%	20%	10%	−10%	0%	20%
24	−20%	−10%	20%	0%	−10%	10%
25	−20%	−20%	−10%	20%	10%	0%

[2] In some cases, the status quo may very well have an attribute with value close or equal to 100% (or 0%). This would constraint a positive % variation (or a negative one). Such a situation is pointed out to the decision maker who should take it into account in his / her preference ranking.

All this is carefully explained at the beginning of the experimental game, and the interviewee is invited to keep in mind the attributes' absolute levels of the reference typical flow.

Given that the interviews are face-to-face with the possibility of helping the decision maker and listening to his/her oral comments, some useful additional information may be gathered. Likewise, the interviewer observation of the actual preference ranking provides a better understanding of its process, as well as insights into whether the decision maker ranks according to a lexicographic order or uses threshold values in assessing alternatives, etc. These observations are useful for interpreting the individual decision maker's preferences and checking the results of ulterior analyses.

It must be underlined that none of the alternatives is explicitly characterised by a specific mode use. However, the status quo solution may very well be associated with its actual mode in the respondent's mind. Clearly, we can presume that the hypothetical solutions preferred by the respondent would be chosen if they were available without any modal switch, but we cannot necessarily infer from the preference order that a modal shift would be accepted. In order to find out whether some preferred alternatives would be chosen even if they required a modal shift, additional questions focusing on that problem are raised in the fourth part of the survey. They investigate whether the respondent has ever considered switching mode, whether there would be obstacles to do so, and whether he/she would actually switch mode if another mode was able to provide one of the preferred alternative. This additional information will permit a more precise interpretation of the stated preference data by allowing to check whether the information conveyed by the individual preference statements can really be used for analysing the modal choice decision of the respondents.

9.3 The UTA Model

Like most multi-criteria approaches, the UTA model aims to estimating a utility function or utility values. This terminology is maintained here and throughout the paper more for convenience than for substance. Actually, a more neutral terminology like "decision function" or "value function" could be appropriate. Indeed, it is not obvious that a competent transport manager thinks in terms of maximizing a utility value. They likely rather try to minimize some measure of the total transport logistic cost, which integrates many internal and external logistic factors that are function of the transport attributes. Hence, the utility terminology does not have any substantial significance for the following analysis, despite the fact that the concept of logistic cost may still involve a somewhat subjective judgment on risk taking, since it is influenced by the management of safety stocks.

As mentioned above, our survey is far from completed, so that we did not yet venture in any aggregate econometric analysis of a sample. However, this multi-criteria method, rather unusual in the field, allows to compute the attributes' weights and equivalent money values for individual decision makers. In this way, it contributes to a better understanding of the interviewed individuals' preference system, permits a double check of the interviews and gives interesting insights in each decision making approach. This is particularly valuable in a first stage analysis, since freight demand is heterogeneous, from firms characterized by different industrial processes and outputs as well as different accessibility to the transport network (Bolis and Maggi 2002). Another advantage of the method is that it estimates non-linear utility functions, whereas the usual discrete choice models provide only a linear utility function with constant coefficients.

It is a model specifically designed to derive utility functions on the basis of a preference ranking. Hence, it is particularly appropriate to our purpose and our data. Indeed, the problem here is to compare, rank and value a set of actions, or choice alternatives, with respect to N different criteria which contribute to the alternatives' utility. The criteria's values are given by the vector $g(a) = (g_1(a), g_2(a),..., g_N(a))$ for any alternative a belonging to A. As an example, for a highway project, the $g_i(a)$'s could be the cost-benefit ratio, its favourable impact on safety, on environment, etc. In our case, the criteria will be the characteristics of the transport solutions under consideration: their Cost, Reliability, Frequency, Flexibility, Time, and Safety. These characteristics were discussed and defined in Sect. 9.2.

The model assumes the existence of a utility function:

$$U(g(a)) = U(g_1(a), g_2(a),..., g_N(a)),$$
(9.1)

which satisfies the classic axioms of decision theory, namely the axioms of comparability, reflexivity, transitivity of choices, continuity and strict dominance.

The utility function is additive,

$$U(g(a)) = \sum_{i=1}^{N} u_i(g_i(a))$$
(9.2)

with

$$u_i(g_i) \geq 0 \text{ and } \frac{du_i}{dg_i} > 0.$$
(9.3)

The additive function implies in particular that the partial utility of a criterion $u_i(g_i(a))$ depends only on the level of that particular criterion.[3] Equation (9.3) guarantees that the functions are monotone increasing with respect to increasing levels of a favourable attribute. Hence, each attribute must be defined as a favourable factor. In our case, this means that the cost and time attributes must be sign-

---

[3] For a discussion about additive utility functions see Fishburn (1967) and Keeney and Raiffa (1976).

inverted to fit in the model. Equation (9.3) can be seen as a minimal requirement of judgement rationality.

The utility function provides an aggregation of the criteria in a common index to compare and value the alternatives under consideration. It ranks the project in a complete weak order R : if P indicates a strict preference and I the indifference between two projects a and b, then

$$U[g(a)] > U[g(b)] \Leftrightarrow aPb \qquad (9.4)$$

$$U[g(a)] = U[g(b)] \Leftrightarrow aIb \qquad (9.5)$$

The UTA method, proposed initially by Jacquet-Lagreze and Siskos (1978, 1982), estimates the function U on a set of reference alternatives projects A, by the method of linear goal programming proposed by Charnes and Cooper (1961, 1977), which provides an approximation by linear intervals of a non-linear function.

In order to apply that method, the field of variation of each criterion $\left|g_{i^*}, g_i^*\right|$, defined by its least favourable value of that criterion (g_{i^*}) and its best value (g_i^*), is divided in α_i equal intervals $\left|g_i^j, g_i^{j+1}\right|$. The variables to be estimated by the program are the partial utilities at these bounds, say $u_i(g_i^j)$. The utility at intermediate values of the criteria are given by linear interpolation. Thus, for $g_i(a) \in \left|g_i^j, g_i^{j+1}\right|$,

$$u_i[g_i(a)] = u_i(g_i^j) + \frac{g_i(a) - g_i^j}{g_i^{j+1} - g_i^j}\left[u_i(g_i^{j+1}) - u_i(g_i^j)\right] \qquad (9.6)$$

For each pair of transport alternatives (a, b) belonging to A, the decision-maker must express his/her preferences or indifferences. Under the version proposed by Despotis et al. (1990), the so-called UTASTAR version, the results of these comparisons are introduced as constraints consistent with Eqs. (9.4–5), i.e.

$$\sum_{i=1}^{N}\{u_i(g_i(a)) - u_i(g_i(b))\} + \sigma^+(a) - \sigma^-(a) - \sigma^-(b) + \sigma^-(b) \geq \delta \Leftrightarrow aPb \qquad (9.7)$$

$$\sum_{i=1}^{N}\{u_i(g_i(a)) - u_i(g_i(b))\} + \sigma^+(a) - \sigma^-(a) - \sigma^+(b) + \sigma^-(b) = 0 \Leftrightarrow aIb \qquad (9.8)$$

with all σ^+ and $\sigma^- \geq 0$.

σ^+ corresponds to a positive error with respect to the difference between utility levels, whereas σ^- indicates a negative error. These errors are all non-negative, they represent the possible errors of an action's utility estimation. The objective function F to be minimised is the sum of these errors:

$$F = \sum_{a \in A'} \left| \sigma^+(a) + \sigma^-(a) \right| \qquad (9.9)$$

The parameter δ on the right side of Eq. (9.7) must be strictly positive. Its value can very well influence the solution of the program. Hence, in the course of estimation, it must not initially be given a high value (Beuthe and Scannella 1996, 2001). The hypothesis that the partial utilities increase with the value of the criteria imposes a series of additional constraints:

$$u_i(g_i^{j+1}) - u_i(g_i^j) \geq s_i \qquad j = 1, 2, ..., \alpha_i, \text{ and } i = 1, 2, ..., N \qquad (9.10)$$

where s_i must be (strictly) positive. Like for δ, it is better initially to give it a small value. Finally the partial utilities are normalised by the conditions

$$\sum_{i=1}^{N} u_i(g_i^*) = 1, \qquad (9.11)$$

and

$$u_i(g_{i^*}) = 0 \quad \forall i \qquad (9.12)$$

Equation (9.10) indicates that the values of $u_i(g_i^*)$'s, the criteria's utilities at their highest levels, correspond to the criteria's relative weights in the utility function.

Putting together all these elements, the following linear program is obtained:

$$\min F = \sum_{a \in A'} \left| \sigma^+(a) + \sigma^-(a) \right| \qquad (9.13)$$

subject to:

$$\sum_{i=1}^{N} \{ u_i(g_i(a)) - u_i(g_i(b)) \} + \sigma^+(a) - \sigma^-(a) - \sigma^+(b) + \sigma^-(b) \geq \delta \Leftrightarrow aPb \qquad (9.7)$$

$$\sum_{i=1}^{N} \{ u_i(g_i(a)) - u_i(g_i(b)) \} + \sigma^+(a) - \sigma^-(a) - \sigma^+(b) + \sigma^-(b) = 0 \Leftrightarrow aIb \qquad (9.8)$$

$$u_i(g_i^{j+1}) - u_i(g_i^j) \geq s_i \qquad j = 1, 2, ..., \alpha_i, \text{ and } i = 1, 2, ..., N \qquad (9.10)$$

$$\sum_{i=1}^{N} u_i(g_i^*) = 1 \qquad (9.11)$$

$$u_i(g_{i^*}) = 0 \ \forall \ i \qquad\qquad (9.12)$$

$$\sigma^+(a) \geq 0, \ \sigma^-(a) \geq 0 \ \ \forall a \in A' \qquad\qquad (9.14)$$

$$u_i(g_i^j) \geq 0 \ \ \forall i, \forall j \qquad\qquad (9.15)$$

where Eq. (9.6) is used to calculate the utilities of the g_i (a) between two consecutive bounds. This is the basic UTA-UTASTAR model that we shall use. The interested reader may find a few other specifications as well as a set of comparative simulations in Beuthe and Scannella (1996, 2001). Some of these specifications include additional constraints for handling additional information that may be given by the decision maker.

The program above may have two types of solution: either all errors have zero values and $F = 0$, or some errors are positive and $F > 0$. In this second case, there does not exist a non-linear additive utility function that perfectly represents the preferences expressed by the decision maker. If we exclude the cases of a decision maker not able to reasonably compare projects, or irrational in the sense of exhibiting intransitive preferences, the presence of errors may indicate that the decision maker preferences are characterised by partial utilities which are not independent of each other or which are not monotonically increasing. But, it may also be the case, more simply, that the intervals chosen should have been more numerous or defined in a different way.

The specification of an additive function and its derivation from separate assessments of partial function supposes an assumption of preferential independence. Its means that, if two projects are characterised by the same values for some criteria, the preferences between them depend only on the values taken by the other criteria. How much this hypothesis is acceptable in practical applications may vary from case to case. Von Winterfeldt and Edwards (1973) are of the opinion that an additive function could be used as a good approximation. Indeed an additive function of non-linear partial utility functions is quite a flexible specification, and it can provide an estimation that implicitly takes into account a certain degree of interdependence among criteria. Stewart (1995) empirically demonstrated that it was indeed a robust specification. Furthermore, through a set of simulations, Beuthe and Scannella (2001) showed that the UTA model is quite able to obtain useful results with F equal or close to 0, even in case of interdependence between criteria.

Whether F equals zero or not, the program's solution may not be unique, as it is often the case in linear programming. This problem must then be solved by a post-optimality analysis. Jacquet-Lagrèze and Siskos (1978) have simply proposed to use a function which is the average of the extreme optimal functions obtained from a sensitivity analysis applied on the last bounds of each criterion.

This sensitivity analysis is made with an additional constraint

$$\sum_{a\in A'} \sigma(a) \leq F^* + \theta, \qquad (9.16)$$

where θ is a small positive number. This procedure was shown to provide a practical and efficient method of estimation.

9.4 Preliminary Results of the Multi-Criteria Analysis

This section will illustrate this multi-criteria methodology and the nature of its results with an application to a set of individual preference observations. This task was performed with the MUSTARD software (Scannella 2001; Scannella and Beuthe 2001, 2002). To begin with, the first line of Table 9.2 gives the average weights computed over the 98 firms that we have already interviewed. They clearly show that transport cost is the most important factor, followed by reliability but with a much lower weight.

The following lines of Table 9.2 give the individual results of nine firms from various industrial sectors. Again the importance of the cost appears quite clearly, as cost is the main factor in seven out of nine cases. Reliability comes next but often receives a very small weight. The other factors take some importance in a few cases according to the particular circumstances of transport; otherwise, they receive small weights. For instance, transport time is important for the textile firm and the producer of electronics, which ship over rather long distances. For these two firms, as well as for the pharmaceutical firm, cost appears less important and the weights are more equally distributed. Reliability is the first factor for the pharmaceutical firm, which also gives a high weight to an absence of losses. This last factor also has some importance for one of the steel making firm that ships by waterway.

It is worth underlining though that these results do not mean that the non-cost quality attributes taken together do not play an important role in decision making. Indeed, together they weight about as much as the cost. This question certainly deserves additional probing.

These results and comments are just descriptive of a few particular situations. Nevertheless, it is clear that there is much heterogeneity in the results; this could be expected as these firms are very different with respect to their products and spatial situation. A rigorous analysis of possible explanatory factors can only be performed on a sample or groups of firms and with the help of appropriate econometric techniques. When the survey is completed, the results obtained for the full sample with this multi-criteria method will be analysed in order to identify additional explanatory variables.

Table 9.2. Relative weights of attributes

Firms	Freq.	Time	Reliab.	Flex.	Loss	Cost	Σ errors	Kendall
Average weights 94 firms	.069	.068	.170	.065	.097	.532	-	-
Steel, multimodal 991 km, 240 hours C:.038, S: 350	.008	.029	.115	.042	.084	.722	.009	.978
Steel, waterway 404 km, 55 hours C:.017, S: 900	.003	.008	.001	.004	.327	.658	.345	.947
Textile, multimodal 2104 km, 120 hours C:.11, S: 15	.081	.267	.145	.060	.146	.301	.163	.933
Electronic, road 800 km, 48 hours C: .12, S: 23	.174	.360	.139	.069	.043	.215	.225	.962
Chemical, Rail 1200 km, 48 hours C: .002, S: 28	.003	0	.001	.004	.001	.983	.011	.909
Cement, road 123 km, 3 hours C: .25, S: 31.5	.001	.001	.011	.002	0	.985	.021	.945
Packing, road 500 km, 10 hours C: .16, S: 12	.003	0	.092	.002	.001	.902	.011	.978
Pharmaceutical, road 240 km, 24 hours C: .96, S: .1	.076	.045	.358	.127	.187	.207	.409	.930
Building mat., waterway 155 km, 48 hours C: .025, S: 1000	0	0	.167	0	0	.833	0	1

C Euro cost per tonne/km, *S* shipment size in tonne.

Also, it will be necessary to compare these results with those obtained by other methods. At this point, we can already mention that a set of experiments were made with classical statistical conjoint analyses that provided similar results: the cost factor again was the most important, albeit with a lower weight, and reliability came second. However, given our experimental design of 25 alternatives, conjoint analyses consume too many degrees of freedom in individual preference estimations. Furthermore, they do not incorporate a minimal rationality specification like monotone increasing partial utility functions. Hence, we abandoned that methodology, which did not obtain reliable results.[4] Another current experiment with a frontier analysis of transport market also confirms that none of the non-cost attributes plays a significant role in the decision-making.

---

[4] For more details: Bouffioux and Beuthe (2004).

Obviously, a larger sample will also allow the use of some discrete choice models like the usual probit and logit models.

Meantime, it is still interesting to further analyse a particular case, in order to illustrate the potential of this multi-criteria methodology for assessing the qualitative factors' equivalent money value. Let us take the case of the steel making plant using a multi-modal solution (barge, rail, truck) for transporting coils towards Italy over a distance of 991 km. As can be seen in Table 9.2, the estimated weights of the additive decision function are: 0.008 for Frequency, 0.029 for Time, 0.115 for Reliability, 0.042 for Flexibility, 0.084 for Loss and 0.722 for Cost. Five alternatives were deemed preferable to the status quo solution, and, in the last part of the questionnaire, the decision maker expressed the intention of switching mode if they would be available.

As explained above, the UTA model permits the estimation of non-linear functions made of a number of linear segments. The following Fig. 9.1 illustrates the partial utility functions estimated by MUSTARD for the various attributes but one, i.e. frequency. In effect, this particular attribute with a negligible weight had an entirely flat partial function; it is not useful to show it. To well understand these graphs, note that:

− The abscissa scale for the attributes is centred around the status quo value of a zero percentage of variation.
− For the Time, Loss and Cost attributes, the abscissas have been defined in negative percentage of increase, so that a higher level on the scale corresponds to a more favourable level. Hence, these attributes are indicated as time saving, absence of loss and saving of cost, respectively, and their utilities are increasing along the scale of variation.
− The utilities are scaled with respect to a zero utility level at the status quo point where there is a 0% variation.

The presentation of the functions on similar size graphs should not lead us to forget the small weights affecting some of these attributes, which hardly play any specific role in actual decision making.

An attractive feature of this non-linear methodology is that it allows the computation of different money equivalent values for an increase and a decrease of an attribute from the status quo level, i.e. different willingness to pay and willingness to accept compensation. For example, the steel making plant would appear ready to pay an additional .07 EURO per tonne for a gain of one day over the present time of ten days, but would demand a compensation, or a reduction, of 2 EURO for a one day increase in transport time. Furthermore, for a one percent improvement in reliability the firm would be ready to pay .08 EURO more per tonne, whereas a one percent loss in reliability would justify a reduction of 1.7 EURO per tonne.[5]

---

[5] For this computation of equivalent money values, the relevant trade-off's were computed over the variations from 0% to +20% and from −20 % to 0%. Shorter variation intervals would have lead to smaller differences between the two willingness.

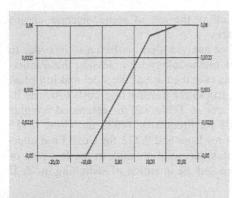

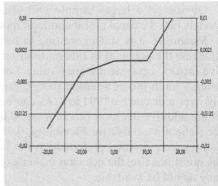

Reliability variation in % (weight: .114)   Time saving variation in % (weight: .029)

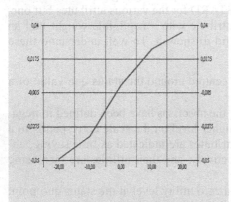

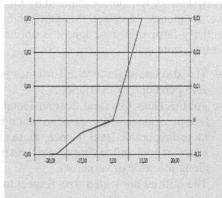

Flexibility variation in % (weight: .043)   Absence of loss variation in % (weight: .084)

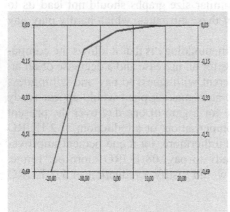

Cost saving in % (weight: .722)

Fig. 9.1. Partial utility functions

These differences indicate that this firm is well adjusted to the option it chose. A shorter transport time or a higher service reliability obviously would be valued to a certain degree, but a longer transport time or a lesser reliability definitely would cause problem. These different valuations mainly result from the concave partial utility function of the inverted cost attribute. For the carriers it means that they should strive to maintain their performance at the expected level, since a degradation of the service level would seriously affect their client and could induce a switch of carrier in this case, unless they can propose a substantially lower tariff. This type of result deserves additional scrutiny over the full sample.

9.5 Conclusion

This is research in progress, and it is too early to draw definite conclusions on the use of this methodology. Let us tentatively state that, this multi-criteria tool provides some interesting insight on the preferences decision makers and aids in the ordering of stated preferences through the levels of the Kendall coefficient and errors. It also provides equivalent money values of the willingness to pay and the willingness to accept compensation. Obviously, with a large sample, the basic weights and the equivalent money values could be averaged over relevant subgroups of firms to provide a more general view of the role transport attributes play in influencing choices. This method also provides global money equivalent value for each alternative. Such estimates could be input to econometric modelling. Further research would permit us to compare the results of this methodology with those that can be obtained with the more usual logistic models.

Provisionally, we can conclude that the cost factor weight varies heavily and the qualitative attributes also play an important role, despite the fact that they weight little when considered separately. This raises an interesting issue about the modelling of the qualitative differences between transport modes, i.e. whether a simpler analysis with an aggregate measure of quality would be worth considering. However, it is important to note that the importance given by transport managers to the various attributes could vary with transport circumstances and industrial activity. This feature would complicate the derivation of a common measure of quality.

References

Abdelwahab WM (1998) Elasticities of mode choice probabilities and market elasticities of demand: evidence from a simultaneous mode choice/shipment-size freight transport model. Transportation Research E 34: 257–266

Addelman S(1962) Orthogonal main-effect plans for asymmetrical factorial experiments. Technometrics 4: 21–46

Bergkvist E (1998) Valuation of time in Swedish road freight, the difference between internal and external transport services. In: Umea Economic Studies 488. University of Umea

Beuthe M, Scannella G (2001) Comparative analysis of UTA multicriteria methods. European Journal of Operational Research 130: 246–262

Beuthe M, Jourquin B, Geerts J-F, Koul à Ndjang' HC (2001) Freight transportation demand elasticities: a geographic multimodal transportation network analysis. Transportation Research E 37: 253–266

Bouffioux C, Beuthe M (2004) Conjoint analysis vs. multi-criteria analysis of rank-ordered data. Working note GTM, January 2004

Carmone FJ, Schaffer CM (1995) Journal of Marketing Research 32: 113–120

Carroll JD, Green PE (1995) Psychometric methods in marketing research: part I, conjoint analysis. Journal of Marketing Research :385–390

Danielis R (ed) (2002) Freight transport demand and stated preference experiments. Franco Angeli, Milano

Department of Transport (UK) (2002) Economic valuation with stated preference technique: a manual. Edward Elgar, Cheltenham Northampton

Fishburn PC (1967) Utility theory. Management Science 14: 335-378

Green E, Srinivisan V (1990) Conjoint analysis in marketing: new developments with implications for research and practice. Journal of Marketing 54: 3–19

Huber J, Zwerina K (1996) The importance of utility balance in efficient choice set designs. Journal of Marketing Research 33: 307–17

INRETS (2000) Intermodal quality. Final report for publication. 4th Framework Programme of the European Commission, European Commission, Brussels

Jacquet-Lagrèze E, Siskos J (1978) Une méthode de construction de fonctions d'utilité additives explicatives d'une préférence globale. Cahier LAMSADE n°6, Université Paris-IX-Dauphine, Paris

Jacquet-Lagrèze E, Siskos J (1982) Assessing a set of additive utility functions for multicriteria decision-making, the UTA method. European Journal of Operations Research 10: 151–164

Jovicic G (1998) Application of models based on stated and revealed preference data for forecasting Danish international freight transports. Tetraplan AS, Aalborg

Keeney RL, Raiffa H (1976) Decisions with multiple objectives: preferences and value tradeoffs, Wiley, New York

Louviere JJ, Street D (2000) Stated-preference methods. In: Hensher DA, Button KJ (eds) Handbook of transport modelling. Elsevier, Amsterdam, pp 132–143

Louviere JJ, Hensher DA, Swait J (2000) Stated choice methods: analysis and application (in marketing, transportation and environmental valuation). Cambridge University Press

Matear S, Gray S (1993) Factors influencing freight service choice for shippers and freight suppliers. International Journal of Physical Distribution and Logistics Management 23: 25–35

NEI (1999) Prijelasticiteiten in het goederenwegvervoer. Rotterdam Delft

Oppewal H (1995a) A review of conjoint software. Journal of Retailing and Consumer Services 2: 56–61

Oppewal H(1995b) A review of choice-based conjoint software: CBC and MINT. Journal of Retailing and Consumer Services 2: 259–264

Sawtooth Software (2002) ACA 5.0. Technical paper, Sequim

Scannella G (2001) Multicriteria assessment of uncertain projects with UTA and quasi-UTA approaches. Ph.D. thesis, Facultés Universitaires Catholiques de Mons, Mons

Scannella G, Beuthe M (2001) Assessing risky public investments with MUSTARD. Journal of Multi-criteria Decision Analysis 10: 287–302

Stewart TJ (1995) Simplified approaches for multicriteria decision making under uncertainty. Journal of Multi-criteria Decision Analysis 4: 246–258

STRATEC (1999) Final report of Task 2, Project "Integration of intermodal transport in the supply chains" of the European Commission DG VII. STRATEC, Brussels

von Winterfeldt D, Edwards W (1973) Evaluation of complex stimuli using multiattribute utility procedures. Research report, Ann Arbor: Engineering Psychology Laboratory, University of Michigan

10 An Adaptive Conjoint Analysis of Freight Service Alternatives: Evaluating the Maritime Option

Angela Stefania Bergantino[1] and Simona Bolis[2]

[1] University of Bari, Bari, Italy
[2] University of Lugano, Lugano, Switzerland

10.1 Introduction

The growing interest towards redistributions of freight traffic across different modes has brought a renewed focus on the use of the maritime mode and, in particular, of ro-ro services, or combined transport by road and sea. In many European countries, ecological concerns, the congestion of most road infrastructure networks, the characteristics of rail freight services and the state of the public finances have redirected attention to the sea as a means for transportation. However, while the great opportunities offered by the development of these types of transport services in re-directing freight flows are widely acknowledged, especially at the Community level (e.g. EU White Paper of 2001, the Marco Polo project, the "quick start" list of projects defined in 2004), little has been done to empirically identify factors which might induce operators to opt for the maritime alternative. The determinants of demand have not yet been the object of a detailed investigation. In order to achieve this, it is important to have information not only on the current movements but also on the potential reallocation of traffic flows to the new alternative routes/services. An estimation of the latter cannot be achieved without an in-depth analysis of the behaviour of traffic operators: identifying the value that the user assigns to the specific transport alternative would strongly contribute to evaluating the possibility of a trade-off between the maritime mode and the other modes. Furthermore, the identification of the factors related to both the mode and the specific organisation of the companies that exert a significant influence on the choice of operators and the magnitude of their impact would represent, in such instances, a necessary prerequisite for any market forecasts and project appraisal.

In this paper we opt for an interactive approach which allows consumers' preferences to be elicited on hypothetical alternatives as well. In particular, we carry out an adaptive stated preference experiment to collect an appropriate database and, given the characteristics of the data, estimate the relevant parameters through a Tobit model. This approach enables us to analyse consumers' preferences for the maritime alternative and to identify service attributes which most influence freight-forwarders' attitudes towards short-sea shipping ro-ro services. The analysis is carried out through two quantitative surveys: a revealed preference study to obtain data on the characteristics of the "typical" transport performed by the company and a stated preference interactive interview with freight forwarders to learn about user preference for the hypothetical alternative.

The rest of this paper is organized as follows. In Sect. 10.2 we describe the methodology used to assemble the dataset, the criteria for identifying the sample and the design of both the revealed preference survey and the adaptive stated preference experiment. Section 10.3 contains a detailed description of the database and an illustration of the estimation procedure and main outcomes. It also contains a brief comparison of the main results of other EU studies. Section 10.4 briefly summarizes the main conclusions.

10.2   Data Base Construction Methodology

10.2.1 Stated Preference Versus Revealed Preferences

In the last few years, significant improvements have been made in the definition of a methodology capable of realistically interpreting the decision-making process of operators with respect to transport service choice. The superiority of stated preference techniques versus revealed preference techniques in these instances is generally accepted, mainly due to the characteristics of the data needed for the experiments. Application of revealed preference methods based on observed behaviour is, generally, not feasible in the context of freight transport since:

- the data on actual choices is usually commercially very sensitive and hence is usually not disclosed;[1]
- the complexity of the freight transport decision requires the collection of large dataset on a number of variables and the observation of a great number of firms' decisions in order to take into account the heterogeneity of the context.

Revealed preference datasets, in fact, are based on the observation of actual choices; need a large number of observations; may include only existing alternatives; and require the choice set to be defined and the level of service information for the discarded option to be calculated. Moreover, important characterising variables (such as, for instance, time and cost) are often correlated and, due to possible measurement error, there might be bias in forecasting. Finally, for the specific scope of the study, the limited use of the maritime alternative, especially for certain routes and products, is an additional reason against the use of revealed preferences in this context. The existence of an alternative which is not sufficiently used

---

[1] In a liberalised environment, freight rates are individually negotiated and held commercially confidential.

is, in fact, analogous to analysing the choice of a new alternative (Tweddle et al. 1996).

Stated preference data, on the other hand, overcome these problems, although questionnaire design and choice of the relevant attributes[2] plays a major role in their efficacy. It has the advantage, with respect to standard revealed preference approaches, of allowing analysis in contexts in which it is not possible to "observe" the real behaviour of operators either for lack of data or because the alternative to be analysed is not yet used or available for use.

More recently, a growing body of literature emphasizes the advantages of combining revealed preference and stated preference data in order to exploit the strengths of both.[3] In the present application, however, given the need to consider hypothetical services as well, this possibility is partially precluded and – although revealed preference techniques are used in gathering data on the current choices of the pilot sample and to select a "typical" transport for each company (the current choice) – the data are mainly collected through stated preference techniques.

The methodology used falls within the broad family of conjoint analysis experiments, as we attempt to determine the value that individuals place on any product as the sum of the utility derived from all the attributes making up a specific transport service. The conjoint alternative scenario approach is a research technique used to measure the trade-offs people make in choosing between products and service providers. It was first developed in the marketing sector and has been largely used to predict consumers' choices for future products and services, and now it is a well-established procedure in transport studies.[4]

In particular, given the need to avoid offering the respondent options which are irrelevant for the respondent, we discard traditional stated preference techniques in favour of the adaptive stated preference (ASP). This interactive data collection technique amends attribute levels offered to the respondent during the experiment on the bases of the responses he gives. One significant advantage of this method in studying freight is that it makes it possible to cope with a wide range of "situations" which are comparable with the real world known by the respondent and that the experiment is trying to recover (type of commodity, time variance of attribute valuation, etc.).

---

[2] On the importance of the correct specification of the influential attributes in SP analysis, the reader is referred to the detailed work of Cullinane and Toy (2000).

[3] For greater details the reader is referred to: Adamowicz et al. (1994, 1997), Ben Akiva and Morikawa (1990), Bradley and Daly (1997), Brownston et al. (1999), Louviere et al. (2000), Stopher (1998), Swait et al. (1994), Wardman (1998).

[4] In particular, in the context of freight transport, since the late seventies – with the pioneering work by Fowkes and Tweddle (1979) – stated preference techniques have been used, among others, by Bates (1988), Bergkvist (2001), Bolis and Maggi (2002, 2003), Danielis and Rotaris (2002), Fowkes and Shinghal (2002), Fowkes and Tweddle (1996, 1997), Fridstrom and Madslien (1994, 2002) and Maier and Bergman (2001, 2002). For a more detailed review of literature on stated preference experiments in the freight transport sector see also Regan and Garrido (2001).

The ASP experiment starts from an existing freight transport option chosen by the interviewed person. Usually this option is defined using revealed preference data and is elaborated in accordance with the person responsible for the mode choice: it is the "typical" transport of the firm (Fowkes and Tweedle 1996). Starting from this option, the ASP exercise implies asking the respondent to rate various hypothetical alternatives for performing the same transport task expressed in terms of the relevant attributes.

To our knowledge, this is the first ASP experiment performed with the scope of determining the preferences of operators in terms of service attributes of sea transport and of studying the potential reallocation of traffic from surface transport services to maritime ro-ro services.[5]

10.2.2 Identification of the Sample: Who and Where

In contrast with many previous studies, which investigate producers or suppliers,[6] the present analysis is carried out on a sample of freight-forwarders. The specific choice is based on the following reasons:

* first, it is increasingly common, especially for medium-long distance transfers, to delegate the decision on the mode to be used outside the firm to third parties: choosing freight-forwarding agencies makes it possible to intercept information from a sector of the industry which accounts, on average, for more than half of the transport decisions, as outsourcing of transport operations is spreading rapidly.[7]
* Secondly, the focus on freight forwarders results in a sample which, although small, is homogeneous with regard to respondents' activity. Given the limited resources available, and in the light of extending the experiment, selecting producers would have limited the scope of the analysis to a specific productive sector or would have excessively constrained the dimension of the dataset for each industrial sector. On the other hand, choosing transporters, given the current situation of the Italian surface transport industry, would have probably led to interpretation problems due to the resistance of small operators to intermodal transport.[8]

---

[5] A previous study carried out on the routes between Sicily and the Continent by Gattuso and Pastorino (1996) adopted standard SP methodology.

[6] Among others: Bolis and Maggi (2002, 2003), Meier and Bergman (2001, 2002) and Danielis and Rotaris (2002).

[7] Recent surveys on the evolution of the freight forwarders business and type of services offered are contained in KNP (2002) and Unescap (2002). At the European level interesting insights are given by Logiq (1999).

[8] Recent studies highlight (Tsamboulas and Kapros 2002) the widely differing expectations different groups of users have for transport service attributes, especially in relation to multimodal transport services, and they indicate that intermediaries have, in general, a more in-depth knowledge of possible alternatives. Moreover, when producers externalise the logistic and/or transport function they tend to be less concerned with the actual

- Finally, recent studies have demonstrated that freight forwarders are becoming "one-stop shop" specialist companies (KNP 2002). According to the results of the market review carried out by Unescap in 2001, this is part of a process that has led to the blurring of boundaries between what were formerly distinct activities. There is a growing body of evidence showing that "freight forwarders, from the perspective of the shipper, assume the role of the carrier; from the point of view of the actual carrier; they assumes the role of the shipper" (Unescap 2001, p. 1).

All in all, selecting freight-forwarding agents instead of producers on the one hand allows insights to be gained from a wider spectrum of possible uses, and on the other hand, to gather a set of information on the subject who is really behind the decision-making process in transport attribute choices. Although the objective function of the freight forwarder would necessarily differ from that of the producer, it could reasonably be argued that, given the recent evolution of the market and of the contractual agreements in force, once the organisation of the transport service has been outsourced the real (final) decision maker, the shipper, would be the freight forwarder herself/himself. S/he would be the residual claimant to any cost-quality advantages obtained.

Also, in line with the scope of our investigation, we have restricted the interviewed sample to those freight forwarders who have a certain familiarity with the maritime mode and, given the purposes of this study, we have focussed the empirical application on a specific geographical context. In particular, we have analysed the preferences of operators localised in the north-west regions of Italy with respect to the possibility of accessing maritime ro-ro services from the port of Genoa. In order to present the participating operators with comparable alternatives, we have considered traffic-flows between origin-destination areas which are reachable from the area of the study both by sea and by land.

10.2.3 Data Collection: The Revealed Preference Survey and the ASP Experiment

Once the participants and the geographical context to be covered by the study were identified, the data was collected in two steps. In the first phase a revealed preference survey was carried out – through the use of a questionnaire – to identify potential participants to the second stage and to obtain data on actual choices used in selecting a "typical" transport for customising the design of the ASP experiment. In the second phase, the ASP experiment was carried out on a subsample of the freight forwarding agencies that participated in the revealed preference survey. The main reason for performing a stated preference experiment, in this context, was the need to test the introduction of a new maritime transport service – on the route of interest for the respondent – alternative to the transport ser-

---

characteristics of the transport service chosen as long as terms and conditions of the contract are respected.

vice currently chosen. The final sample constitutes the pilot group, and the estimations are based on the collected database.

10.2.3.1 The First Phase – The Questionnaire

The aim of the first phase of the interview was to determine whether the company was appropriate for the study and whether it was useful to include it in the second phase of data collection. Inclusion depended not only on the willingness of the company to participate but also on its geographical coverage and on the type of traffic it manages. In order to compare surface and sea transport it was necessary to identify operators where the hypothetical alternative was feasible, given the characteristics of their traffic. For instance, companies with routes from northern Italy to Sardinia would not be appropriate as there are no surface alternatives that are considered viable. Similarly, it would not be appropriate to include those with routes Turin to Trieste since there are practicable sea alternatives.

The questionnaire elaborated contained questions directed at acquiring basic facts (products, destinations, typical modes, and so on) on the company's activity and dimension and to understand its actual commodity and geographical coverage. A specific question was included in order to understand the role of the respondent in the organisation of the transport service, the characteristics of the contract and the level of independency from the producer in choosing the transport service. In particular, a section of the questionnaire was dedicated to the definition of the "typical" transport carried out by the company useful for customising the ASP experiment to the company in the context of maritime transport.

The sample has been obtained from the 165 freight forwarding companies belonging to the association of freight-forwarders related to the port of Genoa. About 20% of the companies did not reply to a first telephone contact (34 companies) and, of the remaining, about 15% affirmed of not having a stable working premise in the area of interest (18 companies) and about 10% had the same management as others in the sample (14). The relevant population was thus reduced to 99 units. Of these, about 39% declared that they were not interested in participating (38) without giving additional information and about 25% (25) declared they were not interested in participating as they specialised only in surface transport or had a geographical coverage which was not compatible with maritime transport. The questionnaire was thus sent to the remaining 36 companies (36% of the relevant population). The overall response rate, although limited with respect to the total population, was relatively good with respect to the restricted group of freight forwarders identified as potentially suitable for the interview: 18 companies out of the 36 contacted replied (50%).[9] From the information collected it appeared that only about 80% of the respondents could be fit for continuing with the second part

---

[9] For a detailed illustration of the outcome of the analysis of the data retrieved through the questionnaires see: Bergantino and Bolis (2002) and Bergantino et al. (2005).

of the study (14); however, at this stage, only 5 gave immediate availability to continue with the experiment (30%).[10]

10.2.3.2 The Second Phase – The Experiment

The second phase of the study, following a thorough pre-test of all instruments, involved an interactive conjoint analysis interview carried out with the managers responsible for the mode choice decisions. The "ASP experiment" was carried out with the support of a portable computer and software which presented a consistent, on-screen, series of scenarios adapting to the respondents' choices.

The interviewing process is described here. On the first screen the respondent was asked to confirm information on a "typical" transport operation performed by the company acquired through the revealed preference survey. The information was then used to customise the "current choice" of the respondent becoming the "reference option", which did not change for the whole experiment. On the basis of the relevant literature[11] and the outcome of the revealed preference survey, four variables were identified as determinants of transport service: price (P), time (T), reliability (R) and frequency (F). This option, which consisted of a value for each of the four service attributes identified, was reported at each iteration on the left-hand side of the screen, column A, and was automatically assigned a rating of 100. It was assumed that among the existing alternatives, this was the preferred one, representing the operators current utility level.

From the second screen and for each subsequent iteration, two more options – B and C – appeared next to column A. They reported hypothetical alternatives which were automatically generated by the software and which were characterised by differing values of their service attributes. Column B always referred to the same mode of transport of the "typical" transport defined by the respondent (column A) while column C referred to an alternative mode of transport. The alternative mode of transport across all experiments was always "maritime ro-ro service".

---

[10] Although a larger sample would have been desirable, even for the pilot study sampling costs are considerable and organising the meetings quite burdensome and time consuming. Interviews with relevant decision makers have to be agreed upon, set up, often postponed and have rarely been short enough to permit more than one to be conducted on the same day. Nevertheless, the interviewing process is still going on and, at the time of revising this paper, the companies contacted have significantly increased, generating a much larger dataset. Preliminary analysis of the integrated dataset show consistency of the results with the outcome of this first pilot study, which took place in September 2002.

[11] Among others, Bolis and Maggi (2002), Danielis and Rotaris (2002), Fowkes and Shinghal (2002), Fowkes and Tweddle (1996, 1997), de Jong (2000), and Maier and Bergman (2001, 2002). Extremely interesting is the ranking of the attributes most commonly used in analysing transport demand and users' preferences contained in the detailed survey of Cullinane and Toy (2000).

The value of the four service attributes of each alternative are determined as follows:

- the first time the alternatives were presented (second screen), the information was taken on the basis of the known characteristics of the firms' original transport service in terms of percentages (e.g. % discount or increase in price, % of shipments currently arriving on time, etc.)
- for the subsequent iterations, on the basis of the choices reported each time by the respondent.

In every repetition of the experiment, the hypothetical alternatives presented in column B and C changed: new computer generated alternatives were presented and the respondent is asked to rank the two alternatives against option A on the basis of the value he/she assigns to the "new" service.

In choosing the rating, the respondent was asked to use a value scale carefully illustrated by the interviewer. The scale was ranged between 0 and 200.[12] The iterations continued until, for each variable in turn, starting with price, indifference was reached. Once variations in prices as a function of the rating given by the respondent in the previous iteration no longer led to a variation in the rating, the process continued with the next attribute screen, presenting options in which the remaining attributes change values following the same procedures. The process continued until convergence was found for all attributes or at the 20th iteration.[13]

10.3 Data Analysis and Estimation Methodology

Given the characteristics of the experiment, the formulation of the two alternatives, and respondents' choices, each answer given during the experiment was taken as a separate observation. The database included 167 observations, with an average of 33.5 observations per respondent.

10.3.1 Descriptive Statistics

The sample used for the estimation was obtained using the observations gathered during the interviews. Table 10.1 contains the main characteristics of the data collected with regards to the "typical" transport services described by each respondent and used as the benchmark for the experiment (column A).

---

[12] It is extremely important that the respondent rank options in their desired order, having a clear understanding of the scaling, so to indicate as accurately as possible their strength of preference (Tweedle et al. 1995).

[13] Each iteration generates two responses therefore, in the case that all 20 iterations are run, we would obtain 40 observations by each respondent.

Table 10.1. "Typical" transport (average values)

Variable	Mean	Min	Max	Measurement unit
Price	1,633	1,215	2,250	(euro)
Time	66	50	90	(hours)
Reliability	82	50	100	(%)
Frequency	19.2	12	40	(times x month)
Mean length	1,260	900	2,000	(km)

Table 10.2. Hypothetical offers: mean values of service attributes

	Cost (Euro)	Cost (Index)	Time	Relia	Freq	Rating
Mean	1,085.7	65.1	69.9	80.5	14.7	109.9
Median	1,035.0	69.0	66.0	81.0	12.0	110.0

Number of observations: 167.

The shipment generally carried out by the "average" company participating in the pilot study lasts three days, it is relatively frequent (every 1.5 days), it is delivered at the expected time more than 80% of the time and costs about 1.3 euros per kilometre.

The data collected seems to be relatively coherent across the five cases. Figure 10.1 highlights the spread, for each variable, across observations. As can be seen, the range of variation is limited.

Table 10.2 shows the mean and the median values of the hypothetical offers presented to the five respondents. Interestingly, although both mean and median values of the variables Time, Reliability and Frequency are all below the values of the current option, the mean value of the rating is always above 100 (the rating of the reference alternative, the "typical" transport): the shippers always prefer the new services offered. It therefore seems that the savings in cost more than compensate for the reduction in the other attributes and that there is no mode-specific preclusion.

The mean and the median of the difference between the value for each attribute of current service and the hypothetical alternative is shown in Table 10.3. Across all experiments, the hypothetical services offered a mean discount of about 35%, a mean reduction in travel time of about 4 hours, a mean decrease in reliability of 3,6% and, finally, a mean reduction of frequency corresponding to a service supplied about four times less per month. The mean probability of choosing the alternative service is about 50%.

Figure 10.2 shows the variations in the ratings across the five experiments: the range is between 0 – the refused hypothesis – and 200, with the reference option valued 100.

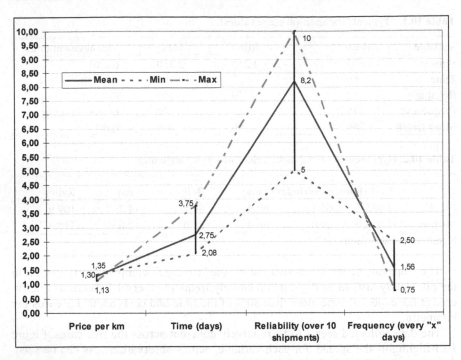

Fig. 10.1. Spread of the values for the main characteristics of the "typical" transport across participating companies

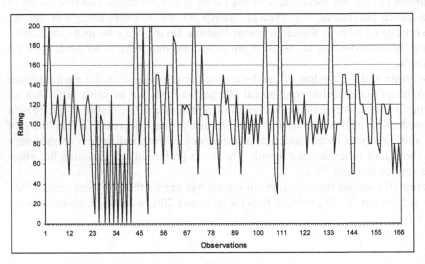

Fig. 10.2. Sequence of ratings. Observations: case 1: 1–41; case 2: 42–69; case 3: 70–101; case 4: 102–132; case 5: 132–167

Table 10.3. Hypothetical offers: mean values of the difference in service attributes

	DiffCostindex	DiffTime	DiffRelia	DiffFreq	Pa
Mean	34.9	−3.9	−3.6	−3.8	0.5
Median	31.0	−2.0	0.0	−4.0	0.5

Number of observations: 167.

It can be seen that the options presented have been considered unacceptable seven times and that all the zero-values are concentrated in the first experiment (see below). From the raw data it is possible to see that these values are related to changes in the level of reliability: the respondent considered the levels of reliability of the hypothetical offers to be too low, notwithstanding any compensatory decrease in price. The respondent considered reliability an essential attribute of the transport service and any alternative transport service which implied significant changes in the level currently guaranteed represented, for her, a non-viable option. As it can be seen, the remaining ratings indicate that convergence was generally found relatively easily.

10.3.2 Estimation Results

The estimation was carried out separately for each company in order to avoid estimation problems linked to the well-known problem of repeated and non independent observations.[14] The procedure chosen to estimate the empirical model is the Tobit ML estimator.[15] The dataset contains a number of zero values corresponding to those alternatives which, given the value of their attributes, have received a rating of zero. Since we can assume that those zero values correspond, in principle, to cases in which the latent variable – the indirect utility – might take negative values (i.e. unacceptable levels of reliability which would compromise the respondent activity), we can treat the zeros as a result of censoring and non-observability and thus apply the Tobit estimator.

The results of the estimation are shown in Table 10.4.

All coefficients (β_i) refer to the effect of a change in the respective variable (i) on the respondent's utility (rating). The coefficients of cost, time, and frequency are generally significantly different from zero. In particular, the coefficient of the variable cost is always significant at the 10% level with an expected negative coefficient. Intuitively, in fact, an increase in cost generates a decrease in the respondents' utility.

---

[14] On the issue of how to tackle the issue in a particular context, the reader is referred to Maier and Bergman (2001, 2002). Although the solutions they adopt are valid and would be relatively easy to apply, in this particular pilot study, given the limited size of the database, we prefer to proceed with separate estimations.

[15] For greater details on the estimation procedure, the reader is referred to Bergantino et al. (2005).

Table 10.4. Estimation results on ASP data

	Case 1	Case 2	Case 3	Case 4	Case 5	Exp.Sign
Intercept (α)	1.290	-15.61^a	-7.67	-4.68	-9.15	+
Cost (β_c)	-0.48^b	-1.13^b	-0.74^b	-1.35^b	-1.11^b	-
Time (β_t)	0.70	-0.13^b	-1.18^a	-1.56^a	0.81^a	-
Reliability (β_r)	1.41	5.42^a	1.99^a	1.64^a	-0.18	+
Frequency (β_f)	1.18^b	-0.71	7.13^b	10.13^a	9.90^b	+
Use RoRo (β_{ro})	-9.11	15.61	-22.64^a	8.05	-12.40	
Adj ρ^2	15%	49%	28%	59%	54%	
N, obs,	41	27	33	31	35	167

^{a}5%.
^{b}10%.

Frequency and time also have, in general, the expected positive sign as an increase in the difference in frequency and journey time between the current option (A) and the alternative (i = B or C) is likely to have a negative impact on the probability of continuing to choose the current service. The only exceptions are for frequency, case 2, and for time, case 1 and case 5. For the first two cases, however, the coefficients are not statistically different from zero.

Given the focus of our study, of particular relevance is the dummy ro-ro, which should pick up the valuation of the willingness to use the maritime mode. Although the coefficient takes quite differing values among the different case studies, it is generally not significantly different from zero. Except for case 3, for which the parameter is negative and significantly different from zero, it is possible to infer that there is no "a priori" reluctance of the respondents to use ro-ro services. In particular, freight forwarders in the pilot study do not seem to have strong preferences either way.

From Table 10.4 it can be noted also that, in general, the coefficients have very low values for all the variables and for all case studies. This implies that the marginal impact of a change in a variable on the propensity to change from the current solution to a hypothetical one is small. The respective elasticities would thus be small as well (see also Bolis and Maggi 2003).

In Table 10.5 we report the monetary valuations of tradeoffs (MVT) between attributes. For each attribute (i), the values are obtained as the ratio of its parameter estimates (β_i) to the cost parameter estimate (β_c).

$$MVT_{ic} = \frac{\beta_i}{\beta_c} \tag{10.1}$$

The values in parenthesis refer to parameters which are not significantly different from zero at least at the 5% confidence level. The corrected average is calculated excluding values which are not significantly different from zero.

Table 10.5. Trade-off ratios of transport service attributes to cost (absolute values – in Euro)

	Case 1	Case 2	Case 3	Case 4	Case 5	Corrected Avrg.[b]
Time	(−1.44)	0.11	1.60	1.16	−0.73	0.53
Reliability	(−2.92)	−4.80	−2.70	−1.22	(−0.16)	−2.91
Frequency	−2.44	(0.63)	−9.68	−7.52	− 8.95	−7.15

[a]The values in parenthesis are not significantly different from zero at the 5% confidence level.
[b]The corrected average includes only the values of the trade-off relative to coefficients which are significantly different from zero, at least at the 5% confidence level.

Each column of Table 10.5 reports the amount of money that the respondent would be willing to pay (in case of a positive value) or to receive as compensation (in case of a negative value) for a one-unit variation in the specific service attribute (MVT). The ratio of the service attributes to the cost coefficient yields, in fact, the monetary values of an attribute at the margin and hence gives an idea of how changes in attributes are traded off against a monetary change in transport costs. In the case of time this is the Value of Time (VOT), in the case of reliability and frequency this is Value of Reliability (VOR) and of Frequency (VOF), respectively. As can be seen, an hour reduction of journey time is on average valued 0.53 euros per ton, while a 1% reduction in reliability would require a compensation of almost 3 euros per ton, and a one step reduction in the frequency supplied would require just above 7 euros per ton.[16]

While the values of both VOR and VOF are relatively high for most cases, in general the VOT is comparatively low. In general, it seems that for the sample analysed, frequency is the most precious attribute of the service required: this is true for cases 3 to 5 in particular. For these operators, the willingness to pay for an increase of frequency is significantly greater than for changes in any of the other variables. In particular, in case 5, the willingness to pay for frequency is more than tenfold the value related to overall journey time. Moreover, the lowest value, corresponding to case 2, is not statistically significant.

Although the sample considered is extremely small and not representative of the category, it is interesting to note that, as expected, freight forwarders tend to give a higher value to factors which enlarge their freedom of choice and the regularity of service than to those elements, like time of journey, which are more easily taken into account in planning their activity.

10.3.3 Comparing the Preliminary Results of the Pilot Study with Those of Other European Studies: A Brief Comment

Although a comparison between the absolute values assigned to the single service attributes by the respondents of different studies might be difficult to carry out be-

---

[16] The reduction in frequency of services varies between twice daily (upper value) and once every two weeks (lower value).

cause of the different approaches used (also in the definition of the specific variables), a comparison of the relative ranking is possible. Some common traits emerge: as can be seen from Table 10.6, which reports the relative ranking of the estimated values of the most relevant variables taken from a selection of recent European studies. There seems to be agreement in assigning the lowest value to the variable time among the three main service attributes considered.

Table 10.6. Ranking of the values of time, reliability and frequency of a selection of European studies

Studies	VOT	VOR	VOF
Maier and Bergman (2002)	C	A	B
Danielis and Rotaris (2002)	C	A	B
Bolis and Maggi (2002)	B	A	C
Our study	C	B	A

The findings of our pilot study seem thus in line with the outcomes of similar research carried out in other European contexts. In particular, the results of our study show that reliability and frequency are the two key determinants in users' choice of transport mode.

In contrast with the other studies, however, the relative importance of frequency and reliability are reversed, with the former assuming a greater weight. The outcome is not unexpected and can be easily justified. Even with all the drawbacks of the exiguity of the sample, the study, focussing on the choice of maritime transport versus currently used alternatives, has highlighted the specificity of the context. In transport services performed by sea the availability of regular transport – i.e. a regular frequency of the service demanded – becomes a strong decisional factor for firms which have to abandon the currently used mode of transport. In this context, reliability assumes a secondary role: a decrease in reliability is easily taken into account by price changes and by contractual agreements. The unavailability of service when needed would, instead, completely preclude the use of the mode.

Increases in journey time, which assume an extremely low value, are considered strictly linked with the maritime alternative and are immediately internalised in the reorganisation of the transport service adopted when deciding to view the ro-ro alternative as viable.

10.4 Concluding Remarks

In this paper we have presented preliminary evidence from a pilot study carried out with the primary objective of testing the validity of adaptive conjoint data collecting methods in analysing operators' preferences when redirecting current on-land transport services to a hypothetical maritime ro-ro alternative. Secondary objectives, though not less important, have been to obtain a preliminary rating of the transport attributes included in the stated preference experiment and a first on-the-field test of the soundness of the selection carried out with respect to the analysis of the maritime ro-ro context.

The application has involved a small sample of freight forwarders localised in the area of influence of the port of Genoa. Freight forwarders have been preferred to producers in order to gain insights from a wider spectrum of possible uses. Choosing freight-forwarding agencies has allowed us to intercept information from a sector of the transport industry which accounts, on average, for more than half of the transport decisions, as outsourcing of transport operations is spreading rapidly. At the same time, it has allowed us to obtain a sample which, although small, is homogeneous as to the type of activity carried out by the respondents and their knowledge endowment. Given the limited resources available, selecting producers would have limited the scope of the analysis to a specific production sector or excessively constrained the dimension of the dataset for each industrial sector. Although the objective function of the freight forwarder would necessarily differ from that of the producer, the recent evolution of the market and of the contractual agreements in force would generally place the freight forwarder in a position to be the residual claimant to any cost-quality advantages obtained. In any case, this is true for the sample interviewed.

The current study has allowed us to test our methodology and the strategies adopted for carrying out the experiment. The specificity of the design used has been to always characterise the alternative service as ro-ro. In so doing we tried to stimulate, during the experiment, an explicit focus on such mode. Although the results presented in this paper relate only to a very limited group of potential users with obvious consequences on sample representativeness, some preliminary considerations on the outcome and on its implications for policy can be drawn. We are aware that, in order to validate the results, it would be necessary to compare them with the final outcomes of a follow-up research project currently being carried out involving freight forwarders localised in northern and in southern Italy.

The study seems to confirm that, as expected, adapted stated preference techniques represent a valid option to estimate the attitude of operators for maritime ro-ro transport services. Overall, initial evidence is encouraging and offers some understanding of the determinants of the maritime transport choice.

First of all, the data collected seems to indicate no *a priori* preclusion of the maritime alternative and, in particular ro-ro services, on the part of operators. The valuations placed on the attributes of the transport services by the freight forwarding companies interviewed are generally consistent. Despite certain important critical variations, in fact, the outcome of the estimation shows a strong and reliable influence of certain characteristics on the decision process. The empirical evidence confirms that freight rates are not the only determinant of modal choice, but that in choosing the sea other factors play a relevant role as well. Most notably, and in line with the results of other studies, reliability and frequency seem to be the key factors in the choice of the transport service alternative. However, between the two attributes, in contrast with other studies concentrating on land transport and producer responses, the ranking of reliability and frequency are inverted. When evaluating the maritime alternative, freight forwarders, in fact, seem to assign a higher ranking to frequency than to reliability.

According to our estimation – which, however, due to the limited database should be taken with the appropriate scepticism – freight-forwarders seem to value a 1% improvement in reliability at about 3 euros per ton and a variation in frequency just above 7 euros per ton. The difference in the findings could be easily justified on the basis of two elements: first, a single producer might consider a change in the frequency of service easier to adapt to than a change in its level of reliability; secondly, a freight forwarder, who often aggregates more than one shipment, might give a higher weight to frequency of service since it contributes more than reliability to solve transport coordination problems and to respond faster to different requests by clients. Journey time, in line with other studies, is significantly less valuable than the time lost for low levels of reliability or for low frequencies. From the sample it appears that it is unanimously considered to be the least relevant attribute: the value of time is calculated to be, on average, about 50 cents per ton.

In conclusion, taking the outcome of the preliminary estimation into consideration, it would appear that in order to improve the use of the maritime ro/ro, maritime transport operators and institutional authorities should focus on actions which improve the reliability and the frequency of service. In particular, any investment or action directed at promoting the development of the "Motorways of the sea" should thus primarily focus on creating the conditions for maritime transport operators to organise their services in order to respond fully to the need for quality put forward by potential users. Investments should be channelled towards those infrastructures, superstructures and services which increase frequency and reliability of sea services.

Acknowledgments

The authors are indebted to Prof. Rico Maggi of the Institute of Economic Research (IRE) of Lugano and to Prof. Carla Canali of the Economics Department of the University of Parma for their support. Our thanks also go to Michel Beuthe, Mons, for his helpful comments on an earlier version of this paper. The authors would like to thank three anonymous referees for their useful comments and suggestions. The usual disclaimer applies for all remaining errors.

Financial support from MIUR – Cofin 2003 grant no. 2003134052 – "Prospectives of short sea shipping in the Mediterranean area" is gratefully acknowledged.

References

Adamowicz, W, Louviere J, Williams M (1994) Combining revealed and stated preference methods for valuing environmental amenities. Journal of Environmental Economics and Management 26: 271–292

Adamowicz W, Swait J, Boxall P, Louviere J, Williams M (1997) Perceptions versus objective measures of environmental quality in combined revealed and stated preferences models of environmental valuation. Journal of Environmental Economics and Management 32: 65–84

Ben Akiva M, Morikawa T (1990) Estimation of switching models from revealed preferences and stated intentions. Transportation Research A 22: 485–495

Bergantino AS, Bolis S (2002) Motorways of the sea: is this a real alternative to all-land transport? Some preliminary valuations on the North Tyrrenian sea routes. Paper presented to the 2nd STRC Conference, Ascona, 21st–22nd March

Bergantino AS, Bolis S, Canali C (2005) A methodological framework to analyse the market opportunities of short-sea-shipping: the adaptive stated preference approach. In: Jourquin B (ed) Towards better performing European Transportation Systems (forthcoming)

Bergkvist E (2001) Freight transportation – valuation of time and forecasting of flows. Ph.D. Thesis, Department of Economics, Umea University, Umea

Bolis S, Maggi R (2002) Stated preference – evidence on shippers' transport and logistics choice. In: Danielis R (ed) Domanda di trasporto merci e preferenze dichiarate – Freight transport demand and stated preference experiments. Franco Angeli, Milan, pp 203–222

Bolis S, Maggi R (2003) Logistic strategy and transport service choices. An adaptive stated preferences experiment. Growth and Change - A Journal of Urban and Regional Policy (Special Issue STELLA FG 1) 34: 492–504

Borruso G, Polidori G (2003) Trasporto merci, logistica e scelta modale. Franco Angeli, Milano

Bradley M, Daly A (1997) Estimation of logit choice models using mixed stated preference and revealed preference information. In: Stopher P, Lee-Gosselin M (eds) Understanding travel behaviour in an era of change. Pergamon Press, London

Brownston D, Bunch D, Train K (1999) Joint mixed logit models of stated and revealed preferences for alternative fuel vehicles. Transportation research part B 34: 315–338

Cullinane K, Toy N (2000) Identifying influential attributes in freight route/mode choice decisions: a content analysis. Transportation Research part E 36: 41–53

Danielis R (ed) (2002) Domanda di trasporto merci e preferenze dichiarate – Freight transport demand and stated preference experiments. Franco Angeli, Milano

Danielis R, Rotaris L (2002) Characteristics of freight transport demand in the Friuli Venezia Giulia region: a summary. In: Danielis R (ed) Domanda di trasporto merci e preferenze dichiarate – Freight transport demand and stated preference experiments. Franco Angeli, Milan, pp 163–182

Danielis R, Rotaris L (2003) Le preferenze degli utenti del servizio di trasporto merci: i risultati di un esperimento di conjoint analysis condotto in Friuli Venezia Giulia. In: Borruso G, Polidori G (eds) Trasporto merci, logistica e scelta modale. Franco Angeli, Milan, pp 115–134

Fridstrom L, Madslien A (1994) Own account or hire freight: a stated preference analysis. Working paper, Institute of Transport Economic, Norway

Fridstrom L, Madslien A (2002) A stated preferences analysis of wholesalers' freight choice. In: Danielis R (ed) Domanda di trasporto merci e preferenze dichiarate – Freight transport demand and stated preference experiments. Franco Angeli, Milan, pp 223–250

Fowkes T, Shinghal N (2002) The Leeds adaptive stated preference methodology. In: Danielis R (ed) Domanda di trasporto merci e preferenze dichiarate – Freight transport demand and stated preference experiments. Franco Angeli, Milan, pp 185–202

Fowkes AS, Tweedle G (1996) Modelling and forecasting freight transport demand. Mimeo, ITS-University of Leeds, Leeds

Fowkes AS, Tweddle G (1997) Validation of stated preference forecasting: a case study involving Anglo-continental freight. In: European Transport Forum – 25th Annual Meeting, Proceedings of Seminar F, PTRC, London

Gattuso D, Pastorino MN (1996) L'applicazione del metodo SP per l'analisi di scenari di mobilità delle merci fra Sicilia e Continente. Serie Rapporti Scientifici, CISUT, Università degli studi di Reggio Calabria, Reggio Calabria

de Jong G (2000) Value of freight travel-time savings. In: Hensher DA, Button KJ (eds) Handbook of transport modelling. Pergamon, London

Louviere J, Hensher D, Swait J (2000) Stated choice methods. Cambridge University Press, Cambridge

Maier G, Bergman EM (2001) Stated preferences for transport among industrial cluster firms. European Research in Regional Science 11

Maier G, Bergman EM (2002) Conjoint analysis of transport options in Austrian regions and industrial clusters. In: Danielis R (ed) Domanda di trasporto merci e preferenze dichiarate – Freight transport demand and stated preference experiments. Franco Angeli, Milan, pp 251–274

Regan AC, Garrido RA (2001) Modelling freight demand and shipper behaviour: state of the art, future directions. In: Hensher D (ed) Travel behaviour research – The leading edge. Pergamon, London, pp 185–215

Stopher P (1998) A review of separate and joint strategies for the use of data on revealed and stated choices. Transportation 25: 187–205

Swait J, Louviere J, Williams M (1994) A sequential approach to exploiting the combined strengths of SP and RP data: application to freight shipper choice. Transportation 21: 135–152

Tsamboulas D, Kapros S (2000) The decision making process in intermodal transport. Transportation Research Record 1707

Tweddle G, Fowkes AS, Nash CA (1995) Impact of the channel tunnel: a survey of Anglo-European unitised freight. Results of phase I interviews. Working paper 443, Institute for Transport Studies, University of Leeds, Leeds

Wardman M (1998) A comparison of revealed preference and stated preference models of travel behaviour. Journal of Transport Economics and Policy 22: 71–91

Part C: Telecommunications and Air Transport

11 Small-World Phenomena in Communications Networks: A Cross-Atlantic Comparison

Laurie A. Schintler[1], Sean P. Gorman[1], Aura Reggiani[2], Roberto Patuelli[1] and Peter Nijkamp[3]

[1] George Mason University, Fairfax, VA, USA
[2] University of Bologna, Bologna, Italy
[3] Free University, Amsterdam, The Netherlands

11.1 Introduction

One of the key features of our modern world is its gradual transition to a network society. This development has prompted many intriguing research questions, not only on the structural properties of networks (e.g., connectivity properties), but also in its evolutionary properties. The present paper will address the latter type of questions.

Many networks like the Internet have been found to be small-world networks possessing so-called scale-free properties exhibited by power-law distributions reflecting their non-linear dynamic features. Scale-free properties evolve in large complex networks through self-organizing processes and more specifically, preferential attachment. New nodes tend to attach themselves to other vertices that are already well-connected. Systems with this topology are generally viewed as falling into a larger class of networks that exhibit a small-world phenomenon. A small-world network is characterized by a high degree of local clustering and a short average minimum path or diameter through the network. Because traffic is routed mainly through a few highly connected vertices, the diameter of the network is small in comparison to other network structures, and movement through the network is therefore efficient. In this context, Watts and Strogatz (1998), two pioneers of "small-world" network analysis, argue that "models of dynamical systems with small-world coupling [for example] display enhanced signal propagation speed, computational power, and synchronisability." While an efficient network topology is good in certain respects, it also presents some problems emerging from its high connectivity. Bad elements such as contagious diseases, forest fires and Internet viruses tend to spread more freely in "small-world networks." Also, a network with "small-world" properties is more vulnerable to major disruption or a shutdown, when super connected nodes are removed either intentionally or through a targeted attack.

This paper examines small-world phenomena in communications systems focusing specifically on three networks each operating in different geographical spheres. The first is the logical IP (Internet Protocol) fibre optic infrastructure that connects major metropolitan areas in the United States (for the years 1997 through 2000), the second a portion of the Italian phone network using outgoing landline calls by district to capture network traffic dynamics, while the third one is a Peer-to-Peer (P2P) data network for the international exchange of music for a particular group of independent people. Power-law distributions are generated for each network to look for scale-free properties. The implications of the results of these experiments for transportation policy and planning, and the way in which they may vary depending on geography – i.e., for example, whether or not a network operates in Europe versus the United States, or whether it is one with no geographical boundaries and rather an international dimension – are hypothesized although a more thorough investigation of this is warranted. Also the paper offers some thoughts about the analytical methodologies, visualization techniques and data that are needed to facilitate a valid and informative cross-Atlantic comparison of communications networks in this context.

The paper contains three sections in addition to the present introduction. In Sect. 11.2, the small-world network concept as it has evolved over the last few decades and the way in which it has been applied to systems in a variety of fields such as transportation and communications is described. Section 11.3 presents the results of the empirical experiments involving the US backbone network, phone traffic in Italy and the P2P musical data exchange system. Finally, Sect. 11.4 presents the implications of the results and directions for cross-Atlantic research in this area.

11.2 Small-World Network Analysis

11.2.1 Prefatory Remarks

The concept of "small-world" networks has recently received much attention, although its origins stem from early work done some forty years ago on large, complex systems under assumptions that the underlying network structure is random (e.g., Erdös and Renyi (ER) 1960). As computing power increased and real world network data began to become available, empirical analysis extended to real-world networks with non-random characteristics. Albert and Barabasi (BA) (2002, pp. 48–49) found that large complex networks possess three properties:

1. Short average path length
2. High level of clustering
3. Power-law and exponential-degree distributions

Short average path length indicates that the distance between any two nodes on the network is short; they can be reached in a few number of hops along edges. Clustering occurs when nodes locate topologically close to each other in cliques that are well connected to each other. Lastly, the frequency distributions of node density, called degrees, often follow power laws.

Watts and Strogatz (WS) (1998) formalized the concept of clustering and short average path length for large, complex networks. Using several large data sets, WS found similar to BA that the real-world networks studied were not entirely random but instead displayed significant clustering at the local level. According to WS, "small-world" networks are characterized by their average path length $L(p)$ and the degree to which there is local connectivity in the network, measured by a clustering coefficient $C(p)$. The variable $L(p)$ measures the average minimum path in the network and $C(p)$ the connectivity of an average neighbourhood in the network. More specifically, $L(p)$ is the smallest number of links it takes to connect one node to another, averaged over the entire network, and clustering is the fraction of adjacent nodes connected to one another. One may view $L(p)$ as a global property of the network and $C(p)$ a local property.

WS (1998) showed that a "small-world" network lies somewhere in between a regular lattice and random network. To demonstrate this, they began with a regular lattice with n vertices and k edges, and rewired it in such a way that it approaches a random network. Specifically, beginning with a vertex, the edge connected to its nearest neighbour was reconnected with probability p to another vertex chosen randomly from the rest of the lattice. No rewiring occurred if there already exists a connection to that vertex. They continued the process by moving clockwise around the lattice, and randomly rewiring each edge with probability p, until the lap was completed. Next, the same process was repeated for vertices and their second nearest neighbours. Because they considered a network with only first-order and second-order connections in each direction of the vertex, they terminated the rewiring process after two laps.

In general, for a network with k nearest neighbours, WS found that rewiring would stop after k/2 laps. As the network is rewired, shortcuts through the network are created, resulting in an immediate drop in $L(p)$. Local clustering, or $C(p)$, remains relatively high up to a point after which it begins to drop rapidly. The results of this process suggest that the global connectivity of a regular network can significantly improve with the addition of just a few shortcuts; in essence, a "small-world" network is one with high degree of local clustering and a short average minimum path.

The third property of large complex networks is that vertex connectivity follows a power-law or exponential distribution. The short cuts across the graph to different clusters of vertices identified by WS introduced a level of efficiency[1] not predicted in the ER model where the distribution is bounded and decayed exponentially for large sets of vertices (Watts and Strogatz 1999).

The finding of WS spurred a flurry of work into understanding the attributes of complex networks, while new findings and discoveries quickly followed. Two parallel studies by Albert, Jeong, and Barabasi (1999) of Notre Dame, and Huberman and Adamic (1999) at Xerox Parc found that when one looks at the World

---

[1] Efficiency in this case refers to the network characteristic of a large number of nodes having a low diameter.

World Wide Web as a graph (web pages are vertices and hyperlinks connecting them are edges) it followed not an exponential distribution, but a power-law distribution. In a power-law distribution there is an abundance of nodes with only a few links, and a small but significant minority that have very large number of links (Barabasi 2002). It should be noted that this is distinctly different from both the ER and WS model; the probability of finding a highly connected vertex in the ER and WS model decreases exponentially, thus, "vertices with high connectivity are practically absent"[2] (Barabasi and Albert 1999, p.510). The reason, according to Barabasi and Albert (1999), was that their model added another perspective to complex networks, incorporating network growth; the number of nodes does not stay constant as in the WS and ER model. The Barabasi-Albert (BA) models added growth over time and the idea that new vertices attach preferentially to already well-connected vertices in the network. The BA model is based on three mechanisms that drive the evolution of graph structures over time to produce power-law relationships (Chen et al. 2001, p. 5):

1. Incremental growth – Incremental growth follows from the observation that most networks develop over time by adding new nodes and new links to existing graph structure.
2. Preferential connectivity – Preferential connectivity expresses the frequently encountered phenomenon that there is higher probability for a new or existing node to connect or reconnect to a node that already has a large number of links (i.e. high vertex degree) than there is to (re)connect to a low degree vertex.
3. Re-wiring – Re-wiring allows for some additional flexibility in the formation of networks by removing links connected to certain nodes and replacing them with new links in a way that effectively amounts to a local type of re-shuffling connection based on preferential attachment.

This leaves the fuzzy question as to what the difference is between a small-world and scale-free network. As stated earlier Albert and Barabasi (2002) see small worlds and scale-free networks as explanations for two different phenomena occurring in complex networks. The WS small-world model explains clustering and the scale-free model explains power-law degree distributions (Albert and Barabasi 2002, p. 49). Their have, though, been other opinions on how small-world and scale-free networks should be classified, Amaral et al. (2000) argue that scale-free networks are a sub class of small-world networks. Further, they argue that there are three classes of small-world networks (Amaral et al. 2000, p.11149):

1. Scale-free networks, characterized by a vertex connectivity distribution that decays as a power law.
2. Broad-scale networks, characterized by a connectivity distribution that has a power-law regime followed by a sharp cut-off.

---

[2] Barabasi and Albert's definition of high connectivity is relative to the number of nodes in the network, and in this context, simply means a large proportion on the total connections in the network. The odds of a node having a large proportion on connections in a network are small enough that they are likely to be "practically absent."

3. Single-scale networks, characterized by a connectivity distribution with a fast decaying tail.

An exact delineation of where small-world and scale-free networks diverge is still somewhat fuzzy in the literature, but the area of study is still evolving. It can be safely said that the two are inter-related and that generally speaking scale-free networks exhibit the clustering and short average path length of small-world networks, but not all small-world networks exhibit the power-law distribution of scale-free networks.

11.2.2 Small-World Network Applications

"Small-world" network phenomena have been explored in the context of many large, complex networks. Not only has the World Wide Web found to fall into a scale-free organization, but so has the Internet. The Faloutsos brothers (1999) found that the Internet followed power laws at both the router level and autonomous system (AS) level. The router level entails the fibre optic lines (edges) and the routers (vertices) that direct traffic on the Internet, and the AS level entail networks (AT&T, UUNet, C&W etc.) as vertices and their interconnection as edges. This meant that the physical fabric of the Internet and the business interconnections of the networks that comprise the Internet both qualified as scale-free networks. Before these discoveries, the Internet had been modelled as a distinct hierarchy or random network and the new finding had many implications throughout the field of computer science. Scale-free theory and BA model have not been without debate. Several arguments have been made stating that the BA model is too simplistic for the Internet and additional corollaries need to be made (Chen et al. 2001). The re-wiring principle was one of Albert and Barabasi's (2000) responses to these criticisms, but overall the model has held. Tests of network generators based on power laws have been found to produce better models and efforts are being made to base new Internet protocols on these discoveries (Radoslavov et al. 2001; Tangmunarunkit et al. 2001). While these discoveries have paved the way for advancements in several fields, the question of the geography and location of these networks remain to be addressed.

Small-world properties have also been found in transportation networks. Amaral et al. (2000) found that the airline network was a small world because of its small average path length, and other transportation networks such as the Boston subway has also been found to be small worlds (Latora and Marchiori 2001). Schintler and Kulkarni (2000) discovered the emergence of "small-world" phenomena in a congested road network. One may argue though that transportation networks are less prone to evolve into a scale-free structure over time given the fact that they tend to be planar. The number of edges that can be connected to a single node is limited by the physical space available to connect them and it is this fact that makes the large number of connections needed for a power-law distribution quite difficult to obtain. But even in some non-planar networks this may be a problem as well. Airline networks, for example, have similar properties. The number of connections is limited by the space available at the airport, and "such constraints may be the controlling factor for the emergence of scale-free networks" (Amaral et al. 2000, p.11149).

Finally, there is an interesting parallel between the study of scale-free networks from a mathematical-statistical perspective and network externalities from an industrial organization perspective. Network externalities refer to unpaid benefits for users or subscribers of a network facility as a result of additional entry of new members. Given the direct and indirect connectivity increase of one additional member, a non-linear evolutionary growth is obtained. This drives the network to a more than proportional performance and explains the rapid introduction rate of new forms of network technologies (e.g., mobile phone).

More applications and experiments aiming to verify power-law behaviour or scale-free assumptions can be found in different fields, ranging from biology, with the study of the metabolic network of the E. Coli bacterium (Jeong 2003), to networks in linguistics (Albert and Barabasi 2002). Appendix 11.A presents a brief review of these applications.

11.3 Empirical Experiments

11.3.1 Introduction

In this section, we examine three communications networks and look at the connectivity distribution of each to assess whether or not they possess small-world network properties and whether or not they are power-law or exponential. Evidence of incremental growth, preferential attachment and rewiring in each network is also explored. The networks examined include the US IP (Internet protocol) fibre optic infrastructure, the landline telephone network in Italy and a P2P musical data exchange network. The results are mixed, most likely owing perhaps to the diversity of the networks examined and differences in the social, economic and political factors underpinning these networks.

11.3.2 Bandwidth Network in the United States

The US IP (Internet protocol) infrastructure is an interesting case to study features of small-world networks. The logical network itself is planar, while the underlying physical infrastructure – i.e., the fibre that is positioned in the ground, is planar, meaning there is a spatial aspect attached to it that may hinder the development of scale-free attributes in the network. This section will examine whether the vertex connectivity of these networks exhibits a power-law distribution over time and whether other scale-free properties such as preferential attachment and rewiring have also taken place.

Data on the US IP fibre optic infrastructure data was collected for the years 1997–2001. While 1997 and 1999 data was obtained from New York University's

Information Technology and the Future of Environment project (SBR-9817778) (Moss and Townsend 2000), the 1998 data was compiled from CAIDA's MapNet application, and the 2000 data was obtained from the University of Florida's The Infrastructure of the Internet: Telecommunications Facilities and Uneven Access project (BCS-9911222) (Malecki 2002). All four data sets cover the backbone layer-three transit providers of the USA Internet and are very similar in composition. It should be noted that data in all three data sources is not always 100% accurate, since carriers often advertise more bandwidth and lines than are actually in service and topological errors have been found in the past. These have been corrected for to the maximum extent. However, for the gross level of aggregate analysis in this paper these data sets are a viable and useful information source.

For all four data sets the total bandwidth connecting to a consolidated metropolitan area (CMSA) was tabulated. For the 1998 and 2000 data sets this was done through the construction of a matrix and the calculation of an accessibility index based on the bandwidth capacity of the links for each CMSA. For 1997 and 1999, the data was provided with total bandwidth connected to the CMSA already tabulated. Capacity was totalled for each CMSA as the total number of mega bits per second (Mbps) of fibre optic connections to the CMSA, running IP. Since binary connectivity data was not available for 1997 and 1999, total capacity was utilized for comparison across the four years of data.

The data for 1997–2000 and 2003 was individually plotted as rank order distributions with log-log plots and fitted with a power law (see Figs. 11.1–5).

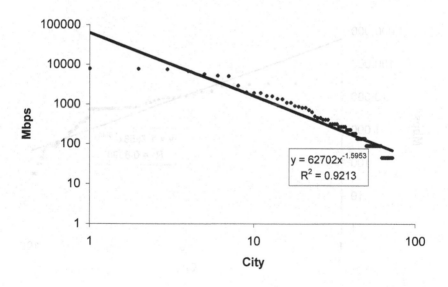

Fig. 11.1. Power-law distribution of the USA Internet 1997

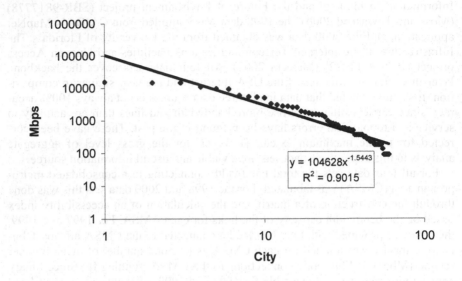

Fig. 11.2. Power-law distribution of the USA Internet 1998

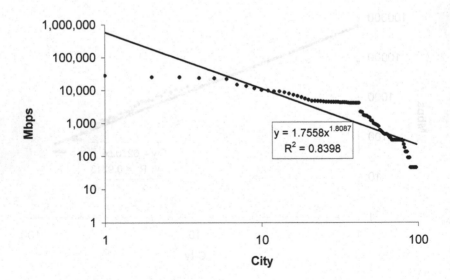

Fig. 11.3. Power-law distribution of the USA Internet 1999

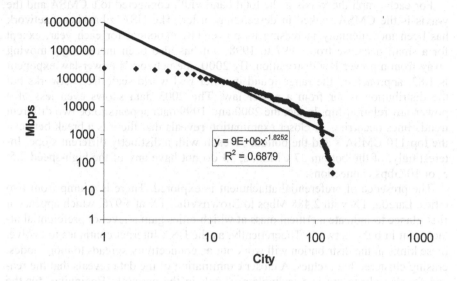

Fig. 11.4. Power-law distribution of the USA Internet 2000

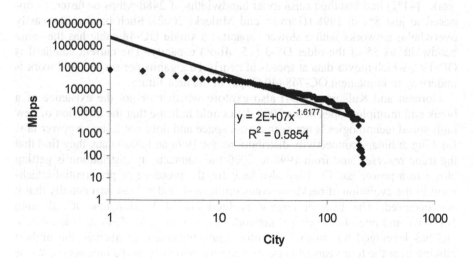

Fig. 11.5. Power-law distribution of the USA Internet 2003

For each graph the x-axis is the total bandwidth connected to a CMSA and the y-axis is the CMSA ranked in descending order. The USA's backbone network has been incrementally increasing its power-law exponent for each year, except for a small decrease from 1997 to 1998, but has also been increasingly moving away from a power-law distribution. By 2000, the network's power-law exponent is 1.82, approaching the range found in other real world scale-free networks but the distribution is far from a power law. The 2003 data shows even less of a power-law relationship. In fact the 2000 and 1999 data appears to be two different trends lines occurring. A closer examination reveals that there is a break between the top 110 CMSA's and the bottom 37 each with a distinctly different slope. Interestingly, of the bottom 37 CMSA's, 33 do not have any of the high-speed 2.5, 5, or 10 Gbps connections.

The presence of preferential attachment is explored. There is a jump from two cities, Laredo, TX with 2,488 Mbps to Brownsville, TX at 4,976, which appears at first glance to indicate a critical mass at which cities gain a level of preferential attachment into the network. Theoretically, as the USA Internet continues to evolve, these kinks in the distribution will work out as connectivity spreads to more nodes, erasing clustered hierarchies. A closer examination of the data reveals that the reason for this clustering is a technology shock in the network. Beginning, for the most part, in 1999 several networks began provisioning dense wave dimension multiplexing (DWDM) lines with capacities of 2448 Mbps in their networks, a large increase in capacity from the more common 45 and 155 Mbps lines. A connection to two cities provides 4,976 Mbps and caused a whole cluster of cities to be bumped up into the 4,976–5,624 Mbps noted in the distribution. Massive investment in Internet backbone capacity has occurred between 1998 and 2000 in the US. In early 1998, only two of 38 national backbones offered bandwidth at OC-48 (2488 Mbps or 2.488 Gbps). By mid-2000, fully 17 of 41 backbone networks (41%) had installed capacity at bandwidths of 2488 Mbps or faster, as opposed to just 5% in 1998 (Gorman and Malecki 2002). Such bandwidths easily overwhelm networks with a slower capacity: a single OC-48 cable has the same bandwidth as 55 of the older DS-3 (45 Mbps) capacity. The current standard is OC-192, which moves data at speeds of nearly 10 gigabits per second, and work is underway to implement OC-768 (40 Gbps) in the near future.

Gorman and Kulkarni (2004) also explore whether or not the existence of a break and multiple slopes in the 2000 data could indicate that the diffusion of new high-speed technologies is not even across space and does not follow a power law. Looking at binary connectivity distributions for 1998 and 2000 data, they find that the trend reverses, and from 1998 to 2000 the connectivity distribution is getting closer to a power-law fit. They also look for the presence of preferential attachment in the evolution of backbone connections and find at least anecdotely that it has occurred. The Internet largely evolved out of Washington DC, through NSFNET and one of the original network access points, MAE East. Washington, DC has leveraged this historical preferential attachment to average the highest ranking over the four years of backbone connectivity data in the time series. While the rank order of the top ten cities has shifted, they have consistently benefited from preferential connectivity to maintain the majority of connections in the network. Although it should be noted, that early first mover advantage for preferential attachment has succumbed to market size in many cases; the most obvious in the data being New York's move from a sixth to a first position. Over the four time series, the top ten cities have on average accounted for 57.4% of total bandwidth. The 1997–2000 time series appears to establish evidence of preferential attachment as one of many factors in the growth of the network. The actual testing of the BA equation to the time series was not possible, since matrix connectivity data was not available for all four years.

Rewiring is also evidenced in the evolution of the IP backbone network (Gorman and Kulkarni 2004). Re-wiring of the Internet occurs at many levels but at dramatically different rates. The backbone network, in general, operates at layer 3 of the OSI (open system interconnect) networking model. This is the layer where routing between networks occurs and rewiring within this virtual network occurs on a very frequent basis. Topologies and routes change frequently as new peering arrangements occur on one hand and the actual path of traffic changes constantly as congestion and traffic fluctuate on the other. The physical fibre that is installed in the ground is re-wired at a much slower pace, but re-wiring does occur. Fibre into a city is typically leased from a carrier's carrier, like Enron, Williams, or Qwest. The long haul transit fibre into a city most often surfaces at a co-location facility, network access point, or a metropolitan area network interchange. At these junctures, the individual conduits leased by multiple different backbone carriers are split off and run by various networks to their customer's locations. This allows for a considerable amount of fluidity in re-wiring topologies within backbone networks without actually digging up, turning off, or laying new fibre. The most dramatic example of this type of re-wiring was the change in Cable and Wireless's network when they acquired MCI's network. The network was significantly re-wired from a star topology focusing on connectivity to coastal cities to a partial mesh topology concentrating connectivity to interior vertices (Gorman and Malecki 2000). While the re-wiring principle occurs at various levels of the data examined and at different rates, it is very much a factor affecting the distribution and connectivity of the network.

11.3.3 Italian Telephone Network

Unlike the U.S. IP backbone network the Italian phone network is largely nonplanar and provides an interesting contrast to the former network. The network examined consists of landline phone calls in Italy, for 101 districts.[3] The data cover the volume of outgoing phone calls by district and their cumulative length. Calls are divided into 4 types: urban, inter-district, international and intercontinental, which provides another interesting dimension in terms of the geographic bounds of the network – i.e., it implicitly brings in a global dimension.

---

[3] Main cities (Milan, Turin, Rome and Naples) are here divided in several districts. In addition, a database using aggregated metropolis has been used, providing similar results.

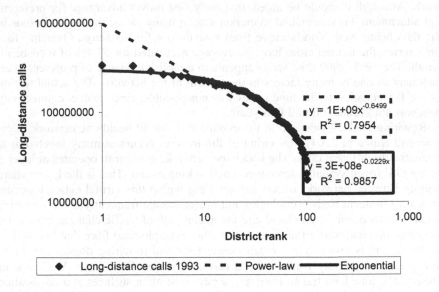

Fig. 11.6. Log-log plotting of Italian landline phone calls for 1993

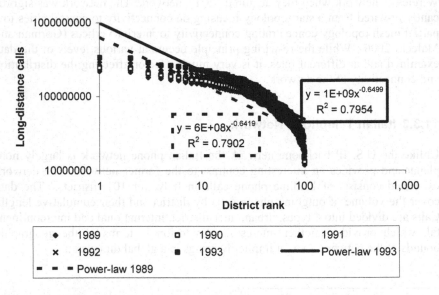

Fig. 11.7. Italian phone calls over time (1989–1993) and interpolating power laws

In order to verify if the Italian telecommunication network, in our case represented by the volume of landline phone inter-district calls, qualifies as a free-scale network, we have to fit the data to a power-law distribution. Telephone use is ranked in ascending order and plotted using a log-log scale to look for a power-law distribution. Figure 11.6 shows the plotting of the phone data on a log-log graph. The data are here interpolated with two functions: a power-law function and an exponential function. The graph shows that the data can be interpolated by a power-law function having a power equal to about 0.65, while the R^2 value for the data adaptation is about 0.795. The exponent of the power-law function is much lower than the value expected for scale-free networks, which is usually found between 2.1 and 3.

The data fit best to an exponential function.[4] The R^2 value of 0.986 shows the high degree of correlation of the phone data to the curve. This result shows that long-distance calls distribute in Italy more as an exponential function than as a power law.

The exponent of the interpolating power-law function does apparently not change over time (see Fig. 11.7). Although the level of calls is increasing, log-log power laws from different years are indeed parallel. This result is due to the strong relationship between number of phone calls and the population size of the cities.[5] In fact, similar exponents for the power-law function can be found plotting city population in the same way as for telephone traffic. Similar results have been obtained using data for cumulative phone time (instead of amount of calls) and different types of calls, like urban, international and intercontinental calls. Splitting the database in order to verify whether the North of Italy had a different behaviour did not generate significant results, as a similar exponent for the power-law function was found.

Concluding, we can say that inter-district phone calls in Italy do not show any appearance of scale-free behaviour. Indeed, the distribution of phone traffic shows a distinct exponential shape, imitating the distribution characteristic of many phenomena, as for instance, city size.

One explanation for these findings may be the institutional framework of the telecommunications market in Italy. This system tends be under-developed especially when compared to other nations like the United States. The SIP-Telecom Italia monopoly on landline telecommunications, the delay in the use of the Internet and the slow decay of the price for long-distance calls avoided a development similar to that in the United States or other European countries. In particular, the lack on competition on the market did not bring about descending prices for long-distance – and international – calls. Only recently, Italy has started a path leading to descending prices and a liberalization of the market. This process is still on its way, and is also strongly supported by the European Union, in an effort to homogenize European telecommunication prices.

---

[4] The equation of the exponential function interpolating the data (for 1993) is $y = 3*10^8 e^{-0.0229x}$, while the power-law equation is $y = 10^9 x^{-0.6499}$.

[5] A second-degree factor can be considered economic activity, creating more than proportional phone traffic, because of office activity.

11.3.4 Peer-to-Peer Sharing Networks: A Sample Case

Peer-to-Peer networks have been on a rising edge in the past years. Although it has been around for a while, only recently this networking model has been pushed to new heights. P2P networks can be seen as a model of a more efficient way for data exchange. In addition, applications of P2P networks in virtual enterprises and Business-to-Business operations are estimated to be potentially successful (Malecki and Gorman 2001; Singh 2001).

Since the inception of Napster, P2P has become the easiest way to share, exchange, find documents and files on the Internet. Endless software had seen birth in the last years, expanding the heritage of the famous P2P software and joining millions of users worldwide in large communities of peers.

More importantly, second-generation P2P software generally shares a new characteristic, which is the following. Information on available files on the network is not treated on centralized servers, as it was the case for Napster. It is instead available through the service given by private users who dispose of broadband connections and are willing to give up a small portion of bandwidth in order to serve as a node for the network.

Each computer serving as a main node to the network receives and passes on file requests – and availability information – to the computers that make a connection to the network through it. In some cases, each computer connected to the network contributes to the passage of the information. This flow expands at any passage, as each node of the network is transmitting file requests on the attached nodes. The process goes on for a predefined amount of levels.[6]

This kind of network seems to be structured in a small-world fashion. In order to properly analyze this issue, a snapshot of online users for a P2P network would be required. This kind of data would let us determine how the files usually available on P2P networks, amounting to thousands of Gigabytes, are distributed on the network's nodes, that is, the users.

In recent literature, Jovanovic et al. (2001) stress that P2P networks (the Gnutella network was used in their case study) have "strong small-world properties", displaying higher clustering coefficients and shorter characteristic path lengths compared to random networks and 2D meshes.[7]

The aspect of P2P networks that we will now investigate concerns the results of a file search on the network.

---

[6] The Time-To-Live (TTL) parameter defines how deep (how many hops) the information and requests of the user will go through the network. For instance, in the case of Gnutella, probably the most known P2P software by now, peers usually keep a default value of 7 hops, which generally provide link up to ten thousand peers and a million files (Malecki and Gorman 2001).

[7] In order to retrieve the Gnutella network's topology, Jovanovic et al. (2001) employed a distributed network crawler based on the software protocol. The Gnutella network's parameters for clustering and characteristic path length are compared to the ones generated by both a random graph and a 2D mesh of the same size.

For our experiment, we used a well-known P2P software and generated a returning list of files by typing a simple keyword and interrogating the network. The list of results obtained (in the month of April 2003) comprises 2801 file matches. More importantly, a portion of the matches – amounting to 270 files – is shared by multiple users.

The data set comprising the files shared by at least two users will now be analyzed. Results range from the most common file, which is shared by 99 users, to 101 files shared by just two users. By creating a descending rank size rule of the amounts of users sharing the matching files, we can plot the data on a two-axis graph (see Fig. 11.8).

The log-log plot of our data shows that the files' sharing seems to follow a power-law distribution.[8] The interpolating function's R^2 value equals to 0.9725, showing good approximation to the data, while the function's equation shows an exponent value of –0.9196. The good fitting of the model is confirmed by analysis of residuals, which show normal distribution.[9]

As we explained above, the data set generating the graph in Fig. 11.8 only comprised files shared by at least two users. Allowing in the remaining cases (single-user shared files), which anyway are the majority of the search results (2531 results on 2801), brings to severe change in the function shape (see Fig. 11.9). The interpolating function's fitting (R^2) decreases down to 0.6441 and the power exponent is only –0.4101.[10] This change in the results can be explained by a simple consideration. The files that are exchanged on the network – especially since we used a keyword for our search – are of a limited number. The remaining files can be considered peripheral in the perspective of the network.[11] If each user's available files are mostly a result of past exchanges on the network, unique files show scarce interest by the network. Furthermore, the choice of the exchange source, for an incoming file request, is not casual. This is usually guided by "preferential connectivity", explainable here as a "the more, the better" behaviour. The user searching for a document or file will likely choose the file that is shared by as many users as possible – and obviously still respecting the search criteria.

---

[8] The equation for the interpolating power-law function (Fig. 11.1) is as follows: $y = 292.77x^{-0.9196}$.

[9] Komogorov-Smirnov normality test carried out on the residuals confirms the goodness of the model.

[10] The resulting equation (Fig. 11.2) is now: $y = 19.77x^{-0.4101}$.

[11] A similar aspect was investigated by Xerox Palo Alto Research Center (PARC). They discovered that up to 50% of the search results on a Gnutella network is actually provided by the top 1% hosting peers, somehow centralizing the sharing process and probably letting peripheral peers serve for less mainstream file requests (Adar and Huberman 2000; Malecki and Gorman 2001).

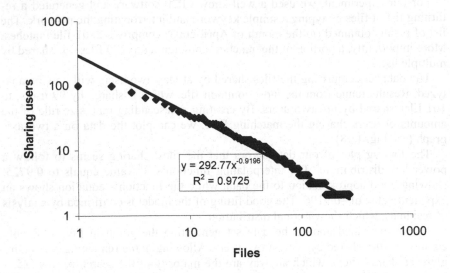

Fig. 11.8. Distribution of shared files over the network users (2003)

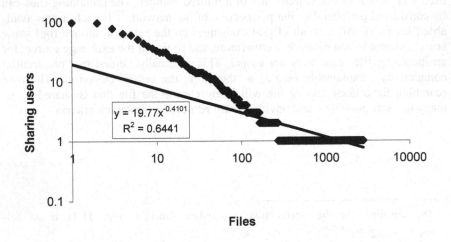

Fig. 11.9. Files' sharing comprising single-user shared files (2003)

Although the power law's exponent in this experiment is low in comparison to scale-free networks (see Sect. 11.3.2), it should be noted that the search results over the P2P network do not represent a 'topological' network, but are just an indirect result of it. The present experiment only stands as a first explorative step towards a more in-depth analysis of P2P communication networks and the data exchange within.

A second – and better – step might be the analyses of the users connected to the network. A snapshot of the network's online users and their file availability would permit to identify the hypothetical presence of super-connectors – users disposing of large bandwidth and archives – who serve a large part of the network demand or equity in file sharing.

11.3.5 Concluding Remarks

The experiments presented in this section demonstrate how "small-world" network properties are not universal across all networks. While a power-law distribution was found to exist under certain conditions in a particular P2P data exchange network and was generally discovered in the US IP backbone network, small-world network properties were not found in the Italian phone traffic network and they appear to have diminished over time in the US IP backbone network. In fact, the Italian phone network, at least with the network indicators used, appears to more closely match an exponential function. These conclusions raise some interesting empirical, theoretical and methodological issues, and demonstrate the need to conduct a more extensive Cross-Atlantic comparison of networks in terms of small-world network properties.

11.4   Conclusions: Towards a Cross-Atlantic Agenda

The results of the experiments undertaken in the previous sections are preliminary and they highlight the need for new data and methodologies to conduct cross-Atlantic comparisons of communications networks. One question that surfaces from the analysis presented here is why in certain cases scale-free properties exist and why in other communications networks they don't, and whether or not the influence of these factors may vary geographically. Would one see differences in the findings when comparing similar networks between the United States and Europe? Thus there is a need for research into this conditioning factor of scale-free features of complex systems.

Furthermore, there are several factors that may contribute to disparities across networks and that may require the use of different data sets on such complex phenomena. First, the underlying spatial structure of the infrastructure – in particular, the question whether it does have aspects to it that are planar – will likely play a prominent role in the ability of a network to evolve gradually into a small-world network. While the logical IP network for the United States may look similar to that in Europe, there may be differences in the spatial layout of the physical fibre in each region. Data on the European IP backbone network and the location of physical telecommunications infrastructure would help facilitate a more thorough study of this issue. Second, there may be social, economic or cultural factors that may contribute to differences in the findings across geographical regions. For example, the macroeconomic structure of Italian telecommunications – in particular, the question whether there is a monopoly, is much different from that in other countries in Europe or the United States. Do these and other factors significantly contribute to differences across regions? And third, there is the question of the quality and appropriateness of data that is currently available to undertake a small-world network analysis. In the case of the telephone network in Italy, outgoing landline calls were used to capture network dynamics indirectly, but in order to measure this more directly inter-district or point-to-point flows would be more accurate and appropriate. Or in the case of P2P data exchange networks, perhaps a breakdown of the networks by region would allow for a more fruitful comparison of these types of networks by region.

Clearly, there are also methodological issues to be resolved. The case study of the US IP backbone network highlighted the fact that the power-law distribution methodology may be too simple for weighted networks. In fact, to date only a few studies have addressed the challenge of developing a robust and statistically sound technique for examining scale-free properties in weighted networks. This should also be explored in future studies.

Acknowledgements

The European authors wish to thank their STELLA colleague Carlo Tesauro (C.N.R., Napoli, Italy) for kindly providing the Italian data set on phone network.

References

Abello J, Pardalos PM, Resende MGC (1999) On maximum clique problems in very large graphs. In: Abello J, Vitter J (eds) External memory algorithms, DIMACS Series, AMS, pp 119–230

Adar E, Huberman BA (2000) Free riding on Gnutella. Technical report, Xerox PARC, 10 Aug. 2000

Aiello W, Chung F, Lu L (2000) A random graph model for massive graphs. In: STOC'00, Proceedings of the ACM Symposium on Theory of Computing, ACM Press, pp 171–180

Albert R, Barabasi A-L (2000) Topology of evolving networks: local events and universality. Physical Review Letters 85: 5234–5237

Albert R, Barabási A-L (2002) Statistical mechanics of complex networks. Review of Modern Physics 74: 47

Albert R, Jeong H, Barabasi A-L (1999) The diameter of the World Wide Web. Nature 401: 130–131

Amaral LAN, Scala A, Barthélémy M, Stanley HE (2000) Classes of small-world networks. Proc. Nat. Acad. Sci. USA 97: 11149–11152

Barabasi A-L (2002) Linked: the new science of network, Perseus Publishing, New York

Barabasi A-L, Albert R (1999) Emergence of scaling in random networks. Science 286: 509–512

Chen Q, Hyunseok C, Govindan R, Sugih J, Schenker S, Willinger W (2001) The origin of power laws in Internet topologies revisited. IEEE Infocom 2002: 602–617

Erdos P, Renyi A (1960) On the evolution of random graphs, Publication of the Mathematical Institute of the Hungarian Academy of Science

Faloutsos M, Faloutsos C (1999) Analysis of the Internet topology. DARPA NMS, no. 00-1-8936

Gorman SP, Kulkarni R (2004) Spatial small worlds: new geographic patterns for an information economy. Environment and Planning B: Planning and Design 31: 273–296

Gorman SP, Malecki EJ (2000) The networks of the Internet: an analysis of provider networks. Telecommunications Policy 24: 113–134

Gorman SP, Malecki EJ (2002) Fixed and fluid: stability and change in the geography of the Internet. Telecommunications Policy 26: 389–413

Huberman BA, Adamic LA (1999) Growth dynamics of the World-Wide Web. Nature: 40: 450–457

Jeong H (2003) Complex scale-free networks. Physica A 321: 226–237

Jovanovic MA, Annexstein FS, Berman KA (2001) Scalability issues in large peer-to-peer networks - a case study of Gnutella. University of Cincinnati technical report

Latora V, Marchiori M (2002) Is the Boston subway a small-world network? Physica A 314: 109–113

Malecki EJ (2002) The economic geography of the Internet's infrastructure. Economic geography 78: 399–424

Malecki EJ, Gorman SP (2001) Maybe the death of distance but not the end of geography. In: Brunn SD, Leinbach TR (eds) The worlds of electronic commerce, John Wiley, New York, pp 87–105

Newman MEJ (2001) The structure of scientific collaboration networks. In: Proc. Nat. Acad. Sci. USA 98, pp 404–409

Radoslavov P, Tangmunarunkit H, Yu H, Govindan R, Schenker S, Estrin D (2000) On characterizing network topologies and analyzing their impact on protocol design. Tech Report 00-731, University of Southern California, Dept. of CS

Redner S (1998) How popular is your paper? An empirical study of the citation distribution. Euro. Phys. Journ. B 4: 131–134

Schintler LA, Kulkarni RG (2000) The emergence of small world phenomenon in urban transportation networks: an exploratory analysis. In: Reggiani A (ed) Spatial economic science: new frontiers in theory and methodology, Springer, Berlin Heidelberg New York, pp 419–434

Singh MP (2001) Peering at peer-to-peer computing. IEEE Internet Computing 5: 4–5

Tangmunarunkit H, Govindan R, Jamin S, Schenker S, Willinger W (2001) Network topologies, power laws, and hierarchy (Submitted for publication)

Watts DJ, Strogatz SH (1998) Collective dynamics of small-world networks. Nature 363: 202–204

Appendix 11.A

Authors	Year	Application	Power-law exp.
Faloutsos and Faloutsos	1995	Pair of nodes within h hops	2.83
	1997	Frequency of outdegree	2.15
	1998	Outdegree of Internet nodes	0.74
	1998	Eigenvalues of adjacency matrix	0.48
Redner	1998	Papers' citations	3
Abello et al.; Aiello et al.	1999–2000	Telephone-call network	2.1
Barabasi and Albert; Amaral	1999–2000	Network of movie actors	2.3
Huberman and Adamic	1999	Distribution of documents on domains	1.8
Jeong et al.	2000	Cellular networks	2.4
Newman; Barabasi et al.	2001	Science collaboration graph	1.2; 2.1; 2.5

12 The Diffusion of Cellular Phones: A Model for Italy and a Comparison with the United States

Domenico Campisi[1], Roberta Costa[1] and Carlo Tesauro[2]

[1] Università di Roma "Tor Vergata", Roma, Italy
[2] C.N.R., Napoli, Italy

12.1 Introduction

Communications' scenario has evolved exceptionally starting from the 80's, when early applications of electronics and computer technologies have caused radical changes: the introduction of digital technologies and the diffusion of Facsimile and Data Transmission systems represented the initial step in the ongoing development of the telecommunications technologies, and resulted in a remarkable impact both in economic and social environment.

Since when Nicholas Negroponte published his book *Being Digital*, in 1995, the forecast on the communication process, and the analysis of resulting effects on the socio-economic environment, found recognition as one of the most interesting international debates, both in the scientific community and in the mass media, where particular attention was paid to issues concerning technological update, diffusion and distribution.

The rapid pace and pervasiveness of the transformation in the communications field can be effectively highlighted analysing two sensational phenomena: Internet and mobile phoning. The main difference between these two technologies is related to the way of usage and technological equipments: in the first one, users access to large amount of information mainly via wireline, whilst in mobile telecommunications, electromagnetic waves (rather than some form of wire) carry the signal over part or all of the communication path, enhancing the mobility of the user.

In both cases, however, a high rate of technological innovation and a process of market liberalisation favoured such revolutionary change. Furthermore, the technological progress strongly reduced infrastructure costs, thus favouring the entering of new competitors in the market and the subsequent reinforcement in the market deregulation.

As it specifically concerns mobile telecommunications, the new investments in technologies, by far less expensive than those needed for wireline communications, have created favourable opportunities for a large number of telecommunications enterprises to access the market. This was also essential for mobile phoning achievements, including the partial substitution of wireline with wireless.

These innovations have encouraged producers of telecommunications equipments and service providers to search for, and implement, systems integrations and standardization, thus leading to the introduction of the so-called 3G "third generation standard". In order to increase profits, marketing power and added value in their services, the principal operators of communication systems have been competing strongly in global markets.

In such a peculiar setting, the European mobile standard was defined as UMTS (Universal Mobile Telecommunication Service). A system that should enable, as opposed to the former one, an effective expansion of the customary and innovative services provided by the wireline network.

This paper presents a study of the different phases of innovation in the Italian telecommunications sector. In particular, analysis of mobile traffic is conducted by means of multi-logistic curves at an aggregate and regional level.

The multi-logistic curve is obtained by the sum of "n" independent logistic curves, each one characterized by three independent parameters: the carrying capacity, the growth coefficient and the midpoint. This model allows the analysis of all those complex growth phenomena that are constituted by distinct processes, both in succession or overlapped. In our case, this enables determining trends and market drives related to the dynamics of technological innovation.

12.2 Model and Data

Correlation between technological innovation and economic development was used by Schumpeter (1939) to explain the long cycle of economy. The behaviour of the couple *"technological innovation* and *market requirement"* is substantially equivalent, even if formally opposite. As a matter of fact, increase of technological offer is strongly linked to an equivalent market demand development.

It is actually often difficult to identify the role played by the technology or by the market, especially when the induced changes achieve a primary relevance. Thus, if similar conditions should take place, a complete redefinition of roles starting from the new reality becomes necessary.

Subsequently, in 1983, Rogers showed how, in the majority of cases, the time distribution of innovation adopters can be represented as a standard normal curve. As a result, the total number of adopters can be obtained by the mathematical integration of the distribution, called "diffusion curve".

The Schumpeter model introduced also the difference between innovation and imitation, rigorously linking the early stage of the diffusion process to "innovators" and leaving to a second phase the "imitation" effect, following the spreading of "innovation" concepts.

12.2.1 The Model

The most utilized representation of technological innovation dynamics is the well-known Pearl-Verhulst equation or logistic "S shaped" curve (Marchetti 1980). This curve starts with a slow-pace growth, followed by a fast growth in the central phase to finally reach an asymptotic behaviour in its last phase.

In particular, from the two "historical" models (*Exponential* and *Coleman*) (Skiadas 1985) describing respectively the initial and final stage of the diffusion process, Fisher and Pry (1971) derived their logistic model defined by:

$$\frac{df}{dt} = C_1 f(a - f) \tag{12.1}$$

with an inflection point at $f = 1/2$.

If the total number of adopters is to be considered, instead of their percentage, we obtain the Blackman (1974) model, that is slightly different than the former one (with inflection point at $f = F/2$):

$$\frac{df}{dt} = C_1 \frac{f(F - f)}{F} \tag{12.2}$$

Fisher-Pry and Blackman equations tend to 0, respectively, as f tends to 1 and to F, reflecting the behaviour of the Coleman model, while as f tends to 0 they mirror the Exponential model. In the intermediate phase, instead, the models in Eqs. (12.1–2) represent the interaction process between real and potential adopters.

Both Fisher-Pry and Blackman equations were widely used to forecast the diffusion of technological innovations, using the market share gained by the introduction of the innovative product/technology as a dependent variable in the global market appraisal.

A more useful formulation of the logistic function of growth is the following:

$$N(t) = \frac{N^*}{1 + e^{-a(t - t_m)}} \tag{12.3}$$

where N^* represents the *carrying capacity*, the asymptotic value that limits the function and therefore specifies the level at which the growth process saturates (it can also identify the potential market), t_m is the *midpoint* and a is the *growth rate*.

Other formulations were later proposed by several other authors in order to gain an insight into a greater number of processes (Skiadas 1985). Finally, Meyer formulated the multi-logistic model (Meyer 1994, 1999) apt to describe systems that experience two o more *operative phases* during the diffusion process.

The multi-logistic model improves the results obtained with the simple logistic one, since several growth processes experience more than one phases of logistic growth, either overlapping or sequentially. The carrying capacity of a system is often limited by the current level of technology, which however is likely to change. If the carrying capacity changes during a period of logistic growth, then a second one, with a different set of parameters, can superimpose on the first growth pulse (Meyer 1994, 1999).

Accordingly, a multi-logistic approach can be used to model the sequence of different innovation phases, since each innovation causes an upward translation of the current carrying capacity (linked to the existing technology). The change of the carrying capacity in time, then, can be represented by a series of logistic curves. The multi-logistic growth model is defined as the sum of n independent logistics, each one identified by a set of 3 parameters (N^*_i, a_i, t_{mi}):

$$N(t) = \sum_{i=1}^{n} \frac{N_i^*}{1 + e^{-a_i(t - t_{m_i})}}$$

(12.4)

We assume, as usually happens, that the measurement errors are independently and normally distributed with constant standard deviation, and that a least-squares method of regression is used to estimate parameters.

Our analysis was performed using a dedicated software tool: the Loglet Lab software (Meyer 1999b). This software implements a non-linear least square algorithm (the Levemberg-Marquandt method) to fit the historical data series to the multi-logistic curve and the Bootstrap method to evaluate the confidence region for each parameter (Campisi and Costa 2002).

12.2.2 The Data Set

Nowadays data related to telecommunications sector are collected more frequently and accurately than in the past. Such a condition however does not imply that their availability is increased. Data collected by providers, in fact, are always considered as *classified* and often researchers have to present only specific results, thus preventing the rebuilding of the original set, in order to ensure providers' privacy.

To analyse the complex evolution of the Italian market, we used aggregate wireline and wireless traffic data from 1996 up to 2000, the number of mobile subscribers from 1993 to 2002 and regional wireless traffic from 1999 up to 2000. In figures and graphics traffic data are expressed in millions of minutes and subscribers are expressed in units.

Finally, to compare mobile phone usage in the United States and Italy we used cellular mobile phone penetration data (measured as the percentage of the total population owning a mobile phone) from *Communications Outlook 2003* of the Organization for Economic Co-operation and Development (OECD 2003).

12.3 The Results

12.3.1 The Italian Telephone Market

The first set of data (wireline and mobile traffic) shows the telephone demand behaviour in Italy during last years. Figure 12.1 illustrates that, despite a small reduction of interpersonal wireline voice usage, there is a remarkable growth of total wireline usage (wireline voice usage and wireline Internet access) and mobile telephone traffic.

Moreover, Fig. 12.1 shows the changes in the market share of the three telephone services during last five years (voice; voice + Internet; mobile). Wireline Internet access and wireless/mobile traffic, reached the 50% of the overall telecommunications demand in 2000, compared to a percentage lower than 10% measured in 1996.

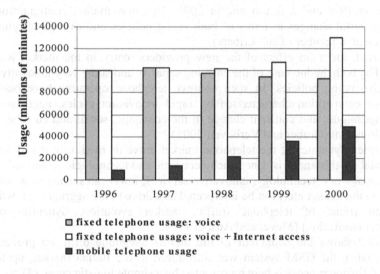

Fig. 12.1. Market shares in telephone usage from 1996 up to 2000

The behaviour of wireline and wireless telephone diffusion (Figs. 12.2 and following) shows that the telecommunications demand is still far from a steady level, as it happens for the demand of Internet communications (Tesauro 2002).

12.3.2 Mobile Telephone Diffusion in Italy

The GSM system was the first common international standard in the market of mobile telephone. It was adopted by all European countries and by most of other continents' countries (excluding North America and Japan) and introduced for the first time the concept of "free circulation" by means of the so called roaming service. This service allows operating a cellular phone outside the usual service area, when travelling outside of the service area defined by a service provider, as in an other country for example (Christensen et al. 2001).

While Europe and Australia adopted a single second generation digital standard (GMS), in USA there have been three different standards in use: TDMA, which is very closely related to GSM; PCS, for personal communication system and CDMA, for code division multiple access (also called IS-95). Obviously, the absence of an unique standard makes a mobile telephone in non-local regions (called roaming) less convenient. In the purest technical sense CDMA is more efficient than GSM, but in actual application, GSM has such widespread following and rich features, such as the near-global coverage available from GSM carriers, to keep CDMA from being much of a threat (Gruber 2001).

Italian mobile market deeply changed starting from 1995 when the process of market liberalisation leaded to the entry of a second national provider, followed by a third one in 1998 and a fourth one in 2000. This new market configuration caused meaningful changes in terms of both rating policies and overall carrying capacity (potential number of subscribers).

As just said, the main effect of the new providers' entry in the market was represented by both the increase of the carrying capacity and some very innovative and attractive rating policies. In such context, telephone operators have been facing fierce competition characterised by rapid innovation cycles, aggressive marketing techniques and constant change in the economic, social and customer-related environment (Gruber and Verboven 2001).

The complex dynamics of the telephone market drove us to choose the multi-logistic model for this analysis, since each economic and technological innovation (introduction of a new technology, innovative services, lower rates, entry of a new competitor in the market etc.) can be interpreted as a drive to the aggregate growth phenomenon (trend of telephone traffic, market evolution, dynamics of technological innovation) (Meyer and Ausbel 1999)

Figure 12.2 shows the behaviour of the mobile telephone diffusion process from 1993, when the GSM system was introduced in the Italian market, up to today. The diffusion process is here represented by a simple logistic curve (3).

The same results (Fig. 12.2) were obtained using different evaluation approaches. In the first case, in fact, a non-linear least square algorithm, the Levemberg-Marquandt method, was used to determine the parameters of the multi-logistic model. The same parameters, then, were evaluated utilizing the Bootstrap method implemented by the software Loglet Lab (Meyer et al. 1999). The Bootstrap operates by synthesizing a new set of data by resampling from the residuals of an initial fit, then fitting a curve to the new set. Loglet Lab reiterates the process of synthesizing and refitting 200 times, producing a sample set of 200 values for each parameter. From these sets of values it's then possible to calculate the confidence interval of each parameter (Meyer et al. 1999).

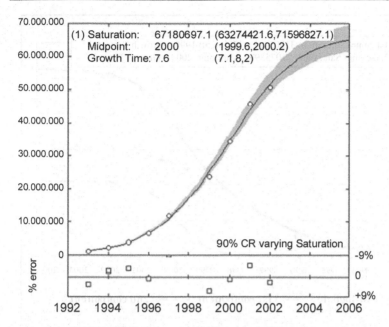

Fig. 12.2. Diffusion of mobile telephone from 1993 to 2002 and its forecast up to 2006 (millions of subscribers). Data source: Mobile Communications Review (1999–2002)

The growth time Δt (fig.2) is a parameter defined as the length of the time interval required for the growth process to grow from 10 to 90 percent of the saturation level N^* (3). The length of this interval is $\Delta t = (\ln 81) / a.$ $\square$

Figs. 12.3–4 show the behaviour of the mobile telephone diffusion process from 1993, when the GSM system was introduced in the Italian market, up to today. The diffusion process is represented by a simple logistic curve (3).

In Fig. 12.2, the estimation of the confidence interval for each parameter (values in brackets) enables the graphical representation of the curve confidence region. In this case, the graphic represents the carrying capacity confidence interval: the 90% estimated confidence region is a function of the real carrying capacity variation.

Our evaluation indicates the saturation of the Italian telephone market for GSM close to 67 millions of subscribers, with a midpoint in 2000 reached in only 7 years (from 1993 – year of the introduction of the European 2G standard). The midpoint is the curve inflection point, that corresponds to the maximum growth rate.

The saturation level forecasted by the multi-logistic model seems consistent , even if it is considerably high, since it shows the value of 51 millions of subscribers sampled in June 2002 close to the 55 millions estimated for the end of the year.

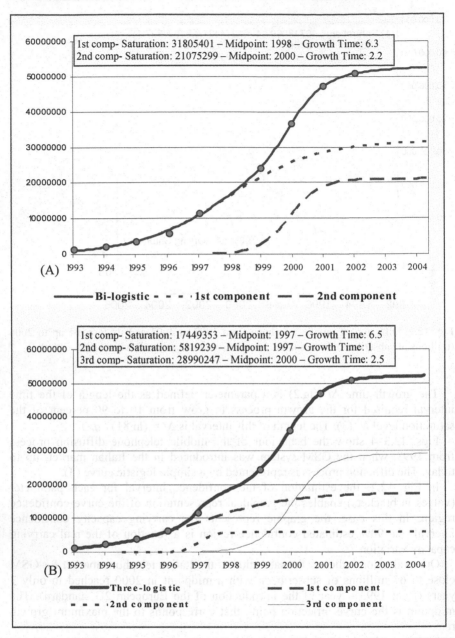

Fig. 12.3. (A) Bi-logistic analysis of mobile telephone diffusion from 1993 to 2002; (B) Three-logistic analysis of mobile telephone diffusion from 1993 to 2002 (data are in millions of subscribers). Data source: Mobile Communications Review (1999-2002).

Figure 12.3A presents the previous analysis, realized however by means of a bi-logistic model, that is two partially overlapping logistic curves. It is easy to observe that the model introduces a second logistic curve (starting from 1998) and substantially modifies both the overall carrying capacity (in this case close to 53 millions of units) and the main curve midpoint that shifts at the end of year 1998.

Finally, Fig. 12.3B depicts the results of the analysis implemented with a three-logistic model. The outcome of this attempt is definitely surprising, since the two added logistic curves correspond to the entry in the wireless/mobile telephone market of the two main competitors of the former monopolist. The estimation of the overall carrying capacity remains about 53 millions of units, but the midpoints of the first two curves seem advanced with respect to former analysis, indicating a postponement in the occurrence of the highest growing rate of the market, due to a fiercer competition between operators.

12.3.2 The Italian Regional Distribution

Figures 12.4A–B show mobile telephone traffic for each Italian region in 1999 and 2000, both in terms of number of calls (sent or received) and call duration. A first element to be considered is the absence of meaningful discrepancies into each regional sample set, in terms of ratio between number of calls and call length. Vice versa, small variations can be observed comparing homogeneous data sampled in different years.

The significant differences among regions can be immediately recognised: there is a group of five regions (Piemonte, Lombardia, Veneto, Emilia-Romagna e Toscana) that absorbs about 50% of mobile telephone usage, with individual values between 8% and 14%.

A second group of five regions (Trentino, Marche, Puglia, Calabria e Sicilia) represents a market share of 25%, with individual values between 4% and 8%, while the remaining 10 regions cover the residual 25% of market share, with individual values below 4%.

The observed values for the regions characterised by an high economic development (see in Table 12.1 Piemonte, Lombardia, Veneto, Emilia-Romagna) were definitely predictable, while the data about Campania and Lazio are absolutely surprising, because former analysis (Campisi 1995) out lighted a special reactivity of these two regions to highly innovative products/services. Instead, the actual sample includes Campania and Lazio in the set of areas less responsive to the mobile telephone market.

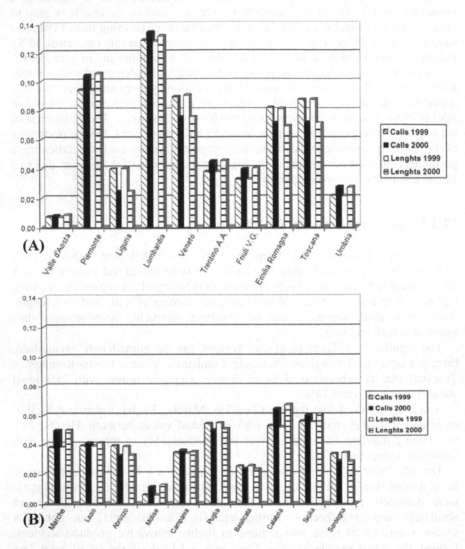

Fig. 12.4. Mobile telephone usage as percentage (1999–2000): number of calls and call length for each Italian region

Table 12.1. Aggregate and per capita families' income , 1995–2000 (Italy Index=100).

Regions	Estimated Regional accounting			
	Per capita expenditure for final consumption of families (1999–2000)	Per capita gross domestic product (1995–2000)	Per capita income for families (1992)	Per capita income (1995–2000)
Piemonte-Val d'Aosta	109	117	118	116
Lombardia	115	131	124	128
Trentino e Friuli	120	122	112	122
Veneto	112	118	109	109
Liguria	117	106	118	120
Emilia Romagna	121	127	124	140
Toscana	111	110	113	120
Umbria	98	97	99	106
Marche	104	102	104	101
Lazio	107	109	105	104
Abruzzo-Molise	88	84	84	87
Campania	73	63	72	64
Puglia	79	66	74	71
Basilicata-Calabria	76	63	70	61
Sicilia	79	66	73	65
Sardegna	84	75	80	82
Italy	100	100	100	100

Source: Bank of Italy Income and Wealth Distribution in the Italian regions 1995–2000, Themes of discussion n. 482, July 2003.

The comparison of yearly values for each region propose another interesting insight. Mobile telephone traffic increased in 2000 against 1999 in twelve Italian regions, but only for four of these (Piemonte, Lombardia, Marche e Calabria) the increase is significant. On the other hand, in the remaining eight regions the usage percentage declined, and for five of these (Liguria, Veneto, Emilia-Romagna, Toscana e Abruzzo) the decrease was remarkable.

12.3.4 Comparison Between Cellular Phone Diffusion in the United States and Italy

As an introduction to the comparison of mobile phone diffusion in the United States and Italy we first provide a brief history of wireless telecommunications in the US and EU countries.

Early on in the US, the Federal Communications Commission (FCC) initially gave away radio spectrum licenses for cellular communications (Christensen et al. 2001). AT&T, the inventor of cellular technology, lobbied heavily for exclusive use of a large portion of the spectrum. However, because of the politics surrounding monopoly ownership at that time, the FCC allowed non-telephone companies to compete with AT&T for licenses. After deciding that cellular should be competitive, the FCC, in 1982, stated that it would accept applications for spectrum licenses to run mobile phone systems for the 30 largest US cities (Murray 2001). The 40 MHz spectrum was divided in half: one for the local telephone company and the other for non-telephone companies (Christensen et al. 2001; Kim and Litman 1999; Murray 2001). A diverse group of companies and entrepreneurs sought to become a part of the new industry and applied for the non-telephone company licenses, including MCI, Graphic Scanning (a communications company), and Western Union. In October 1983 the first system went on- line in Chicago, which helped to jumpstart the cellular revolution in the US (Murray 2001).

In the ten years that followed, 13 million mobile telephones were sold to US consumers (Rogers 1995). By 2000, the US had 100 million mobile subscribers. This statistic was a surprise to many analysts; it was more than 100 times what AT&T had predicted in 1980 and two and a half times what Donaldson, Lufkin, Jenrette, a major investment banking and securities firm, predicted as late as 1990 (Murray 2001).

The development of digital wireless technology proceeded more smoothly in Europe (Christensen et al. 2001) and contributed to a steady increase in mobile phone penetration in the EU. Wireless market penetration rates were increasing by 1.5 percent every month during 2000 in Europe (Murray 2001). In 2000 penetration rates (measured as the percentage of the total population owning a mobile phone) in EU were about twice those of the US: Finland was at 73 percent, Norway at 81 percent, Sweden at 76 percent (Murray 2001) and Italy at 74 percent (OECD 2003). The high percentages in these countries, however, come as no surprise. Scandinavia, including Denmark, Finland, Norway, and Sweden, was where mobile service was first introduced in 1981 by the Nordic Mobile Telephone System. This was followed by systems in Great Britain, West Germany, France, and Italy, each using a different frequency range (Farley 2000–2004). Due to the national systems' incompatibility with one another, plans were underway in the early 1980s to build an all-digital mobile service to allow 'roaming' between countries and other advanced services (Farley 2000–2004). Then, the development of GSM (Global System for Mobile communication) was begun by twenty-six European national phone companies (Christensen et al. 2001; Farley 2000–2004). The European Telecommunication Standards Institute (ETSI) eventually took over the planning of GSM and commercial GSM networks began operating in the early 1990s (Christensen et al. 2001, p. 21; Farley 2000–2004).

In addition to Europe's GSM standardization, the evolution of its wireless industry and geography contributed to Europe's earlier advances in wireless technology relative to the US. In Europe, the evolution of cellular systems was first initiated by monopoly telephone companies owned or subsidized by the government (Murray 2001). Technology standards were therefore dictated by government agencies, which aided in the adoption of new innovations (Murray 2001). Additionally, geography played a role in Europe's rapid advances in the cellular industry. In fact, during the advancement of wireless telecommunications, the US contained many geographically distinct markets licensed to different operators using incompatible technologies, like Europe prior to GSM standardization. In contrast, Europe's compact boundaries and large population density allowed for easier standardization within its national markets (Murray 2001). However, despite these differences in the history and growth of the mobile industry, both the US and EU currently boast enhancements in mobile communication that are important for future mobile phone applications.

To compare mobile phone usage in the US and Italy we used cellular mobile phone penetration data (measured as the percentage of the total population owning a mobile phone) from Communications Outlook 2003 of the Organization for Economic Co-operation and Development (OECD 2003). Using this data, we compared phone trends in the US and Italy by means of a bi-logistic curve (the analysis of residuals indicated that this model was the more feasible to fit the dataset) (see Fig. 12.5).

Figure 12.5 illustrates steady increases in mobile phone usage in both the US and Italy. While the future is uncertain, it is apparent that Italy currently has more wireless subscribers than the US. Forecasts suggest that this is likely to remain this case for some years to come. Europe's commitment and coordination in creating one universal standard has given it an edge over the US mobile phone market (Walters and Kritizinger 2000). In addition, European producers of telecommunications equipment have proven to be more successful when there is also a regulatory element (Gruber 2001). This is partially due to the regulatory element, as the act of coordinating GSM implementation across the EU, offering a crucial incentive for making GSM the most extensive digital mobile communications technology worldwide (Gruber 2001). But whatever the reason for Europe's advantages over the US, the crucial point is that Europe is definitely leading in the diffusion of mobile telecommunications (Gruber 2001).

The first component of the bi-logistic curve in fig. 5 represents the ongoing phenomenon of cellular mobile diffusion, in both the US and Italy, beginning in the early 1990's. The second, instead, embodies an impulse to the growth process due to the liberalisation (in US and Italy) and the introduction in the Italian market of prepaid cards. Actually, in the EU the rapid expansion of mobile penetration rates owes more to the popularity of prepaid cards than any other factor. Prepaid card were introduced in the southern Mediterranean countries in 1996 and immediately fostered very high growth rates. In 1996, for example, United States' mobile penetration was 16,6 percent while Italy's rate only 11,3 percent, but by 2001 Italy had nearly doubled United States' penetration (see figure 5). This was not because US' mobile market ceased to grow, rather, it reflects that growth rates were much higher in Italy where prepaid cards became popular (OECD, 2003).

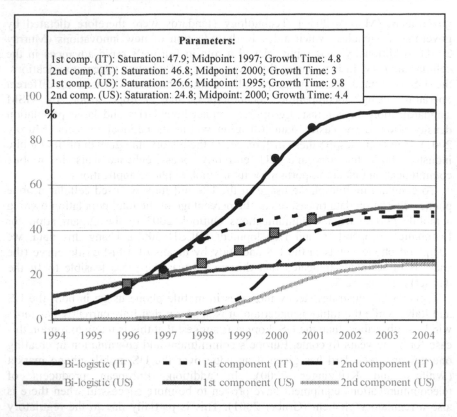

Parameters:

1st comp. (IT): Saturation: 47.9; Midpoint: 1997; Growth Time: 4.8
2nd comp. (IT): Saturation: 46.8; Midpoint: 2000; Growth Time: 3
1st comp. (US): Saturation: 26.6; Midpoint: 1995; Growth Time: 9.8
2nd comp. (US): Saturation: 24.8; Midpoint: 2000; Growth Time: 4.4

Fig. 12.5. Bi-logistic analysis of cellular mobile penetration in the US and Italy. Data Source: OECD (2003) (Dots are Italy's penetration data and squares are United States' ones)

At the close of 1996 only around 1% of mobile users were prepaid customers, by the end of 2001 in Italy more than 70% of users opted for prepaid service. In contrast, United States has a relatively low proportion of prepaid cards (9%) with most users being on post-paid tariff plan.

There are many possible explanations for the relative popularity of prepaid cards in different countries. In United States the relatively low use of prepaid cards may be due to this pricing structure, which is less popular in countries where the receiving party pays. Cellular operators in the United States generally bundle large amounts of minutes for a fixed monthly charge. Operators in Europe generally prefer to meter usage and include lower amounts of bundled minutes in the most widely used tariff plans. The latter of these two systems lends itself more to prepaid cards. As a result, the penetration of cellular mobile phones is much higher in Europe, and more specifically in Italy, than in Canada and United States. Also the existence of unmetered local calls on the fixed network in North America has probably contributed to lower mobile penetration rates, united with a highly performing fixed network. So an efficient and inexpensive fixed network lessens the need for users to also take up mobile service in tenuous.

12.3 Conclusions

The telecommunications sector is characterized by an ongoing market growth and it seems bound toward the most innovative systems in terms of technological equipment for both personal communication (mobile telephones) or information retrieval (Internet). The growth rates and the related market opportunities remain remarkably high, even if the fastest-growing phase is over.

In this situation, the telecommunications market is still highly dynamic and consequently it remains attractive for further investments. On the other hand, marketing and commercial initiatives can modify the market responsiveness and thus give new impulse to the mature growth process creating good openings for business.

The multi-logistic approach has resulted to be highly effective especially for the analysis of the evolution process of phenomena. In particular, the bi-logistic model seems to partially accomplish the aim of the analysis, even if it produces a percentage error slightly greater than the simple logistic model (12% instead of 9%). Actually, the second component of the bi-logistic starts when the second provider entered the market, which, of course, provides an overall assessment of the competition environment. Moreover, the midpoint of the first component matches the same occurrence, indicating a newfound vigour in the telecommunication market, because of the fiercer competition between market players.

The three-logistic model appears to provide more meaningful insights, since this model highly reduces the percentage error of the estimates (negligible values) and shows a characteristic dynamic that mirrors the telephone market behaviour in a faithful way.

Nevertheless, the forecasting attitude of multi-logistic model seem less reliable of the simple logistic one, at least for the used software tool. As a matter of fact, the sampled Italian values of about 51 millions telephone subscriptions in 2002 is not compatible with the overall market dimension estimated by the multi-logistic model at 53 millions of units.

On the other hand, the market potential estimate obtained by the traditional model (about 67 millions) seems excessive considering the national population.

Moreover, the regional analysis of mobile telephone usage in Italy represents an overall scenario substantially close to expectations. Only for a couple of regions the obtained results were different with respect to a general perception of their receptiveness to the telecommunications market.

This prediction shows a different market scenario where the amount of people using different operators and simultaneous telephone numbers will increase the present growth dynamics.

The introduction of the innovative UMTS standard will surely bring about a turnaround in the dynamics of the telecommunications market. GSM operators have already made major contributions to wireless/wireline substitution and this process will be reinforced as the mass market is developed and new UMTS players enter the market with aggressive business development plans. In particular, UMTS players will reinforce competition on the market of wireless voice and specific wireless data services. In terms of Internet, for example, the technical possibilities of UMTS will enable or accelerate the substitution initiated in GPRS services.

Until recently, the phenomenal growth of cellular mobile phone and mobile data services in Europe (such as SMS) had not translated in the USA. This was partly due to the fragmentation of the American mobile industry, but now with over 1 billion text messages per month, there is clear evidence that Americans are embracing mobile applications, much as their European counterparts have done. The US market is waking up to the potential of mobile marketing. Mobile phone penetration in America is currently about 50% with over 150 million subscribers. Although the level of penetration lags behind the majority of European and Asia markets, the sheer number of subscribers makes this a very attractive market for those who want to use the cellular as an interactive channel for communication with these consumers.

References

Blackman AW (1974) A mathematical model for trend forecasts. Technological Forecasting and Social Change 6: 41–63

Bank of Italy (2003) Income and wealth distribution in the Italian regions 1995–2000. Themes of discussion n. 482, July

Campisi D, Tesauro C (1995) Telecommunication usage, socio economic environment and spatial hierarchies: methodology, empirical evidence and simulation from the Italian case. 35th E.R.S.A. Congress, Odense, 21–25 august

Campisi D, Costa R (2002) A new paradigm for TLC assets in Italy. In: Proceedings of the 6th World Multiconference on Systemics, Cybernetics and Informatics SCI 2002, Vol. IV, pp 1–6

Christensen G, Florack PG, Duncan R (2001) Wireless intelligent networking. Artech House, Boston, Massachusetts

Farley T (2000–2004) Wireless telephone history. Available at http://www.telecomwriting.com/PCS/history.htm

Fisher JC, Pry RH (1971) A simple substitution model of technological change. Technological Forecasting and Social Change 3: 75–88

Gruber H, Verboen F (2001) The diffusion of mobile telecommunications services in the European Union. European Economic Review 45: 577–588

Gruber H (2001) The diffusion of information technology in Europe. Info – The journal of policy, regulation and strategy for telecommunications 3: 419–434

Kim S, Litman B (1999) An economic analysis of the US wireless telephone industry: responses to new technologies. Telematics and Informatics 16: 27–44

Marchetti C (1980) Society as learning system: discovery, invention, and innovation cycles revisited. Technological Forecasting and Social Change 18: 267–282

Meyer PS (1994) Bi-logistic growth. Technological Forecasting and Social Change 47: 89–102

Meyer PS, Ausbel JH (1999a) Carrying capacity: a model with logistically varying limits. Technological Forecasting and Social Change 61: 209–214

Meyer PS, Yung JW, Ausbel JH (1999b) The Loglet software: a tutorial. Technological Forecasting and Social Change 61: 273–295

Mobile Communications (1999–2002) Business intelligence for mobile industry executives: Fortnight review of Informa Telecoms Group, UK

Negroponte N (1995) Being digital. Sperling Kupfer

OECD (2003) OECD communication outlook. Organization for Economic Co-operation and Development, Paris

Rogers EM (1983) Diffusion of innovation. 3rd edn. The Free Press, New York

Rogers EM (1995) Diffusion of innovation. 4th edn. The Free Press, New York

Schumpeter JA (1939) Business cycles. McGraw -Hill, New York

Skiadas C (1985) Two generalized rational model for forecasting innovation diffusion. Technological Forecasting and Social Change 27: 39–61

Tesauro C, Campisi D (2002) Internet diffusion vs. the crisis of the new economy. 42nd E.R.S.A. Congress, Dortmund, 27–31 august

Walters LO, Kritizinger P (2000) Cellular networks: past, present, future. ACM Crossroads Student Magazine. Available at http://www.acm.org/crossroads/xrds7-2/cellular.html

13 Congestion Charging at Airports: Dealing with an Inherent Complexity

Milan Janic[1] and Roger R. Stough[2]

[1] Delft University of Technology, Delft, The Netherlands
[2] George Mason University, Fairfax, Virginia, USA

13.1 Introduction

Congestion occurs when the volume of people needing to travel by a given transport mode at specific times during the day, week, and/or year exceeds the available capacity of the infrastructure to support these needs. One of the main reasons for congested travel patterns is that people, while maximising benefits of their choice, often neglect the interest and choice of others. Consequently, among other factors, they cluster around service facilities without being aware that they can do so because they are not paying the full social cost of their choice.

During the past decade in both Europe and the U.S. air transport congestion has increased mainly due to an increase in travel preferences on the part of the public and constraints in the capacity of air transport infrastructure to appropriately accommodate them. Because air transport demand continues to grow, efficient measures for matching capacity to growing demand are needed. The physical expansion of infrastructure is one of the long-term measures. Two short-term measures particularly useful for airports are enhanced utilisation of existing airport capacity through technological and operational innovations, and demand management.

At many airports, physical expansion of infrastructure may be difficult or even impossible in the short-term due to political and environmental constraints such as excess noise, air pollution, land use, patterns and conventions. And more efficient utilisation of existing airport capacity based on adoption of new technologies and procedures produces limited effects. However, demand management has recently been considered to be a potentially useful short-term measure (Adler 2001; De-Cota 2001; Federal Aviation Administration 2001).

Generally, demand management at an airport consists of the administrative and economic instruments used to ensure that congestion is maintained at an acceptable level. The administrative measures include negotiations among airlines, the airport, and air traffic control about the volume of demand, its distribution during the day, and the acceptable level of congestion. Consequently, the airport is "fully co-ordinated" with access limited exclusively to slot holders, i.e., access to gates for loading and unloading passengers. Recently, this administrative system has been criticised as being anti-competitive and for being in opposition to rapidly spreading air transport liberalisation policies. Economic instruments that include measures such as slot auction and congestion charges, are being considered as alternatives. Auction of slots can enable efficient usage of existing slots and provide more efficient distribution any new slots. Congestion charges can be applied to price-sensitive demand when other demand-management measures are inefficient. At present, scheduling flights at congested airports to handle passenger preferences in terms of the arrival and departure times takes into account only the private benefits of flights and not the external costs they impose on society. These external costs are the costs of marginal delays, which each flight imposes on other flights during a congested period. In order to deter or 'penalise' such flights a charge equivalent to the total cost of marginal-external delays is suggested. Together with private cost, this charge constitutes the total social cost of each flight during a congested period. In any case, these social costs include the cost of delay time of both the airline (aircraft) and the passengers. From the airline's point of view, if the total social costs of a given flight are higher than its perceived benefits, the flight will not depart indicating the efficiency of the congestion charge, and vice versa.

This paper deals with modelling charges for congestion at a capacity-constrained and congested airport with free access. The objective is to illustrate: i) the nature of congestion to be charged; ii) convenience of the models applied during realistic conditions; iii) effectiveness of the congestion charge; and iv) sensitivity analysis applied under alternative congestion scenarios and varying demand conditions in terms of flight-aircraft types and airport capacity.

In addition to this introduction, the paper consists of four parts. Section 13.2 examines the problem of congestion and delays at European and U.S airports. Section 13.3 elaborates on the conditions under which congestion charging could be implemented, i.e., internalised. Section 13.4 considers models for congestion charges. Section 13.5 provides numerical examples to demonstrate the modelling procedure and its potential utility. Section 13.6 presents conclusions.

13.2   Demand Capacity and Congestion at European and U.S. Airports

13.2.1 Background

Currently, most European and U.S. airports are "fully-coordinated" or managed through administrative measures. At these airports, demand and capacity are balanced through these measures to maintain congestion within prescribed limits. In case of an increase in demand for flights, administrative priorities are used to select the flights to be allowed access to the airport, those to be rejected, as well as the level of congestion at which a moratorium for any number of new flights is introduced. Sometimes, in the name of fairness, the economic measure called 'slottery' is applied in combination with administrative prioritising. Under such circumstances, at some airports, despite the relatively high level of congestion, this measure compensates for non utilization of another economic measure - charging for congestion. In addition, for example, at some U.S. airports with free access, congestion is relatively low, which does not justify demand management of any kind including charging for congestion. As well, at most airports the current system of service pricing is mainly based on the aircraft weight and is designed to recover airport costs, and bears little relation to managing demand (Adler 2002; Airport Council International 2001; Doganis 1992).

However, under conditions of very high prospective demand that, for example, happened at New York LaGuardia airport between the summer 2000 and January 2001, administrative prioritising combined with slot lottery was used as a temporal demand management instrument until new more efficient economic measures such as congestion charging developed. Such circumstances actualised debate about introducing charging for congestion to regulate access to this as well as to all other severely congested airports in the U.S. (Odoni and Fan 2001).

Nevertheless, introducing congestion charging as a revolutionary measure inevitably calls for a priory evaluation suitability assessment of an airport for application of the measure. This usually includes analysis of demand, capacity, the nature of congestion and related delays.

13.2.2 Demand and Capacity

At an airport, demand is represented by flights scheduled during a given period of time to support travel needs. Usually, at most large European and the U.S. airports the largest number of flights is scheduled by one or a few airlines, their subsidiaries and alliances. The available arrival and departure slots, i.e., the airport declared capacity[1] enables handling these flights at the airport. Demand for flights and the airport capacity may have differing relationships over time which may cause congestion and consequently delays of incoming and outgoing flights.

Demand is usually balanced or equated to the declared capacity of an airport in an effort to prevent unacceptable congestion. In both Europe and the U.S this is carried out as a multi-stage process (ATA 2002; EUROCONTROL 2002; Federal Aviation Administration 2001, 2002a; Janic 2003; Liang et al. 2000).

In general, congestion occurs when demand exceeds airport capacity. Periods of congestion are called peaks. Peaks at airports tend to occur in the early morn-

---

[1] In Europe, the number of arrival and departure flights accommodated at an airport during a given period of time (usually one hour) under specified conditions determines the airport's 'declared' capacity. This capacity is based on IMC (Instrumental Meteorological Conditions) and IFR (Instrumental Flight Rules). Usually, this capacity is an agreed value between airlines, airports and air traffic control (EUROCONTROL 2002). In the U.S., the agreed airport capacity usually has two values: the 'optimal' one determined for VMC (Visual Meteorological Conditions) and VFR (Visual Flight Rules), and the 're-duced' one determined for IMC and IFR (Federal Aviation Administration 2001).

ing, at midday and in the late afternoon/early evening reflecting preferences to travel at some times more often than at others. At most airports peaks are recognisable, but at some no congestion exists during the whole day.

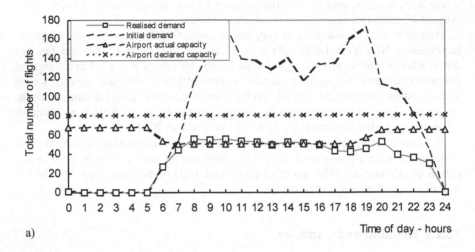

a)

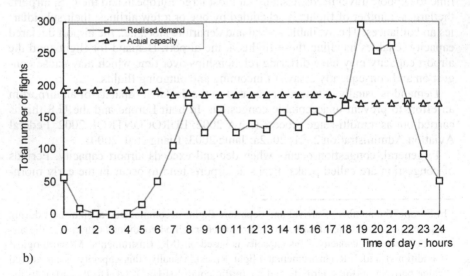

b)

Fig. 13.1. Examples of relationships between demand and capacity at two U.S. airports: a) New York LaGuardia airport; b) Atlanta Hartsfield airport (Compiled from Federal Aviation Administration 2002a)

Figure 13.1 illustrates two examples of congestion at U.S. airports. Figure 13.1a shows congestion at New York LaGuardia airport (U.S) during one peak or high demand day – 30 June 2001, i.e., at the beginning of the Independence Day holiday (Federal Aviation Administration 2002a). As can be seen, congestion spreads over the whole day despite balancing of demand and capacity. Initially, demand with three highlighted peaks appears to be much higher than airport capacity for most of the day. After balancing, demand is reduced closer to the expected airport capacity but still remains above it until the midday.

Figure 13.1b illustrates conditions at the U.S. Atlanta Hartsfield airport during the same day – 30 June 2001. As can be seen, the pattern of demand is quite different than at LaGuardia airport. It materialised in the form of the artificially created peaks during the morning and afternoon hours by hub-and-spoke operations of the dominant airline – Delta Airlines. During each of these peaks, demand was lower than the airport declared capacity, except during the late afternoon/evening hours (18–22) when it was considerably greater than capacity thus reflecting severe congestion and delays.

13.2.3 Congestion and Delays

The time and spatial interactions between demand and capacity may cause congestion and flight delays at airports. Physically, congestion occurs and delay emerges when at least two flights interfere with each other while intending to simultaneously pass through a given 'reference location' or space. Due to the safety requirements only one flight can occupy the reference location at a time. Thus, the latter one waits while the former moves through the reference space. Since the time of the flight's passing through the reference location is always scheduled, the deviation of the actual from this scheduled time is called delay. At most airports, the agreed delay threshold of either arrival or departure flights is a period of 15 minutes. The reference location can be the airport runway threshold and/or the arrival/departure gate (Association of European Airlines 2001; Bureau of Transport Statistics 2001; EUROCONTROL 2001; Federal Aviation Administration 2002a).

At European and the U.S. airports, congestion and delays have become a common and inherent operational characteristic. Table 13.1 presents some delay statistics at these airports. As can be seen, the percent of delayed flights is different for the two regions. In Europe, it varies between 17% and 30% for arrivals, and from 8% to 24% for departures. In the U.S. it varies between 22% and 40% for arrivals, and from 19% to 38% for departures. In general, more frequent delays happen at U.S. than at European airports.

Delays are generally expressed as average delay per flight as well as the average delay per delayed flight. The former is the total delay divided by the number of all flights during a given period of time. The later is the number of delayed flights divided by the total number of flights per period of time (EUROCONTROL/ECAC 2002; Federal Aviation Administration 2002a). In addition, delays can be classified as arrival and departure delays as well as according to the specific causes. A convenient statistical analysis shows that the average delay per flight – departure or arrival – is generally longer at the U.S than at European airports.

Table 13.1. Flight delays at congested European and U.S. airports

European airports (2001)	(%) of delayed flights arr	dep	U.S. airports (1999)	(%) of delayed flights arr	dep
Paris CDG	24.6	21.8	Chicago-O'Hare	33.6	29.9
London Heathrow	17.4	21.0	Newark	38.4	31.0
Frankfurt	30.8	18.9	Atlanta	30.9	26.8
Amsterdam	25.7	23.2	NY-La Guardia	40.1	28.9
Madrid/Barajas	19.6	20.0	San Francisco	32.1	21.5
Munich	19.0	19.0	Dallas-Ft. Worth	21.7	23.7
Brussels	29.8	27.7	Boston Logan	37.7	29.3
Zurich	23.2	23.8	Philadelphia	40.4	37.9
Rome/Fiumicino	-	12.5	NY-Kennedy	28.0	19.0
Copenhagen/K	17.8	10.3	Phoenix	29.6	30.8
Stockholm/Arlanda	-	8.0	Detroit	24.6	26.3
London/Gatwick	19.6	24.3	Los Angeles	26.1	20.8

arr arrivals, *dep* departures.
Sources: EUROCONTOL/ECAC 2002; Federal Aviation Administration 2002a.

At U.S. airports, the average departure delays are generally longer than average arrival delays. The former delays vary between 10 and 20, and the latter between 5 and 15 minutes. At European airports, there is not a significant distinction between the average delay per arrival and per departure flight. Almost all these delays are shorter than 15 minutes. At airports in both regions, there is a small increase in delays as the demand/capacity ratio increases, i.e., utilisation of the airport capacity for both arrival and departure flights can be observed (EUROCONTROL/ECAC 2002).

The picture is different when the average delay per delayed flight is considered. This delay – arrival and departure – is again longer at the U.S. than at European airports, 40–60 minutes compared to 15–25 minutes, respectively. In both regions, for aggregate flight operations this delay is similar (EUROCONTROL/ECAC 2002).

The same statistical analysis also shows that the average demand/capacity ratio varies between 25% and 65% at European, and from 35% to 75 % at U.S. airports. This indicates that, at almost all airports, on an average annual scale, demand is generally kept lower than the capacity implying a lack of any severe congestion and delays (EUROCONTROL/ECAC 2002; Odoni and Fan 2001; Welch and Lloyd 2001). The above figures show that average congestion is still well managed by current administrative measures including prioritising and moratoria on new entries, if necessary, at many European and the U.S. airports. Most delays due to congestion to be eventually controlled by additional economic measures of demand management are not due to the relationships between demand and capacity, but mainly due to other causes out of the control of air transport operators. For example, in the U.S., bad weather causes about 70–75% delays. Airspace and airport congestion causes about 20–30% of delays (Bureau of Transport Statistics 2001; Federal Aviation Administration 2001, 2002a). In Europe, bad weather causes only 1–4% delay while airspace and airport congestion causes about 30–40% delays (Association of European Airlines 2001; EUROCONTROL 2001).

In addition to the amount of congestion, the nature of congestion may also be relevant when considering the potential introduction of economic measures of demand management. For example, at a hub airport with only one dominant airline, congestion and delays occur due to airline scheduling policies and practices. In this case, external congestion costs are already internalised and any further charge may either destroy the present schedule or constrain its further development. In the case of two-dominant airlines operating at the same hub airport, caution is needed in judging or measuring the real interference level of their flights. Despite operating simultaneously at the airport and flights competing among each other, flights might not interfere if separate parts of both airport airside and landside area are used. In this case, the situation is similar as in the case of a single dominant airline and therefore there is no desire to additionally manage demand and congestion by economic measures. Consequently, it appears that economic demand management measures including congestion charging may be effective only at airports with relatively free access of a large number of airlines operating point-to-point networks with a large number of flights.

13.3 Charging Congestion at Airports

13.3.1 Background

During peaks, particular flights may interfere with each other. The demand/capacity ratio is a measure of this type of interference, i.e., the capacity utilisation ratio, defined as the quotient between demand and capacity, which may take values lower, equal to or greater than one. Specifically, if the number of flights is equal to the airport capacity, this ratio is equal to 1.0 or 100% (Newell 1982). As well, during some peaks this ratio may reach or even exceed this value indicating the potential for long delays (Federal Aviation Administration 2001, 2002a). Therefore, such cases deserve or warrant additional demand management, capacity or both. Congestion charging may be considered as one of the short-term helpful measures (Vickery 1969).

13.3.2 Inherent Complexity of Implementation

Despite being a theoretically mature economic concept, congestion charging is still not implemented at any of the congested airports. The main reasons seem to be a conflict with the overall airport objectives, complexity of measurement of the charging-relevant conditions, present ambiguity of the concept and barriers within the industry.

13.3.2.1 Ultimate Collision with the Airport Objectives

The prime aim of most airports is to grow due to their internal – economic – as well as wider external – economic and political – regional and national interests. This policy combined with regional and local development policies stimulate attraction of the greatest possible traffic volumes. If such traffic occurs according to expectations, physical expansion of airport capacity is the usual long-term solution for a congestion problem despite the various temporal short-term social, political and environmental barriers. At present two factors favour such policy at many airports: first, pricing of services based on recovering average or marginal operational costs neither controls nor deters access of excessive demand, i.e., this pricing mechanism does not force user flights to cover the full social costs of their choice; second, the benefits of airport growth often shadow the real dimension of the associated environmental and social costs – damages. Consequently, any constraint of demand due to congestion charging might be seen as a threat to the prospective growth.

Nevertheless, this attitude is likely to change particularly at those congested airports characterised by the lack of non-congested alternative, a lack of land for further physical expansion and with the current short-term environmental and social barriers, which may become permanent. Under such circumstances, a reasonable not-threatening measure for managing growth appears to be stimulating change of the fleet structure by introducing larger aircraft carrying out smaller numbers of flights but serving almost the same or larger numbers of passengers. Charging for congestion combined with other measures of demand management would appear to be able to stimulate such fleet changes including redistribution of demand during the day. Both of these measures should mitigate congestion and reduce delay.

13.3.2.2 Complexity of Measurement and Relevant Conditions

Peaks in which the demand/capacity ratio may be very high differ from airport to airport in terms of frequency and duration, type of operations, and airlines and aircraft involved.

Short, sharp and frequent peaks are mostly artificially created by airline hub-and-spoke operations. Infrequent and sometimes long but less sharp peaks are created by airline point-to-point operations. In the former case, a single airline or a few airlines operating hub-and-spoke network(s) are assumed to internalise the costs of marginal delays of their flights. Thus, it is questionable if such peaks should be 'modified' by eventually imposing a congestion charge on existing and new-additional flights since it might compromise efficiency and development of these networks. Even, some airlines not willing to accept such compromise may simply consider leaving the airport. In this latter case, flights of several airlines interfere and impose marginal delays on each other during congestion. Since the costs of these delays are not internalised, this situation seems to be convenient for charging. For such a purpose, a criterion for determining the level and causes of congestion for charging needs to be precisely specified. Currently, congestion causing delays up to 15 minutes are not relevant. At most airports, such delays occur when the demand/capacity ratio rises to around 85–90%. Much greater congestion causing longer delays happens when demand/capacity ratio rises to or exceeds 100%. Consequently, this level could be considered to be a congestion-charging threshold. However, such increase is very often caused by a combination of factors, some being out of control of air transport operators such as, for example, bad weather. This factor may particularly affect airport capacity and thus increase the demand/capacity ratio above the threshold. The partial contribution of this as well as of other factors is often difficult to measure or estimate, to assign responsibility and charge (Airport Council International 2001, Janic 2003; Odoni and Fan 2001).

According to the type of operations, airlines and aircraft involved, congestion and delays caused by regular – planed – and irregular – disturbed – operations of one or several airlines may be transferred between arrival and departure flights, spill out from one peak into another, and are transferred between airports along the aircraft's daily itinerary. Under such circumstances, allocation of responsibilities for contributions of each flight to the marginal delays of other flights throughout the network and setting up local congestion fees would be extremely complex.

13.3.2.3 *Present Ambiguity of the Concept*

From this perspective charging for airport congestion seems to be an ambiguous concept for several reasons. First, a charge should be equivalent to the cost of marginal delays that a given flight imposes on other flights during a congested period. The aim is to make this flight unprofitable and thus prevent its access to the airport during congested periods. This seems to be in conflict with the currently guaranteed freedom of unlimited access to airports under ICAO agreements (Corbett 2002). Second, the congestion charge is expected to be effective, which in the case of market imperfections may not be the case, i.e., the charge simply may either be too low to be effective or too high to unwillingly dampen the extra elastic demand. Third, the relations between congestion charges and the other airport internalised externalities such as noise and air pollution including eventual relations of these to existing schemes of charging for the airport services base, for example, on the aircraft take-off weight, are not sufficiently clear and transparent. Fourth, a real benefit from a congestion charge may be questionable since, for example, under current conditions passengers, the airline and the airport benefit from a given flight while the flights and passengers being imposed upon with marginal delays lose. If a charge is introduced, a flight might not be realised and flights and passengers remaining in congestion would benefit while passengers from a flight, airline and airport would lose. In any case, if a flight is not realised a congestion fee will not be collected. Thus, it appears to be a virtual fee. This gives rise to the question of a fair distribution of benefits and losses due to congestion charging.

Another question relates to spending or allocation of the congestion fee revenue. On the one hand, the airport may use this for capacity expansion. If expansion happens, the congestion charge source of airport revenues will probably vanish, at least for a while. On the other, under current policies, it is less likely to consider the possibility of an allocation of the fee outside the industry – for developing non-air alternatives to handle airport congestion either through cooperation or competition. Finally, at this time, it seems rather insensitive to impose additional charges on the economically and financially vulnerable airline industry despite, from the social perspective, this might contribute to more efficient utilisation of scarce airport infrastructure capacity and thus improve overall system performance.

13.3.2.4 Barriers Within the Industry

The above reasons have already contributed to building strong barriers against adoption of congestion charges at airports. For example, Adler (2002) identifies three groups of barriers as follows:

- Institutional, organisational, political and legal barriers intended to protect monopolistic powerful hub airports in Europe, and hub bed airlines both in Europe and the U.S. These barriers also include the lack of harmonisation of charging conditions across European countries and across the airports of different sizes both in Europe and the U.S.;
- Unacceptability of the concept for large airlines, their alliances and lobbing groups due to the lack of similar concepts deployed by other transport modes including roads both in Europe and the U.S.; and
- Technological barriers in collection of relevant data on the actual causes of airport congestion and delays including the precise data on the capacity for European airports under different circumstances. However, relatively useful databases for this purpose exist in the U.S. (FAA 2002a).

13.4 Modelling Congestion Charging at an Airport

13.4.1 Previous Research

The concept of congestion charging at airports has been substantially investigated.

Economic theory supports a thesis that the optimal use of a congested transport facility – in this case an airport – can not be achieved unless each user-flight pays social costs equivalent to the marginal delay costs imposed on all other users-flights during a congested period. In the 1990s, the cost of marginal delays was considered as externality to be internalised together with other externalities such as air pollution, noise and air traffic accidents (Adler 2002; Brueckner 2002; Daniel 1995; Daniel 2001; Daniel and Pahwa 2000; EC 1997; European Conference of Ministers of Transport 1998; Odoni and Fan 2001; Vickery 1969). In this context, some researchers proposed charging for the marginal delays caused by hub-and-spoke operations, which due to the lack of direct interference between flights of different airlines appeared to be inappropriate. They used steady-state time-dependent queuing models to estimate congestion, delays and associated marginal costs to be internalised. Nevertheless, it was not quite clear why congestion charging was suggested in some specific cases because the airports, the airlines and passengers had already found a balance of interests within many such situations (Daniel 1995; Daniel 2001). Specifically, a comparison of different models for congestion charging provided some interesting results on performance. However, the reasons for suppressing congestion by a charge were not emphasised (Daniel and Pahwa 2000). Recently, the problem of congestion charging at airports where the airlines might have different levels of dominance in terms of market share and under an assumption that they have already internalised their congestion cost has been elaborated (Bruckener 2002).

Nevertheless, despite being theoretically sophisticated and advanced, almost all above referenced economic models remain within the academic domain. One of the reasons is the above-mentioned strong opposition of the industry. Another seems to be, with the partial exception of the work of Daniel (1995, 2001) and Brueckner (2001), existence of an analogy between congestion and delays at airports and roads, which except similarity in the type of 'predictable' queues do not have anything else in common (Hall 1991). Furthermore, the previous models do not seem to pay attention to the nature of congestion to be charged as well as to the conditions of effectiveness of the charging system. For example, Adler, (2002) suggests implementation of congestion charging combined with other externalities non-selectively at all or almost all European airports. Since the criteria for distribution of the overall welfare obtained by congestion charging is also questionable, it is probably unacceptable for airports, airlines, and passengers, who, at present, look mostly after their individual interests and just a little bit after wider social interests.

13.4.2 Assumptions

In this paper, modelling of congestion charging at an airport builds upon previous research and is based on several assumptions, which seem to support analysis of the more realistic traffic scenarios than previous models as follows:

- At a candidate airport, demand and capacity change over time. They both are known for a typical or representative period of congestion. There are noticeable variations that occur even during short periods of time such as one hour or less.
- The demand profile during the congestion period can be obtained either from the published airport and airline schedule or by recording the process of handling flights at the airport in question.
- Each flight taking part in congestion is specific regarding the average operational cost and revenue, both of which depend on the airline, aircraft type-capacity, and the number of passengers on board. This implies differences in

user-flights, which has not always been sufficiently emphasised in previous research, particularly not in the models based on the road congestion analogy.
- The airport runway system is a critical element of flight congestion and delays. Its capacity may change during the congestion period. The runway system capacity can be determined for given IMC or VMC conditions using the past, current or forecasted data obtained from the airport and/or air traffic control operator. This capacity reflects the service time of specific arriving and/or departing flights.
- Congestion is assumed to occur at a demand/capacity ratio close to or above 1.0 (100%). At this level there is potential for serious delays and congestion at this level or above is considered to be relevant for charging. This congestion can be of any type in terms of the form and duration, which enables dealing with airports serving both point-to-point and hub-and-spoke networks but with the later only if reasonable. These characteristics of congestion can be used as criteria for selecting candidate airports for congestion charging, which is not particularly well discussed in earlier research (Adler 2002).
- The number of flights is large, at least several dozen, which makes congestion predictably dependent on the variations and positive difference between demand and capacity.[2] This enables application of a queuing model based on the diffusion approximation that is considered in this paper as the most convenient analytical tool to estimate congestion and delays relevant for charging (Hall 1991; Newell 1982).

13.4.3 The Modelling Components

Modelling congestion charging at an airport embraces estimation of the system's total social cost of delays during a congested period, which include i) the private cost of delay of each flight; and ii) the cost of marginal (additional) delay each flight imposes on other-subsequent flights (Ghali and Smith 1995; Hall 1991). For this purpose, the modelling procedure includes development of three component-models: i) a model for congestion; ii) a model for the system delays and their costs; and iii) a model for assessment of feasibility of realisation of each flight during congestion period after imposing a charge.

13.4.3.1 Model for Congestion

Currently, congestion at transport facilities is usually modelled by using queuing and simulation models. Newell (1982), Odoni et al. (1997), and Hall (1998) describe one of the models based on a diffusion approximation to deal with severe congestion conditions. In this paper, this model is modified in order to appropriately handle the problem of quantifying congestion to be charged at an airport.

---

[2] For example, for the non-stationary Poisson arrival/departure processes, if the numbers of users-customers during a given period are greater, the random variations of such greater numbers will be smaller (Hall 1991).

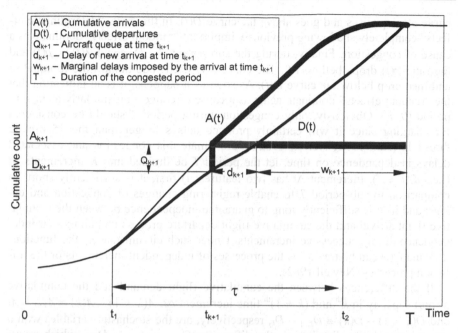

Fig. 13.2. Typical process of congestion at an airport

Figure 13.2 illustrates visualisation of this model as a graphical representation of a typical congestion process at an airport during a dynamic period of congestion, period T. For the 'point-to-point' airport, period T may last for several hours or even for the whole day.

For the hub-and-spoke airport, period T may relate to duration of one 'wave' of incoming and outgoing flights of one or few airlines. As can be seen, the lines $A(t)$ and $D(t)$ represent the cumulative count of those flights requesting service and those being served, respectively, by time t. Since the cumulative number of flights is assumed to be large ($>> 1.0$) both types of counts, actually being the step functions of time, can be considered as their continuous (smooth) counterparts. The curves $A(t)$ and $D(t)$ can be derived either as a single realisation or as the average of many realisations during period T. Since both curves change in time, their relationship also changes. By deriving functions $A(t)$ and $D(t)$ with respect to the variable t the intensity of demand and the capacity can be obtained, respectively, as follows: $\lambda(t) = dA(t)/dt$ and $\mu(t) = dD(t) / dt$. Consequently, the demand capacity ratio $\rho(t)$ as the time-dependent function can be obtained as $\rho(t) = \lambda(t) / \mu(t)$.

In Fig. 13.2, dependence on the values of function $\rho(t)$ compared to the 'critical' value 1.0, three sub-periods can be observed. In the first one $(0, t_1)$, $\rho(t)$ is less than 1.0, i.e. $\lambda(t) < \mu(t)$ implying that only "random effects" cause congestion. The curve $A(t)$ lies bellow the curve $D(t)$. During the second sub-period $\tau \equiv (t_1, t_2)$, $\lambda(t)$ becomes first equal to and after that greater than $\mu(t)$, the function $\rho(t)$ first equalises to and then becomes greater than 1.0, respectively. Consequently the curve $a(t)$ equalises and goes above the curve $D(t)$. In this case, "deterministic effects" completely shadowing previously important "random effects" dominate as a cause of congestion. Finally, during the sub-period (t_2, T), again $\lambda(t) < \mu(t)$ and the ratio $\rho(t)$ drops bellow 1.0. The curve $A(t)$ needs additional time to equalise and then drop below the curve $D(t)$. As soon as it happens, it is an indication that the "random effects" dominate again as a cause of congestion similarly as in sub-period $(0, t_1)$. Obviously, only congestion during period T should be considered for charging since it will certainly produce delays longer than the 15 minute threshold (Hall 1991; Newell 1982). To estimate this congestion and associated delays in dependence on time, let the period T be divided into K increments Δt (i.e., $K\Delta t \approx T$). Increment Δt has two features: i) first, it is sufficiently short[3] in comparison to sub-period T to enable registering changes of congestion and delays; and ii) it is sufficiently long to guarantee independence between the cumulative flight arrival and the cumulative flight departure process including their independence during successive increments. Under such circumstances, the functions $A(t)$ and $D(t)$ can be treated as the processes of independent increments or the diffusion processes (Newell 1982).

If the differences between the cumulative flight demand and the cumulative airport capacity in k^{th} and $(k + 1)^{th}$ time increment Δt, $A(k + 1) - A(k) \equiv A_{k+1} - A_k$ and $D(k + 1) - D(k) \equiv D_{k+1} - D_k$, respectively, are the stochastic variables with a normal probability distribution, the difference $Q_{k+1} = A_{k+1} - D_{k+1}$, which represents the queue in the $(k + 1)^{th}$ increment Δt, will also be the stochastic variable with normal probability distribution ($k \in K$) (Newell 1982). Consequently, the queue of flights in $(k + 1)^{th}$ increment Δt can be approximated as follows:

$$Q_{k+1} = Q_k + \overline{Q}_{k+1} + B_{k+1} = Q_k + (\lambda_{k+1} - \mu_{k+1})\Delta t + B_{k+1} \qquad (13.1)$$

$$\text{for } k = 0, 1, 2, \dots , K - 1$$

where Q_k is the actual queue in k^{th} increment Δt; $\overline{Q}_{k+1}$ is the average queue in $(k + 1)^{th}$ increment Δt; λ_{k+1} is the intensity of flight demand in $(k + 1)^{th}$ increment Δt; μ_{k+1} is the airport capacity, i.e., the flight service rate, in $(k + 1)^{th}$ increment Δt; B_{k+1} is the anticipated deviation of the flight queue from its average value in $(k + 1)^{th}$ increment Δt.

As can be seen, the average queue of flights either increases or decreases in accordance with the behaviour of $\lambda_{k+1} > \mu_{k+1}$ or $\lambda_{k+1} < \mu_{k+1}$.

The anticipated deviation B_{k+1} in Eq. (13.1) can be estimated as follows (Newell 1982):

---

[3] For example, if T is a period of several hours during the day, Δt will certainly be a quarter, a half or an hour.

$$B_{k+1} \cong \sqrt{\Delta t(\sigma_{a,k+1}^2 / \bar{t}_{a,k+1}^3 + \sigma_{d,k+1}^2 / \bar{t}_{d,k+1}^3) * C} \qquad (13.2)$$

$$\text{for } k = 0, 1, 2, \ldots, K - 1$$

where $\bar{t}_{a,k+1}; \bar{t}_{d,k+1}$ is the average inter-arrival and service time, respectively, of a flight in $(k + 1)^{th}$ increment Δt; $\sigma_{a, k+1}$; $\sigma_{d, k+1}$ is the standard deviation of inter-arrival and service time, respectively, of a flight in $(k + 1)^{th}$ increment Δt; C is a constant $(C = \Phi^1(1 - p)$, where Φ^1 is the inverse Laplace function and p is the probability that the queue in $(k + 1)^{th}$ increment Δt will spill out of the confidence interval $(\overline{Q}_{k+1} \pm B_{k+1})$.

In Eq. (13.2), the variance of distributions of the flight inter-arrival and flight service time are assumed to be independent in the successive k^{th} and $(k + 1)^{th}$ increment Δt (Newell 1982).

In Eq. (13.1) and Fig. 13.2, at the beginning of period T, the function $\rho(t)$ takes the value one [1] for the first time, and the deterministic queue begins to build up. However, this queue continues to be built up due to the previously dominating "random effects". The already existing queue $\overline{Q}_0$ can be approximated as follows (Newell 1982):

$$\overline{Q}_0 \equiv Q_{m/(\lambda_m = \mu_m)} =$$

$$= \left\{ \left(\frac{1}{\left[(\sigma_{a,m} / \bar{t}_{a,m})^2 + (\sigma_{d,m} / \bar{t}_{d,m})^2 \right]^2} \right) * (1 / \mu_m) * (d\rho_m / dt) \right\}^{-1/3} \qquad (13.3)$$

where m is the time increment Δt in which the intensity of flight demand becomes for the first time equal to the flight service rate, i.e., to capacity $(m \square K)$.

Other symbols are analogous to those in the previous equations.

Similar Eqs. (13.1–3), if reasonable, can be applied to determine the flight queue for the frequent congestion periods in which the demand/capacity ratio $\rho(t)$ is close, equal to or greater than one, which is the characterisation of the hub-and-spoke operations.

13.4.3.2 Model for the System Delays and Their Costs

From Eqs. (13.1–3), delay of a flight joining the queue in $(k + 1)^{th}$ increment Δt can be approximated as follows:

$$d_{k+1} = Q_{k+1} * (\bar{t}_{d,k+1} + B_{d,k+1}) = Q_{k+1} * \left[\bar{t}_{d,k+1} + \sigma_{d,k+1} * \Phi^{-1}(1 - p) \right] \qquad (13.4)$$

where the symbols are as in the previous equations.

Equation (13.4) assumes that the flight service rate (i.e., the airport capacity) does not change during the service of queue Q_{k+1}.

In Fig. 13.2, the marginal delay of a flight that arrived during the $(k + 1)^{th}$ increment Δt is imposed on all subsequent flights until the end of the congested period T can be determined as:

$$w_{k+1} \cong T - [(k+1)\Delta t + d_{k+1}] \equiv (\bar{t}_{d,k+1} + B_{d,k+1}) * \sum_{l=k+1}^{K} [1/(\bar{t}_{a,l} + B_{a,l}] * \Delta t =$$

(13.5)

$$= [\bar{t}_{d,k+1} + \sigma_{d,k+1} * \Phi^{-1}(1-p)] * \sum_{l=k+1}^{K} \{1/[\bar{t}_{a,l} + \sigma_{a,k} * \Phi^{-1}(1-p)]\} * \Delta t$$

where all symbols are as in the previous equations.

From Eq. (13.5), the marginal delay that a flight imposes on other flights is proportional to the product of its service time, i.e., the airport service rate or capacity at the time the flight is served, and the number of the subsequent affected flights. In such a context, for example, falling of airport capacity combined with increased volatility will certainly increase marginal delays. As well, if the flight is scheduled closer to the beginning of a congestion period, the marginal delays will be longer, and vice versa.

If a given flight belongs to the group of $N_i(T)$ uniformly distributed flights scheduled by airline i during the period T together with the flights of other $M - 1$ airlines, i.e., $N(T) = \sum_{i=1}^{M} N_i(T) \equiv A(T)$, the total cost of marginal delays it imposes on all succeeding flights during congested period can be determined as follows:

$$C_{m,k+1}^{i} = [1 - N_i(T)/N(T)] * [\bar{t}_{d,k+1} + \sigma_{d,k+1}\Phi^{-1}(1-p)] *$$

(13.6)

$$* \sum_{l=k+1}^{K} c_l(n_l) * \{1/[\bar{t}_{a,l} + \sigma_{a,l}\Phi^{-1}(1-p)]\} * \Delta t$$

where $c_l(n_l)$ is the average cost per unit of delay of a flight of the seat capacity n_l scheduled in l^{th} increment Δt, in monetary units per unit of time.

Other symbols are as in the previous equations.

The cost per flight $c_l(n_l)$ may include the cost of aircraft and passenger delay. Equation (13.6) shows that the total marginal cost imposed on the succeeding flights by a flight of an airline i will increase with decreasing airport service rates (capacity) and increases in volatility as well as with an increase in the number and capacity of flights during the congested period. Under the other constant conditions, this marginal cost will decrease with increasing numbers of flights of a given airline that are assumed to already be internalised. This implies that congestion charging seems to favour a stronger airline presence and disfavour the airlines endeavouring to strengthen their market position with additional flights or new entrants currently with no flights. This outcome smacks of protection for airlines that have already gained rights and would promote monopolistic or oligopolistic oriented outcomes.

13.4.3.3 Model for Assessment of Feasibility of a Given Flight

The congestion charge is efficient if it compromises the expected profitability of a new flight. Thus, if the charge deters access of a new flight or removes a flight from the airport during congested period. If the charge is $C^i_{m,k+1}$ and if the average cost per unit of time of a given flight of capacity n of airline i in $(k + 1)^{th}$ increment Δt is $c^i_{k+1}(n)$, the total social cost imposed by this flight will be as follows:

$$C^i_{f,k+1} = c^i_{k+1}(n) * \left[t^i_{f,k+1} + d_{k+1} \right] + C^i_{m,k+1} \tag{13.7}$$

where $t^i_{f,k+1}$ is the duration of a given flight of airline i scheduled in the $(k + 1)^{th}$ increment Δt.

Other symbols are as in the previous equations.

If the airfare includes the congestion charge, the expected revenue of a flight can be estimated as follows:

$$R^i_{f,k+1} = p^i_{k+1}(L, C^i_{m,k+1}) * \lambda^i_{k+1} \left[p^i_{k+1}(L, C^i_{m,k+1}) \right] * n^i_{k+1} \tag{13.8}$$

where $p^i_{k+1}(L, C^i_{m,k+1})$ is the average airfare "corrected" by the congestion charge $C^i_{m,k+1}$ imposed on a given flight scheduled by airline i on route L in $(k + 1)^{th}$ increment Δt; $\lambda^i_{k+1}[p^i_{k+1}(L, C^i_{m,k+1})]$ is the expected load factor influenced by the "corrected" airfare of a given flight of airline i in $(k + 1)^{th}$ increment Δt; n^i_{k+1} is the seat capacity of a given flight of airline i in $(k + 1)^{th}$ increment Δt.

The "corrected" airfare $p^i_{k+1}(L, C^i_{m,k+1})$ in Eq. (13.8) can be determined as follows:

$$p^i_{k+1}(L, C^i_{m,k+1}) = p^i_{k+1}(L) + C^i_{m,k+1} / n^i_{k+1} \tag{13.9}$$

where $p^i_{k+1}(L)$ is the basic average airfare at a given flight of airline i on route L in $(k + 1)^{th}$ increment Δt.

As can be seen, if the airfare $p^i_{k+1}(L)$ is constant, its relative increase due to the congestion charge will be higher for smaller-cheaper flights. As well, its relative increase will be higher when a smaller-cheaper flight imposes longer marginal delay on the greater number of the more expensive succeeding flights, than otherwise. In practice, this means that small regional airplanes intending to operate at congested airport(s) in the morning peak(s) will certainly be charged more and thus deterred from accessing the airport at that time. In addition, if demand is elastic, increase in the airfare due to the congestion charge will generally diminish the number of passengers, certainly cause a fall in the total flight revenue below the total cost despite the higher average airfare and thus force the airline to give up from a flight at the intended time. This will occur despite the fact that some passengers may still benefit from travelling at that time.

From Eqs. (13.7–8) it follows that a given flight will be unprofitable under following condition:

$$R^i_{f,k+1} - C^i_{f,k+1} = p^i_{k+1}(L, C^i_{m,k+1}) * \lambda^i_{k+1} \left[p^i_{k+1}(L, C^i_{m,k+1}) \right] * n^i_{k+1} -$$
$$- c^i_{k+1}(n) * \left[t^i_{f,k+1} + d_{k+1} \right] - C^i_{m,k+1} \leq 0$$

(13.10)

where all symbols are as in the previous equations.

If charge $C^i_{m,k+1}$ determined by Eq. (13.6) does not fulfil the condition in Eq. (13.10), it should be increased to at least make the expected profit per flight negative, other factors remaining constant.

13.5 An Application of the Proposed Models

13.5.1 Setting up the Case

The proposed models for charging congestion at an airport are applied to the case of New York (NY) La Guardia airport. This is an example of a heavily congested airport and with the most advanced ideas on introducing this concept (Odoni and Fan 2002). As one of the three largest airports in the New York area LaGuardia serves the U.S. domestic short- and medium-distance 'point-to-point' traffic. Most of its traffic is origin or destination (about 92% of the total number of flights) and about 45–55% are business passengers. One of the main driving forces of this type of traffic is closeness of the airport to Manhattan in the centre of New York City – about 18km away. After the September 11, 2001 terrorist attack followed by an immediate sharp decline, the traffic has gradually recovered and reached an annual number of about 22 million passengers and 358 thousand flights (by the end of 2002). The average number of passengers per flight has been relatively stable during the past five years at between 58–62 (PANYNJ 2003).

Currently, 20 airlines operate at the La Guardia. Three have the greatest market share in terms of the number of flights and the number of passengers, respectively: US Airways (38%; 14.2%), Delta (18%; 17.2%), and American (17%; 18.5%). Two right angle-crossing runways, each 7000ft (2135 m) long, mostly influence fleet type and length of routes and markets served to/from the airport. The fleet mostly consists of B737/717 with a capacity of 100–150 seats, and of smaller regional jets and turboprops with a capacity of 70–110 seats. The average route length to/from LaGuardia airport is about 1200 km (Backer 2000; Port Authority of New York & New Jersey (PANYNJ) 2003).

The airport runway capacity is about 80 (40/40) aircraft movements or flights per hour under VMC (Visual Meteorological Conditions) and 64 (32/32) aircraft movements per hour under IMC (Instrumental Meteorological Conditions) rules. The aircraft are accommodated at 60 apron parking stands.

The intensity of hourly flight demand frequently exceeds airport capacity of both the runway system and the apron, and thus causes severe congestion. Because there is no additional land available, options for relieving congestion through physical airport expansion given predicted growth of about 19% between 2002–2010 are limited to nil. The possible options include stimulating an increase in the average aircraft size and of increasing of the runway capacity by innovative operational procedures and technologies. The first option already occurred in 2001 after the reintroduction of flights by B767-400ER aircraft with seat capacity of about 280 seats (AIRWISE NEWS 2001). The runway capacity expansion option is still awaiting implementation but is expected to raise the runway capacity about 10% under VMC and about 3% under IMC rules when implemented (Federal Aviation Administration 2003b). None of the options includes demand management through modification of the current service charging system that is based on aircraft weight. The unit charge for this system is $6.55 for each five hundred kilograms or thousand pounds of the aircraft maximum take-off weight. Each flight is additionally charged a fixed amount of US $100 if it arrives between 8 o'clock in the morning and 9 o'clock in the evening (PANYNJ 2003a). Nevertheless, neither of the above-mentioned options efficiently cope with the prospective long-term growth of demand beyond the year 2010. This may again initiate a search for measures of demand management based on past experience. For example, the initial trials of slot auction, i.e., 'slottery' substantially mitigated congestion in the year 2000. For the future, congestion charging might be reconsidered. The following numerical example illustrates possible effects of congestion charging.

13.5.2 Description of Inputs

Two groups of inputs are used for application of the proposed models: i) inputs on the demand and capacity for estimation of congestion and delays under given circumstances; ii) inputs on aircraft operating costs and airfares for assessing profitability of particular flights.

13.5.2.1 Inputs for Estimating Congestion and Delays

The distributions of the hourly number of flights and the corresponding capacity at NY La Guardia airport for every day of July 2001 are used as inputs for the proposed diffusion approximation queuing model to estimate congestion and delays. These distributions are determined by using 31 daily traffic distribution data sets at NY La Guardia airport (Federal Aviation Administration 2003a, 2003b).

Table 13.2. Parameters of distributions of the flight inter-arrival and inter-departure time in a given example - NY LaGuardia airport (U.S.)

Time of the day	Demand Flight inter-arrival time		Capacity Flight service time	
Hour (k)	Mean ($t_{a,k}$) (s/flight)	St. dev.($\sigma_{a,k}$) (s/flight)	Mean ($t_{d,k}$) (s/flight)	St. dev.($\sigma_{d,k}$) (s/flight)
1	-	-	-	-
2	-	-	-	-
3	-	-	-	-
4	-	-	-	-
5	-	-	-	-
6	50.72	9.972	52.56	7.488
7	52.20	3.942	52.92	7.524
8	50.76	3.123	52.20	4.608
9	49.68	4.716	52.56	7.776
10	50.04	4.860	52.20	7.164
11	50.40	1.764	51.12	6.912
12	50.76	2.376	51.12	6.984
13	48.96	3.096	50.76	6.912
14	51.84	3.744	50.76	6.336
15	50.04	3.312	50.40	7.056
16	48.24	2.916	50.40	7.020
17	48.60	5.148	50.04	7.022
18	51.48	8.640	50.04	7.020
19	50.76	5.292	50.40	7.704
20	51.84	7.992	49.68	6.624
21	59.67	5.220	49.32	6.012
22	78.12	16.236	49.32	5.976
23	23.84	36.468	50.40	7.308
24	-	-	-	-

s seconds.
Source: Federal Aviation Administration 2003a.

Each distribution for each hour is assumed to be normal or nearly normal and independent from each other. Table 13.2 gives the main parameters of these distributions for an average day. In addition, constant C is set to be 1.96 in all experiments, which implies that the queues stay within given confidence boundaries with a prescribed probability of 0.95 (Newell 1982).

13.5.2.2 Aircraft Operating Costs

Aircraft operating costs are standardised according to a seat capacity metric and are expressed in monetary units per block hour. The cost relevant data related to the U.S. airlines are given in Fig. 13.3 (Federal Aviation Administration 1998) where it shows that this cost increases almost linearly with increasing aircraft seat capacity.

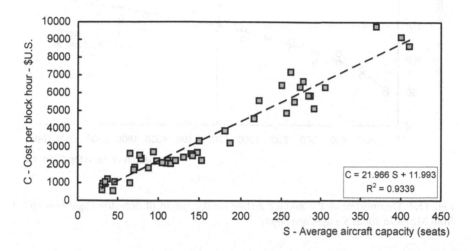

Fig. 13.3. Dependence of the operating cost on the aircraft seat capacity (Compiled from Federal Aviation Administration 1998)

For example, at NY LaGuardia airport the average cost of an aircraft with 100–150 seats such as B737 or B717 varies between $US 2209 and $US 3307 per hour or from $US 37 to $US 55 per minute, respectively. The average cost of an aircraft of 280 seats such as for example B767-400ER is $US 6162 per hour or $US 103 per minute. This cost does not include the cost or value of passenger time.

13.5.2.3 *Airfares*

The average airfare per passenger at NY La Guardia airport is determined by using 1998 U.S. data. Figure 13.4 illustrates the results are modified due to changes in the value of the US dollar by the year 2002 (Mendoza 2002; Sheng-Chen 2000). The average airfare increases at a decreasing rate with increasing route length, which reflects a decrease in the average aircraft unit cost with an increase of the non-stop flying distance (Janic 2001). At NY La Guardia airport, for an average flight of about 1200 km the corresponding airfare is $US 152 (Mendoza 2002). These airfares do not include congestion charges.

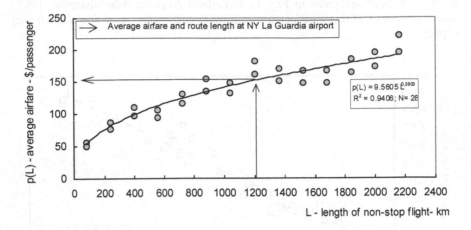

Fig. 13.4. Dependence of the average airfare on the length of non-stop flight (Compiled from Mendoza 2002; Sheng-Chen 2000)

13.5.2 Analysis of Results

The results from the experiments with the model are shown in Figs. 13.5–7. Figures 13.5a–c show congestion and delay created by a flight joining a queue at different times during the day.

Figure 13.5a shows that during an average day the queue of flights starts to develop early, immediately after opening the airport at 6 o'clock in the morning. If the airport operates at declared capacity, the queue grows gradually during the day and reaches a maximum at about 8 o'clock in the evening. Since after that time the intensity of demand significantly diminishes, this long queue disappears relatively quickly one hour before midnight. In this case, on average 35 flights and a maximum of 59 flights wait in the queue. If the airport declared capacity decreases, for example, by 10%, during the second half of the day – from one o'clock in the afternoon on, the queue of flights will increase faster, reach the maximum of 93 flights between 8 and 9 o'clock in the evening, and consequently persist until the midnight.

Figure 13.5b illustrates flight delays during the day. As can be seen, delay of the last flight in the queue changes directly with the change of queue length. When the airport operates at the declared capacity, the average and maximum delay per flight is about 35–40 and 65 minutes, respectively. In the case of deterioration of the airport capacity, the average and maximum delay per flight will increase to about 55–65 and 105 minutes, respectively.

a)

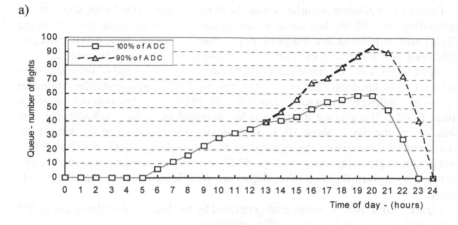

b)

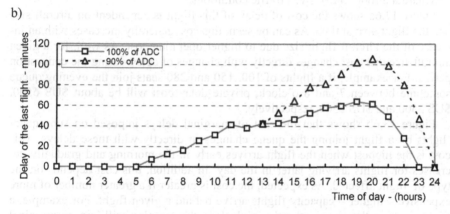

c)

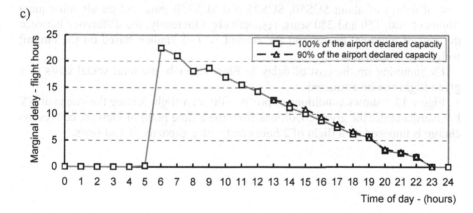

Fig. 13.5. Congestion and delays in a given example: a) Queue of flights; b) Delay of the last flight; c) Marginal delays imposed by the last flight

Figure 13.5c illustrates variations of the marginal delay due to the changing of scheduling time of the last flight in the queue. As can be seen, early morning flights will impose longer marginal delay than otherwise. In a given example, scheduled at 6 o'clock in the morning, the flight will impose additional delay of about 22 flight-hours on subsequent flights that arrive by the end of the congestion period. If scheduled later during the day, the flight will impose smaller additional delays as intuitively expected because it will affect a smaller number of subsequent flights. The average marginal delay imposed by a flight scheduled at any time during the day is about 10–12 flight-hours. Deterioration of the airport declared capacity contributes to an increase in system delays, both marginal delays and private flight delay. As well, Figs. 13.5b–c show that the total marginal delays imposed by a given flight on other flights are significantly greater than the private delay.

Figure 13.6 shows the social cost generated by the last flight in the queue at NY La Guardia airport under given traffic conditions.

Figure 13.6a shows the cost of delay of this flight is dependent on aircraft size and the flight arrival time. As can be seen, this cost generally increases with an increase of the aircraft flight size due to higher operating cost. As well, for a given aircraft size this cost changes directly with changes of delay during the congestion period. For example, if a flights of 100, 150 and 280 seats join the evening queue sometime between 7 and 8 o'clock, private delay cost will be about $US 6500, $US 3500 and $US 2300, respectively.

Figure 13.6b shows that the cost of marginal delays imposed on subsequent flights by a flight joining the queue changes in directly with these delays. This cost is the highest when the flight arrives early in the morning and gradually decreases for flights arriving latter in the day. In addition, this cost depends on the type of flight affected. As expected, the cost is greater if a greater number of more expensive – higher – capacity flights arrive behind a given flight. For example, a flight entering the queue around 6 o'clock in the morning will impose marginal cost of delays of about $US50, $US75 and $US150 thousand on all subsequent flights of 100, 150 and 280 seats, respectively. Obviously, the difference between the cost of marginal delays and the current cost of landing based on the aircraft weight is considerable.

By summing up the cost of delay in Figs. 13.6a–b, the total social costs of a given flight can be estimated.

Figure 13.7 shows conditions of profitability of a flight joining the queue at NY LaGuardia under the given conditions from the airline point of view. A congestion charge is imposed on a flight of 2 hours and with a capacity of 150 seats.

a)

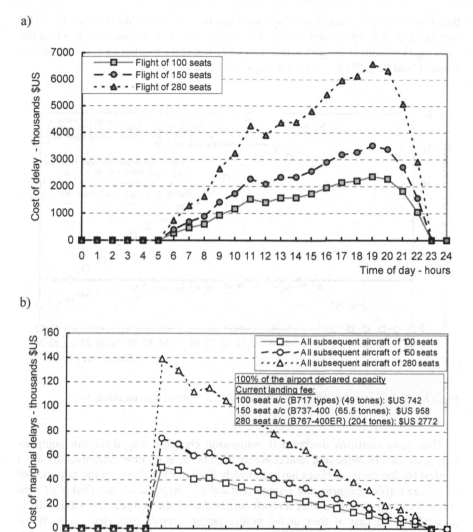

Fig. 13.6. The system cost of the last new flight in a given example: a) Cost of delay of new flight; b) Cost of marginal delay imposed by new flight

The flight operational cost not including the cost of passenger time is $US3300. If the average load factor is 60% and the average airfare is $US 152, the revenue of this flight will be $US13680 (heavy line in Fig. 13.7). When an airline has no market share at the airport, the flight fully burdened by the congestion charge based on the cost of marginal delays imposed on all succeeding flights with a 100 seat capacity will be unprofitable if it arrives at any time before 10 o'clock in the evening. However, if the given airline already has significant market share, for example, about 85–90% or more, the flight might be profitable.

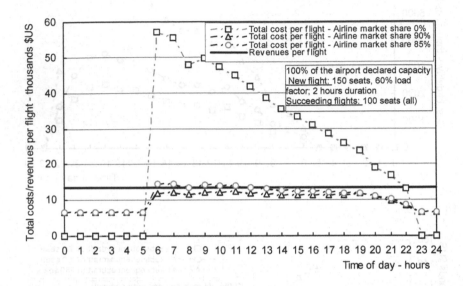

Fig. 13.7. Conditions of profitability of an additional flight in a given example

This result confirms doubts that congestion charging may disfavour competition at airports by imposing unacceptably high burdens on new entrants and only a modest burden on the airlines having already high market shares at the airport. For the given traffic scenario, the charge particularly discourages the flights of new entrants carried out by smaller aircraft earlier during the congested period. This is particularly the case if they arrive before larger aircraft, and vice versa. When such flights are launched by airlines with an already high market share, they will strengthen the position of these airlines at the given airport.

13.6 Conclusions

Models for estimating the effects of congestion charging at an airport have been developed and tested, *ex ante*, in this paper. Currently, congestion charging is not practised at airports despite the introduction of different charging mechanisms for peaks and off-peak periods. In addition to an analysis and comparison of airport delays in Europe and the U.S., different conditions influencing airport congestion have been examined. It has been emphasised that reliable and transparent estimation of relevant parameters have been essential for developing the models and the system of congestion charging.

The models include: a queuing model based on diffusion approximation to quantify the relevant congestion and delays during congestion periods; a model of marginal delays and delay costs imposed by each flight on other flights during congested periods; and a model to estimate the profitability of each flight burdened by the congestion charge. The models were applied to the case of New York (NY) La Guardia airport.

An application of the models indicates that they could be used to efficiently help guide the implementation of congestion charges at airports like NY La Guardia. In particular, the queuing model has enabled quantification of flight queues and delays realistically. The other two models have estimated the costs, congestion charge and profitability of a particular flight for given traffic (congestion) scenarios.

The results obtained from the models have shown that congestion charging could be used as a demand-management measure under conditions when congestion as an exclusive consequence of the relationships between demand and airport capacity cause delays longer than the threshold of fifteen minutes, i.e., in cases when the demand/capacity ratio moves to and exceeds the value one. Further, congestion needs to be created by many flights of different competing airlines in order to raise the need for internalising the marginal costs of delays flights impose on each other because a single airline with many flights has already internalised costs of the marginal delays of its flights. In this context, airports with many competing airlines performing point-to-point operations appear to be more likely to benefit from congestion charging than airports with a few airlines operating hub-and-spoke networks despite the fact that in both cases it may be relevant to impose congestion charging.

Congestion charges appear to be effective in preventing access of earlier flights during a congestion period carried out by smaller aircraft and before flights carried out by larger aircraft, and vice versa. This implies that congestion charging stimulates exclusion of earlier arrivals by smaller-regional aircraft and instead favours the use of larger aircraft not particularly sensitive to arrival time.

Congestion charges appear to stimulate additional flights of airlines having a significant amount of airport market share, i.e., those with more flights and this with already internalised cost of marginal delays. In this case, it contributes to consolidation of the market position of the incumbents, discourages new entries and thus compromises competition at the airport.

Despite being theoretically correct regarding the distribution of benefits and losses, implementation of congestion charging at airports will be complicated. Further, implementation poses a number of problems.

References

Airport Council International (Europe) (2002) Airport charges in Europe. Report of Airport Council International, p 39

Adler N (2002) Barriers and implementation paths to marginal cost based pricing: rail, air and water transport. 3rd MC-ICAM Seminar, 2–3 September, p 5

Association of European Airlines (2001) Yearbook 2000. Association of European Airlines, Brussels, p 80

AIRWISE NEWS (2001) Delta launches Boeing 767-400ER at La Guardia. (http://news.aiwise.com)

Air Transport Association (2002) System capacity: part I: airline schedule, airport capacity, and weather. Air Transport Association Industry Information, USA. Available at http://www.air-transport.org/public/industry

Backer C (2000) Airports: top 1000 ranking. Airline Business, pp 55–86

Brueckner JK (2002) Internalisation of airport congestion. Journal of Air Transport Management 8: 141–147

Bureau of Transport Statistics (2001) Airline service quality performance data. US Department of Transportation, Bureau of Transportation Statistics, Office of Airline Information, Washington, D.C.

Cheng-Shen AH (2000) An analysis of air passenger average trip lengths and fare levels in US domestic markets. Working paper UCB-ITS-WP-2000–1, NEXTOR Aviation Operations Research, Institute of Transport Studies, University of California, Berkeley, p 14

Corbett JJ (2002) Small communities are concerned about congestion pricing. The Air and Space Lawyer 17: 17–21

Daniel JI (1995) Congestion pricing and capacity of large-hub airports: a bottleneck model with stochastic queues. Econometrica 63: 327–370

Daniel JI, Pahwa M (2000) Comparison of three empirical models of airport congestion pricing. Journal of Urban Economics 47: 1–38

Daniel JI (2001) Distributional consequences of airport congestion pricing. Journal of Urban Economics 50: 230–258

DeCota W (2001) Matching capacity & demand at LaGuardia airport. NEXTOR, Airline & National Strategies for Dealing with Airport & Airspace Congestion, p 26

Doganis R (1992) The airport business. Routledge, London

European Commission (1997) External cost of transport in ExternE. European Commission, Non Nuclear Energy Programme, IER Germany

European Commission (2001) Concerted action on transport pricing research integration. CAPRI, Final Report, European Commission, Transport RTD of the 4th Framework Programme, ST-97-CA-2064, Brussels

European Conference of Ministers of Transport (1998) Efficient transport for Europe: policies for internalization of external costs. European Conference of Ministers of Transport, OECD-Organisation of Economic Co-operation and Development, Paris

EUROCONTROL/ECAC (2001) ATFM delays to air transport in Europe. Annual Report 2000, CODA, EUROCONTROL, Brussels

EUROCONTROL (2002) An assessment of air traffic management in Europe during calendar year 2001: performance review report. Performance Review Commission, EUROCONTROL, Brussels

EUROCONTROL/ECAC (2002a) ATFM delays to air transport in Europe: annual report 2001. EUROCONTROL, Brussels

Federal Aviation Administration (1998) Economic values for evaluation of federal aviation administration investment and regulatory decisions. Report FAA-APQ-98-8, Federal Aviation Administration US Department of Transportation, Washington, D.C.

Federal Aviation Administration (2003a) Airport capacity benchmarking report 2001. Federal Aviation Administration, Washington, D.C.

Federal Aviation Administration (2003b) Aviation policy and plans (APO). FAA OPSNET and ASPM, Federal Aviation Administration, Washington, D.C.

Fron X (2001) Dealing with airport and airspace congestion in Europe. ATM Performance, the paper presentation, Brussels, EUROCONTROL meeting, March, p 25

Ghali MO, Smith MJ (1995) A model for the dynamic system optimum traffic assignment problem. Transportation Research B 29: 155–170

Hall RW (1991) Queuing methods for services and manufacturing. Prentice Hall International Limited, London

Janic M (2003) Large scale disruption of an airline network: a model for assessment of the economic consequences. The 82nd Transportation Research Board (TRB) Conference, January, Washington, D.C., p 25

Liang D, Marnane W, Bradford S (2000) Comparison of the U.S. and European airports and airspace to support concept validation. 3rd USA/Europe Air Traffic Management R&D Seminar, Napoli, 13–16 June, p 15

Mendoza G (2002) New York State airport air fare analysis. Aviation Service Bureau, NYSDOT, Washington, D.C., p 4

Nash C, Sansom T (2001) Pricing European transport system: recent developments and evidence from case studies. Journal of Transport Economics and Policy 35: 363–380

Newell GF (1982) Airport capacity and delays. Transportation Science 13: 201–241

Odoni A, Bowman J (1997) Existing and required modelling capabilities for evaluating ATM systems and concepts. NASA/AATT Final Report, International Centre for Air Transportation, Massachusetts Institute of Technology, Massachusetts, p 206

Odoni AR, Fan TCP (2002) The potential of demand management as a short-term means of relieving airport congestion. 4th USA/Europe Air Traffic Management R&D Seminar, Santa Fe, 3–7 December, p 11

Port Authority of New York & New Jersey (PANYNJ) (2003) La Guardia airport: traffic statistics. Report, The Port Authority of NY&PJ, New York, p 2

Port Authority of New York & New Jersey (PANYNJ) (2003a) Schedule of charges for air terminals. Report, The Port Authority of NY&PJ, New York, p 40

Schiphol Group (2002) Annual report-2001. Amsterdam Schiphol Airport, Amsterdam

Vickery W (1969) Congestion theory and transport investment. American Economic Review 59: 251–260

Welch JD, Lloyd RT (2001) Estimating airport system delay performance. 4th USA/Europe Air Traffic Management R&D Seminar, Santa Fe, 3–7 December, p 11

14 Short- and Long-Term Reaction of European Airlines to Exogenous Demand Shifts[1]

Marco Alderighi[1] and Alessandro Cento[2]

[1] Università della Valle d'Aosta, Aosta, Italy; Università Bocconi , Milan, Italy
[2] KLM Royal Dutch Airlines, Milan, Italy

14.1 Introduction

In less than 10 years, the liberalisation of the European airline industry has moved flag carriers in highly competitive environment. The reason for this clearly follows from the peculiarity of this industry: airline carriers have to produce one of the most perishable goods (passenger transport) in one of the most dynamic industries. This fact has forced carriers to implement and refine practices and strategies to react promptly to the ups and downs of the demand. It is common practice that daily fluctuations are usually controlled by advanced pricing policies, called 'yield management', while long-lasting demand shifts require a reaction in terms of advanced capacity strategies, called 'tactical planning'.

In this paper, we focus on this second aspect. Exploring the behaviour of carriers in such a complex context seems to be very difficult unless it is based on particular situations as important demand shifts. Recently, two terrible events have characterised the world economy: the September 11 terrorist attack on the Twins Towers in New York and on the Pentagon in Washington in 2001, and the SARS epidemic in East Asia which begin in February 2003. These events have produced two dramatic crises especially in the North American and the Asian market, respectively. By analysing these two important demand shifts, we are able to detect some determinants of the carriers' conduct. In particular, we have split the carriers' conduct into short- and long-term determinants to capture information about carrier's strategies (internal policy, expectations for the evolution of the markets, etc.) and its specific characteristics (structure of the network, adjustment costs, financial situation). To be comprehensive, an analysis based on short- and long-term components needs to be both theoretical and empirical. From a theoretical point of view, we show that, if capacity variations are costly, it is optimal to base a

---

[1] This paper has benefited from suggestions by Kenneth Button, Anton van Dasler, Peter Nijkamp, Aura Reggiani and Piet Rietveld and participants at the ERSA 2003 Congress 27-30 August, Jyväskylä, Finland. The authors' opinions do not necessarily reflect the official KLM viewpoints.

capacity reaction on both short- and long-term profitability where the right mix depends upon the importance and duration of the shock. From an empirical point of view, we can explain the carrier's capacity choices with two variables: the passenger reduction due to the shock, and the expected profitability of the market.

To clarify the first point, suppose that an unexpected shock reduces the demand. A carrier can react by decreasing its offer but incurring a cost of adjustment. If the shock is brief, the carrier's choice during the crisis period is mainly based on the expected situation after the crisis. In fact, its reaction aims to limit the costs of reducing and restating the capacity. On the contrary, when there is a long-lasting shock, the carrier focuses on the crisis period as post-crisis profits are far away and their discounted value is low. Adjustment costs also induce carriers to behave strategically. In fact, a carrier that increases (or decreases less) the capacity during the crisis period, forces its competitor to reduce its capacity offer in the post-crisis period. This phenomenon is known in the literature as 'pre-emption'. Pre-emption reduces the reactivity of the carrier to the shock during the crisis.

Theoretical results are based on the assumption that carriers encounter adjustment costs in changing the network configuration, so that their choice depends on short- and long-term variables. Empirically, we observe that any modification of the flight supply involves costs. For instance, a carrier that decides to enter a new route needs to have new rights at the airport (slot), organise new staff, promote and advertise the new route, launch price actions and so on. Moreover, in the short-term, the aircraft for the new route should be moved from another route to the new one, and the logistic activity should be adjusted to the new aircraft rotations. Moreover, reducing frequencies or closing a route is a costly decision seeing that a carrier needs to change the aircraft rotations or definitely ground a plane. It is worth noting that adjustment costs are first of all set-up costs and hence are higher when carriers want to enter or expand a route than when they want to exit from or reduce it.

Adjustment costs are usually high for large carriers (carriers with higher market shares), since they employ local ground staff, but are low for small carriers that usually outsource ground activities. In addition, closing and opening an intercontinental route imply a re-optimisation of the network, which is more complex and costly for larger carriers. Other factors such as specific network characteristics and the flexibility of the fleet, i.e. the number of aircraft that can operate both on short and long haul routes can have an impact on the importance of the adjustment costs. The existence of adjustment costs motivates the decision to change the capacity supply only few times a year and in the meantime to compete in prices. Data support our conjecture that there is a positive relation between market shares and costs of adjustment, even if this result is clearer for the North American crisis than for the Asian crisis.

In these two crises, the typology of the shocks and the characteristics of the markets are different. Nevertheless, some related results seem to emerge. The empirical analysis confirms that there is a trade-off between short- and long-term goals among carriers facing the same crisis, for both the first and the second crisis. We may note that after the first shock, some carriers: namely British Airways and

Air France, shifted from long-term to short-term reaction. There are many explanations for this unexpected result. For example, it may originate from an underestimation of the duration of the crisis in the first shock and an overestimation in the second shock. Another interpretation may be that carriers believe the American market is more strategic than the Asian market. Alternatively, high operating costs and low margins, combined with continuing turbulences have induced carriers to focus on the short-term rather than on the long term.

Carriers determine the capacity supply through a process called network planning. This process is usually organised on three levels: 1) strategic planning: alliances, buying/selling new aircraft, anticipating new routes, usually every 1–3 years; 2) tactical planning: scheduled timing, numbers of frequencies and aircraft size, which will takes place every semester; 3) operational actions: pricing strategies and small adjustments of the network to improve operations such as reducing connections time at the hub, ad-hoc changes of the aircraft size on a few days. This process follows the short-term demand fluctuation and competitor moves. Each step of network planning is widely analysed in the literature. Chang and Williams (2002) and Janic (1997) investigate the relation between the liberalisation, alliance and performance of the airlines. Chin and Tay (2001), Smith (1997), and Bruning and Hu (1988) focus on the profitability and investment decision of North American and Asian carriers. Finally, Borenstein (1989), Windle and Dresner (1995, 1999) give attention to operational choices, i.e. pricing equilibrium and market competition.

Our analysis attempts to propose an integrated model which considers operational, tactical and strategic decisions in a crisis situation. Specifically, we present a dynamic game-theoretical framework organised into three stages, which are a time-continuous sequence of periods. In each period, carriers take operational actions (i.e. they choose a price); in each stage, they choose their tactics (corresponding to a capacity offer); and, in the entire game, they follow a strategic plan (i.e. the choice of a strategy to solve the overall game). The empirical model does not consider operational decisions but focuses on tactical and strategic plans that are driven by short- and long-term indicators, respectively.

Recently, the literature has proposed new research in the field of the airline crisis. In particular, Alderighi and Cento (2004) and Hätty and Hollmeier (2003) present a view of the airline crisis after the September 11. The first contribution is strongly related to this paper, being divided into two parts, one dealing with theoretical framework and an other with the results of the North American crisis. The second contribution originates from the internal debate in the crisis management unit at Lufthansa Airlines. In this study, it is shown that the reduction of air traffic demand was matched by industry capacity reduction. When demand declines, capacity can not be adjusted immediately due to the insufficient flexibility. These authors conclude that managing the crisis aims not only to restore the pre-crisis state but rather to form a more healthy business environment. In addition, Gillen and Lall (2003) examine shock transmission in the airline industry after September 11. Their research attempts to identify three main propagation channels: the trade effect; the alliance effect; and the wake-up call effects.

The remainder of this paper is organised as follows: Sect. 14.2 presents a brief description of the airline sector during the North American and Asian crises. In Sects. 14.3 and 14.4, we provide the theoretical model and the empirical analysis, respectively. The final conclusions are presented in Sect. 14.5.

14.2 Exogenous Demand Shifts: The American and Asian Crises

The September 11 terrorist attack on United States and the SARS epidemic in Asia had a strong impact throughout the airlines sector. The North America crisis has been the most tragic shock that the industry has faced in its recent history. The SARS shock strongly hampered the carriers' expectation for the development of the Asian market. In the next two sub-section we provide some facts and figures that describe the shocks and the subsequent reactions of the European carriers. The description is also necessary to support some of the methodological decisions that have been taken in the econometric analysis.

14.2.1 The September 11 Terrorist Attack

On 11 September 2001, one Boeing of American Airlines and one of United Airlines were diverted by terrorists to crash on the Twin Towers in New York City, and a third Boeing of America Airlines was diverted to crash on the Pentagon in Washington. For security reasons the North American air space was closed for the next five days. Eight days after the terrorist attack the Lufthansa Chief Executive Officer Jurgen Weber, made the following statement:

"The losses incurred due to the closure of US and Canadian airspace, flight diversions, cancellations and drop in demand have made it necessary for companies to revise their profit forecast and capacity supply. The forecasting was dependent on an economy upswing in the last quarter of the year, which was no longer anticipated in the wake of the 11th September event. The aviation industry has been hit badly by the consequences of the terrorist attacks. It will require immense efforts on the part of Lufthansa staff if we are to avoid an operating loss this year " (Lufthansa Chief Executive Officer Jurgen Weber, 19 September 2001).

The revenue passenger kilometres (RPK)[2] and the available seat kilometres (ASK)[3] are two relevant market indicators to understand the impact of the crisis on the airline industries. The indicators refer to the transatlantic traffic generated by European carriers to North Atlantic destinations; they are seasonally adjusted and

---

[2] The RPK is the number of passengers who generated revenue (free travellers are excluded) normalised by the length of the journey in kilometres.

[3] The ASK is the number of seats offered by the carriers on a certain route multiplied the route length (in kilometres).

observed as a year-to-year index. Before the terrorist attacks, the RPK between Europe and North America had a zero growth, afterwards RPK dropped significantly in October (–26%) and reached its lowest point in November (–33%). The European carriers' reacted to adjust their capacity in November (–15%). Afterwards the capacity reduction continued until January 2002, when it reached the lowest point of the crisis (–26%).

The indicators are plotted in Fig. 14.1. The two series are clearly affected by a strong downturn, in October for the RPK, and in November for ASK. The market had fully recovered from the crisis in terms of RPK in February 2003, and in terms of ASK in March 2003. The crisis had therefore lasted about 17 months, but it is clear that the carriers did not know this in September 2001, as at that time Mr. Jurgen Weber (Lufthansa CEO) stated that:

"… there is uncertainty about the length and effect of the crisis and the future developments in the aviation industry."

Nevertheless management expected that the crisis would be long. KLM President & CEO Leo van Wijk reported in a press release that:

"…many passengers are cancelling their reservations and we can expect diminishing load factors as result. Demand is diminishing on various intercontinental routes and I do not expect this to change in the near future…"

In general, carriers reduced their capacity supply by cutting the frequencies and the aircraft size, or closing routes. For example, KLM adjusted its flights to the US by reducing weekly frequencies to New York (from 13 to 11), to San Francisco (from 7 to 6), to Miami (from 7 to 5), and to Detroit (from 4 to 3). It also closed the Amsterdam-Atlanta route, and reduced the aircraft size to Canada (Montreal: from Boeing 747 to Boeing 767; Toronto: from Boeing 747 to McDouglas 11). The year-to-year index of ASK decreased to below 100 in the last quarter of 2001 (Oct–Dec), immediately after the September demand shift. Some carriers, such as British Airways, Alitalia or KLM, seemed to reduce their capacity already in September 2001, as the index fell lower than 100. Nevertheless, these indexes showed the same negative growth even before the crisis. These carriers were already in a capacity- reduction process, regardless of the forthcoming crisis. On the other hand, other carriers such as Air France, Aer Lingus, and SAS had an index above 100 in the third quarter, since they were registering a positive trend before the crisis. In this perspective, the indices cannot be compared among the carriers but only in terms of the trend over time. In the last quarter of 2001, the carriers reduced their capacity supply, and the cut ranged from –39% of Swiss[4] to – 4% of SAS.

---

[4] The name "Swiss", as opposed to " Swiss Air", has been adopted throughout this paper, as SwissAir went bankrupt after September 11 crisis, after which a new airline with the name Swiss was created.

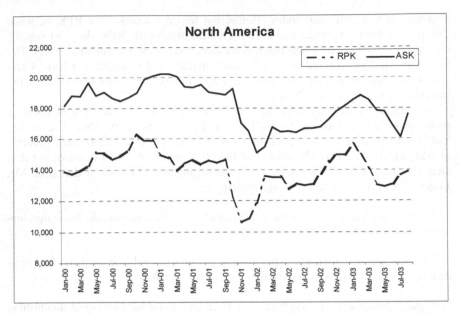

Fig. 14.1. RPK and ASK from Europe to North America (Source: AEA seasonally adjusted)

14.2.2 The SARS Epidemic

The severe acute respiratory syndrome (SARS) is a respiratory illness caused by a virus. SARS was first reported in Asia in February 2003. Over the next few months, the illness spread to more than two-dozen countries in North America, South America, Europe, and Asia. According to the World Health Organisation, during the SARS outbreak of 2003, a total of 8,098 people worldwide became sick with SARS; and of these, 774 died. Most of the SARS cases in Europe were among travellers returning from other parts of the world, particularly from Asia. As the main way that SARS appears to spread is by close person-to-person contact, fears of contagion and the official travel advice to defer non essential travel generated a shock in the demand, mainly for air transport to Asia and Canada.

Before the epidemic spread, the RPK from Europe to Asia was still recovering from previous crises (September 11, the Afghanistan war and the October 2002 Bali terrorist attack) and showed positive growth. After these crisis, the negative trend is again evident in March (–8%), just one month after the first SARS case was reported. During the succeeding months, the demand sank (–22% in the April RPK), and reached its lowest point in May 2003 (–30%). The European carriers reaction is captured by the ASK index. The capacity adjustment started two months later in May 2003 (–15%) and continued in the next two months (June 2003 –15%, July –8%).

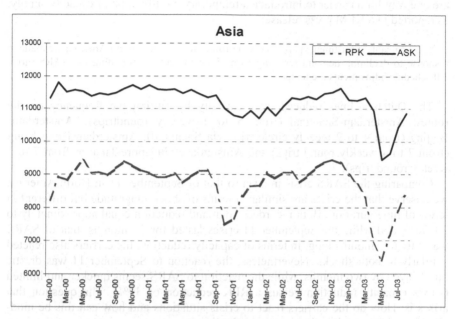

Fig. 14.2. RPK and ASK from Europe and Asia (Source: AEA seasonally adjusted)

The two indicators are plotted in Fig. 14.2. The time path is clearly affected by the two big crises, i.e. September 11 and SARS. Both negative shocks can be detected in the plotted time series; nevertheless, the effects were different in terms of both magnitude and the recovery path to the pre-crisis situations. Due to the September 11 attack, the RPK decreased to the lowest value of 7499, while the lowest point reached in the SARS crisis was even lower (6403). In the first crisis, the downturn of the RPK come in October 2001. A minor shift was registered in December 2002 due to the announcement of the Iraqi war, which generated negative expectations of travel security and economic development in the Asian areas. In the second crisis the drop was in March 2003 and became strong in April 2003. Later, in August 2003, the crisis does not seem to be completely absorbed by the market. Over the first quarter of 2003 (Jan–Mar), the carriers considered were still enjoying a phase of expansion the only exception being British Airways which was stable for almost all 2002 with an index of 81–87. In the second quarter of 2003 (Apr–Jun), ASK fell drastically for every carrier, with different magnitudes, ranging from 18% for Swiss to 8% for KLM and British Airways.

As in the previous crisis, European carriers reduced their capacity in term of frequencies, aircraft size, and routes. Additionally, airlines also adjusted their capacity also by introducing triangular services. The Asian routes are on average 3000 longer than those in North America, and passengers are willing to tolerate a stop service in order to keep the same number of frequencies. Triangular flights are one way for a carrier to introduce a temporary modification of capacity supply, as reported in a KLM press release:

> "..the capacity adjustments particularly on routes to Asia and North America are made in response to declining demand resulting from developments surrounding the SARS virus. All schedule adjustments are temporary..."

The Dutch airlines reduced their capacity by cutting the frequency on the routes: Amsterdam-Shanghai (from 5 to 4 weekly roundtrips),[5] Amsterdam-Beijing (from 4 to 2 weekly circle trips via Shanghai); Amsterdam-Hong Kong (from 7 to 4 weekly round trips) and Amsterdam-Singapore-Jakarta (from 7 to 5 weekly round trips).

Comparing the SARS crisis in Asia to that of September 11 in North America, we observe that the crises are similar in terms of shock magnitude but different in terms of time duration. Both recorded a demand reduction equal approximately to 30–36%, and while the September 11 crises lasted for 17 months, that of SARS was only 6–7 months long. In terms of capacity reduction, the carriers also reacted similarly to both shocks. Nevertheless, the reaction to September 11 was drastic but delayed by two months, while the reaction to SARS seems quicker and limited (−15% capacity reduction versus a RPK reduction of 30%). The question that arises is: How do the carriers react to crisis situations and how can this be modelled in order to explain their general behaviour?

14.3 The Theoretical Model

We consider duopolistic market[6] consisting of two firms: namely, A and B. They compete in quantities (capacities), and we assume that firms revise their capacity supply only rarely since, in modifying their flight supply, they incur adjustment costs.

The model is set in a continuous time framework, and firms are profit maximises. To keep things simple, we assume that at date 0 there is an unpredicted negative shock (that is described as a temporary reduction of the demand), and that firms modify their capacity supply only twice, once when the shock has occurred and again when it ends. In what follows, we present a basic version where we assume that the duration of the crisis is known just after the shock has occurred. At the end of the section, we informally present some extensions which do not substantially change the main results of the model. Therefore, we start by assuming no uncertainty regarding the duration of the crisis, no financial constraints, and no differences in the adjustment costs. The timing of the game is as follows:

---

[5] A round trip flies there and back on the same route. A circle trip flies from the origin on the outward journey, stopping at one or more places on route, and it flies straight back from the final destination without stopping on route.

[6] In this model, we focus on a single market that corresponds to a single intercontinental route.

- (Stage 0) Before time 0, the market is on a long-term equilibrium. That means the capacity that firms A and B have chosen is the solution of a Cournot game.[7] The outcome of this stage-game is J_0, K_0 and p_0, where J_0 and K_0 are, respectively, the capacity choice of firm A and B at Stage 0, and p_0 is the equilibrium price at Stage 0.
- (Stage 1) At time 0, there is an unpredicted (negative) shock in the demand with a certain duration $\theta > 0$. Firms change their capacity.[8] The outcome is J_1, K_1 and p_1.
- (Stage 2) At time θ, the negative shock ends. Firms modify their capacities with a cost that is increasing in the capacity change.[9] In this case, the outcome is J_2, K_2 and p_2.

We solve the model backwards, starting from Stage 2, and then we move to Stage 1.

We will only focus on the behaviour of firm A, since there is an analogous solution for firm B. The overall profit of firm A can be described as the sum of the discounted instantaneous profits. We call π_1^A and π_2^A the instantaneous profit of firm A at Stage 1 and 2, respectively.[10] The overall profit for firm A, namely Π^A, is:

$$\Pi^A = \int_0^\theta e^{-rt}\pi_1^A dt + \int_\theta^\infty e^{-rt}\pi_2^A dt = r^{-1}\left(1 - e^{-rt}\right)\pi_1^A + r^{-1}e^{-rt}\pi_2^A \qquad (14.1)$$

where r is the interest rate, and e^{-rt} is the discount factor.

The Stage 2 equilibrium is computed assuming that firms have already chosen their capacity in the first stage.

The inverse demand in the second Stage 2 is $p_2 = a - Q_2$, where Q_2 is the quantity supplied by both firms. During the crisis period $(0,\theta)$, the demand was $p_1 = b - Q_1$ with $0 < b < a$. At time $t \in [\theta, \infty)$, firms A and B maximise their profit given J_1 and K_1, where J_1 and K_1 are, respectively, the capacity choice of firm A and B in Stage 1. At time $t = \theta$, they choose the capacity J_2 and K_2 to maximise their profits.

In the Stage 2, the period profit of firm A is:

$$\pi_2^A = (b - c - J_2 - K_2)J_2 - D(J_1, J_2, \delta) \qquad (14.2)$$

---

[7] Because no costs of adjustment are assumed in Stage 1, the equilibrium levels before time 0 do not have an impact on the choices in Stage 1 and 2, but we maintain this assumption because it is necessary to consistently compute the capacity change.

[8] For simplicity, in Stage 1, the capacity adjustment is costless.

[9] See, a. g. Gould (1968).

[10] Because firms can not change their capacity supply during these stages, their per period profit is constant.

where c is the unit-cost for the installed capacity and $D(J_1, J_2, \delta) = (J_2 - J_1)^2$ are the (per-period) adjustment costs.[11] We define $J_2^* = J_2^*(J_1, K_1)$ the optimal capacity level in the second Stage 2 as a function of J_1 and K_1. Hence, after some computations, the solution of the Stage 2 of the game is:

$$J_2^*(J_1, K_1) = \frac{(1 + 2\delta)(a - c) + 4\delta(1 + \delta)J_1 - 2\delta K_1}{4(1 + \delta)^2 - 1}. \tag{14.3}$$

Note that the optimal level J_2^* is affected by the costs of adjustment and by the decisions taken in Stage 1: namely, J_1 and K_1. The Stage 1 instantaneous profit of firm A is given by:

$$\pi_1^A = (b - c - J_1 - K_1)J_1 \tag{14.4}$$

The firms' behaviour in the Stage 1 is determined by the optimisation of the overall profit described by Eq. (14.1). For firm A, this is equivalent to maximisation of the following equation:

$$\max_{J_1} R\pi_1^A(J_1, K_1) + \pi_2^A(J_2^*, K_2^*, D), \tag{14.5}$$

where $R = (1 - e^{-r\theta})/e^{-r\theta}$, $J_2^* = J_2^*(J_1, K_1)$ and $K_2^* = K_2^*(J_1, K_1)$ are the optimal capacity levels of A and B respectively, in Stage 2 and D are the adjustment costs of A. The solution of this optimisation problem is the reaction function of firm A in Stage 1.

The first order condition implies that:

$$re^{rt} \frac{d\Pi^A}{dJ_1} = R\frac{d\pi_1^A}{dJ_1} + \frac{d\pi_2^A}{dJ_1} = 0. \tag{14.6}$$

When firm A maximises the overall profit it balances its choice between the short-term effect and long-term effect. The short-term effect is the traditional result of the duopoly theory: $\frac{d\pi_1^A}{dJ_1} = (b - c - 2J_1 - K_1)$, while the long-term effect

---

[11] For technical reasons, we assume that the adjustment costs are persistent, i.e. they span the interval $[\theta, \infty)$. Similar results can be obtained under the assumption that these costs are only realised at time θ.

$$\frac{d\pi_2^A}{dJ_1} = \frac{\partial \pi_2^A}{\partial J_1} + \frac{\partial \pi_2^A}{\partial J_2}\frac{\partial J_2^*}{\partial J_1} + \frac{\partial \pi_2^A}{\partial K_2}\frac{\partial K_2^*}{\partial J_1} + \frac{\partial \pi_2^A}{\partial D}\frac{\partial D}{\partial J_1} \tag{14.7}$$

is composed of 4 different impacts. The first and second terms of the RHS of Eq. (14.7) are null because J_1 does not directly affect π_2^A, and because of the envelope theorem: $\frac{\partial \pi_2^A}{\partial J_2} = 0$. The third term captures the strategic effect and corresponds to the impact of J_1 on π_2^A due to a change in K_2^*: $\frac{\partial \pi_2^A}{\partial K_2}\frac{\partial K_2^*}{\partial J_1} = J_2^* \frac{2\delta}{4(1+\delta)^2 - 1}$. The sign of the strategic effect is always positive because Stage 2 actions are strategic substitutes (i.e. the reaction curves are downward sloping[12]). In fact, through increasing the capacity in Stage 1, a firm forces its competitor to reduce its capacity in Stage 2. In the literature, this effect is called 'pre-emption'. In the limit case (when $\delta=0$), the strategic effect is not present.

The fourth term corresponds to the impact of J_1 on π_2^A due to a change in D:

$\frac{\partial \pi_2^A}{\partial D}\frac{\partial D}{\partial J_1} = 2\delta(J_2^* - J_1)$, and is positive as soon as $J_2^* - J_1 > 0$. It captures the resistance of a firm in reducing its capacity in Stage 1 since it has to bear high costs in Stage 2 for increasing the capacity. Also this term is null when $\delta = 0$.

The presence of adjustment costs D complicates the optimisation problem. In fact, the equilibrium solution in the Stage 1 is characterised by strategic considerations as well as cost considerations regarding the choice of Stage 2. The optimisation problem is clearly simplified when $\delta = 0$, where the equilibrium solutions are the usual ones of a static duopolistic game: $J_1^* = J_b = \frac{b-c}{3}$ and $J_2^* = J_a = \frac{a-c}{3}$. In the general case, when $\delta > 0$, the optimal solution J_1^* is given by:

$$J_1^* = \frac{1}{3}\frac{R(1+2\delta)(2\delta+3)^2(b-c) + 8\delta(1+\delta)^2(a-c)}{R(1+2\delta)(2\delta+3)^2 + 8\delta(1+\delta)^2 - \frac{2}{3}\delta(2\delta+3)} \tag{14.8}$$

Rearranging previous equation, we have:

$$J_1^* = (1+o)(\lambda J_b + (1-\lambda)J_a) \tag{14.9}$$

where

$$\lambda = \frac{R(1+2\delta)(2\delta+3)^2}{R(1+2\delta)(2\delta+3)^2 + 8\delta(1+\delta)^2}, \tag{14.10}$$

and

---

[12] See Fundemberg and Tirole (1984), and Bulow et al. (1995).

$$o = \frac{\frac{2}{3}(2\delta + 3)}{R(1 + 2\delta)(2\delta + 3)^2 + 8\delta(1 + \delta)^2 - \frac{2}{3}(2\delta + 3)} . \tag{14.11}$$

In order to simplify the discussion of Eq. (14.9), we will focus on the second part of the equation.[13] The second bracket indicates that the solution is a combination of the long-term solution and the short-term solution of the static game. The weights λ and $(1 - \lambda)$ depend on θ (the adjustment costs) and R (the duration of the crisis). Different values of these parameters modify the weights of the short- and long-term solution of the static problem. If λ is close to 0 (R low or θ high) the solution J_1^* is close to J_a, i.e. the long-term solution; on the other hand, if λ is close to 1 the solution J_1^* is close to J_b, i.e. the short-term solution.

Hereafter, we investigate the relationship between long-term and short-term profitability and the variation of the capacity supply.

We define $\Delta S = J_1^* - J_0^*$ as the variation of the capacity supply, $\Delta P = (b - a)$ the fall in the short-term profitability, and $y = (a - c)$ the long-term profitability. Using Eq. (14.8), after some computations, we have:

$$\Delta S = \frac{1}{3} \frac{R(1 + 2\delta)(2\delta + 3)^2 \Delta P + 8\delta(1 + \delta)^2 Y}{R(1 + 2\delta)(2\delta + 3)^2 + 8\delta(1 + \delta)^2 - \frac{2}{3}(2\delta + 3)} . \tag{14.12}$$

We define α_S and α_L as the reactivity of the capacity variation to a change of the short and long-term indicator, respectively. They are defined as follows:

$$\alpha_S = \frac{\partial(\Delta S)}{\partial(\Delta P)} = \frac{1}{3} \frac{R(1 + 2\delta)(2\delta + 3)^2}{R(1 + 2\delta)(2\delta + 3)^2 + 8\delta(1 + \delta)^2 - \frac{2}{3}\delta(2\delta + 3)} \tag{14.13}$$

and

$$\alpha_S = \frac{\partial(\Delta S)}{\partial Y} = \frac{1}{3} \frac{8\delta(1 + \delta)^2}{R(1 + 2\delta)(2\delta + 3)^2 + 8\delta(1 + \delta)^2 - \frac{2}{3}\delta(2\delta + 3)} . \tag{14.14}$$

Hence, replacing α_S and α_L in Eq. (14.12), we have:

$$\Delta S = \alpha_S \Delta P + \alpha_L Y \tag{14.15}$$

---

[13] The first bracket is greater than 1 when $\delta > 0$, but is approximately 1 whenever R is not too small, so that we can neglect it from our discussion. In fact $o < 0.01$ when $R > 0.6$ for every value of δ, and $o < 0.1$ when $R > 0.2$.

Equation 14.15 shows that the capacity reduction (or expansion) is a mixture of short- and long-term profitability,[14] and Eqs. (14.13–14) indicate that α_S and α_L depend on δ and R.

A change of the adjustment costs and of the duration of the crisis modifies the composition of the optimal reaction of the firms.

The ratio $\alpha_S/\alpha_L = \dfrac{1}{8}\dfrac{R(1+2\delta)(2\delta+3)^2}{\delta(1+\delta)^2}$ provides some indications of the firm's responsiveness to a change in the adjustment costs. It is simple to verify that the ratio is decreasing in δ, meaning that an increase in the adjustment costs shifts the attention from the short-term to the long-term goals. Therefore, firms care more about the future situation since higher adjustment costs imply more preemption and more expenditure to adjust to the long-term equilibrium.

The ratio α_S/α_L can be also used in order to analyse the impact of the duration of the crisis on the strategy composition. When the duration is short, α_S/α_L is large, while when the duration is long, α_S/α_L is small. This point has a very simple interpretation. If the shock is long, each firm will focus on the crisis period by reacting to the demand reduction. If the shock is short, the decision can be based on the post-crisis perspective, and hence on the long-term market profitability. Therefore, when the duration is short the capacity reaction is driven by long-term profitability, while if the duration is long, the capacity reaction depends on short-term profitability.

Analogously, an increase of the interest rate r affects the α_S/α_L ratio positively.

Finally, we have to stress that as δ increases the carriers are less flexible. When carriers have low adjustment costs, they react strongly to a shock, and when they have high adjustment costs they react weakly. We will clarify[15] this argument in Sect. 14.4.3.

---

[14] In Sect. 14.4, we will base our empirical analysis on Eq. 14.15. In Sect. 14.4.3, Fig. 14.3, we will provide a graphical representation of α_S and α_L as a function of R and δ. Note that the model we propose fits for the duopolistic case, but in the empirical part there are situations including different market structures, e.g. in the North American case there are some routes with more than two carriers. As qualitative results do not change, we assume that the model holds in any situation.

[15] A formal interpretation of flexibility is as follows. Let $J^*(\delta, R)$ be the capacity when the adjustment costs are δ and the length of the crisis is R. For any δ and δ' such that $\delta' < \delta$, for every $R \in (0, \infty)$, there is a $R' \in (0, \infty)$ such that

$$\text{(a)} \quad \frac{d}{da}J^*(\delta, R) < \frac{d}{da}J^*(\delta', R')$$

and

$$\text{(b)} \quad \frac{d}{db}J^*(\delta, R) < \frac{d}{db}J^*(\delta', R').$$

Moreover, under the same conditions, there is no R' such that both the inequalities hold if $\delta' > \delta$.

In what follows, we present the main conclusions of the extension of the previous analysis in an informal way. We focus on four different situations: (1) when there is uncertainty about the crisis duration; (2) when carriers have different discount factors; (3) when firms have different adjustment costs; and (4) when firm B has a financial constraint. In these cases, we also observe different combinations of the short- and long-term indicators for the determination of the equilibrium choice.

First, we consider the case where firms have uncertainty about the duration of the crisis.[16] Each firm can base its predictions on its private information (for example, the result of their research team and of the task-force created to tackle the crisis). Each firm formulates its expectations independently from the other and chooses a capacity level. We assume that there are only two possible states of nature with known probabilities: $\theta = \{\theta_L, \theta_S\}$, where $\theta_L > \theta_S$.[17] We assume that each firm does not have knowledge of the opponent's expectations and bases its choice on its own information. If the firm expects $\theta = \theta_L$, it will focus more on the short-term aspects, and hence α_L is low and α_S is large. If the firm expects $\theta = \theta_S$, it will be the opposite: α_S is low and α_L large.

Second, firms may have different discount factors, for example $r_A > r_B$. This situation occurs when carrier A values its future profits more (and hence is more interested in being on the market in future) than carrier B. Clearly, carrier A will focus more on the long-term aspects and less on short-term aspects than carrier B.

Third, we consider the case where firms have different adjustment costs, for example $\delta_A > \delta_B$. In this situation, firm A will be more reactive to the long-term, while firm B will be more reactive to the short-term.

Finally, we now assume that firm B cannot choose to react as before, since it has a financial constraint (that may depend on low liquidity or high pressure from investors, high debts, and so on). In particular, firm B can find it difficult, all things being equal, to maintain high K_1^* in conditions of low short-term profitability, even if long-term profitability is high. Therefore, firm B is characterised by low reaction to long-term indicators and strong reaction to short-term indicators, which means high values of α_S and low values of α_L.

14.4 The Empirical Analysis

The hypothesis that the capacity choice on a certain route depends on short- and long-term profitability is tested in two different markets: Asia and North America. The empirical procedure in divided into three steps: 1) the basic properties of the theoretical model are tested (the capacity-supply reaction to a demand shift and to

---

[16] See also Bashyam (1996).
[17] Where L stands for 'long' duration, and S for 'short' duration.

the potential yield; 2) the impact of a demand shift is decomposed per carrier; 3) the impact of the potential yield is decomposed per carrier.

14.4.1 Data

Two databases referring respectively to the 11 September 2001 crisis and the SARS crisis were collected. They contain information on the number of passengers per city-pair (traffic flow), available seats, average revenue per destination and distance in kilometres from Europe to the top 10 North American and the top-20 Asian destinations. Data are related to European carriers, which are selected by network (max. 1 stop on route service) and high market share. Every carrier operates with a hub and spoke configuration. Therefore, the traffic flows have been aggregated, as described in the following example (see: Fig. 14.3).

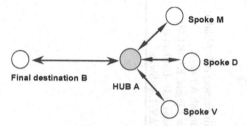

Fig. 14.3. Hub and spoke airline network

One carrier flying to destination B carries passengers from the hub A and the spokes M, D, V. In order to determine the number of intercontinental passengers flying on the route A-B, we add up the passengers originating from points A, M, D and V.

Data on capacity supply is retrieved from the Official Airline Guide (OAG database). The yield information is collected from the Bank Settlement Payment (BSP) database and concern the average revenue generated from Europe to the each North American and Asian destination.

On the basis of the above mentioned data, we compute the following variables:

- ΔS_{ij} : CAPACITY (percentage variation of seats supplied) is the percentage variation of the number of seats offered by carrier i to destination j due to the crisis.

Table 14.1. Variables description

Variable	Description	September 11th	SARS epidemic
ΔS_{ij} : CAPACITY Percentage variation of seats supplied	Total number of seats offered by carrier i to destination j during the crises versus the period before the crisis	$\Delta S_{ij} = \dfrac{S_{ij}^{NOV01} - S_{ij}^{SEP01}}{S_{ij}^{SEP01}}$	$\Delta S_{ij} = \dfrac{S_{ij}^{JUN03} - S_{ij}^{NOV02}}{S_{ij}^{NOV02}}$
Y_{ij} : YIELD Yield per available seat kilometre before crises	Total revenue divided by the total passengers flow from Europe to the destination j times the distance d_{ij} and the lf_{ij} for the carrier i	$Y_{ij} = \dfrac{r_{ij}^{APR-AUG01}}{p_{ij}^{APR-AUG01} d_j} lf_{ij}^{APR-AUG01}$	$Y_{ij} = \dfrac{r_{ij}^{MAR02-FEB03}}{p_{ij}^{MAR02-FEB03} d_j} lf_{ij}^{MAR02-FEB03}$
ΔP_{ij} : PAX Percentage variation of Passengers due to the crises	Percentage variation of bookings made during the lowest downturn of the crisis for the carrier i to the destination j versus the same period of previous year	$\Delta P_{ij} = \dfrac{P_{ij}^{NOV01} - P_{ij}^{NOV00}}{P_{ij}^{NOV00}}$	$\Delta P_{ij} = \dfrac{P_{ij}^{MAY03} - P_{ij}^{MAY02}}{P_{ij}^{MAY02}}$
XX_i : AIRLINES Dummy variable	Dummy variable designating the airlines i included in the analysis	AF=Air France; AZ=Alitalia; BA=British Airways; EI=Aer Lingus; KL=KLM; IB=Iberia; LH=Lufthansa; SK=SAS; LX=Swiss	AF=Air France; AZ=Alitalia; BA=British Airways; KL=KLM; OS=Austrian Airlines; LH=Lufthansa; LX=Swiss

- Y_{ij}: YIELD (yield per available seat kilometre before the crisis) is calculated as the total revenue r_j generated by the total market (all points of sale in Europe) to destination j divided by the total passengers p_j flown to destination j times the distance d_j. Finally, to better approximate the real yield (per flight), the expression is corrected for the load factor (lf_{ij}), i.e. the percentage of the occupied seats in the aircraft of airline i flying to destination j. In the empirical analysis, we assumed that the YIELD per ASK (see Sect. 14.2.1) is the measure of the long-term profitability. Other authors have used a similar measure of long-term profitability. For instance, Bruning and Hu (1988) measured the profit by a passenger profitability index, which was the product of the revenue to cost ratio and the load factor. Indeed, information before the crisis is likely to be the basis to generate a forecasting of the market situation after the crisis.
- ΔPij: PAX (percentage variation of bookings) is the percentage variation of bookings generated during the lowest downturn of the crisis for carrier i to destination j. This variable provides a measure of the exogenous demand shift.
- XX_i: Dummy variable designating airlines with AF=Air France, AZ=Alitalia, BA=British Airways, EI=Aer Lingus, KL=KLM, IB=Iberia, OS=Austrian Airlines, LH=Lufthansa, SK=SAS, LX=Swiss.

Table 14.1 provides a summary of those descriptions of the variables related to the two crisis periods.

The third and fourth columns present, respectively, the market share and the number of destinations in the carrier's network. In North America, Lufthansa and British Airways are the major European players, with 10.8% and 10.1% Table 14.2 presents some descriptive statistics of the main variables for both crises (North America, Asia). Specifically, two columns display the capacity and passenger percentage reduction per carriers for both crises. We observe for the September 11 crisis that Alitalia, Iberia, and Swiss faced the highest passenger reduction (about 35%) and as a consequence their capacity was decreased by 24% for Alitalia, and by 35% for Swiss, but increased by 1% for Iberia. The reason for the Iberia increase lies in the first reaction of Iberia. The Spanish carrier drastically reduced the frequencies to New York and switched the aircraft to operate to Miami instead.

The third and fourth columns present respectively the market share and the number of destinations in the carrier's network. In Asia, the major players are Air France and KLM, with 4.6% and 4%, respectively of the market share, and 14 and 12 direct-service destinations. Different market positions can influence the carrier strategy. If market share is a proxy variable of adjustment costs, then, in Asia, carriers can reduce their capacity at lower costs than they can in North America.

Table 14.2. Descriptive statistics

Carrier	Sept.11				SARS			
	Capacity[a]	Passengers[b]	Dests in North America	Market shares[c]	Capacity[a]	Passengers[b]	Dests in Asia	Market shares[d]
AF	−18%	−20%	10	6.6%	−22%	−24%	14	4.6%
AZ	−24%	−36%	7	3.0%	−15%	−4%	3	1.8%
BA	−17%	−22%	10	10.1%	4%	−23%	11	7.1%
EI	−15%	−10%	5	1.6%				
IB	1%	−37%	3	1.8%				
OS					−19%	−49%	9	3.0%
KL	−18%	−20%	10	5.2%	−12%	−28%	12	4.0%
LH	−8%	−16%	10	10.8%	−8%	−15%	13	3.4%
SK	−12%	−6%	3	1.5%				
LX	−35%	−34%	8	3.2%	−11%	−25%	5	2.3%

Source: elaboration of OAG and KLM data.
[a]Difference in number of seats after and before the crises.
[b]Percentage difference in bookings before the crisis.
[c]Apr01-Jun01.
[d]Jul02-Feb02.

14.4.2 Econometric Analysis

Three models are specified to test the hypothesis that capacity choice on a certain route depends on short- and long-term profitability.

Equation 14.16 relates the capacity change to the variation of the YIELD and PAX variables, as presented in Eq. (14.15):

$$\Delta S_j = \alpha_0 + \alpha_1 Y_j + \Delta P_j + \varepsilon_j. \tag{14.16}$$

In the next two equations, the specific reactions of the carriers to short-term and long-term profitability are decomposed by means of the dummy variables XX. In Eq. (14.17), the dummies are multiplied by the PAX variable:

$$\Delta S_j = \alpha_0 + \alpha_1 Y_j + \sum_j \beta_i \Delta P_j XX_i + \varepsilon_j. \tag{14.17}$$

In Eq. (14.18), the dummies are multiplied by the YIELD variable in order to decompose its impact per carrier:

$$\Delta S_j = \alpha_0 + \alpha_1 P_j + \sum_j \beta_i Y_j XX_i + \varepsilon_j. \tag{14.18}$$

Table 14.3. Estimated coefficients of Eqs. (14.11–13) for the September 11 and SARS crises

Variable	Equation 1		Equation 2		Equation 3	
	Sept.11 A	SARS B	Sept.11 C	SARS D	Sept.11 E	SARS F
Intercept	−0.37 (0.14)	−0.34 (0.08)	−0.45 (0.15)	−0.25 (0.08)	−0.43 (0.14)	−0.39 (0.07)
YIELD	5.96 (1.94)	3.60 (0.08)	6.51 (2.12)	2.91 (1.05)	-	-
PAX	0.61 (0.14)	0.49 (1.06)	-	-	0.75 (0.15)	0.45 (0.08)
AF	-	-	0.43 (0.51)	0.65 (0.18)	7.31 (2.69)	3.82 (1.45)
AZ	-	-	0.62 (0.33)	−0.10 (0.22)	9.15 (2.47)	1.48 (1.71)
BA	-	-	0.00 (0.31)	0.29 (0.17)	10.55 (3.33)	7.50 (1.36)
EI	-	-	1.12 (0.48)	-	7.42 (2.95)	-
IB	-	-	1.19 (0.40)	-	8.96 (6.12)	-
OS	-	-	-	0.93 (0.13)	-	2.14 (1.32)
LH	-	-	0.43 (0.54)	0.44 (1.70)	5.75 (2.4)	4.48 (1.26)
KL	-	-	0.70 (0.29)	0.39 (0.21)	5.81 (2.09)	5.49 (1.68)
SK	-	-	0.45 (0.71)	-	6.10 (3.49)	-
LX	-	-	0.69 (0.37)	0.47 (0.32)	2.31 (2.85)	3.56 (1.43)
Statistics	$R^2 = 0.29$	$R^2 = 0.49$	$R^2 = 0.43$	$R^2 = 0.61$	$R^2 = 0.44$	$R^2 = 0.60$
	$AdjR^2 = 0.27$	$AdjR^2 = 0.47$	$AdjR^2 = 0.32$	$AdjR^2 = 0.56$	$AdjR^2 = 0.33$	$AdjR^2 = 0.55$
	Obs = 67	Obs = 70	Obs = 67	Obs = 70	Obs = 67	Obs = 70

Note: standard error is in brackets

The equations are estimated by means of Ordinary Least Squares, and the results are presented in Table 14.3. The adjusted R^2 value ranges from 0.29 to 0.56.

The R^2 is higher for the three SARS related equations than for the equations referring to September 11 crisis. The reasons can be either that the models better fit the SARS crisis than that of September 11, or they are related to a better data collection. In both cases, we can confirm the validity of our methodology to analyses two crises over different time periods and markets (North America vs. Asia). We take it as the first result that reinforces our theoretical conjectures. Furthermore we proceed to investigate the specific carriers' conduct.

Hereafter we compare the coefficients for each equation:

Equation 14.16: both PAX and YIELD are significantly different from zero, and their magnitude is higher for the September 11 crisis than for that of the SARS.

The PAX variable measures the passenger variation that occurred immediately after the crisis. As no carrier has changed its capacity supply in the months after the crisis, PAX does not depend on the change in the capacity supply[18] as it cap-

---

[18] To be more precise, in certain cases, data on the PAX variation may present some endogeneity as some capacity variations had already occurred at the date on which we measure passenger reduction. Nevertheless, the endogeneity issue does not seem too severe since passengers usually take decisions in advance, and hence before capacity change. Passengers who have booked for a time schedule that is not available are reallocated to another flight. Usually, for low fares, there is no reimbursement. For highest

tures an exogenous demand shift. Consequently, no identification problems are generated due to simultaneous changes in demand and supply behaviour. For the North American destinations, when the coefficient PAX equals 0.61, it means that a 10% reduction of the total demand in the market induces the carriers to reduce their capacity by 6.1%. This value decreases to 4.9% for the Asian destinations. The YIELD coefficient is 5.7 for September 11 and 3.6 for SARS, which means that to have a capacity increase of 1%, the yield per passenger (average price) should increase by €12 on a flight of 6500 km for North America and by €18 on a flight of the same length for Asia. This difference increases if we take into account that the average distance from Europe to North America is 6500 km and to Asia 9100 km. In the latter case, the yield per passenger has to increase by €24 in order to have a capacity increase of 1%.

Equation 14.17: the regression explains, 43% and 61% respectively of the variance of the dependent variable although not all the coefficients are statistically significant at 90%. The dummy coefficients of the September 11 equation can be clustered in three groups with similar reactions to the demand shift (short-term reaction). The first group, composed of Air France, British Airways, Lufthansa and SAS, presented a low or null reaction, a second group including Alitalia, KLM and Swiss had a medium reaction and a third group formed by Aer Lingus and Iberia had the strongest reaction. In the SARS equation, where the number of carriers is smaller, we are able to identify two groups, one, including British Airways, Lufthansa, KLM and Swiss, with a low reaction, and a second including Air France and Austrian Airlines with a stronger reaction. Therefore, Air France, KLM and Alitalia have reacted differently to the SARS crisis than to the September 11 crisis. A theoretical interpretation of this result is provided in the next section.

Equation 14.18: the regression analysis explains, respectively, 44% and 60% of the variance of the dependent variable. As in Eq. (14.12), we identify three groups. The first group includes Swiss and Iberia, with no significant YIELD coefficients (low or null reaction), the second includes KLM, SAS, Lufthansa with a medium reaction to the YIELD variable: and the last group, formed by Aer Lingus, Air France, Alitalia, British Airways, with a strong reaction. On the SARS equation we are able to identify one group including Air France, Austrian Airlines, Swiss and Lufthansa with low reaction to long term profitability and a second group including British Airways and KLM, with stronger reaction. In this case we notice that again that KLM, Air France and Alitalia have reacted to this second crisis differently.

In the next section, the results are discussed and interpreted in relation to the theoretical framework, in order to draw a picture of the airlines conduct during exogenous demand shift

---

fares, carriers usually provide extra-benefits to counterbalance the discomfort of the change of departure time. Alternatively, we note that the carriers' decisions are based on the observed demand, as well as on the expected demand. Thus, we need to use the realised passenger demand as a proxy for the expected demand.

14.4.3 Results

The main outcomes of the theoretical model can be explained by means of a simple scatter plot[19] (Fig. 14.4).

The sensitivity of the carriers to short- and long-term profitability is displayed, respectively, on the horizontal and on the vertical axis. A point located on the upper left side identifies a carrier with long-term goals. On the other hand, a point plotted in the lower right side identifies a carrier which pursues short-term goals. Carriers plotted in the middle adopt a mixed conduct.

The graph shows three different lines, each one referring to a different level of adjustment costs. The closer the line is to the origin, the higher the adjustment costs. The first line on the left side represents a carrier with high adjustment costs; the second represents a carrier with intermediate adjustment costs; and the third represents a carrier with low adjustment costs. The three markers on each line identify carriers with different expectations of crisis duration (or different interest rates[20]) but with the same adjustment costs. The upper-left plot on the line indicates expectation of short crisis duration, the lowest plot on the same line indicates expectation of long crisis duration. The financial situation also modifies the markers' location in the graph: the stronger is the financial constraint, the higher the sensitivity to short-term profitability, and the lower the sensitivity to long-term profitability.

The main factors affecting the carriers' conduct and hence their positioning on the graph are adjustment costs and expectation of the crisis duration. We expect that flexible carriers are located on an upper line, while non-flexible carriers are on a lower line.

As mentioned in the Introduction, market shares[21] are a proxy for the costs of adjustment. We observe the market shares of the nine European carriers flying between Europe and the North Atlantic over the period April–June 2000. Lufthansa and British Airways are the carriers with the highest adjustment costs in the North American market (with 10.8% and 10.1% of the market, respectively), followed by Air France (6.6%), KLM (5.2%), Swiss (3.2%), Alitalia (3.0%), and, finally, Iberia (1.8%), Aer Lingus (1.6%) and Scandinavian Airlines (1.5%).

---

[19] This graph is generated assuming $R = 0.1, 0.2, 0.3$ and $\delta = 0.5, 1, 1.5$.

[20] We present the results as depending on different expectations of the duration of the crisis but, looking at the interest rate the conclusions are exactly the same. In fact, the discount factor depends on both these variables and it is not possible to separate the two effects.

[21] A referee suggested that the cost of adjustment should reflect the opportunity cost. This means that fleet flexibility, network structure and other relevant variables should also be included in the explanation of the adjustment costs. In this paper we limit our analysis to consider market share as a proxy for adjustment costs, but we agree with the point.

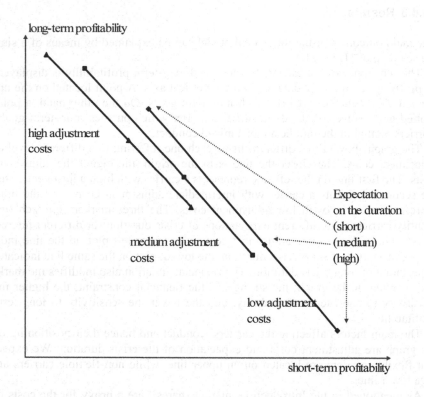

Fig. 14.4. Expected impact of short and long-term profitability reaction depending on the adjustment costs and the duration of the crisis

In the Asian market, British Airways has the largest market share (7.1%,) followed by Air France (4.6%), KLM (4.0%), Lufthansa (3.4%), Austrian Airlines (3%), Swiss (2.3%) Alitalia (1,8%). The relationship between market shares and adjustment costs seems less strong in the Asian market.[22]

---

[22] As suggested by a referee, it is possible to estimate the impact of market shares (*MS*) on the capacity choice. Equations. (14.19–20) present the results of September 11 and SARS, respectively:

$$\Delta S = -0.49 + 5.56Y + 0.61\Delta P + 1.97MS \qquad (14.19)$$

and

$$\Delta S = -0.40 + 3.53Y + 0.51\Delta P + 0.53MS \qquad (14.20)$$

All the coefficients have the correct sign and are significant at 5% with the exception of *MS* for the Asian Crisis.

Hereafter, we present the results of the econometric analysis. We assumed in the previous paragraphs that the YIELD variable is the measure of the long-term profitability, and the PAX variable is the measure for short-term profitability. Therefore, we can use the framework of Fig. 14.4 and by displaying the PAX coefficients of Eq. (14.17) on the horizontal axis and the YIELD coefficients of Eq. (14.18) on the vertical axis. The estimated coefficients are plotted in Fig. 14.5. Black diamonds represent the carriers' reaction to the US crisis and the white diamonds their reaction to Asian crisis.[23]

To investigate the functioning of the model, we focus on the carriers' reaction to the shock of September 11. Assuming a linking line is created between British Airways and Lufthansa, and moving out of the origin with other parallel lines, we can order the different behaviour of carriers depending on their flexibility. On the lowest line, we locate Lufthansa and British Airways. On the next lines, we locate Air France and KLM, followed by Alitalia. Aer Lingus and Iberia are located on the highest lines.

The behaviour of Swiss and Scandinavian Airlines does not fit the model. Scandinavian Airlines has 1.5% of the market share and should be plotted somewhere closer to Iberia and Aer Lingus. However, the Nordic carrier is plotted very close to Lufthansa. This might be explained by the strong commercial relationship between the two carriers. Apparently, SAS is mimicking the Lufthansa strategy and the partnership affects not only commercial activities but also strategic actions.

The position of Swiss on the graph might be explained by the financial situation that the carrier was facing at the time of the American crisis. In fact, the theoretical model suggests that the financial constraints move carriers towards a short-term strategy. This is evident from the scatter: Swiss reacts to the crisis with a short-term strategy.

The expectation of the crisis duration is the second factor that affects the carrier' conduct. In December 2001, no carrier revealed its network planning for the next 12 months. As the crisis prediction is a strategic variable the carriers avoided as much as possible giving any external signal to the competitors. For this reason, it was impossible to collect reliable data to measure this variable. We have no choice but to assume that the theoretical model is correct, and make some kind of qualitative considerations. Combining Figs. 14.4–5, we notice that British Airways expected a much shorter duration than Lufthansa. They lie on the same line, but have opposite behaviour. Air France and Alitalia were more optimistic than Lufthansa. If it is not the case, the YIELD reaction of the two carriers should be lower than the one of Lufthansa. The same considerations can be applied to the other carriers. For example, Iberia and Aer Lingus expected a longer duration of the crisis than KLM, and KLM expected a shorter duration than that of Lufthansa. Swiss should have the shortest expected duration of the crisis but again its strategy

---

[23] Alitalia conduct for the SARS crisis is out of the graph (the PAX coefficient is negative). We do not provide any interpretation of this result, but we see that Alitalia has only two routes.

might result from the financial problems of the company that forced its reaction in the short-term.

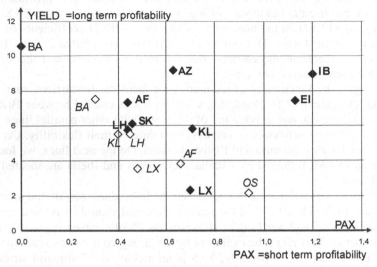

Fig. 14.5. Classification of firms in terms of short- and long-term reaction. The black diamonds indicate the carrier's reaction due to September 11, while the white diamonds indicates the carrier's reaction due to SARS

Alternatively, we can interpret a different positioning on the line as a different evaluation of the 'strategic' importance of the market. A carrier evaluating a market as 'very strategic' has a low discount rate on this market, and hence it will focus on the long-term more than the short-term returns. This could explain the positioning of British Airways with respect to the other large carriers. Since the North American market is very strategic for British Airways, it reacts only to long-term but not to short-term aspects.

Figure 14.5 also provides a representation of carriers' conduct induced by the Asian crisis. Before analysing specifically the behaviour of the carriers, we try to emphasise the main differences between the first and the second crisis.

As a general remark, we observe that compared with the North American crisis where only 1/3 of the capacity choice variation is explained by the PAX and the YIELD variables, in the Asian crisis about 2/3 of the capacity variation is explained by the same variables. This is due either to better data collected on the Asian crisis or to the fact that carriers' strategies are based more on the short- and the long-term variable in Asian crisis than in the North American crisis. If the second point is true, it may mean that carriers in the second crisis had gained experience of the previous crisis and therefore they could better calibrate their strategies on short- and long-term parameters. There are also other interpretations of a better fit of the second model, such as the fact that carriers in the North American market have a more complex strategy involving other variables more strongly than in the Asian market.

There are three main differences in the carriers' conduct in the two crises.

First, the reaction in the Asian crisis was lower than in the North American crisis. This emerges by comparing column 1 with column 2 of Table 14.3 where PAX values are respectively, 0.49 and 0.61, and YIELD values are respectively 3.60 and 5.96. On the graph, the white diamonds are closer to the origin than the black diamonds. Following our conceptual framework, it means that, on average, the adjustment costs of carrier are higher in the Asian market.

Second, the reaction to the Asian crisis was focused on short-term aspects and not on long-term aspects. There are many explanations for this result. A first explanation that we do not entirely believe is that the expectation of the crisis duration was shorter for the American crisis that for the Asian crisis. This is true if we think that carriers underestimate the duration of the crisis in the first shock and overestimate the duration of the crisis in the second shock. A slightly different interpretation can be provided by assuming that carriers can learn from the past, and thus a sort of mimicking behaviour of carriers emerges. Hence, British Airways having had a wrong reaction to the first shock has decided to recalibrate its conduct in the second shock. KLM having been too much reactive to the PAX variable after September 11 chose to adopt a strategy similar to Lufthansa after the SARS epidemic. The same argument is valid for Swiss. Lufthansa having been right has decided not to change. A third explanation for the different behaviour in the two crises is given by the fact that Asian market is not so crucial as the North American market for European carriers. This explains the shift towards the short-term choice of British Airways and Air France. Finally, a more fundamental explanation for the short-term attention of carriers is in the differences of the markets. The Asian market is characterised by higher operating costs and lower margins, meaning that the reduction of profitability (revenue – costs) when there is a demand shift in the short term is higher for the Asian market than for the North American market. Moreover, the crises affecting the Asian market before March 2003 (i.e. not only September 11 but also the Afghanistan war and the October 2002 Bali terrorist attack) might have induced carriers not to focus on the long-term indicators.

Thirdly, it does not seem that there are important adjustment-costs differences among carriers since they lie very close to the same line. Just as in the American crisis, during the SARS epidemic, we see that there were some carriers which followed the ordering as expected from the model, but there are some exceptions. Here, British Airways, KLM and Lufthansa are on the same line with Air France slightly higher and Austrian Airlines a little bit higher still. Swiss is out of the scheme and has the same behaviour as in the first shock. Financial constraints forced this carrier to focus on the short-term rather than long term.

Applying the theoretical framework to detect the behaviour during the Asian crisis, we note that all carriers can be easily sorted in terms of expectation of the crisis duration. Austrian Airlines expected longer crisis duration than Air France. Lufthansa and KLM have similar expectations. Then British Airways expected the crisis would have a short duration. Finally, assuming that Swiss was financially constrained, its expected duration was closest to those of Lufthansa and KLM. As already mentioned, expectation of the crisis duration can be also interpreted as the strategic or non-strategic goals of the carriers.

Now we compare the conduct of the four main carriers in the two situations. First of all, we observe that Lufthansa did not change its behaviour. British Airways that was very optimistic in the North American crisis has changed its strategy, and aligned with the one of other players. Also, KLM aligned with its main competitor, Lufthansa. These three carriers moved towards or kept on a balanced conduct by mixing short- and long-term goals. On the contrary, Air France did not seem to be confident of a quick recovers from the crisis and assumed a longer duration of the crisis

14.5 Conclusions

This paper provides a theoretical and empirical analysis of the conduct of European carriers during the North American and Asian crises. An important assumption of the model is the existence of positive adjustment costs, i.e. the costs required to re-expand capacity. Adjustment costs introduce rigidity in the carriers' conduct. Indeed, non-flexible carriers typically present, a small reaction to short- and long-term variables. This behaviour results from the fact that a non-flexible carrier sets high capacity levels during the crisis to push its competitors out of the market and to reduce the set-up costs of re-entering. On the other hand, flexible carriers present high responsiveness to both short- and long-term profitability. They can be small during the crisis period to reduce the losses, and free to expand in the post-crisis period. In the North American market, we observe that the conduct of non-flexible carriers is oriented to long-term profitability, while in the Asian market they have a more balanced choice. Carriers' strategies are also affected by expectations of the crisis duration and on the strategic importance of the market. If a carrier expects the crisis to have a long duration (or the market is not strategically important), then its conduct shifts to the short-term variable. If the expected duration is short (or the market is strategically important), then the carrier bases its strategy on the long-term variable.

Empirical analysis suggests that the theoretical model is useful to interpret both crises. The main differences we find for the two crisis situations are: the carriers' reaction to the Asian crisis was lower than in the North American crisis; it was focused on short-term aspects; and there were less adjustment costs differences among carriers.

An open question is whether or not carriers gain experience from the past events. We think that it is possible, and this is supported by our results. If we assume that carriers base their strategies only on short- and long-term gains, we see that these two variables explained 2/3 of the capacity choice in the Asian crisis but only 1/3 in the North Atlantic crisis. Hence, carriers have been more consistent in managing the Asian crisis than the North American crisis. Some more evidence comes from the behaviour of British Airways. In fact, it seems that British Airways modified its strategy by changing from a situation where it only cared about long-term variables toward a more balanced situation, closer to the Lufthansa/KLM strategy.

References

Alderighi M, Cento A (2004) European airlines conduct after September 11. Journal of Air Transport Management 10: 97–107

Bashyam TCA (1996) Competitive capacity expansion under demand uncertainty. European Journal of Operational Research 95: 89–114

Borenstein S (1989) Hubs and high fares: dominance and market power in the US airline industry. RAND Journal of Economics 20: 344–365

Bruning RE, Hu MY (1988) Profitability, firm size, efficiency and flexibility in the U.S. domestic airline industry. International Journal of Transport Economics XV

Bulow J, Geanakoplos J, Klemperer P (1993) Multimarket oligopoly: strategic substitutes and complements. Journal of Political Economy 93: 488–511

Chang Y, Williams G (2002) European major airlines' strategic reaction to the Third Package. Transport Policy 9: 129–142

Chin ATH, Tay JH (2001) Development in air transportation: implication of investment decisions, profitability and survival of Asian airlines. Journal of Air Transportation Management 7: 219–330

Fudenberg D, Tirole J (1984) The fat-cat effect, the puppy-dog ploy, and the lean and hungry look. American Economic Review 74: 361–366

Gould JP (1968) Adjustment costs in the theory of investment of the firm. Review of Economic Studies 35: 47–55

Gillen D, Lall A (2003) International transmission of shocks in the airline industry. Journal of Air Transportation Management 9: 37–49

Hätty H, Hollmeier S (2003) Airline strategy in the 2001/2002 crisis: the Lufthansa example. Journal of Air Transportation Management 9: 51–55

Janic M (1997) Liberalisation of European aviation: analysis and modelling of the airline behaviour. Journal of Air Transportation Management 4: 167–180

Smith GH (1997) The European airline industry: a banker's view. Journal of Air Transportation Management 4: 189–196

Windle R, Dresner M (1995) The short and long run effects of entry on US domestic air routes. Transportation Journal 35: 14–25

Windle R, Dresner M (1999) Competitive responses to low cost carrier entry. Transportation Research Part E: Logistics and Transportation Review 35, 59–75

Part D: Sustainable Transport and Policy Perspectives

15 Taxes and the Environmental Impact of Private Car Use: Evidence from 68 Cities

Keiko Hirota[1] and Jacques Poot[2]

[1] Japan Automobile Research Institute; Tsukuba, Japan
[2] University of Waikato, Hamilton, New Zealand

15.1 Introduction

Many countries have implemented measures to reduce greenhouse gas emissions and other environmental costs resulting from the transport sector. Energy consumption, CO_2 emission and other environmental impacts of the transport sector depend on the modal split in transportation, which in turn is strongly influenced by the relative cost and convenience of each transport mode.

In this chapter we focus on private car use. The global demand for private car use may be expected to continue to expand as incomes in most countries continue to increase. Figure 15.1 shows the relationship between car density (the number of private cars per 1000 of the population) and per capita income. Figure 15.1 combines two samples: one sample of cities in Europe, North America and the Asia-Pacific region and one sample of the corresponding country information. The figure illustrates two points. First, the demand for private cars clearly increases with the level of development. Second, at each level of development there is considerable variation in car ownership. The latter variation is *inter alia* due to local geography, available infrastructure, private cost in use of motor vehicles, congestion levels and local regulations, taxes and fees. We exploit the variation in these conditions across cities in this chapter in order to identify the effect of the user cost of private cars and tax incentives on car ownership and use.

The incidence of car ownership and vehicle kilometres travelled (VKT) are likely to be related, but the relationship is not necessarily a close one. This is illustrated in Fig. 15.2. As car ownership increases, the average annual distance travelled per capita increases, but the variance increases too. A high rate of ownership is likely to reflect a low user cost and a high level of income. In some cities a high rate of car ownership is accommodated by an extensive infrastructure that encourages car use. On the other hand, congestion may arise where the infrastructure is inadequate, leading to a relatively lower level of distance travelled.

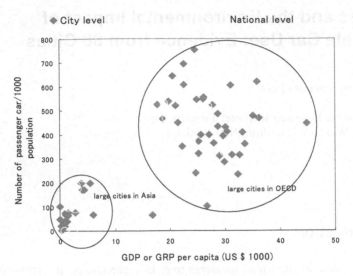

Fig. 15.1. Per capita income and car density, 1990

While Fig. 15.2 depicts pooled data for 1990 and 2002 from a range of cities in North America, Europe and the Asia-Pacific region, the same relationship holds for more homogeneous subgroups of cities.

Given that GDP and other factors affect car ownership and that car ownership affects aggregate VKT, the question arises to what extent these relationships are modified by transportation and environmental policies. In this chapter we analyse the responsiveness of demand to the user cost per kilometre in order to identify which vehicle tax policy might be effective for an improvement of environmental conditions. User costs are divided into fixed and variable costs. An example of fixed cost is a lump sum levy such as an acquisition tax. Variable costs have an influence on the distance travelled and the driving habits. For example, fuel taxes and road charges such as tolls are variable costs. In theory, we expect lump-sum taxes and charges to be less clearly linked to environmental outcomes than taxes related to use, although it is possible to differentiate fixed charges in order to encourage the purchase and use of environmentally-friendly vehicles (e.g., ECMT 1998). Generally, vehicle tax policy has shifted in Europe from fixed to variable taxes. In Asia's emerging-market countries, there may be an opportunity to reform the vehicle tax structure in tandem with trade liberalization and income growth.

Our empirical analysis in this chapter is based on a study of large cities in Europe, USA, Canada and the Asia-Pacific region. Our data set consists of 68 large cities, of which 49 are located in OECD countries (including Japan) and 19 in other Asian countries. Data are primarily available for 1990, in some cities for 2002, and in a few cases for both years.

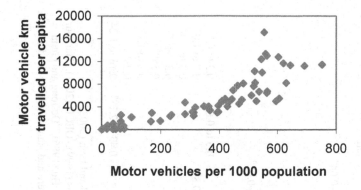

Fig. 15.2. Car ownership and use in an international sample of large cities, 1990 and 2002 pooled data

The population density, the number of passenger vehicles per 1000 persons and the available public transport infrastructure are all expected to influence VKT and greenhouse gas emissions. The sample of Asian cities was selected by means of the following criteria: (i) private car density of less than 200 passenger vehicles per 1000 people; (ii) population density of at least 150 people per ha; and (iii) public transport expenditure of less than US$200 per capita annually.

The chapter is organized as follows. The next section provides a brief survey of the literature on price elasticities of the demand for car travel. Section 15.3 describes the data. In Sect. 15.4 we report some simple regression models of the relationship between car use, pollution and tax incentives. In the final section we sum up and suggest how the tax structure can be improved.

15.2 Previous Research and Theoretical Considerations

15.2.1 Travel Demand Elasticities

There is considerable spatial variation in the incidence of car ownership and use. For example, urban areas in Asia are experiencing a considerable growth in the number of vehicles, but these countries often differ from OECD countries in terms of vehicle usage, because of different land use patterns, a different population density gradient in urban areas, etc.

302   K. Hirota and J. Poot

Table 15.1. A selection of typical elasticity estimates

Impact of → on	Fuel cost / Fuel tax		Acquisition cost/tax		Ownership cost/tax		Road capacity	
	Short term	Long term	Short term	Long term	Short term	Long term	Short term	Long term
Car stock		−0.3[a] −0.41 to −0.15[b] −0.4 to −0.2[c] −0.2 to −0.1[d] −0.18 to 0.36[e] −0.18 to 0.36[j]	−0.38[i]	−1.6 to −0.4[g] −0.24 to −0.09[f] −0.253[h] −0.77 to −0.6[i] −0.57 to −0.28[e] −0.31 to −0.22[d]		−0.081[h] −0.08 to −0.04[d]		
Fuel consumption	−0.28 to −0.27[a] −0.23 to −0.1[f] −0.6 to −0.5[l] −0.26[k]	−0.84 to −0.71[a] −0.702[h] −0.77[f] −0.86[k]		−0.529[h]		−0.055[h] −0.16 to −0.02[d]		
Car use(km)	−0.16[a]	−0.33/−0.29[a] −0.262[h] −0.55/−0.05[i] −0.3[k]		−0.287[h]		0.062[h] −0.04 to 0.8[d]	0.3 to 0.6[n]	0.3 to 0.9[o] 0.7 to 1.0[n] 0.3 to 1.0[p] 0.3 to 0.5[q] 0.559[r] 0.8 to 1.1[s] 0.29[t]
Public transport (km)	0.18 to 0.37[m]	0.34[a] 0.18 to 0.24[m]					0.43 to 2.78[m]	0.16 to 1.24[m]

Sources: Research cited in ECMT (1998), de Jong and Gunn (2001), Graham and Glaister (2002) and Noland and Lem (2002). [a]Goodwin (1992). [b]Hensher (1992). [c]Tanner (1992). [d]Johansson and Schipper (1997). [e]Dargay and Vythoulkas (1999). [f]OECD (2001). [g]Harbour (1987). [h]Storchmann (1998). [i]Vaes (1982). [j]European Commission (1996). [k]Sterner et al. (1992). [l]Greene and Hu (1986). [m]De Jong and Gunn (2001). [n]Noland (2001). [o]Hansen and Huang (1997). [p]Noland and Cowart (2000). [q]Fulton et al. (2000). [r]Cervero and Hansen (2001). [s]Rodier et al. (2001). [t]Strathman et al. (2000).

Although people may change their behaviour for various reasons, the price elasticity of demand is the most important factor to take into account when considering tax incentives. Standard economic theory would suggest that an increase in the price of private motor vehicle transportation – e.g., to reduce congestion on urban motorways – will indeed reduce VKT, although the consumer may also change his or her driving behaviour by taking an alternative route or by driving at off-peak times. In general, vehicle-related taxes can lead to a wide range of responses which may each have an environmental impact. Besides a possible change in VKT by means of a change in route and destinations and/or trip frequencies, these include the value of the car to buy and the related size of the engine, the age at which to replace the car, the number of passengers in the car (e.g. car pooling), the time of travel, the speed of travel, and other driving habits. Consequently, the calculation of travel demand elasticities is complex and has led to a wide range of different approaches in the literature. A range of typical estimates is reported in Table 15.1.

Espey (1998) carried out a meta-analysis of a large number of estimates of the price elasticity of the demand for fuel in the US and other countries. She finds that elasticity estimates are sensitive to the inclusion or exclusion of some measure of vehicle ownership. Elasticities of demand do appear to vary across countries. She also finds that gasoline demand appears to be getting more price-elastic and less income-elastic over time.

A more recent survey by Graham and Glaister (2002) draws some general conclusions that appear to be robust in the literature (but see also, for example, Dodgson et al. 2002). Firstly, short-run elasticities of fuel consumption with respect to price are in the region of –0.3 and in the long run between –0.6 and –0.8. However, the elasticity of VKT with respect to the price of gasoline is in the short run only about –0.15 and in the long run –0.3. Consequently, motorists (and manufacturers of motor vehicles) do find ways of economising on the use of fuel.

It is clear from these estimates that an increase in the gasoline price leads to behavioural responses such that gasoline consumption is much more affected than car traffic. Graham and Glaister conclude that changes in gasoline prices are more likely to affect fuel consumption rather than road congestion. de Jong and Gunn (2001) find that commuting and business travel is less sensitive to changes in fuel prices than travel for other purposes.

As can be expected, the available capacity of the road network also affects VKT. For example, Hansen and Huang (1997) found a lane mile elasticity of 0.9 in California metropolitan areas for a 4 to 5-year time period. Noland and Lem (2002) similarly concluded that new transportation capacity tends to induce an increase of travel in both the short and the long run, with UK elasticities ranging between 0.5 and 0.9 for metropolitan data.

In Eltony's (1993) study of household gasoline demand in Canada from 1989 to 2000, 75 percent of households reduced their travel by car within one year after a fuel price increase, which averaged at 2.7 percent over this period (compared with a 3.6 percent increase in prices of manufactured goods). Fifteen percent of households shifted from large vehicles to small vehicles. Ten percent of households switched from less fuel-efficient vehicles to more efficient vehicles.

However, a weakness of some studies is that they focus on behavioural changes in car usage, but do not take modal choice into account. Drollas' (1984) survey of gasoline elasticities for European countries found that people switched from gasoline to LPG or diesel-powered vehicles, or used a different mode of transport as gasoline prices increased. The author's results yield a short run price elasticity estimate of –0.26 and a long run elasticity of –0.6. Hence, consistent with the evidence of others, Drollas (1984) finds that the demand for fuel is more elastic in the long run than the short run due to the wider range of behavioural responses available to the motorist in the long run. The long-run effects include destination and frequency choices (i.e. they respond to a price increase by making shorter and/or less frequent trips).

As we saw in Fig. 15.2, VKT is positively related to car ownership. In turn, car ownership is positively related to GDP per capita (Fig. 15.1) and to the real price of cars. Consequently, the responsiveness of observed traffic with respect to fuel price is often blurred due to economic growth and changes in the price of a car relative to other goods and services. Noland and Cowart (1999) find that the elasticity of VKT with respect to the total user cost of a car varies in the USA between –0.8 for a 5-year period and –1.0 for a 20-year period.

The responses of consumers to a change in the price of anything that affects the cost of a private car trip can be exploited for the formulation of economic instruments for the improvement of environmental quality. However, across countries there is considerable variation in the composition of the cost in use of a car. This variation is exploited in this chapter to assess the impact of a marginal change in any of these components on VKT, CO_2 emissions and the stock of cars.

15.2.2 Tax Policies

Economic incentives for reducing the environmental impact of private car transportation can take the form of a 'carrot' (i.e. a subsidy) or a 'stick' (i.e. a tax or fee). In the United States, the federal government offers consumers tax deductions ranging from $2,000 to $50,000 towards incremental expenditure for the purchase or conversion of an approved clean fuel vehicle. In a similar manner, the Japanese government reduces the acquisition tax for clean energy vehicles, such as electric or natural-gas powered vehicles. Japan also offers a separate reduction in the acquisition tax for vehicles that meet certain emission targets. Vehicles that achieve a 25 percent emission reduction below the 2000 emission standard obtain a 13 percent rebate of the motor vehicle tax. For 50 percent and 75 percent emission reductions these rebates increase to 25 percent and 50 percent respectively. As a consequence, the number of low-emission vehicles significantly increased from 2000 to 2001 (Ishak 2001).

In some other Asian countries, the environmental impact of private car transportation has been modest until now due to the combination of high population density, low passenger car ownership and high use of public transport. However, in these countries increased income is likely to induce growing private car use although improvements in public transport services may moderate this growth. Modal choice is of course often influenced by equity consideration: governments may subsidize or encourage the use of some types of vehicles, or maintain low public transportation fares.

For example, sales tax in the Philippines is lower for diesel vehicles than for gasoline vehicles. Malaysia has tax incentives for environmental reasons: conversion kits for alternative fuel vehicles are exempt from import duties and sales tax. In addition, the Malaysian Department of the Environment has been encouraging the use of natural gas in public service vehicles in urban areas, and the road tax is reduced for alternative fuel vehicles (50 percent off for monogas vehicles, 25 percent off for dual fuel vehicles), with some success (Ishak 2001).

Among European countries, the UK has the highest fuel tax rate. The rate of fuel tax was increased to compensate for the abolition of a car purchase tax. In contrast, Italy has the highest tax on heating oil while its fuel tax rate is not as high as that of the UK (OECD 2001). These examples illustrate that there is considerable variation in tax incentives across countries.

Private motor vehicle tax levels vary also often by engine capacity, vehicle gross weight and price. The existence of a vehicle taxation system based on engine capacity or vehicle weight would be a potential incentive to purchase or keep vehicles with a smaller engine capacity or lighter weight. It is useful to compare this with, for example, the UK system where an annual circulation tax and the company car taxation system are based on CO_2 emissions. When taxing cars based on market value, the incentive structure does not respond to environmental concerns as older, and therefore more polluting, vehicles are taxed at a lower level. The idea of increasing the tax with age has been adopted in Japan, where Tokyo and some other prefectures charge a higher tax for older vehicles.

In the Netherlands, the government reformed vehicle-related taxes to meet environmental objectives, but the total energy consumption since 1990 has been stable and not decreasing (Robert et al. 2001). Car ownership has not decreased. In addition, the average vehicle gross weight of new cars increased by 1.9 percent annually from 1987 to 1991 and average engine capacity of new cars increased by 4 percent from 1985 to 1997. The government of the Netherlands plans to impose an acquisition tax based on CO_2 emissions, which is expected to reduce CO_2 emission by 4 percent.

Another policy example is provided by Denmark. The Danish government decided in 1997 to reform its ownership tax system from a weight-based system to a fuel-economy based one. Fuel-efficient vehicles are taxed at a lower rate. Since implementation of this policy, the average fuel economy of new cars has been improved by 0.5 km/l for gasoline vehicles and by 2.3 km/l for diesel vehicles. As a result, CO_2 emissions have been reduced from 183 g/km to 176 g/km (based on test vehicles). In addition, the green tax system in Denmark imposes higher taxes on diesel vehicles.

The examples above illustrate that taxes and subsidies which affect the price of car use do lead to a range of behavioural responses in the 'right' direction, i.e. demand is price elastic. In order to quantify effects on car ownership, VKT, and CO_2 emissions, we exploit the variation in conditions across a wide range of large cities to estimate a simple regression model of the impact of various components (purchase, ownership and use) of the user cost of cars. The data are described in the next section and the regression results are reported in Sect. 15.4.

15.3 Data Description

15.3.1 Defining the Cost of Motor Vehicle Use

Economic theory shows that private motor vehicle users should pay the marginal social cost of their transportation. Such first best pricing is in practice rarely feasible and, instead, governments attempt to implement a set of taxes, charges and subsidies that bring the full price that the traveller pays closer to the marginal social cost. What is the price paid per km travelled? In many countries this question is answered regularly by various transport-related agencies or consumer groups who calculate and combine the fixed and variable costs of motor vehicle use. In order to make valid comparisons across cities and countries, we must define precisely the 'commodity' for which the responsiveness to price is investigated. Consequently, we standardize by focusing on popular and ubiquitous global cars, such as the Toyota Corolla. Given the fierce competition between car manufacturers, price variation at any given location between comparable models of different car makes is very little and it is possible to calculate the cost in use of a 'generic' new gasoline passenger vehicle, defined as a four door manual sedan with a weight of 1300 kg, engine capacity 1600 cc, power 110 HP and CO_2 emission of 188 g/km. This also permits international comparison of various taxes. While acquisition taxes are generally based on car prices, ownership taxes are imposed on emissions, fuel economy, weight, or engine capacity in many countries. Registration fees are included in the acquisition tax. Fuel taxes differ by type of fuel.

Data were collected on car ownership, use and costs in a range of cities. The data referred primarily to 1990, but for some cities an update for 2002 was readily available. An example of the cost-in-use calculation is given in Table 15.2. The data in the Table are for Tokyo in 2002. The cost in use of the generic car per kilometre travelled is similarly determined for all other cities. However, it should be noted that a wide range of sources was consulted to compile our city-level data base and the available information is of rather variable quality. In addition, it was not possible to include road user tolls (such as the cordons and congestion charges in Singapore, London and Oslo), or the motorway tolls (in e.g. France and Japan).

Table 15.2. An example of cost-in-use calculations: Tokyo, 2002

Generic 1600 cc car	Yen	Real US$ cost at PPP exchange rate of 153.7
Purchase price	1,453,000	9,453.48
Acquisition tax	72,650	472.67
Car price including acquisition cost	1,525,650	9,926.15
Total taxes, duties and delivery costs	296,050	1,926.15
Real interest rate	2.20%	
Life of the car in years	9.96	
Annuity factor	8.86	
Annual equivalent of purchase price	164,042	1,067.29
Annual equivalent of acquisition tax	8,202	53.36
Annual ownership (licence) tax	60,983	396.77
Vehicle kilometres travelled (VKT) per capita	2,357	
Vehicle kilometres travelled (VKT) per car	8,504	
Gasoline price per litre at pump	97	0.63
Gasoline tax per litre (included in price)	59	0.38
Car fuel consumption: kilometres per litre	12.5	
Annual gasoline cost excluding fuel tax	25,907	168.55
Annual fuel tax	39,799	258.94
Annual maintenance and repair cost	96,984	631.00
Annual insurance cost	16,467	107.14
Total annual cost in use	412,384	2,683.04
Cost in use per km travelled	48	0.32
Cost in use excl taxes per km travelled	33	0.21
Acquisition tax per km travelled	4	0.03
Ownership tax per km travelled	7	0.05
Fuel tax per km travelled	5	0.03
Income per capita	5,721,974	37,228.20
Car units per 1000 persons	232	
CO2 emission per capita	1,763	

Nonetheless, cities were only included in the database when the data were considered to be of adequate quality. For international comparison, local prices in any given year were converted to US dollars at the purchasing power parity (PPP) exchange rate for that year, using IMF data. With respect to taxes and duties paid at purchase, two alternative approaches were adopted. The first approach accounts as a tax only the explicitly stated vehicle acquisition tax. In the case of Tokyo in 2002, this tax, which is related to the vehicle price, was 72,650 yen for a Toyota Corolla type car (Table 15.2). The alternative approach is to consider the full gap between the retail price and the assumed pre-tax world factory price of US$8000 for this type of vehicle as representing total taxes, duties and delivery costs. This gap between the world factory price and the local delivery price was in PPP terms about $1900 in Tokyo in 2002.

Lump sum costs were converted to annual equivalents by the standard annuity formula:

$$x_A = \frac{E_0}{\sum_{k=1}^{n} \frac{1}{(1+i)^k}} = \frac{E_0 i (1+i)^n}{(1+i)^n - 1}$$ (15.1)

In this formula, E_0 is the lump sum cost, n the expected life of the car in years, i the real interest rate and x_A the annual equivalent cost. In Tokyo, the expected life of a car of 9.96 years combined with a real interest rate of 2.2 percent leads to the annual equivalent of the purchase price of about 164,000 yen, or US$1067 in PPP terms.

The annual costs of ownership and use are then added to the annualised purchase cost in order to compute the full cost per kilometre travelled. The annual fuel cost was calculated by means of data on fuel economy. Even for the generic car, this varies across cities due to different driving conditions.

Fuel economy for cities in European countries is based on European Conference of Ministers of Transport data. Fuel economy for the USA was derived from the CAFÉ standard (FTP mode), while for Japan data can be found in EDMC statistics. The estimated fuel economy for Asian countries varies between 8.73 km/l and 12.3 km/l, depending on local conditions (using data from IRF 2002 and IEA 2001). The annual fuel cost is estimated from data on VKT per vehicle divided by fuel economy and multiplied by the local price of unleaded gasoline.

VKT per capita was estimated from the total traffic volume (private car passenger kilometres) divided by city population. Where city-level data were not available, national averages were inserted. CO_2 emission data from the transport sector were obtained from IEA (2001) and are available only at the national level. However, car stock data (cars per 1000 persons) were available at city level.

The annual maintenance, repair and insurance costs are often available from various Automobile Association websites. When unavailable from this source, expenditure survey statistics were used instead. The pre-tax total vehicle cost in use per km consists of the following components: the annual equivalent of the purchase price (excluding acquisition taxes), the annual gasoline cost excluding fuel tax, the annual maintenance and repair cost, and the annual insurance cost. In the Tokyo example of Table 15.2, the total cost in use per km travelled is 32 cents (PPP terms) including taxes and 21 cents excluding taxes, so that the various types of government fees and taxes add 52 percent to the cost in use. Of these, the ownership tax is the largest component (44 percent), while the annualised acquisition tax and the fuel tax are similar. Figure 15.3 shows the share of the different types of taxes in the total user cost per km for selected large cities.

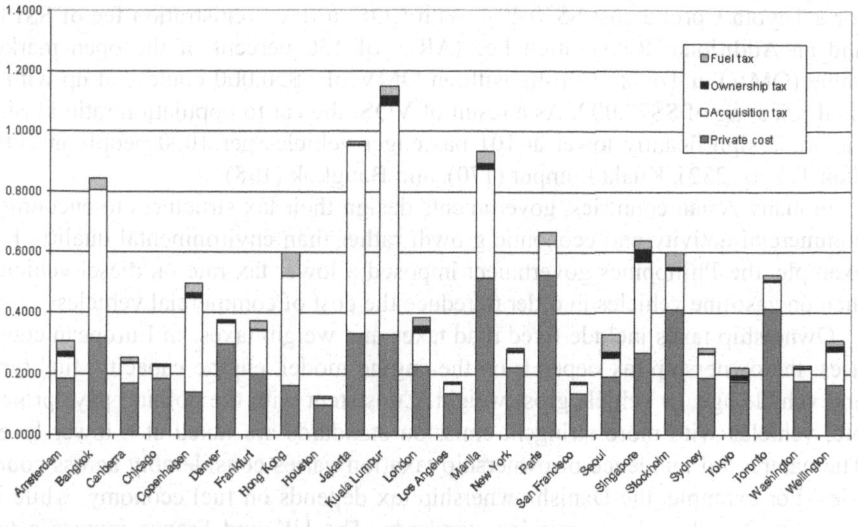

Fig. 15.3. The total cost in use per kilometre travelled in selected cities, for a generic mid-sized type (e.g. Toyota Corolla) car, 1990

Figure 15.3 shows that the total cost in use per km is the lowest in cities in the United States. The cost in use exceeds 60 cents (in PPP terms) primarily in Asian cities (Bangkok, Jakarta, Kuala Lumpur, Manila and Singapore), but also in Paris. In the latter city, the annualised pre-tax cost of purchase, maintenance and insurance is quite high, but in the other cities the generalised acquisition tax (which is based on the difference between the retail price and the world price) is primarily responsible for the high cost in use. The ownership tax is noticeably high in Singapore, while the fuel tax component is the highest in Hong Kong and Stockholm.

15.3.2 Examples of Acquisition, Ownership and Fuel Tax Schemes

Across cities, different criteria can be found for levying an acquisition tax. For example, the high acquisition tax in Denmark (see Copenhagen in Fig. 15.3) is based on the value of the car. For cars costing less than 48,800 DKr, the acquisition tax is 105 percent of the value. Above this amount, the tax increases to 180 percent. Clearly, a tax of this nature is based on the assumption that the environmental cost of large cars is greater. There is also built-in progressivity in the tax, as buyers of larger cars tend to have higher incomes.

Many countries have a lower acquisition tax level for clean energy vehicles. In Singapore, taxes and charges on car acquisition are a significant component of transportation expenditure for middle and upper-income households. Singapore's

Vehicle Quota System (VQS) has been applied since 1990. The VQS controls the car stock with Certificate of Entitlement (COE) quotas. In August 2003, a COE for a Toyota Corolla cost S$30,497. With COE, a fixed registration fee of S$140 and an Additional Registration Fee (ARF) of 130 percent of the open market value (OMV), a Toyota Corolla with an OMV of S$20,000 could end up with a final price tag of S$77,000. As a result of VQS, the car to population ratio in Singapore is significantly lower at 101 passenger vehicles per 1000 people in 2002 than Tokyo (232), Kuala Lumpur (170), and Bangkok (198).

In many Asian countries, governments design their tax structures to encourage commercial activity and economic growth rather than environmental quality. For example, the Philippines government imposed a lower tax rate on diesel vehicles than on gasoline vehicles in order to reduce the cost of commercial vehicles·

Ownership taxes include fixed road taxes and weight taxes. In European countries, the ownership tax depends on the engine model, engine capacity, fuel type and vehicle age, or vehicle gross weight. Consistent with the polluter pays principle, vehicles with more stringent emission standards are taxed at a lower level. The nature and incidence of ownership taxation varies considerably across countries. For example, the Danish ownership tax depends on fuel economy, while in Germany it is based on emission standards. The UK and France impose a tax based on CO_2 emissions. In the UK, a single rate road tax has been replaced by a tax with four categories based on CO_2 emission levels. In France, the ownership tax depends on vehicle age and the region where the car is registered. In the Netherlands and Sweden, the ownership tax is based on vehicle gross weight and fuel type. In the US, all states impose an annual registration fee which varies by state and depends on vehicle size/weight, private/contract carrier, farm/non farm, etc. Most states and local governments also have property taxes and licence fees which vary from state to state.

In Malaysia, a rather large ownership tax depends on engine capacity. In Thailand and the Philippines, it depends on vehicle gross weight. An ownership tax did not exist in Indonesia in the 1990s. In the Philippines and Thailand, older vehicles are taxed less.

IEA (2001) statistics provided the fuel tax data required to estimate the gasoline tax per VKT. A fuel tax is a widely used instrument of taxation to raise general government revenue. In OECD countries, many vehicle taxes and fuel taxes have been redesigned to better reflect environmental objectives. Finland, Sweden and Denmark have shifted from energy taxes to 'carbon taxes' that could reduce CO_2 emissions. In Denmark, a tax rebate of 0.1 DKK/litre is granted for light diesel oil but not for normal diesel oil. In Asian developing countries, the political impact of a gasoline fuel tax on low to middle income households is often given considerable weight.

The discussion above illustrates the wide variety of tax schemes and motivation for these schemes across countries, regions and cities. An important question is the extent to which such schemes modify behaviour and specifically lead to better environmental outcomes. Given the diversity in social-economic, institutional and spatial conditions, there is no simple answer to this question. However, some broad conclusions can be drawn from a cross-section regression analysis based on our data collected from 68 cities. The results are presented in the next section.

15.4 Regression Results

Using the data obtained for 68 large cities in Europe, North America and Asia, a cross section of 77 estimates (with two observations for some cities) of the annual cost in use of the generic mid-sized car was obtained. We decomposed the annual cost in use into the pre-tax private cost in use, the acquisition tax, the ownership tax and the fuel tax. Given standard consumer demand theory, demand for car ownership and use is also expected to be related to real income per capita.

The regression model was estimated with four dependent variables: car owner-ship per 1000 population, VKT per capita per year, average distance travelled per car per year (VKT per car) and CO_2 emission per capita. The equations were es-timated by Ordinary Least Squares (OLS). However, errors in cross-section mod-els of the type used here may be expected to be heteroscedastic due to large varia-tion in city sizes and varying levels of quality of the data. This was confirmed by a series of heteroscedasticity tests which were generally significant at the 5 or 1 percent level. Consequently, robust standard errors were computed using White's (1980) method. The natural logarithm was taken of all variables so that the results can be interpreted as elasticities. The estimation results are reported in Table 15.3.

The private user cost per km – which is a measure of the pre-tax price of pri-vate car transportation – is inversely related to car ownership and use, as standard demand theory would predict. The elasticity of private car ownership per 1000 population to our measure of the annualised price per kilometre is about –0.5 (and significant at the 10 percent level). Hence a 10 percent increase in the private user cost per kilometre reduces ownership by 5 percent, all else being equal. Vehicle kilometres travelled per car decrease too with a user cost increase, but the elastic-ity is a little smaller (about –0.4). The coefficients of vehicle kilometres travelled per capita and CO_2 emission per capita are also negative but not significant.

Real income per capita has, as expected, a strongly positive effect on car own-ership. The elasticity of about 0.7 is significant at the 1 percent level. Conse-quently, economic growth of about 3 percent per annum would induce a growth in car ownership of about 2 percent. Higher income also increases higher mobility in terms of vehicle kilometres travelled per capita. The elasticity is about 0.5 (sig-nificant at the 1 percent level). Interestingly, however, the average distance trav-elled per car per year is not related to income in our cross sectional sample of cit-ies. Two offsetting factors play a role here. On the one hand, higher incomes lead to greater demand for transportation. On the other, road infrastructure usually does not keep pace with increased car use as incomes increase and large high in-come cities often face severe congestion problems that lead to modal switches in commuting behaviour and reduce the average distance travelled per car per annum.

Table 15.3. The responsiveness of car ownership, use and CO_2 emission to income, user cost and taxes in a cross section of cities ($n = 77$)

	Car ownership per 1000 population	Vehicle kilometres travelled per capita	Vehicle kilometres travelled per car	CO_2 emission per capita
Private user cost per km	-0.489[*] (0.283)	-0.128 (0.194)	-0.397[***] (0.089)	-0.059 (0.270)
Real income per capita	0.684[***] (0.179)	0.479[***] (0.098)	-0.003 (0.035)	0.383[***] (0.096)
Acquisition tax	0.200 (0.234)	0.002 (0.116)	-0.018 (0.038)	-0.010 (0.115)
Ownership tax	0.173 (0.109)	0.037 (0.049)	-0.036[*] (0.021)	-0.004 (0.062)
Fuel tax	-0.648[***] (0.110)	-0.631[***] (0.077)	-0.105[**] (0.047)	-0.561[***] (0.129)
Constant	-3.058	0.988	8.218	1.3887
$\overline{R}^2$	0.58	0.64	0.53	0.47

Estimated standard errors in parentheses. *, **, and *** indicate significance at the 10%, 5% and 1% levels respectively.

Our results also reconfirm that the process of development increases CO_2 emission per capita, a major issue in the quest for reducing further growth in greenhouse gas emissions and in the implementation of the Kyoto protocol to combat global warming.

With respect to acquisition tax and ownership tax, most of the coefficients are not significant. Our results therefore confirm a common finding in the literature that fixed car costs, whether annualised or not, have far less impact on transportation than variable costs. The annual ownership tax does reduce the vehicle kilometres travelled per car, with a coefficient significant at the 10 percent level, but the elasticity is very small. Another interesting observation can be made nonetheless. By being both components of the fixed cost, we have theoretically little reason to expect a difference in elasticities between the acquisition tax and the ownership tax. This is in a sense confirmed by Table 15.3. The elasticities of the impact of the two taxes are of the same sign and similar magnitude in each of the four equations.

A very clear result from Table 15.3 is that our results confirm the importance of the fuel tax as an effective policy instrument in transportation. The fuel tax coefficient is highly significant in all four equations. A 1 percent increase in the fuel tax per kilometre travelled reduces car ownership density, VKT per capita and CO_2 emission all by about 0.6 percent. The results are consistent with the expectation that increased fuel taxes discourage further growth in car ownership, lead to switches to other transportation modes and also lead to manufacturer and driver responses that lower CO_2 emission per capita. The impact on average annual vehicle kilometres travelled per car is much less, however. The elasticity is –0.1 (significant at the 5 percent level). This low elasticity is due to the so-called rebound effect: the increasing price of fuel has led manufactures to design and sell new cars with ever-more economical engines. Consequently, the disincentive of the higher fuel price is partially offset by the greater economy, leading to a lower overall impact on average VKT travelled per car per year.

While the results suggest the greatest responsiveness of private car ownership and use to the fuel tax, they do not preclude that a combination of tax instruments would be more effective than a single one. In addition, even if certain vehicle taxes may have little quantitative impact on the indicators considered here, they may still have a useful signalling role (as well as being a low-distortionary source of public revenue) to raise public awareness of the need for environmental sustainability.

15.5 Final Comments

In this chapter we revisited the issue of the effectiveness of taxes in modifying behaviour and improving environmental outcomes in the private car transportation sector. In contrast with earlier studies that have tended to focus on samples of revealed or stated preference data from specific highly developed countries (or small groups of countries), we compiled and used a database of car costs and use across 68 cities in OECD countries and some additional Asian cities.

Our econometric analysis suggests that taxes on variable costs have a greater impact on car ownership and use than taxes on fixed costs and that the former can be an effective way to reduce CO_2 emission levels, despite the rebound effect. However, given the complexity of the transport sector and the wide range of behaviour responses that can take place in any given socio-economic and institutional setting, a 'one size fits all' conclusion should not be drawn from the rather low-dimensional analysis conducted here.

Nonetheless, some lessons can be drawn, particularly for developing countries. As motorization proceeds, all such economies must work to conserve energy consumption, and reduce greenhouse gas emissions, while maintaining economic growth. While some countries have achieved environmental results through negative reinforcement (i.e. tax policies which discourage certain behaviour), a positive incentive-based system that rewards higher environmental performance may in fact be preferable. For example, it could be argued that such a system has helped to achieve the environmental objectives in some Asian economies, without hindering further economic growth in these economies.

One way to encourage the benefits of technological advances in the sector (in terms of reduced environmental impacts of new vehicles in manufacturing, use and disposal) is to provide a stronger link between vehicle taxes and vehicle age.

This creates the incentive for the accelerated replacement of the existing stock by newer vehicles with better environmental outcomes. This type of incentive would help to speed up the introduction of clean/fuel efficient vehicles, clean fuels, alternative fuels and overall vehicle replacement.

References

Association des Constructeurs Europeens d'Automobiles (ACEA) (2001) Tax guide, ACEA, Brussels

Badan Pusat Statistik (BPS) (2000) Statistik Indonesia, BPS, Jakarta

Beijing Municipal Statistical Bureau (BMSB) (2001) Beijing statistical yearbook, China Statistics Press, Beijing

Cervero R, Hansen M (2001) Road supply-demand relationships: sorting out casual linkages. Paper No.01-2527. Paper presented at the 80th Annual Meeting of the Transportation Research Board

Dargay J, Vythoulkas P (1999) Estimation of a dynamic car ownership model: a pseudo-panel approach, Journal of Transport Economics and Policy 33: 287–302

Department of Land and Transport (DLT) (2001) Motor vehicle inspection and taxation in Thailand, DLT, Bangkok

Dodgson J, Young J, Van der Veer JP (2002) Paying for road use, Commission for Integrated Transport, London

Drollas L (1984) The demand for gasoline: further evidence, Energy Economics 6: 71–82

Eltony M (1993) Transport gasoline demand in Canada, Journal of Transport Economics and Policy 27: 193–208

Espey M (1996) Watching the fuel gauge: an international model of automobile fuel economy, Energy Economics 18: 93–106

Espey M (1998) Gasoline demand revisited: an international meta-analysis of elasticities, Energy Economics 20: 273–295

European Commission (1996) Urban transport, pricing and financing of urban transport (APAS), DG VII Transport Research, Brussels

European Conference of Ministers of Transport (ECMT) (1998) Social costs: study of differentiation and variabilization of taxation related to vehicle ownership and use, ECMT, Paris

Fulton LM, Noland RB, Meszler J, Thomas JV, (2000) A statistical analysis of induced travel effects in the US mid-Atlantic region, Journal of Transportation and Statistics 3: 1–14

Goodwin PB (1992) A review of new demand elasticities with special reference to short and long run effects of price changes, Journal of Transport Economics and Policy 26: 155–169

Graham DJ, Glaister S (2002) The demand for automobile fuel: a survey of elasticities, Journal of Transport Economics and Policy 36: 1–26

Greene D, Hu P (1986) A functional form analysis of the short-run demand for travel and gasoline by one-vehicle households. Transportation Research Record 1092, Transportation Research Board, National Research Council, Washington D.C.

Gulde AM, Schulze-Ghattas M (2003) Purchasing power parity based weights for the World Economic Outlook. Available at www.imf.org

Hansen M, Huang Y (1997) Road supply and traffic in California urban areas, Transportation Research A 31: 205–218

Hensher DA (1977) Value of business travel time, Pergamon Press, Oxford

Hirota K, Minato K (2001) Impact on the cost of living by feebate system in the Japanese automobile market. In: Further than ever from Kyoto? Rethinking energy efficiency can get us there, vol 1. ECEEE, Paris, pp 551–556

Hirota K, Minato K (2002) Regional trade and emission gases in the Asian automobile industry, SAE

International Energy Agency (IEA) (2001) Energy taxes and prices, IEA, Paris

International Road Federation (IRF) (2002) World road statistics 2002, IRF, Switzerland

Ishak A (2001) Urban air quality management: motor vehicle emission control in Malaysia. In: Proceedings of the Clean Air Regional Workshop February 12–14, Clean Air Initiative in Asia, Bangkok

Johansson O, Schipper L (1997) Measuring the long-run fuel demand of cars: separate estimations of vehicle stock, mean fuel intensity, and mean annual driving distance, Journal of Transport Economics and Policy 31: 277–292

de Jong G, Gunn H (2001) Recent evidence on car costs and time elasticities of travel demand in Europe, Journal of Transport Economics and Policy 35: 137–160

Kenworthy J, Laube FB (1999a) The millennium cities database for sustainable transport [CD-ROM], Union Internationale des Transport Publique (UITP)

Kenworthy J, Laube FB (1999b) An international source book of automobile dependence in cities 1960–1990, Colorado University Press, Colorado

Magda L (1996) Phasing out lead from gasoline: world-wide experiences and policy implementations. Paper No.40, Environment Department

National Bureau of Statistics of China (NBSC) (2002) China statistical yearbook, Beijing, NBSC

National Center For Transportation Studies (NCTS) (2000) A research paper on the proper automobile usage strategy towards environmental impact abatement in large cities in Asia, NCTS, Manila

National Statistical Coordination Board (NSCB) (2001) Philippines statistical yearbook, NSCB, Manila

Newman P, Kenworthy K (1999) Sustainability and cities, Island Press, Washington, D.C.

Noland RB (2001) Relationship between highway capacity and induced vehicle travel, Transportation Research A 35: 47–72

Noland RB, Cowart WA (2000) Analysis of metropolitan highway capacity and the growth in vehicle miles of travel. In: Proceedings of the 79th Annual Meeting of the Transportation Research Board, TRB, Washington, D.C.

OECD (2001) Environmentally related taxes in OECD countries: issues and strategies, OECD, Paris

Robert MM, den Brink V, van Wee B (2001) Why has car-fleet specific fuel consumption not shown any decrease since 1990? Quantitative analysis of Dutch passenger car-fleet specific fuel consumption, Transportation Research Part D 6: 75–93

Rodier CJ, Abraham JE, Johnston RA (2001) Anatomy of induced travel: using an integrated land use and transportation model. Paper No.01-2582. Paper presented at the 80th Annual Meeting of the Transportation Research Board

Sankei Shinbun (2001) Vehicle related tax, Sankei Press

Shanghai Municipal Statistics Bureau (SMSB) (2001) Shanghai statistical yearbook, China Statistics Bureau, Shanghai

Social Republic of Vietnam General Statistical Office (SRVGSO) (1996) Statistical year-book, Social Republic of Vietnam General Statistical Office, Vietnam

Speck S, Ekins P (2000) Recent trends in the application of economic instruments in EU member states plus Norway and Switzerland and an overview of economic instruments in Central and Eastern Europe. Report to DG Environment. No. B43040/99/ /123779/MAR/B2

Sterner T, Dahl C, Franzén M (1992) Gasoline tax policy: carbon emissions and the global environment, Journal of Transport Economics and Policy 26: 109–119

Strathman JG, Dueker KJ, Sanchez T, Zhang J, Riis A-E (2000) Analysis of induced travel in the 1995 NPIS. Final Technical Report to the US Environmental Protection Agency, Office of Transportation and Air Quality

Tanner J C (1978) Long-term forecasting of vehicle ownership and road traffic, Journal of the Royal Statistical Society A 141: 14–63

The Energy and Resources Institute (TERI) (2000) Energy data directory and yearbook, TERI, New Delhi

UNEP (1997) Environmental impacts of trade liberalization and policies for sustainable management of natural resources, United Nations, New York

United Nations (1997) Statistical yearbook, United Nations, New York

Vaes T (1982) Forecasting petrol consumption. Paper presented at PTRC Summer Annual Meeting, University of Sussex

White H (1980) A heteroscedasticity-consistent covariance matrix estimator and a direct test for heteroscedasticity, Econometrica 48: 817–838

Working Group of Vehicle-Related Taxes (WGVRT) (2001) A report of vehicle-related taxes, Working Group of Vehicle-Related Taxes, Tokyo

World Bank (2002) World development indicators, The World Bank, Washington, D.C.

World Bank (2003a) World development report, The World Bank, Washington, D.C.

World Bank (2003b) Global economic perspective, The World Bank, Washington, D.C.

Appendix 15.A

Information has been collected from the following cities: Adelaide (1990); Amsterdam (1990); Auckland (1990); Bangkok (1990, 2002); Beijing (1990, 2002); Boston (1990); Brisbane (1990); Brussels (1990); Busan (2002); Calgary (1990); Canberra (1990); Chiba (2002); Chicago (1990); Chongqing (2002); Copenhagen (1990); Calcutta (2002); Deli (2002); Denver (1990); Detroit (1990); Edmonton (1990); Frankfurt (1990); Fukuoka (2002); Hamburg (1990); Hanoi (2002); Ho Chi Min City (2002); Hiroshima (2002); Hong Kong (1990, 2002); Houston (1990); Jakarta (1990,2002); Kathmandu (2002); Kobe (2002); Kuala Lumpur (1990, 2002); London (1990); Los Angeles (1990); Manila (1990, 2002); Melbourne (1990); Montreal (1990); Mumbai (2002); Munich (1990); Nagoya (2002); New York (1990); Osaka (2002); Ottawa (1990); Paris (1990); Perth (1990); Phoenix (1990); Portland (1990); Sacramento (1990); San Diego (1990); San Francisco (1990); Sapporo (2002); Seoul (1990, 2002); Shanghai (2002); Singapore (1990, 2002); Stockholm (1990); Surabaya (1990); Sydney (1990); Tianjin (2002); Tokyo (1990, 2002); Toronto (1990); Urawa (2002); Vancouver

(1990); Vienna (1990); Washington (1990); Wellington (1990); Winnipeg (1990); Yokohama (2002); Zurich (1990).

The statistical sources consulted include ACEA (2001), BPS (2000), BMSB (2001), DLT (2001), Gulde and Schulze-Ghattas (2003), IEA (2001), IRF (2002), Kenworthy and Laube (1999a, 1999b), Magda (1996), NBSC (2002), NCTS (2000), NSCB (2001), Newman and Kenworthy (1999), OECD (2001), Sankei Shinbun (2001), SMSB (2001), SRVGSO (1996), Speck and Ekins (2000), TERI (2000), UNEP (1997), WGVRT (2001), World Bank (2002, 2003a, 2003b).

16 European Perspectives on a New Fiscal Framework for Transport

Stephen Potter[1], Graham Parkhurst[2] and Ben Lane[1]

[1] The Open University, Milton Keynes, UK
[2] University of the West of England, Bristol, UK

16.1 The Purposes of Taxation

In all developed economies, taxation measures serve a mix of the following purposes:

A) To raise general government revenue
B) To pay for specific collective goods and services
C) As an instrument of economic policy
D) As an instrument of other policy areas

Category (A) has existed for thousands of years, with tax funding goods and services that are collectively consumed, such as defence and policing, together with transfer payments, public debt servicing and the whole range of other state expenditure. Category (B) is where a tax is hypothecated (dedicated) to a particular purpose. This often takes the form of a charge rather than a tax (e.g. a road toll). However, in many countries, road transport taxation was initially introduced specifically to fund improvements to the road infrastructure, with the revenue being ring fenced for that purpose. In most instances, such taxes soon merged into (A), which is the longest-established rationale for taxation. As such, transport taxation has evolved to be one of a range of tax measures that fund general state expenditure. There is now no reason for transport taxation being related to transport expenditure any more than the tax on alcoholic drinks might be compared to funding drink related healthcare.

The third rationale (C) emerged in the wake of Keynesian economics after the Second World War and, informed by various economic philosophies, has been with us ever since. The fourth rationale (D), that the design and implementation of taxation measures should serve other policy aims is a recent and only tentatively established purpose of taxation, which includes the use of fiscal instruments for environmental policy.

There are three key issues that arise with adapting taxes to address environmental goals:

- The environmental tax measures may be counteracted by other tax instruments for general income raising and economic policy which have negative environmental impacts (e.g., a small tax concession for fuel economy will be overwhelmed by a large concession on, say, large-engined cars to promote economic development).
- Measures designed to fulfil general income raising and economic policy may be difficult to adapt to address environmental policy concerns. There is a design issue here in that traditional measures such as taxation on income, expenditure and wealth are not the sort of thing that can actually influence environmental performance. To do this, tax needs to charged on environmental impacts. This key design issue is behind the concept of *Ecological Taxation Reform* – that tax should be on environmental impact and not wealth or income.[1]
- Individuals and corporations respond differently to fiscal incentives. For example, individuals are less disposed than corporations to pay higher capital costs for vehicles that have lower running costs (e.g. energy efficient and cleaner fuel technologies). This chapter largely focuses upon tax measures affecting individuals. There are others that primarily impact organisations.

Finally there is the crucial point that the way central (and also local) government revenue is collected can only exert a partial influence. In particular, how that revenue is spent is crucial. For example, if reducing taxation on cleaner vehicles is insufficient to influence car purchasers, then using revenue to provide grants would be needed – as indeed has featured in the UK with grants from the Energy Savings Trust through the *PowerShift* programme (Hinnells and Potter 2001).

Recognising the limits of fiscal measures is as important as identifying their potential. How they can fit with and support other policies (regulation, standards, procurement and subsidy) is thus an important issue.

16.2 Fiscal Measures to Promote Cleaner Cars

16.2.1 The Range of Measures

The above context needs to be understood as we examine how transport taxation measures have been adapted to promote cleaner vehicles.

Within the European Union (EU), the role of the taxation system in managing transport demand has been the subject of a number of policy development reports. Typical of these is the European Council of Ministers of Transport report *'Internalising the Social Costs of Transport'* (ECMT 1997), which advocates a synergistic mix of taxation and charging instruments, including a number of local tar-

---

[1] The concept of ETR was developed by German and Dutch authors in the late 1980s. See von Weizsäcker et al. (1992) and Whitelegg (1992).

geted mechanisms, such as road pricing. Broadly the view is taken that a carefully designed mix of various economic instruments (see Table 16.1) and regulations is needed to achieve political acceptance and practicality.

Table 16.1. Vehicle, fuel and traffic market-based incentives

Vehicle	Tradable permits
	Differential vehicle taxation
	Tax allowance for new vehicle
Fuel	Differential fuel taxation to promote cleaner fuels
Emissions	Carbon taxation
	Emission fees
Traffic	Fuel taxes
	Congestion charges
	Parking charges
	Subsidies for less polluting modes

Source: ECMT 1997.

In exploring the role of taxation, this chapter adopts a slightly different typology that categorises tax measures at points in the life cycle use of cars. There are:

- Tax on the initial purchase of a vehicle
- Annual registration tax
- Tax on the use of vehicles (fuel, roadspace and company cars)

16.2.2 Purchase

Measures on car purchase are crucial to determining the composition and fuel efficiency of a nation's car stock. The standard purchase taxation measure in EU states is Value Added Tax (VAT), with the rate for cars being at between 15% and 25% (Vanden Branden et al. 2000 – see Table 16.2). With a standard rate for all cars, VAT exerts no influence upon purchasing decisions. The only exception is a longstanding differential rate in Italy, where VAT is charged at 19% on cars with an engine capacity of less than 2,000cc (2,500cc for diesels), and at 38% above this threshold.

In addition to VAT, most EU countries have a specific car purchase or registration tax. In Belgium it is graded finely according to the power of the car, and in Finland there is a reduction for low emission vehicles. A notable example is the Netherlands, which has a car purchase tax is 45.2%. This may seem high (although at 105% Denmark's is higher), but there are counterbalancing tax reductions on this – of €1540 for petrol and LPG cars, €580 for diesel cars and other allowances for cleaner vehicles. The net effect is that this fixed tax reduction cuts the tax charge significantly for smaller and more fuel-efficient cars and raises the price of larger and less fuel-efficient vehicles.

Table 16.2. VAT rates on cars in the EU

Member State	VAT rate
Austria	20.0
Belgium	21.0
Denmark	25.0
Finland	22.0
France	20.6
Germany	16.0
Greece	18.0
Ireland	21.0
Italy	19.0 / 38.0
Luxembourg	15.0
Netherlands	17.5
Portugal	17.0
Spain	16.0
Sweden	25.0
United Kingdom	17.5

Source: Vanden Branden et al. (2000).

Table 16.3. Registration (or other purchase) taxes in EU states

Member state	Type of tax	Basis of charge
Austria	Fuel consumption tax	Value and fuel consumption
Belgium	Registration tax "tax de mise en circulation"	Fiscal horsepower
Denmark	Registration tax	Retail price: 105% of first DKr 50 800, 180% of balance
Finland	Registration tax	Value of vehicle: 100% of value minus FM 4 600
France	Registration tax	Fiscal horsepower: FF 95–195 per fiscal horsepower
Germany	None	
Greece	Special consumption tax	Combination of value and cylinder capacity
	Registration tax	Taxable value
Italy	Registration tax	Fiscal horsepower
Ireland	Registration tax	Retail value and cylinder capacity
Netherlands	Registration tax	Net list price
Portugal	Vehicle tax	Cylinder capacity
Spain	Registration tax	Market price
Sweden	Sales tax	Environmental classification of vehicle
United Kingdom	None	

Source: Vanden Branden et al. (2000).

Table 16.4. On-road fuel economy of cars 1970 and 1998 (litres per 100 Km) (gasoline or equivalent)

	1970	1998	% improvement
UK	9.6	9.1[a]	5.2
France	8.5	8.4[a]	1.2
Germany (West)	10.2	9.2[a]	9.8
Italy	8.5	6.8	14.7
Denmark	9.0	7.7[a]	16.9
Netherlands	9.5	8.1	14.7
Norway	10.3	8.9	13.6
Sweden	10.4	9.4	9.6
Finland	9.6	8.4[a]	12.5
Japan	10.8	11.5	2.8
Australia	12.3	11.1[a]	−6.4
USA	17.8	11.8	33.7

Source of data: Schipper and Marier-Lilliu (1999), Schipper et al. (2000).
[a]1995 figures.

Germany has no car purchase tax (and VAT is only 16%). In the UK, until 1991, there was a Car Purchase Tax of 10% on five-sixths of the list price value of a new car. This was reduced to 5% in 1991 and abolished altogether in 1992. It was replaced by the UK policy for higher fuel duty, whereby up to 2000, fuel duties rose higher than the rate of inflation.

In June 2004, France announced proposals to reform their car registration tax into a 'feebate' scheme. Under this measure, cars that emit over 180g/km of CO_2 or diesels without a particulates filter will face a surcharge of €1,500–3,500, whereas cars that emit under 140g/km of CO_2 and diesels with particulate filters will receive a rebate of €200 to €700 (Henley 2004). Cars emitting between 140 and 180g/km of CO_2 will be liable to neither a surcharge nor rebate.

Given these different purchase tax measures, it is interesting to make a comparison between the UK, the Netherlands and Italy. Table 16.4 shows the long term trend in actual on-road car fuel economy in a number of developed countries. This is a better indicator than the often quoted test figures on new car fuel economy. A key observation is that the average car fuel economy in Italy, Denmark and the Netherlands is better than the UK (by 11%, 15%and 25% respectively). Furthermore, since the 1970s, there has been little change in actual fuel economy in the UK, with the Netherlands registering a 15% improvement and 20% for Italy.

With the UK, Italy and the Netherlands being comparable economies, and the UK and Netherlands having similar fuel prices, other explanations are needed for the notably better environmental performance of Dutch and Italian cars. The Dutch car purchase tax and the Italian VAT measures appear to play an important role. It is notable that Denmark, which also has a graded purchase tax for cars, is another country that registers good fuel economy. It appears that purchase measures can be very powerful.

The European Commission has tentatively examined the idea of whether goods with an Ecolabel could qualify for a lower level of VAT. An alternative might be to adapt the Italian system to vary VAT by the environmental performance of cars. This would not just provide a cost reduction for cleaner cars, but combine it with a cost penalty for purchasing 'environmentally dirtier' cars. However, there are political difficulties as the main trend is for VAT harmonisation. Furthermore, the effectiveness of a VAT measure would be reduced due to the effects of company car purchases (see below), as companies can reclaim VAT. Overall, there is a strong case for a dedicated purchase tax, separate from VAT, varied by a car's environmental performance (as is used in the Netherlands and proposed in France).

16.2.3 Annual Registration ('Circulation')

All EU countries have a graded annual registration (or 'circulation') tax which entitles owners to drive a car on the public highway. In the USA and some other countries this takes the form of a 'number plate' tax. This longstanding tax is often varied by engine size or power of a car, but some nations have implemented an eco-reform to this tax. In Denmark the tax varies with fuel consumption, whereas Germany links the tax liability directly to the Euro emission standards, with the least polluting car paying only 20% of the rate of the most polluting car. However, the overall level of the tax is so low (only about €50 per car), that its impact on car choice is negligible.

Until 1999, the UK was unique in Europe in having a fixed-rate annual registration tax. In 1999 a lower rate was introduced for cars under 1,100cc. This was £100 (€140) compared to £155 (€220) for the standard rate. From 1 July 2001 this is extended to all cars of up to 1,549cc. For cars registered from 2001 the UK adopted a CO_2 emission-based system in four bands (A–D), with the charge varying from £100–160 (€140–230). Alternative fuel cars are evaluated on the same bands, but have a slightly lower charge of between £90–150 (€130–220). In 2003 two further bands were added for very low CO_2 emission vehicles (Table 16.5), with the charge range widened to £55–165 (€81–243)

Annual circulation taxes have proved to be readily amenable to eco-reforms, with even the traditional engine-size method indirectly providing an incentive for more fuel efficient vehicles. However, if the tax is at a low rate (as in Germany) any effect will be insignificant.

Table 16.5. UK vehicle excise duty (circulation) tax rates (£ and €), 2003

Band	CO_2 (g/km)	Diesel	Petrol	Alternative Fuels
			£	
AAA	Up to 100	75 (€110)	65 (€96)	55 (€81)
AA	101 to 120	85 (€125)	75 (€110)	65 (€96)
A	121 to 150	115 (€170)	105 (€155)	95 (€140)
B	151 to 165	135 (€199)	125 (€184)	115 (€170)
C	166 to 185	155 (€228)	145 (€213)	135 (€199)
D	Over 185	165 (€243)	160 (€235)	155 (€228)

Source: UK Inland Revenue.

16.2.4 Taxes on Vehicle Use

Although motor fuels in the EU are subject to varying rates of VAT, additional road fuel duties make up the main tax on vehicle use. In Europe, tax on fuel is high by international standards, particularly when compared to North America. Northern European countries tend to have higher fuel taxes than southern EU members (Table 16.6).

Table 16.6. Tax on unleaded petrol in selected EU states, 2001

	Retail price per litre	Tax as % of retail price
UK	€1.19	76
Belgium	€0.98	67
Denmark	€0.98	68
Germany	€0.99	72
Greece	€0.73	55
Finland	€1.08	68
Italy	€1.02	66
Netherlands	€1.12	69
Spain	€0.80	59
Sweden	€0.99	68

Source: *Transport Statistics Great Britain*, UK Department for Transport 2002.

Tax on fuel is the main fiscal measure on use. In many EU states there are lower tax rates for cleaner 'alternative' fuels and some Scandinavian countries have introduced CO_2 tax as well as fuel duty. In Belgium there is no road fuel duty on LPG and Natural Gas. In Denmark, LPG is taxed at a very low rate (6% of that of unleaded petrol), but they have a CO_2 tax as well as excise duty on road fuels. Finland also has a CO_2 tax. In the Netherlands three different types of tax apply to fuel: the excise duty, an environmental tax,[2] and a tax on the stock to finance emergency stockpiles. Germany taxes LPG and natural gas, but at a lower rate than for petrol and diesel.

As noted previously, in the UK following the abolition of car purchase tax, there was a policy to raise fuel duties (the 'Fuel Duty Escalator'). This began under the Conservative government's 1993 Budget and was justified at the time as a major contribution by the government towards the reduction of carbon dioxide emissions. Within this general policy of raising fuel tax there have also been measures to favour cleaner road transport fuels, particularly to provide a duty differential between gaseous fuels (CNG and LPG) and petrol and diesel. These differential were retained when, following blockages of oil refineries by lorry drivers and farmers in 2000, petrol and diesel duty was cut and the Fuel Duty Escalator policy abandoned.

Taxes and charges on using roadspace include bridge/tunnel tolls, road tolls and cordon/congestion charging in city centres. Bridge and tunnel tolls are common-

---

[2] This is an energy and carbon dioxide tax where the rates are based on carbon (50%) and energy (50%) content.

place, but road tolls (usually only for motorways) are used in seven EU states (Austria, France, Germany, Greece, Italy, Portugal and Spain) and also in Norway. In general these are not related to the environmental performance of a vehicle, but they could be. City centre congestion charging is one of the new car tax measures specifically designed to manage traffic and address environmental aims. It has been introduced in three Norwegian cities (albeit mainly to fund transport infrastructure rather than manage traffic, see Ieromonachou 2004) and recently in Durham and London in the UK. The London scheme includes an exemption for cleaner fuel vehicles and has led to an increase in their purchase and use.

16.2.5 Company Cars

In some countries cars are purchased by companies for their staff as 'income-in-kind' rather than for employees who need vehicles to undertake their work duties. In some cases such company cars constitute the majority of new car purchases and hence are the main determinate of the car fleet.

In the UK, over half of all new cars are purchased by companies and not individuals. Finland also has a high proportion of new cars purchase by companies, at about 40%. What type of car is purchased has come to be strongly influenced by the tax treatment of the 'benefit in kind' to the individual employee who is allocated a company car. In general, the company car effect has stimulated the purchase of more powerful and less fuel-efficient cars (Hinnells and Potter 2001; Vanden Branden et al. 2000), which has a major effect upon the fuel economy of the whole of the UK car stock. Gradually reforms have cut down this negative effect, but it is still present.

The treatment of company car benefits varies significantly across EU member states (Vanden Branden et al. 2000). In Greece the benefit is entirely untaxed, and also effectively so in Portugal. Other EU member countries largely tax the benefit of a company car as a proportion of the car's value, although in some countries this is very low. In Germany it is 12% of the car's value per annum, in Spain 15%, the Netherlands 20–24%, Denmark 25% and Ireland 30%.

In the UK, a major reform in company car taxation took effect from 2002. Up until then tax was 35% of the car's value per annum, with discounts for high business travel. This was estimated to be approximate parity to income as cash (which suggests that most EU states do not value company car benefits at realistic levels). From 2002 the tax charge on company cars was modified to weight the percentage of the car's price according to the level of the car's carbon dioxide (CO_2) emissions. The charge builds up from 15 per cent of the car's price, for cars emitting 165 grams per kilometre (g/km) CO_2, in 1 per cent steps for every additional 5g/km over 165g/km. The maximum charge is on 35 per cent of the car's price. Diesel cars not meeting Euro IV emissions standards incur an additional charge of 3%, up to the 35 per cent ceiling. There are further reductions for company cars using cleaner fuels and technologies. Bi-fuel cars (gas/petrol) and hybrid-electric cars receive a 1% and 2% discount respectively, plus a further 1% discount for every 20 g/km below the minimum percentage level. Cars solely powered by electricity (battery-electrics and fuel cell cars) are charged at 9% of their list price. In addition, from 2002 discounts for high business mileage were abolished together with age-related discounts, which had provided an incentive to drive further and to use older, more polluting cars.

This reform has affected the use and type of cars within the UK company car fleet. The number of business miles has reduced by over 480 million kilometres per year and the average CO2 emissions of new company cars decreased from 196 g/km in 1999 to 182 g/km in 2002, only the first year of the new system (Inland Revenue 2004). The overall effect has been to reduce the emissions of carbon from the company car fleet (by around 0.5% of all CO2 emissions from road transport in UK). However, the company car tax reform has not stimulated demand for cleaner fuelled cars by the company car sector, nor have it encouraged car manufacturers to develop new low-emission designs, which was also an objective of the reform.

As was noted previously, because companies can reclaim VAT, any VAT mechanism to encourage cleaner cars would not be effective for company purchases. But there is another way. A neglected side of company car taxation is how they are treated for corporate taxation. It would be possible to vary the extent to which expenditure on company cars counts for calculating profits (and hence taxation) by the environmental performance of the car. As this is being done in several countries for personal taxation of the car's user, then applying the same method to company tax would appear to be a relatively straightforward measure that would usefully reinforce the use of cleaner company cars. A relatively minor tax reform in the UK is that cleaner car technologies qualify for enhanced capital tax allowances.

16.3 Eco-Reform or Eco-Transformation?

16.3.1 The Purchase Cost Problem

Despite some evidence that the eco-reforms to car taxation have promoted a degree of useful change, the effects to date have been relatively marginal. The reason appears to be the deeply entrenched fact that the market simply does not view fuel economy or low-environmental impact cars as an important issue. In particular, engine design and other fuel *efficiency* improvements have been used mainly to improve the performance of cars rather than their fuel economy. Furthermore, the power of cars has increased; in 1980, the average power of new cars sold in the UK was 55 kW; by 1995 it had risen to 68 kW. The average power of German cars has risen a little above the UK figures to 70 kW in 1995. By way of contrast, in Italy average power has risen from 43 kW in 1980 to 55 kW in 1995. The power of Australian and USA cars is almost twice this level, having risen to over 100 kW by 1995 (Schipper and Marie-Lilliu 1999). The fashion for four-wheel drive cars and 'Sports Utility Vehicles' is also pushing up the power of cars and worsening fuel consumption; these vehicles average little better than 12–14 litres per 100 km. Added to this, what developments there have been in alternative fuel cars have not been combined with improvements in fuel economy. Petrol gas guzzlers have been replaced by LPG gas guzzlers.

Associated with this behaviour in car purchase is cheap fuel. In real terms the price of petrol and diesel remains lower than it was 20 or 30 years ago. These big structural changes overwhelm the relatively small tax eco-reforms. Tax reforms to date seem unlikely to make a substantial change and certainly do not create enough of a difference to promote radical new clean technologies.

One structural problem is cost. The basic situation is that the cleaner the car is, the more it costs to buy, and adjustments to the existing tax system can only go so far. If you cannot cut the cost by tax concessions, then using tax revenues to subsidise the more radical technologies needs to come into play. This is a strategy that the UK Energy Savings Trust have used to 'kick start' the market for a number of energy saving technologies such as compact fluorescent lightbulbs and condensing gas boilers. The idea was to get the market developed to a point where the subsidies could be removed. In 1996 this approach was adopted for clean fuel vehicles with the launch of the *TransportAction PowerShift* programme.

PowerShift offers grant support to help with the purchase of vehicles running on natural gas (CNG and LNG), liquefied petroleum gas (LPG) and electricity (including hybrids). PowerShift has a budget of £30m from 2001–4. The key assumption behind the PowerShift programme is that a temporary subsidy programme can allow the market to mature to the point that the cleaner technologies can effectively compete. It is a good strategy to carve out an initial market presence. Hopefully once the initial cleaner technologies get established (like particulate traps on diesels, and LPG/CNG engines), they can be left to their own devices and the subsidies concentrated on the next generation of cleaner technologies (e.g. hybrids) and then moved again to concentrate on fuel cell vehicles. The problem with this approach is if there is more than a transitional problem and a subsidy is needed on a permanent basis. If so, unless cheap 'dirty' cars are regulated out of existence, a subsidy will always be needed.

The need for a permanent cleaner car subsidy is a distinct possibility, and brings us to the nub of the problem regarding the cost structure of cleaner vehicles. They have, and it appears will always have, higher initial purchase costs than conventional vehicles. They do tend to have lower running costs, particularly if their fuel is taxed less than for petrol and diesel. But to what extent are people and companies willing to pay more in capital costs for lower running costs? There is a big difference here between individuals and companies. Companies generally take a life cycle costing approach, and as such trading off capital and revenue costs to minimise the overall annualised cost is normal practice. Even so companies are not buying many cleaner technology cars (even given the sort of company car tax concessions that have been provided in the UK). Individuals are even less inclined to pay up front for cleaner vehicles. For individuals, the initial purchase price is crucial, and people are very reluctant to pay anything at all in purchase cost for reduced running costs. Furthermore, if they sell a car after a two or three years (as is normal for private new car purchasers), even quite substantially lower running costs will only pay for a modest increase in the purchase price.

This suggests that far more attention should be paid to fiscal measures that result in the initial price of the car being varied by its environmental performance. A more radical option is whether the way we pay for cars should not be split into capital and running costs, but that both of these are rolled into a leasing charge. Thus the higher capital and lower running costs would be automatically balanced out. However, the prospect of eliminating private car ownership is not politically realistic, except for niche applications (like 'car clubs').

16.3.2 Changing the Basis of Vehicle Taxation

There do appear to be limitations as to the policy effectiveness of reforming vehicle taxation within the existing taxation regime. Useful effects seem achievable and could be developed further – but it seems that these are insufficient to address the major environmental, congestion and transport problems that we face today. It is not that eco-tax reforms are failing to work. It is that more is needed. In addition, there are a further series of issues that are gradually building up a case for a more radical approach. This is one of not simply reforming the transport taxation regime, but changing the basis of vehicle taxation altogether.

The first stimulus stems from the fact that the above discussion has concentrated upon greening the car as a vehicle. Once the focus shifts to the *car-based transport system*, a greater need for change becomes very apparent. Numerous studies (summarised in Potter et al. 2001) have indicated that unless measures are put in place to manage the growth in road vehicle use, the increase in the number and distances travelled by car will largely counterbalance the improvements from vehicle design.

Secondly there is a significant consequence of stimulating cleaner cars. This is that it will produce a diversity of transport fuels, which will become administratively more difficult to tax. How does one enforce that gas or electricity is taxed at one rate for domestic use and at a much higher rate for road transport use? This is linked into possibly the most politically important stimuli. As governments give tax incentives for greener cars and fuel they are starting to lose revenue from the car sector.

This combination of factors is the focus for a project undertaken by this chapter's authors[3] for the UK Economic and Social Research Council (ESRC) under its Environment and Human Behaviour programme. Entitled *Transport Taxation for Sustainable Mobility*, the project has included an estimate of the effect upon tax revenue of the UK's existing policies to clean up cars. Incentives to promote cleaner fuels and general road fuel duty tax cuts, have reduced road fuel tax revenue by 13% since 2000 (Department for Transport 2003). However, the full range of UK incentives to green vehicles and car fuels are set to cut government taxation revenues even further. As shown in Fig. 16.1, estimates made by Graham Park-

---

[3] Together with Barry Ubbels of Amsterdam's Free University, Marcus Enoch of Loughborough University and James Warren at the OU. For details and the project report see http://design.open.ac.uk/potter.htm.

hurst for this project indicate, depending on traffic growth, government revenues from car taxation are set to drop by up to a fifth in ten years (see Parkhurst 2002, 2005 for details). To this will need to be added losses from parallel actions in the road freight sector.

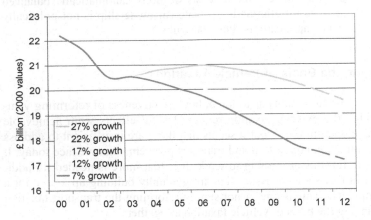

Fig. 16.1. Effect of existing policies on UK car tax revenues, 2000–2012. The projected decline in revenue varies according to different traffic growth assumptions. Source: Parkhurst (2005)

And this is not all. Lane and Potter estimate that further tax losses will be incurred as further new fuels emerge. Zero fuel tax would need to be maintained on hydrogen for some considerable time for fuel cell cars to be an economic reality (Lane and Potter 2003). This would produce a £100m (€140m) tax loss by 2012 if fuel cell cars take a 10% share of new car sales, but if they were to be 10% of the car fleet, the tax loss would rise to £750m (€1050).

With an emphasis shifting to price signals within the existing tax regime to favour cleaner vehicles, the basic function of taxation – to generate government revenue – has started to be undermined. Tax revenues from cars and fuels has started to drop, and is set to dramatically decline with the level of tax incentives that will be needed to stimulate the market for radically cleaner low carbon technologies of hybrids and hydrogen fuel cell cars. There is therefore a growing and seemingly intractable problem of personal mobility and the environment. Because car ownership is such a central feature of our lives it is becoming accepted wisdom that it would be political suicide for any government to raise vehicle or fuel taxation to a level that will produce significant behavioural change. Added to this the level of tax concessions needed for the adoption of cleaner car technologies (which alone will not deliver sustainable mobility) will result in a large drop in tax revenues.

The question therefore arises as to whether a different form of road vehicle taxation would be more appropriate to 21st century environmental, transport and fiscal needs than the 20th century regime of taxing road vehicle purchase, ownership and the fuel that the vehicles use. In a number of countries this has already been recognised for freight transport, with Germany, Austria, New Zealand and Switzerland using or proposing distance/weight based systems to replace circulation taxes. The UK is due to introduce a GPS-based distance charging system for heavy goods vehicles in 2008, including a differential change for motorways and other roads. In the UK a number of studies have advocated generalised road user charging as the basis of a new road user taxation regime. These include a report by the UK Commission for Integrated Transport *Paying for Road Use*, which suggested a charging scheme balanced by a 21 per cent cut in fuel duties and circulation tax (Dodgson et al. 2002). This report was shortly followed by the Independent Transport Commission's report, *Transport Pricing* (Glaister and Graham 2003), which showed how taxes on road use would produce substantial user benefits and significant cuts to congestion. An earlier study in the Netherlands has explored the car use and environmental impacts of replacing car purchase, annual, and fuel taxes with four variations of a fiscally-neutral kilometre charge (Ubbels et al. 2002). Simply redistributing fixed taxes to a kilometre charge resulted in a modelled reduction in car traffic for the four alternative charging systems of between 18 per cent and 35 per cent compared with the 'business as usual' base case. Their results suggest that a different tax regime would be more effective in stimulating behavioural change than reforms to existing car taxation measures. Additionally, this study indicated that growing frontier effects in the EU were reducing the effectiveness of traditional car taxation measures.

In the UK, the concept of a generalised road user charge was supported by the House of Commons Transport Select Committee and, in July 2004, UK Transport Secretary, Alistair Darling, announced that replacing road fuel duty and vehicle excise duty (VED) with some form of widespread road user charging was now envisaged (Department for Transport 2004). This is seen as a key policy tool to deal with transport 'pressures over the next 20–30 years'. Tax regime change is thus rapidly moving up the political agenda as the successor to the eco-reform of existing tax measures.

The UK is far from alone is considering the eventual replacement of its car and fuel taxation regime. The State of Oregon in the USA is in the process of developing a 'Road User Fee' for introduction in 2007. Neighbouring states are also interested in using the system. The main motivation for Oregon's action is the decline in fuel tax revenues. This scheme will also use a novel 'opt-in' charging method. When motorists call at filling stations, if an on-board distance-charging unit is detected, fuel tax is substituted by a distance charge (Oregon Department of Transport 2003). The Oregon example shows that the replacement of the current car taxation regime has long-term structural causes, with a tax regime change towards a car road user charge occurring, or being seriously considered, in societies as varied as a rural state in the USA, the Netherlands, Switzerland and the UK.

However, in developing a new road user charging taxation regime, amongst all the concern of maintaining income and addressing traffic congestion, there is a danger of losing the environmental reforms that have been built into existing taxation measures. If congestion is the only criteria for varying a kilometre charge, and a new clean fuel car faces the same congestion charge as a large gas guzzler, what incentive will there be for going green? This need not be so. The Transport Taxation Futures research (Potter et al. 2004) showed that it would be a relatively simple matter to have banded kilometre rates according to a car's environmental performance. The move towards a new car taxation regime based on road user charges could be an effective eco-reform as well

16.4 Conclusions

A number of changes in the framework of car taxation have resulted in some useful environmental gains. However, these changes are limited because the transport tax system has been designed to produce a substantial income from internal-combustion-engine vehicles in an easily administered form. A major restructuring of transport taxation is required to fully address a different goal – that of stimulating improvements to environmental performance. A number of reforms have taken place to existing taxation measures and useful lessons can be learned from how these have worked in practice. But in addition to reforming the existing car taxation regime, there are now signs that some nations are moving towards the creation of a new tax regime based upon generalised road user charging. Such a system is now seen by several European countries and some USA states as the transport taxation regime for the 21st century.

Tax regime change is emerging onto the transport policy agenda as a vital long-term strategy. Largely by default, transport policy-makers are coming to realise that road taxation regime change is inevitable if traffic and congestion management is to be a reality. The way we taxed vehicles and fuel in the 20th century is simply not appropriate for the transport challenges we face today. However, a key issue is to ensure that this new tax structure takes fully into account the environmental impacts of transport.

References

Department for Transport (2003) Press Release Confirmation of inflation increase of fuel duties, Department for Transport, 25th September
Department for Transport (2004) Feasibility study of road pricing in the UK: a report to the Secretary of State, Department for Transport, July
Dodgson J, Young J, van der Veer JP (2002) Paying for road use. Commission for Integrated Transport, London, February
European Council of Ministers of Transport (ECMT) (1997) Internalising the social costs of transport. OECD, Paris
Glaister S, Graham D (2003) Transport pricing: better for travelers. Independent Transport Commission, Southampton, June
Henley J (2004) France launches radical green tax on bigger cars. Guardian Unlimited, 23rd June. Available at http://www.guardian.co.uk/france/story/0,1182,1245187,00.html (accessed 27th July 2004).

Hinnells M, Potter S (2001) Don't tax more, tax different: a tax paradigm for sustainability. Centre for Reform, London

Inland Revenue (2004) Report of the evaluation of company car tax reform. Inland Revenue, London, April 2004

Ieromonachou P (2004) Norway's urban tolls: evolving towards congestion pricing? Transport Policy (forthcoming)

Lane B, Potter S (2003) A submission to the Department for Transport consultation: road fuel gases and their contribution to clean low-carbon transport. The Open University, Milton Keynes

Oregon Department of Transport (2003) Road User Fee Task Force Available at http://www.odot.state.or.us/ruftf (accessed 20th January 2004)

Parkhurst G (2002) The top of the escalator? In: Lyons G, Chatterjee K (eds) Transport lessons from the fuel tax protests of 2000. Ashgate, Aldershot, pp 299–321

Parkhurst G (2005) Taxation measures for sustainable mobility in the UK roads sector: progress, problems and prospects. In: Mendrisio MobiliTI: towards the portrait of a new urban mobility. Mendrisio, 14 May 2004 (in press)

Potter S, Enoch M, Fergusson M (2001) Fuel taxes and beyond: UK transport and climate change. London, World Wide Fund and Transport 2000

Potter S, Parkhurst G, Lane B, Ubbels B, Peeters P (2004) Taxation futures for sustainable mobility. Final report to the ESRC. Available at http://design.open.ac.uk/potter.htm

Schipper LJ, Marie-Lilliu MA (1999) Carbon-dioxide emissions from transport in IEA countries: recent lessons and long term challenge. International Energy Agency, Paris

Schipper LJ, Unander F, Marier-Lilliu MA (2000) The IEA energy indicators: analysing emissions on the road from Kyoto. International Energy Agency, Paris

Ubbels B, Rietveld P, Peeters PM (2002) Environmental effects of a kilometre charge in road transport: an investigation for the Netherlands, Transportation Research D 7: 255–264

Vanden Branden T, Potter S, Enoch M, Ubbels B (2000) Fair and efficient pricing in transport – The role of charges and taxes. Report for European Commission DG TREN, Oscar Faber, Birmingham. Available on the DG TREN website

Weizsaecker E, Jesinghaus J (1992) Ecological taxation reform. Zed Books, London

Whitelegg J (1992) Ecological taxation reform. In: Whitelegg J (ed) Traffic congestion: is there a way out? Leading Edge, Hawes, pp 169–183

17 Time and Travel

David Banister

University College London, London, UK

17.1 Introduction

When putting together a book based on detailed research carried out by a huge range of authors, it is often difficult to give it a clear structure as the inputs are so varied. That diversity is often an advantage as it gives the reader a clear perspective on the nature and range of work being carried out in North America and Europe on transport and telecommunications. However, the really difficult task is given to the individual writing the final chapter, whose task it is to draw the very disparate themes together and to make some new insights into where research effort should be directed in the future. This is a challenging task, and the approach adopted here is to build upon some of the key common themes that have come out of the contributions to the book. The intention is to both give a flavour of the diverse material in the book and to focus on a series of related key questions that still need to be addressed by transport researchers on both sides of the Atlantic.

More useful is the possibility of highlighting important themes that seem to reoccur in several of the chapters. Often they are raised in very different contexts, and their use in this chapter has really been to trigger thoughts on future research directions.

The title of this concluding chapter reflects its main theme, namely the issue of time, but it also alludes to some of the main issues facing decision makers with respect to transport and telecommunications. Three themes will be developed. The first relates to the treatment of time in transport analysis, as this has been a crucial driving force. Related to this is the theme of congestion and the means by which delays can be addressed not just in land transport, but in all forms of travel. Is there a limit to the amount of travelling that people (and goods) are prepared to undertake? The third theme is more of a composite one as it relates to recent concerns over security in travel and the risks involved, with the opportunities that are presented by ICTs (Information and Communications Technologies). The new technology is relatively risk free, at least in a life threatening way, and it does now offer a new virtual mobility to complement physical movement. There may be mutual lessons to be learned.

17.2 The Nature of Time

Traditionally, time has been treated as a framework or an "environment" within which social activities are carried out (Giddens 1979), rather than as a central focus of social theory. This means that time (and space) has really existed independently. The focus of the scientific approach has been based on the use of neo classical economics to build models to help explain the physical structure and functioning of cities. This logic has led to the unavoidable need for travel and transport, and the analysis of both the amount of travel and the evolution of cities have been shaped by distance, time and the Euclidean landscape (Graham and Marvin 1996). The question raised in this chapter is whether these physical constructs are still valid as the temporal (and spatial) boundaries have collapsed with the use of near instantaneous telecommunications and fast transport, as the world moves towards an "integrated global cultural system" (Harvey 1989).

In addition to these traditional physical constructs of time, there are more sociological constructs (Hassard 1990) that explore the variable experiences of shorter and longer term time. These are sometimes also called instantaneous and glacial time (Macnagthen and Urry 1998). Here it is argued that traditional constraints of time have been relaxed, as more activities are no longer "time bounded". This new flexibility includes social actions, such as work shift patterns, leisure opportunities, and career changes. It also includes valued time in between activities and time alone, or time spent waiting and listening (to music). At the macro level it relates to the globalisation of markets and the importance of time for production and distribution processes, and the expected lifespan in terms of product disposability. All these factors have in large part resulted from improvements in transport and communications technologies (Viger 2002).

Peoples' expectations of the distances that can be covered and the activities available have all been expanded. But importantly, the question raised by the sociologists is whether this is occurring through choice or whether this has been imposed as a result of necessary lifestyle changes. The simple trade-off, between job and home location as moderated by distance, has been replaced by a more complex equation involving housing affordability, location of schools and services, multiple workers, and flexible employment patterns (by time and location). Short-term constraints result in demand patterns that can accommodate all these requirements. Macnagthen and Urry conclude that "feelings of powerlessness appear to be compounded by the apparent mismatch between competing temporalities, with peoples' longer-term desires and aspirations developing in opposition to the "short-termism" and instantaneous time imperatives largely brought about by living in a globalised society" (1998, p. 232).

Time use has become immediate, and many of the longer term issues relating to the environment are not considered. O'Neill (1993) refers to this as the "temporal tragedy", as irreparable damage is imposed on the ecological conditions as the time horizon for these concerns is much longer. This chapter tries to unpack some of these concepts so that insights can be given into how new notions of time can be accommodated into transport modelling and analysis.

17.3 The Treatment of Time

We now have the experience of 50 years of urban transport models, since the pioneering research of Mitchell and Rapkin (1954) at the University of Pennsylvania. They put forward the theory that the demand for travel was a function of land use, and following on from this basic premise, it was argued that if land use could be controlled, then the origins and destinations of journeys could be determined – "urban traffic was a function of land use". There followed a series of large-scale land use transportation studies using this basic relationship (including the classic Chicago and Detroit studies), with changes in land use being taken as the principal exogenous variable. The large scale aggregate city-wide studies marked the genesis of transport planning as a modelling activity.

Underlying much of the subsequent analysis has been a concern about saving travel time. Much of the modelling and evaluation work concentrated on testing options that reduced travel time. The theoretical justification was that travel was a derived demand and that the value of the activity at the destination outweighed the costs of getting there. This meant that journey lengths should be as short as possible (in the sense of their generalised costs), but the recent empirical evidence seems to contradict the theory. As a result of investment in the transport infrastructure, congestion would be reduced and travel times would improve, but by making transport cheaper (faster) longer journeys would also be encouraged and new trips would take place. The question that this raises is whether there is any individual or societal benefit from this new situation.

At the individual level, the travel time saved can be used to visit other destinations (or more distant attractive destinations) or carrying out non travel activities, and the overall utility is enhanced and travel can still be seem as a derived demand (Mokhtarian and Chen 2002). At the aggregate level, an investment could encourage greater agglomeration, then the net effect might be positive, but conversely if it encouraged greater sprawl there may could increase social and environmental costs. This in turn relates back to the land use and transport relationships established in the 1950s. More recently, there has been the equally difficult challenge of linking transport investment to economic development, and bringing additional non-transport benefits to the local economy. If such a relationship can be established there is a double dividend from the transport investment, but if the net effect is merely a transfer of economic activity from one location to another, then there may only be transport benefits (Banister and Berechman 2000).

One underlying future issue is the treatment of time. From much of the analytical research carried out, the concern over travel time reduction has been overestimated, and researchers should begin to look at more sophisticated measures of time that are related to particular situations, and to develop more sociological constructs to complement the physical interpretations of time. Two different points will be made here.

17.3.1 Transport as a Derived Demand or as a Valued Activity

With respect to the work journey, travel time is important, but as travel patterns change and there is an increase in leisure based travel, travel time may become a positively valued activity. The notion that all travel is a derived demand is becoming weaker, as incomes rise and as leisure time becomes more valuable (Mokhtarian and Salomon 2001). Escape theory (Heinze 2000) hypothesises that leisure mobility is an attempt to compensate for a declining quality of life and travel opportunities are sought to get away from ones everyday environment to do something completely different. Such a line of argument leads to a fundamental dilemma about whether all travel is a derived demand. The traditional view that travel is only undertaken because of the benefits derived at the destination is no longer generally applicable. Substantial amounts of leisure travel are undertaken for its own sake and the activity of travelling is valued.

If this conclusion is correct, it has enormous implications for transport analysis as most conventional analysis is based on the premise that travel distances should be short and that travel time should be minimised. A corollary concerns the impact of the new technology on travel flexibility. The new technology provides tremendous opportunity and choice in leisure activities, whether this means time spent in the home at the terminal, or taking the opportunity to book a last minute holiday overseas, or adapting existing activities (such as shopping). In each case there seems to be a strong complementarity between the old (transport) and the new (ICT) technologies. Travel can be replaced by more "at home" activities, whilst in other cases more spontaneous travel is generated, and in a third group there is a modification of existing activities, as shopping for example becomes a multitasking activity through a combination of the Internet (e.g. viewing, deciding and buying) and travel (e.g. collection or delivery).

The knowledge base is extended and this may again result in more travel, but more important is the transfer of power from the producer to the consumer. Increasingly, users will control their leisure and shopping activities tailored to their own specific requirements (at a price). Consumers will determine what type of leisure activity they participate in, where and when it takes place, and who actually goes with them – and the range of alternatives will also increase substantially.

17.3.2 Time Minimisation and Reasonable Travel Time

The second point is the increasing contradictions between the desire to speed up and the desire to slow traffic down. For evaluation purposes, much of the user benefit (often over 80 per cent of total benefits) is derived from the savings in travel time, which in turn is based on the desire to travel as fast as possible between two places. Several conclusions can be drawn from the empirical literature on the subject. First, having higher flexibility, relative to the various time constraints, tends to increase the value of time. For example, the study by MVA (1987) has shown that people with variable work hours have values of time, which are 15–20 percent higher than that of other workers. Similarly, the ability to schedule activities tends to increase estimated values of time (Small 1982). Higher tax rates have an opposite effect (Forsyth 1980).

A second major conclusion is that non-linear relationships exist between income and value of time. Thus, studies have shown that values for in-vehicle time is less than the hourly gross wage rate, but it is an increasing function of income since rising income implies larger opportunity costs of time-saved. Waters II (1992) has estimated the elasticity of value of time with respect to income to be about 0.8, though this general elasticity value depends on trip length, mode use and trip purpose. Gunn (1991) reports smaller effects of income on values of time, except for business travel.

A further conclusion is that users place a higher weight on wait and walk time relative to in-vehicle time. Usually, the value of these time components is 2–3 times that of in-vehicle time. In this regard, inter-modal transfers, which implies additional wait time, entail heavy opportunity costs of time and therefore should be weighted accordingly (Small 1992).

Finally, the common practice is to use the same values of time for small and for large blocks of time saved. This practice has been challenged on the grounds that small time blocks saved (e.g., 5–10 minutes) are valued less by trip makers than larger ones (e.g., 20–25 minutes). Following this rationale it might be argued that the total value of time saved for a large group of people where each saves only 3–5 minutes is negligible. Obviously, it is possible to introduce counter arguments, for example, that for some activities small time savings are a sufficient prerequisite for undertaking them. In general, the use of average value of time across people probably accounts for this problem, mainly because a small but a significant number of people place a very high value even on small time blocks.

This is not the place to enter the debate on how these values are time-saving are derived, or how they are used by the beneficiaries or in the analysis. But there does seem to be an inconsistency in the travel time savings argument within cities, where much effort is now going into slowing traffic down for environmental and safety reasons. Although it is not explicitly stated, a certain level of congestion on roads is now seen as "desirable" and in many locations (e.g. residential streets and around schools), new low speed limits have been introduced, together with appropriate enforcement measures (e.g. speed cameras).

So on the one hand, there are the perpetual complaints from industry that the time lost in congestion is costing business money, and on the other hand as a contradictory transport strategy that both tries to speed traffic up and slow it down. The notion of a transport system with no congestion has never been a realistic objective, and much of the recent debate has been over what should be considered as a reasonable level of congestion. The key policy objectives now becomes that of reasonable travel time, rather travel time minimisation. People and businesses are already concerned about knowing how much time it should take to travel to their destination with a reasonable degree of certainty. It is the reliability of the system that is crucial.

These two points are both important in terms of the rationale behind transport planning, as many of the methods used cannot handle travel as a valued activity or travel time reliability. But they also have important implications for travel planning, if it is to embrace the concepts of a sustainable urban development. It strongly argues for the sister disciplines of urban planning and transport to become fully integrated as one subject area. It also means that the focus for research has switched from the physical dimensions (urban form and traffic) to the social dimensions (people and accessibility). The variable impact of ICT is also a new dimension as activities that traditionally required travel can now be carried out remotely at an almost zero cost to the user. Lyons and Kenyon (2003) have argued that the growth in virtual mobility has substituted for the increase in physical mobility, and that it should also be included in new concepts of accessibility.

It is not just in passenger travel that new interpretations of time need addressing. In the freight sector, time is also a key element in distribution costs and the design of robust logistics systems. Time itself seems to be more easily accounted for in the planning of freight distribution systems, but it is the frequency and to a lesser extent the reliability of the service that is important to shippers (Chap. 9). But here there is variation in terms of the importance of costs, time, reliability and frequency by commodity type, value, mode and distance of haul. With respect to the long distance maritime alternative for example, frequency and reliability improvements are more important than time reductions (Chap 10).

A recent UK survey of 65 freight haulers, representing several market sectors, all types of operators and a wide geographical distribution, was carried out to assess the incidence and impact of network unreliability (CfIT 2002). For about 22 per cent of haulers, journey time unreliability was less than 10 per cent, and these were mainly operators in agricultural businesses in rural areas or those with night time distribution arrangements. A further 52 per cent of haulers recorded a 10–25 per cent range of journey time unreliability, and these operated in general haulage and distribution. The next 22 per cent reported journey time unreliability of between 25 and 50 per cent, and the operators here were mainly in food and retail distribution and construction supplies. The final 4 per cent recorded journey time unreliability of over 50 per cent of scheduled times. Overall, the additional costs to industry averaged 5 per cent, but this ranged between 1–2 per cent in 24 per cent of cases to over 10 per cent in 13 per cent of cases. The main compensating reactions of operators have been to time shift with an earlier departure time (79 per cent), or to deliver out of peak hours (65 per cent), or to plan for additional journey times (75 per cent), or to have some rerouting to less congested roads (57 per cent).

All this debate seems to suggest that the renewed interest in travel time budgets may be misplaced (e.g. Hupkes 1982; Schafer and Victor 2000). The argument that local destinations are being replaced by more remote destinations as travel speeds increase within a fixed 70 minute time constraint may only tell part of the story. As leisure time and incomes increase, the time available for travel also increases so that there is no budgetary constraint. This may already be happening if international travel is included in the national statistics for travel time. For example, in the UK travel time per person per year has been increasing only slowly over the last 18 years (Table 17.1 – total increase about 12 per cent), but this only covers national travel, not overseas travel, where most increase in distance and time has been taking place. Air travel by UK residents in the EU accounts for a further 45 billion passenger kilometres (+6 per cent).

Table 17.1. Travel time in the UK

Year	Travel Time per Trip	Travel Time hours per person per year
1985/86	19.8	337
1991/93	20.5	361
1996/98	20.4	357
1999/01	21.2	360
2002	22.5	378

Source: Office of National Statistics (2003).

Table 17.2. Travel time variability in the UK by age, gender and purpose variables (1998–2000)

Age and gender	Average trip time (mins)	Hours per person per year	Trip purpose	Average trip time (mins)	Hours per person per year
<17	18	270	Commuting	24	66
17–20	23	388	Business	38	22
21–29	22	423	Education	19	22
30–38	21	424	Escort education	12	9
40–49	22	443	Shopping	17	61
50–59	22	406	Other escort	15	21
60–69	21	349	Personal business	17	29
70+	21	245	Visit friends at home	22	50
				18	14
			Visit friends other	21	22
Male	22	387	Sport/entertainment	55	27
Females	20	334	Holiday/day trip other including walk	23	18
All ages	21	360		21	360

Source: ONS (2002), Table 4.4.

In their comparative review of travel time budgets, Mokhtarian and Chen (2002) came to two clear conclusions, namely that at the aggregate level there does seem to be some stability in travel time, but at the disaggregate level, there is considerable variability. This variability can be seen as a function of social characteristics, location and the characteristics of the destination. Table 17.2 gives some comparable data for the UK on the variability in travel times by age, gender and trip purpose. To this list, we would add the problem of measurement, as in the UK time use studies have concluded that published National Travel Survey data underestimates travel time by 24 per cent (Noble et al. 2000). The reason for this is the recording of time in 15 minute time periods that do not have sufficient detail to allow for short (walk) trips. This means that for 2001, the average time spent travelling each day in the UK is 80.1 minutes, as compared with 64.5 minutes recorded in the National Travel Survey, and that the average trip time is about 30 minutes per trip rather than 22 minutes (Table 17.1).

17.4 Congestion Charging

The second theme also relates to travel time and the problem of matching supply and demand. In the roads sector, it is now accepted that new construction will not solve the problem of congestion, and that even if there were resources available it would not be desirable. Hence, there has been a clear move away from supply based solutions to those that rely on demand management through giving priority to particular users of road space, and by raising the costs of travel more generally. But in most situations, space is still allocated inefficiently through time and congestion, rather than through price.

Paying for road use is the one means by which congestion and travel time variability can both be reduced (with corresponding increases in speed). The most recent UK evidence suggests that congestion accounts for between 41 and 81 per cent of the marginal external costs (Table 17.3), with operating costs, accidents and environmental costs also contributing in different proportions. All these external costs are difficult to measure, but with respect to congestion and travel time variability, the normal expectation is the difference between actual travel time and free flow travel time, together with estimates of the standard deviation around that value (Oscar Faber 2002). Under uncongested conditions, the expectation is that the variability in travel time is about 5 per cent of the average journey time, but as the road becomes more congested, this variability increases to between 15 and 45 per cent of the average journey time[1]. More generally, it seems that on UK motorways (1998/99), about 66 per cent of delays are due to congestion, 10 per cent to roadworks, and 24 per cent to other traffic incidents (accidents and adverse weather) (Frith 1999).

It is here that there is a clear distinction between the researcher and the policy maker. If there was any one issue in transport that is clear, it is that pricing policy should be the principal means by which road space is allocated. Where direct pricing methods have been used (for example in Singapore, London and Oslo), the results have been dramatic, with short-term elasticities being much higher than expected. Yet action seems to be slow, and many decision makers seem reluctant to accept the risks, and to take action despite the clear messages coming from the research community and the demonstration effects from the successful schemes that have been implemented.

---

[1] These empirical values were taken on sections of the M25 London orbital route under congested and uncongested conditions, see Abou-Rahme et al. 1998).

Table 17.3. Marginal external costs by vehicle type (2000)

Vehicle Type	Operating costs %	Congestion %	Accident Costs %	Air Pollution %	Noise %	Climate Change %	Total (pence per vkm)
Car	0.5	81.3	9.1	4.4	2.2	2.5	11.95
LDV	0.5	72.5	5.2	14.8	3.7	3.3	13.71
HGV-Rigid	14.0	56.5	5.4	15.9	4.7	3.5	31.17
HGV-Artic	20.2	57.1	2.8	10.5	5.2	4.2	42.92
PSV	14.8	41.1	12.7	22.8	5.2	3.4	40.62

LDV light delivery vehicle, *HGV* heavy goods vehicle, *PSV* public service vehicle (bus).
Operating costs include depreciation.
Source: Sansom et al (2001).

The barriers of public and political acceptability still remain (Banister and Pucher 2004), and this must be an issue that the research community should address. It is not just carrying out high quality technical analysis with a set of interesting conclusions. Part of the total package must be to strengthen the links between research and practice, looking at the means by which research findings can be translated into practice. Too much good research is presented on a "take it or leave it basis". As Hall (2003) has perceptively commented "it is easy to Talk the Talk: the real challenge is to Walk the Walk". History will judge the success of the research by what impact it has had in changing thinking and actual outcomes in terms of successful implementation.

Transport research is full of good ideas and high quality analysis, but its impact does not seem to have been as dramatic as might have been expected. This may in part be due to the complexity of the issues being investigated, the different approaches used, and the varying outcomes of the research, but even where there does seem to be almost unanimous view (for example on demand management and congestion charging), it is not translated into practice. But then again, many policy processes take time to develop from the ideas stage to the implementation stage, and in transport it seems that most innovative and radical ideas are either not implemented at all, or are introduced in a weakened form so as to be ineffective (Rietveld and Stough 2004).

The same arguments about congestion are now being debated with respect to air transport, where capacity utilisation rates are in excess of one. It seems appropriate that some form of congestion charging and slot auctions should be introduced to allocate priority. In Europe, delayed flights account for between 17–30 per cent of all arrivals and 8–24 per cent of departures, somewhat less than the US levels of 22–40 per cent of arrivals and 19–38 per cent of departures. The average delay for the delayed flights in the US is about 50 minutes as compared with the 20 minutes average in Europe. Weather and congestion are the two most important causes in the US, but it is mainly just congestion in Europe (Chap. 13).

Unconstrained growth with large scale infrastructure expansion has been the strategy adopted at many international airports, but demand at certain points in time is still exceeding supply, and this continues to create delays, particularly when combined with the limitations of air traffic control systems. Interestingly here, it seems that the costs arising from delays of up to 15 minutes are not counted, nor is the tendency for the scheduling of longer flight times between congested hub airports to accommodate delays and unreliability in actual travel times. The situation is similar to the targets set for reliability and punctuality of rail services, which have to be within 5 minutes of scheduled time on the UK railways. Again, the scheduled times are being extended, partly to achieve greater reliability.

The question here is over the transferability of methods from one sector to another, both in the theoretical sense that ideas are equally relevant, and in the operational sense of the actual techniques used. Demand management is now commonly applied in many cities and on the railways, and it is now being increasingly used for long distance road travel. Its application to the fast growing air sector is now a priority so that the full social and environmental costs can be internalised. This will mean substantial increases in the costs of air travel, and at the same time will redress some of the imbalances between the charging structures used for the different modes of transport. Some (rail and bus) contribute more to their full social and environmental costs than others (air and car).

Recent world events have also resulted in substantial reductions in demand for air travel. Terrorist action (11th September 2001) resulted in US airspace being closed for 5 days and another more general event (the SARS virus in 2003), both substantially reduced air travel (by over 30 per cent) on routes across the North Atlantic and to the Far East (Chap. 14). Such dramatic reductions in demand suggest that some air travel is discretionary or can be delayed, but it also has important lessons for the airlines in terms of their reactions and learning about the risks involved. The global uncertainties and risks provide a new dimension to the questions of the methods used for demand forecasting for the airlines, both at the strategic level, and at the tactical and operational levels. It also raises longer term implications about whether increasing runway capacity, based on these optimistic demand forecasts, is the most appropriate solution to airport congestion.

17.5 Transport and ICT

In an uncertain world, any strategy should involve risk assessment and the use of complementary means to achieve objectives. This is where transport should be seen as working together with ICTs to provide systems that both work efficiently and are robust. There seem to be strong similarities between transport and ICT, in terms of the processes of diffusion and market penetration, as levels of knowledge and skill increase, and as costs are reduced. But ICT penetration seems to be occurring at a much faster rate, particularly recently. Although in transport there are capacity limitations, it seems that with broadband and satellite communications there are potentially no capacity limits for ICTs. The main risks with ICT are the external factors such as terrorism or a virus (spam mail must be included as a form of virus) disrupt the system or effectively "block the infinite capacity".

It also reflects the need to stay connected and highly accessible, both in a physical (transport) context, and in a virtual (ICT) context. But more important is the complementarity found within networks. Accessibility tends to be viewed as the impact of one new link on the network as a whole. However, many investments are strongly complementary and they do not need to be consumed in fixed proportions as they form systems. Competition is really taking place between systems and not individual products. So accessibility should not only be viewed as the changes in one particular system (e.g. rail), but the new competitive position of that system in relation to other systems (e.g. road). The real value of improvements in the quality of the network is that it provides the opportunity for people and businesses to take part in the network, even if they choose not to. There is an optional benefit. The value of membership to one user is positively affected when another user joins and enlarges the network (Katz and Schapiro 1994). New concepts of networks and accessibility are required to determine under what conditions the competitive position of one network will be changed as compared with another on at least three dimensions – to influence expectations, to facilitate coordination and to ensure compatibility.

Such innovations are evidenced in the scale free and small world network properties that evolve in large complex networks through self organising processes and preferential attachment (Chap. 11). New nodes tend to attach themselves to other vertices that are well connected, and traffic is routed through a relatively few highly connected vertices. This means that the diameter of the network is small in comparison with other network structures and movement is more efficient, as there is a substantial amount of local clustering. But there is also an increase in the risks if one or more of the highly connected nodes become disconnected.

The impact of investment (or lack of it) is important in establishing the image of an area and hence its attractiveness to new development. This in turn will impact on the local labour market so that high quality (and high income) labour will be attracted. Transport and ICT investment may act as the trigger mechanism to this process. The alternative explanation seems to lead to the conclusion that only existing locations will ever be attractive, as they have first mover advantages and will always be more accessible in this broader sense than other new or peripheral locations.

This discussion again brings us back to the notion of time, but in a composite form that allows an activity to be carried out efficiently and reliably within a reasonable time. Time is also not being used in a "single" physical sense but increasingly in a "multi" physical and social sense. As more time is being devoted to travel activities and more time is wasted in congestion and delay, manufacturers and individuals have become more creative in providing the means to use travel time to communicate, to work, to play games and to organise one's life. The notion that travel time is wasted time needs to be reconsidered, and this is one area where ICT has been instrumental in allowing multitasking.

This is where ICT has complementarity with transport in its ability to substitute for travel under certain conditions and also to provide a service for transport (for example through integrated ticketing and journey planning). Increasingly it seems that the weakest link in any travel activity is at the interchange points, as this is where uncertainty arises. As noted earlier, the higher values of time assigned to wait time and interchange time are well researched. But with increasing delays in the system, these interchange links become more important. Apart from the dilemmas it poses for individual travellers or shippers, it raises questions on the amount of redundancy there should be in the system. It also helps explain the rationale behind taking a mode of transport that minimises the number of changes, even though it may not provide the "best" alternative. The use of the car rather than rail or taking a direct flight rather than hubbing are two examples of this phenomenon. The goal of a "seamless" transport system is dependent on the quality of the services provided, the information about the systems including the ease of using it, and the expectation that you will arrive safely and on time.

17.6 Conclusion

Two main conclusions can be drawn from this chapter as it relates to the broader theme of the book, namely methods and models. The first is that the growing integration of transport and telecommunications modelling means that there is a convergence of approaches, so that a new generation of methods are needed that combine elements of each. Some of the chapters demonstrate such an approach, but there are problems with data and more importantly the key variables to be included in such an analysis. The concept of time and its use seems to be central to both transport and telecommunications, and it can perhaps be used as the driving force (or key variable) in explaining patterns of travel and the use of telecommunications.

But there is also a necessity to move beyond current thinking about time as a constraint, to exploring its role as providing new opportunities for travel and activity participation. New concepts of time are required that combine the traditional physical measures with approaches that embrace notions of choice in time use, control over time, multitasking in time, time immediacy, and time dependence. Most of these concepts relate to instantaneous use of time, and more attention also needs to be given to longer term (glacial) time, and the changing patterns of time use over time. The social constructs of time seem to be equally important as the physical constructs of time. This is the second issue.

This concluding chapter has tried to extract some common themes from the other preceding chapters and place them within a wider framework. This has been done for two main reasons. One is to suggest that there are common strands that can be drawn between the often disparate transport analysis that is being carried out on both sides of the Atlantic. The other is to put the case that researchers must place more emphasis on the communication and dissemination of results of their work. They must move on from too much of an isolationist view of research towards engagement with policy makers and other key actors to explain and convince them of the need to take action. Delay and inaction are sometimes appropriate, but in the transport sector it seems to be the norm even where there are very clear and consistent messages arising from the research. In the past, too much emphasis has been placed on research output and publication, almost for its own sake. That must change. The new challenge for researchers in North America and Europe must be to make their knowledge and understanding of transport more relevant and accessible to decision makers, and for it to be presented in such a way that they cannot afford not to act on it.

References

Abou-Rahme N, Rees T, Dixon C, Paulo D (1998) Monitoring of the M25 controlled motorway (March 97–March 98) including the implementation of HIOOC. Highways Agency and Transport Research Laboratory, report PR/TT/083/98, August

Banister D, Berechman J (2000) Transport investment and economic development. University College London Press, London

Banister D, Pucher J (2004) Can sustainable transport be made acceptable? Paper presented at the Transportation Research Board Annual Meeting, Washington, D.C., January

Commission for Integrated Transport (CfIT) (2002) Paying for road use. Report published 25th February 2002, CfIT, London

Commission of the European Communities (CEC) (2001) European transport policy for 2010: time to decide. The white paper on transport policy, Brussels, 12 September 2001. Available at http://europa.eu.int/comm/energy_transport/en/lb_en.html

Forsyth PJ (1990) The value of time in an economy with taxation. Journal of Transport Economics and Policy 14: 337–362

Frith B (1999) The estimation of recurrent congestion and congestion due to roadworks and incidents: 1995/96 to 1998/99. Transport Research Laboratory report PR/TT/160/99, December

Giddens A (1979) Central problems in social theory. Macmillan, London

Graham S, Marvin S (1996) Telecommunications and the city: electronic spaces, urban places. Routledge, London

Gunn H (1991)Research into the value of time savings and losses: The Netherlands 1985–1991. Hague Consulting Group, final report

Hall P (2003) Talking the talk, walking the walk: how to make paper plans real. The Royal Town Planning Institute's Annual Lecture, December, London

Harvey D (1989) The condition of post modernity. Blackwell, Oxford

Hassard J (ed) (1990) The sociology of time. Macmillan, London

Heinze GW (2000) Transport and leisure. Paper prepared for presentation at the ECMT Round Table 111 on Transport and Leisure, Paris, pp 1–51

Hupkes G (1982) The law of constant travel time and trip-rates. Futures 14: 38–46

Katz ML, Schapiro C (1994) Systems competition and network effects. Journal of Economic Perspectives 23: 177–200

Lyons G, Kenyon S (2003) Social participation, personal travel and Internet use. In: Proceedings of the 10th International Conference on Travel Behaviour Research, Lucerne, August

Macnagthen P, Urry J (1998) Contested natures. Sage, London

Mitchell R, Rapkin C (1954) Urban traffic - A function of land use. Columbia University Press, New York

Mokhtarian P, Chen C (2002) TTB or not TTB, that is the question: a review and analysis of the empirical literature on travel time (and money) budgets (Report prepared by the authors for the DaimlerChrysler Corporation, University of California, Davis, July)

Mokhtarian P, Salomon I (2001) How derived is the demand for travel? Some conceptual and measurement considerations. Transportation Research A 35: 695–719

MVA (1987) The value of time savings, a report of research undertaken for the Department of Transport by the MVA Consultancy. With the Institute of Transport Studies, University of Leeds, the Transport Studies Unit, University of Oxford, Newbury

Noble B, Dickson M, Gershuny J, Fugeman D (2000) Using Omnibus surveys to investigate travel. In: Transport trends 2000, The Stationery Office, London, pp 55–68

Office of National Statistics (2002) Focus on personal travel. The Stationery Office, London

Office of National Statistics (2003) Transport statistics bulletin: national travel survey: 2002 provisional results. ONS, London, December

O'Neill J (1993) Ecology, policy and politics. Routledge, London

Oscar Faber, National Economic Research Association, Institute for Transport Studies (Leeds) (2002) Paying for road use: technical report for the 10 year Transport Plan Monitoring Study. Report for the Commission for Integrated Transport, February

Rietveld P, Stough R (eds) (2004) Barriers to sustainable transport: institutions, regulation and sustainable transport. Spon, London

Sansom T, Nash C, Mackie P, Shires J, Watkiss P (2001) Surface transport costs and charges: Final Report. Institute for Transport Studies, University of Leeds report for DETR/DTLR, Leeds

Schafer A, Victor DG (2000) The future mobility of the world population. Transportation Research A 34: 171–205

Small K (1982) The scheduling of consumer activities: work trips. American Economic Review 72: 467–79

Small K (1992) Urban transportation economics. Harwood Academic Publishers, New York

Vigar G (2002) The politics of mobility: transport, the environment and public policy. Spon, London

Waters WG, II (1992) The value of time savings for the economic evaluation of highway investments in British Columbia. Center for Transportation Studies, University of British Columbia, Vancouver

List of Contributors

Alderighi, Marco
IEP and CERTeT, Bocconi University
Via Gobbi 5, 20136, Milano
Italy

Balta, Nazmiye
Regional Economics Applications Laboratory, University of Illinois at Urbana-Champaign
Urbana-Champaign, IL 61820
USA

Banister, David
The Bartlett School of Planning, University College London
London
UK

Bergantino, Angela Stefania
Department of Economics, University of Bari
Via C. Rosalba, 53, 70124 Bari
Italy

Beuthe, Michel
Groupe Transport & Mobilité (GTM), Facultés Universitaires Catholiques de Mons (FUCAM)
151 Ch. De Binche, B-7000 Mons
Belgium

Black, William R.
Department of Geography, Indiana University
Student Building 120, Bloomington, IN 47405
USA

Bolis, Simona
IRE - Department of Economics, University of Lugano
Via G. Buffi, 13, 6900 Lugano
Switzerland

Bouffioux, Christophe
    Groupe Transport & Mobilité (GTM), Facultés Universitaires Catholiques de
    Mons (FUCAM)
    151 Ch. De Binche, B-7000 Mons
    Belgium

Boyce, David E.
    Department of Civil and Environmental Engineering, Northwestern University
    2149 Grey Avenue, Evanston, IL 60201
    USA

Button, Kenneth
    School of Public Policy, George Mason University
    4400 University Dr., Fairfax, VA 22030
    USA

Campisi, Domenico
    Department of Business Engineering, Università di Roma "Tor Vergata"
    Via del Politecnico 1, 00133 Roma
    Italy

Cento, Alessandro
    Revenue Management Department, KLM Royal Dutch Airlines
    Via Modigliani 45, 20090 Segrate (MI)
    Italy

Costa, Roberta
    Department of Business Engineering, Università di Roma "Tor Vergata"
    Via del Politecnico 1, 00133 Roma
    Italy

De Maeyer, Jan
    Dept. of Transport and Regional Economics, University of Antwerp
    Antwerp
    The Netherlands

Donaghy, Kieran P.
    Regional Economics Applications Laboratory, University of Illinois at Urbana-
    Champaign
    Room 314 Temple Buell Hall, 611 Taft Drive, Champaign, IL 61820
    USA

Friesz, Terry L.
    The Pennsylvania State University
    University Park, PA 16802
    USA

Gorman, Sean P.
School of Public Policy, George Mason University
4400 University Dr., Fairfax, VA 22030
USA

Hewings, Geoffrey J.D.
Regional Economics Applications Laboratory, University of Illinois at Urbana-Champaign
Urbana, IL 61801-3671
USA

Hirota, Keiko
General Research and Development Division, Japan Automobile Research Institute
2530 Karima, Tsukuba, Ibaraki 305-0822
Japan

Holguín-Veras, Jose
Department of Civil and Environmental Engineering, Rensselaer Polytechnic Institute
12180 Troy, NY
USA

Janic, Milan
OTB Research Institute, Delft University of Technology
Delft
The Netherlands

Kim, Tschangho John
Department of Urban and Regional Planning, University of Illinois at Urbana-Champaign
111 Temple Buell Hall, 611 East Lorado Taft Drive, Champaign, IL 61820
USA

Lane, Ben
Department of Design and Innovation, Technology Faculty, The Open University
Walton Hall, Milton Keynes, MK7 6AA
UK

Li, Kaidong
Department of Geography, University of Calgary
2500 University Dr. NW, Calgary, Alberta T2N 1N4
Canada

Nijkamp, Peter
  Department of Spatial Economics, Faculty of Economics, Free University
  De Boelelaan 1105, 1081 HV Amsterdam
  The Netherlands

Parkhurst, Graham
  Faculty of the Built Environment, University of the West of England
  Frenchay Campus, Coldharbour Lane, Bristol BS16 1QY
  UK

Patuelli, Roberto
  School of Public Policy, George Mason University
  4400 University Dr., 22030 Fairfax, VA
  USA

Poot, Jacques
  Population Studies Centre, University of Waikato
  Private Bag 3105, Hamilton
  New Zealand

Potter, Stephen
  Department of Design and Innovation, Technology Faculty, The Open
  University
  Walton Hall, Milton Keynes, MK7 6AA
  UK

Reggiani, Aura
  Department of Economics, Faculty of Statistics, University of Bologna
  Piazza Scaravilli 2, 40126 Bologna
  Italy

Santamaria, Giovanna
  Institut de Statistique, Catholic University of Louvain
  Louvain
  Belgium

Schintler, Laurie A.
  School of Public Policy, George Mason University
  4400 University Dr., Fairfax, VA 22030
  USA

Stough, Roger R.
  School of Public Policy, George Mason University
  4400 University Dr., Fairfax, VA 22030
  USA

Tesauro, Carlo
    Istituto di Pianificazione e Gestione del Territorio, CNR
    Via Pietro Castellino, 111, 80131 Napoli
    Italy

Vandaele, Els
    Department of Geography, Ghent University
    Ghent
    The Netherlands

Vandresse, Marie
    Institut de Statistique, Catholic University of Louvain
    Louvain
    Belgium

Vial, Jose F.
    Regional Economics Applications Laboratory, University of Illinois at Urbana-
    Champaign
    Urbana-Champaign, IL 61820
    USA

Waters, Nigel M.
    Department of Geography, University of Calgary
    2500 University Dr. NW, Calgary, Alberta T2N 1N4
    Canada

Williams, Huw C.W.L.
    Department of City and Regional Planning, Cardiff University
    Glamorgan Building, King Edward VII Avenue, Cardiff CF10 3WA
    UK

Witlox, Frank
    Department of Geography, Ghent University
    Krijgslaan 281, S8, B-9000 Ghent
    Belgium

You, Jinsoo
    InComKorea Co., Ltd.
    Hankwang Building 3rd FL
    1625-2 Seocho-Dong, Seocho-Ku, Seoul
    South Korea

List of Referees

Alderighi, Marco
  IEP and CERTeT, Bocconi University, Italy

Anderson, Bill
  Center for Transportation Studies, Boston University, USA

Banister, David
  The Bartlett School of Planning, University College London, UK

Berechman, Joseph (Yossi)
  Tel Aviv University, Israel, and University Transportation Research Center,
  The City College of NY, USA

Beuthe, Michel
  Groupe Transport & Mobilité (GTM), Facultés Universitaires Catholiques de
  Mons (FUCAM), Belgium

Bolis, Simona
  IRE - Department of Economics, University of Lugano, Switzerland

Boyce, David E.
  Department of Civil and Environmental Engineering, Northwestern University,
  USA

Button, Kenneth
  School of Public Policy, George Mason University, USA

Cento, Alessandro
  Revenue Management Department, KLM Royal Dutch Airlines, Italy

Donaghy, Kieran P.
  Regional Economics Applications Laboratory, University of Illinois at Urbana-
  Champaign, USA

Fischer, Manfred M.
  Department of Economic Geography and Geoinformatics, Vienna University of
  Economics and Business Administration, Austria

Gorman, Sean P.
   School of Public Policy, George Mason University, USA

Hirota, Keiko
   General Research and Development Division, Japan Automobile Research Institute, Japan

Janelle, Donald G.
   Center for Spatially Integrated Social Science, University of California at Santa Barbara, USA

Janic, Milan
   OTB Research Institute, Delft University of Technology, The Netherlands

Kim, Tschangho John
   Department of Urban and Regional Planning, University of Illinois at Urbana-Champaign, USA

Kulkarni, Rajenda G.
   School of Public Policy, George Mason University, USA

Lloyd, Michael
   The Alliance of Maritime Regional Interests in Europe (AMRIE), Belgium

Mattsson, Lars-Göran
   Department of Infrastructure, Royal Institute of Technology, Sweden

Miller, Harvey J.
   Department of Geography, University of Utah, USA

Nijkamp, Peter
   Department of Spatial Economics, Free University, The Netherlands

Pan, Qisheng
   School of Public Affairs, Texas Southern University, USA

Pels, Eric
   Department of Spatial Economics, Free University of Amsterdam, The Netherlands

Poot, Jacques
   Population Studies Centre, University of Waikato, New Zealand

Potter, Stephen
   Department of Design and Innovation, The Open University, UK

Reggiani, Aura
  Department of Economics, University of Bologna, Italy

Russo, Giovanni
  Department of Economic and Policy, Utrecht University, The Netherlands

Schintler, Laurie A.
  School of Public Policy, George Mason University, USA

Stough, Roger R.
  School of Public Policy, George Mason University, USA

Waters, Nigel M.
  Department of Geography, University of Calgary, Canada

Wegener, Michael
  Institute of Spatial Planning, University of Dortmund, Germany

Subject Index